D0368475

AN INTRODUCTION TO WORLD POLITICS

AN INTRODUCTION TO WORLD POLITICS

By

W. FRIEDMANN, LL.D.

Professor of International Law and Director of International Legal Research, Columbia University

FIFTH EDITION

ST. MARTIN'S PRESS
New York
1965

First Edition 1951
Second Edition 1952 Reprinted 1953
Third Edition 1956 Reprinted 1957
Fourth Edition 1960
Fifth Edition 1965

Library of Congress Catalogue Card No. 62–17721

PRINTED IN UNITED STATES OF AMERICA

CONTENTS

APPENDICES

PREFACE TO THE FIFTH EDITION

THE present revision is much the most thorough undertaken since the book first appeared in 1951. Since the publication of the last edition in 1960, the structure of international politics has undergone more profound and far-reaching changes than at any time since the end of the Second World War. These were the years when the monolithic structure of the Communist bloc gave way to open and bitter rivalry between the two Communist giants, and to growing independence and diversity in the policies of the smaller Communist States. At the same time, within the Western Alliance, France under de Gaulle moved more and more strongly towards an independent national policy, often in direct conflict with that of the United States, by withdrawing most of her forces from NATO control, blocking Britain's proposed entry into the European Community, recognizing Communist China and aiming at a neutralization of South-east Asia where the United States — and, to a lesser extent, Britain — are heavily engaged. These were the years when an explosive increase in the number of nominally independent new States drastically altered the structure of international diplomacy and of the United Nations. Numerical preponderance shifted to the Asian and African States, whose accession to the family of nations also greatly complicates the balance of international politics. The emergence of so many new nation-States, coupled with the spread of modern weapons and technology, creates many new and acute dangers to peace. It was another characteristic of the last few years that they showed a shift in emphasis from the 'bipolar' aspect of the Cold War, dominated by the almost continuous tension between the United States and the Soviet Union, to a multitude of diverse threats, most of them emanating from medium or smaller States engaged in regional and national conflicts, with the danger of 'escalation'.

Finally, these were the years in which two great leaders, for a tragically short span of a few years, decisively influenced the life of men and the structure of international relations. During a reign of less than five years, an octogenarian Pope altered the image of the Catholic Church by strongly and simply asserting the primacy of its Christian and humanitarian objectives, liberalizing its philosophy, processes and relations to non-Catholic faiths and States. At the same time, in less than three years, a young and vigorous American President showed to his country and to the world that intellect and leadership could go together, that wisdom was not an antithesis to vigour and youth. By the personal impact which President Kennedy made on millions of Americans, Europeans and other nations, by his understanding of the need in the nuclear age for the big Powers to combine the use of power with restraint — as shown by his masterly handling of the Cuban crisis of October 1962 — by what he stood for rather than what he achieved, Kennedy was beginning to exercise a profound influence on the peoples of the world, when the bullet of an assassin tragically cut short his work.

And hardly had the world recovered from the shock of Kennedy's death when the sudden fall from power of Nikita Krushchev, the detonation of Communist China's first atomic bomb, and a change of government in Britain — all occurring in October 1964 — reminded mankind of the precariousness of the balance of power and fear which has until now preserved it from total destruction.

Because of the importance of all these and other changes, the book has been largely rewritten. It is now divided into three parts. The first part, in four chapters, surveys the basic factors of contemporary world politics, including in the fourth chapter a survey of the evolution of the international power conflict, especially the relations between the United States and the Soviet Union, since the last war.

The survey of European policy problems has been taken out of that chapter, and it now forms the first of six chapters on 'Regional Aspects of World Politics', which constitute Part II. The many changes that have occurred in the last few years have necessitated an almost complete revision of that part. The chapter on Africa has been completely rewritten and a new chapter on 'Latin America and World Politics' has been added, in view of the growing involvement of Latin America in world affairs.

The third part deals with some of the long-term problems of

mankind. A chapter on 'Economic Aid and International Development' has been added in view of the close and vital link between the problems of international politics and those of economic development.

As in all previous editions, detailed notes, statistics and texts of international documents have been put into the Appendices so that the narrative could be kept almost entirely free of footnotes and references. Statistics and maps have been brought up to date. The list of international documents has been considerably expanded.

New York, December 1964 W. F.

ACKNOWLEDGMENTS

I AM indebted to Mr. George Kalmanoff and to Mr. Robert F. Meagher for having read and made valuable suggestions in regard to the chapters dealing with Africa and Latin America. Mr. Robert E. Stein, LL.B., has revised the reading-list and Mr. Aaron Etra has assisted me in the preparation of the index. My secretary, Mrs. Maxine E. Mizrahi, has rendered most valuable assistance in the preparation of the manuscript.

New York, December 1964 W.F.

FOREWORD

In Goethe's *Faust*, a German citizen taking his Easter Sunday walk speaks with smug satisfaction of wars in other lands:

> 'When Sunday comes, or times of holiday,
> Let's talk of fights — there's nothing I like more
> Than news of Turkey or lands far away,
> Where malcontents have loosed the dogs of war.
> You stand at windows with your drop of drink,
> And watch the river's coloured traffic gliding —
> And then when evening comes, go home,
> And think how good it is to live in peace abiding.'[1]

In 1964 we can hardly comfort ourselves in this way. A Four-Power clash in Berlin, a Communist move in Vietnam, an adverse vote in the United States Senate on assistance to India, an economic blockade of Cuba, racial strife in Cyprus, are all matters which will directly, and within a short time, affect the peace and happiness of each of us.

The global and all-pervading character of contemporary world politics makes a generally understandable introduction to its main problems both urgent and difficult. Never has it been more necessary for the ordinary citizen of the surviving democracies to have an intelligent interest in world affairs. On the other hand, the close political interdependence of different continents and conflicts, as well as the increasing importance of economics in international politics, make the subject more and more complicated. It is difficult to find the middle way between complexity and over-simplification. Nor does this book offer a patent solution. Few serious students of international affairs will still be content to postulate a master solution: world government, international federation, a Charter of Human Rights. Nor can the statesman put his whole faith in conversion to pacifism, moral rearmament or human brotherhood. We have never been in greater need of faith, and a firm belief in values. But the respon-

[1] *Faust*, Pt. I, 'Vor dem Tor'. Translated by Philip Wayne.

sible democratic citizen must put himself into the position of a statesman, a Member of Parliament, a civil servant and others responsible for the shaping of international relations. And for them, a belief in world government, or an international Bill of Rights, or even in the federal union of Europe, can be no more than a general guiding light. Their problem is how to meet a given situation, how to adjust their ideals and wishes to the military, economic and psychological realities of the moment. A firm scale of values and ideals distinguishes the statesman from the opportunist. But idealism alone will not solve a single one of the grave problems confronting the statesmen of the Western democracies.

The emphasis in this book is therefore on the analysis of the different elements inherent in contemporary international problems. Distortion by over-simplification is one of the most dismal features of present-day international propaganda. Each move, each problem, is interpreted according to taste, as one of pure idealism or of economic greed; of national egotism, or of international humanitarianism; of warmongering, or of love of peace. And one of the greatest threats to democracy is the increasing temptation to imitate the totalitarian example, by singling out an arch-enemy, as a substitute for sober thinking. The present book is not, of course, free from beliefs and, perhaps, prejudices, but I hope that it has succeeded in discussing the main issues dispassionately, and without the over-simplification of the 'love–hate' approach.

PART I — BASIC FACTORS IN WORLD POLITICS

CHAPTER I

MOVING FORCES IN WORLD POLITICS

WHAT are the forces which guide world politics? A generation which has experienced two world wars, fought 'to end wars' but leading to more power politics and strife; which has witnessed the rise and fall of the League of Nations as well as of Hitler and Mussolini; which sees the Allied Powers of the last war engaged in a bitter struggle of power and ideology; which witnesses a proliferation of new, mostly weak, national States, where modern communications and conditions of our world have made the national State an anachronism; such a generation might well feel bewildered and lose all hope of discovering any clear guiding principles. The very disillusionment and apathy produced by all these disappointments, and by the feeling that all the sacrifice and bloodshed may have been in vain, are in themselves a great obstacle to any progress towards a better international order.

Power Interpretations and Ideological Interpretations

Perhaps the most fundamental conflict in the diagnosis of politics and world events is that between 'power' interpretations and 'idealistic' interpretations. A powerful school of students of international affairs argue that the struggle for power supremacy and its maintenance by those who profess it is the guiding theme of world politics. This trend of thought has received much support from recent international events, which time and again have dealt severe blows to idealists and fighters for a new and better international order, while they seem to vindicate those who regard the ruthless exercise of superior power as the one really important factor in the shaping of political affairs.

Where 'power' philosophers see a struggle for control between popes and kings, or the ruthless ambition of a Napoleon, idealists think in terms of a clash between mediæval Christian ideas and the ideology of the modern national State, or between the new ideas of the French Revolution and the conservative political order of early nineteenth-century Europe. Similarly, as a subsequent chapter will show, the greatest conflict of our own day may be interpreted in terms of the conflicting ideologies of democracy and totalitarianism, or as a struggle for world supremacy between the two most powerful States of our time and the groups which control the power of these States. 'Power' interpretations of history tend to emphasize the role of individuals, of a Napoleon, Hitler or Stalin. Ideological interpretations see individuals more as expressions of forces greater than themselves. But the analysis of politics in terms of power is not necessarily a 'great man' analysis. It may equally be concerned with the actions and influences of bankers or international steel interests, of trade unions or churches, of clubs or pressure groups. Ideological interpretations, on the other hand, may be pacific or warlike, fanatic or tolerant, but in all cases they would see persons, groups or forces as instruments in the service of ideas: the Spanish Inquisition as a means to ensure the supremacy of the true Christian faith; the conquests of the Nazis as a means of ensuring the supremacy of the nobler over the inferior races; the struggle of the Soviet bloc against the Western democracies as a struggle for the establishment of the classless society.

The analysis attempted in this chapter will show that ideological and power motivations are almost invariably mixed, and this, of course, makes the interpretation of world events a far more complex affair than it seems, for example, to the mind of a fanatic Marxist or Catholic. But it is not only the mixture of motives and pulls in the behaviour of persons, groups or nations which makes a balanced approach to world politics so difficult. Politics is by its very definition concerned with the activities of organized communities of men and their mutual relations. Ideas do not fight each other in pure space, but through organized groups — and this involves the control of some by others. A Stalin may be convinced that, without absolute control by himself and a small group of the Politburo over the Soviet nation, it may be impossible to achieve world Socialism. American Air Force generals and industrial leaders may think that unless they have the decisive say over armaments and the use of atom bombs, democracy may be destroyed by aggressive Communism. Only rarely the naked desire for power emerges unashamed, as in some of the confidential utterances of Hitler, or in the last days of the Nazi regime. As was then shown, the naked lust for power is often very close to a nihilistic urge for destruction, even self-destruction. Not only are men's motives usually mixed and complex, but the organization of society, especially in our own times, demands increasing control, that is, a degree of power vested in relatively few people over many others.

It is with these considerations in mind that we must approach an analysis of the different aspects of power and ideology in world affairs, and of the ways in which they react on each other.

There are various aspects and forms of power. Bertrand Russell[1] distinguishes between traditional authority; 'naked' power, based on sheer physical force; revolutionary power, derived from the hold of a new creed over men; economic power, based on the legalized control of economic resources; and power over opinion, which may base itself on political and social propaganda, or on religious creeds. In modern politics all these forms are of decisive, though not of equal, importance. The Nazi regime, for example, used as one of its two main weapons 'naked' power — that is, the coercion of the community by the ruthless use of armed forces and police action. But no less important was the control of the people's minds, exercised through a complete State censorship over all vehicles of public opinion, such as Parliament, the Press, the radio, and all forms of political organization. The Nazi regime also, though in a manner far more concealed than that adopted by the Communist Government of Russia, used economic power — that is to say, the control over production and the livelihood of men. But in order to gain control over the economic resources of nations as well as over their constitutional and political life, the Nazis relied on a combination of the revolutionary appeal with the appeal to legality and tradition. Instead of openly repealing the existing democratic constitution of Germany, they preferred to emasculate it by a pseudo-legal process. Having first outlawed the Communist Party and exercised strong pressure upon other parties, the Nazi Government obtained some sweeping constitutional amendments which enabled it to discard allies and opponents alike, and to rule henceforth without opposition. Instead of nationalizing industry, the Nazis preferred to maintain the capitalist owners of industry in nominal control, by

[1] *Power*, 7th imp., 1958.

linking them closely to the regime, through the bribery of profits and power over the workers. The Soviet Revolution has put much greater emphasis on the direct acquisition of economic power. We find the various aspects of power reflected in international affairs. The great majority of power conflicts within a State do not directly touch the world outside, but usually the concentration of power in a person or a group within a strong and powerful State has been followed, sooner or later, by attempts to extend this control to other States and peoples.

The pursuit of political or economic power has been the main dynamo of international movements and conflicts. A State — and that means the most powerful group in the State — has been tempted by the prospect of control over other States and peoples to launch wars and other campaigns of subjection. In modern times the attempt to maintain a privileged position in international trade, to protect financial investments in other countries, or the desire to meet a threat to the social structure of society from abroad, have played an increasingly important part.

Personal megalomania is one of the most powerful causes of conquest and bloodshed. But, unlike the Renaissance tyrants or even Napoleon, modern dictators have to operate in a complex and articulate society, which has at least tasted the greater liberties of a democratic age and which must consider the 'common man' as more than mere cannon-fodder. This means rule by a clique rather than by a single man, and the underpinning of the quest for power by some sort of political philosophy. With Hitler, the idea of the supremacy of a race of master rulers over inferior and subject peoples provided this 'philosophy'. It supplied a bare cover for the merciless lust for power of a small group of people who wanted to establish themselves as the undisputed masters over the bodies and minds of Germany and Europe, and, if possible, the entire world.

The growth of international trade and international financial and industrial development in the nineteenth century, against a background of stark social inequalities, has led to the widespread belief, most articulately formulated in Marxist theory, that the quest for economic power is the main source of international conflict. There is no doubt that the international ramifications and alignments of industrial and business interests have in modern times often had a powerful influence on the trend of international events. The fear of growing German industrial competition on international markets greatly aggravated the tension which eventually brought Britain into war against Germany in 1914. But no sober historian could assert that this tension would have led to war without the German bid for continental hegemony and the aggressive policies of the German Emperor. Business interests have frequently favoured State actions against foreign Powers where the inequality of strength was such as to make a major war unlikely. The clearest example is perhaps the joint action by the European Powers in the Chinese Boxer Revolt of 1900, which threatened the extra-territorial and trading privileges of the European Powers. On other occasions naval demonstrations by the fleets of Western creditor nations have reminded smaller States of the serious view taken of defaults on international loans. But 'vested interests' are very unlikely to push towards a major international war, the destructive effects of which will far outweigh any gain. On the contrary, in recent years economic interests have increasingly been associated with appeasement, sometimes in disregard of national interests. A telling example is the continued supply of iron ore from France to Germany between October 1939 and April 1940, through the then neutral countries of Belgium and Luxembourg. The steel industries of these countries had been associated in an international steel cartel. Similarly American steel industries were indicted in 1942 by the Department of Justice for having attempted to secure continuation of business associations with Japan even in the case of war, and for having disclosed an American patent for the manufacture of synthetic rubber to a German chemical concern under a mutual patent agreement, while they withheld it from the American authorities.

Again, the search for export markets in order to avoid domestic unemployment or to buttress pressure groups in industry or agriculture is a far from negligible factor in international affairs. But there is no reason to regard it as the major cause of international conflict. Whether or not we are witnessing the end of 'economic man', it is beyond doubt that in our own time direction of economic policy is becoming more and more subservient to political power. In a completely Socialist State like Soviet Russia this is obvious. The whole trend of production, the share allotted to consumers, the volume and direction of foreign trade, are all controlled by the master minds who plan the nation's economy in accordance with the general policy of the State. The Fascist regimes of Germany, Italy and Japan ensured a hardly less decisive supremacy of politics over economics by different means. They preserved capitalist ownership, but associated the captains of industry and business with the aggressive policies of the Government by a partnership of loot which promised them rich gains through conquest abroad, and complete control at home over their workers, who had been deprived of free trade unions and been organized in compulsory State-controlled 'Labour Fronts'. This Fascist alternative to the Socialist revolution was relatively easy in States where the rise of industry had from the outset been fostered by active State policy. Germany, Italy, Japan all became powerful modern nation-States in the second half of the nineteenth century, and they nurtured their industries by deliberate policies of protectionism and international expansion.

In the democracies, too, the primacy of politics is becoming more and more evident. Political and military State policies increasingly control the developments of technical research and industrial production, international loan policies and other foreign ventures. United States aid to Europe through the Marshall Plan brought some support to American shipping, to cotton- and tobacco-growers. But the predominant purpose of Marshall Aid has been political — the consolidation of Western European nations against Communism and Soviet expansion. In the pursuit of this objective, the United States made considerable economic sacrifices to aid European economic recovery, not with the purpose of making the assisted nations permanently dependent on American supplies, but with the opposite objective of making them more self-reliant. So successful was this effort that the nations of Western Europe — economically prosperous and financially strong — are now in a position to defy the political leadership of the United States.

The economic development of certain areas in Africa, the Middle East and India forms part of the world-wide contest which will be analysed more fully later. It is, in fact, as a necessary result of the steadily growing importance of economic strength in international affairs that the control and direction of economic forces are increasingly harnessed to State policy. In the balance of international forces the relative importance of purely military skill, organization and prowess is steadily decreasing by comparison with the economic potential of a State. Industrial resources and raw materials, agricultural self-sufficiency, the productivity of the worker, scientific and technical development, financial assets and development potential are today factors which more than any other ensure the predominant power of both the Soviet Union and the United States. On the other hand, the dependence of a country on the import of vital raw materials, lack of agricultural self-sufficiency, scarcity of foreign exchange and technological backwardness are today more vital causes of national weakness than the ready armed strength. But these economic factors are not today allowed to govern the destinies of a nation by autonomous laws, such as the price mechanism, unemployment and the laws of supply and demand were supposed to produce them in the classical economy of the liberal era. Lack of raw materials, deflation, unemployment, are not allowed to work themselves out without political interference. A national economic and financial crisis is counteracted by a national Government through a policy of regulating imports and boosting exports according to national priorities. Employment is actively promoted by the location of industries and, if necessary, public works. The social effects of depression are countered by controlled prices, social insurance and various other relief actions. And despite its lingering economic philosophy of *laissez-faire*, the United States cannot afford to let these economic laws take their course, because too great an economic weakening of friendly nations (such as Turkey or South Vietnam) would upset the international balance of power. *Laissez-faire* has never been absolute, nor can State action today entirely wipe out the laws of supply and demand. But the emphasis has shifted decisively. In so far as it is within the power of organized political action to mitigate or counter the effects of economic movements, this is now increasingly done. And as E. H. Carr[1] has pointed out, many of the practices of Soviet Russia, urged upon her not by the theory of Marxism but by the necessities of impoverishment, scarcity and isolation, are now increasingly accepted by non-Communist countries: five-year plans, Government control of trade, differentiated currencies for external and internal purposes, direction of labour.

Appreciation of this transformation is all the more important

[1] *The Soviet Impact on the Western World.*

as Communist dogma stubbornly adheres to theories developed half a century ago or more, by such leading Marxist thinkers as Engels, Lenin, Hobson or Kautsky, blandly ignoring the tremendous changes in the character of Capitalist as well as Socialist society.

Ideological Forces in World Politics

Most international conflicts show a mixture of power politics and ideological factors. The last two world wars were marked by such a mixture. Some of the most ardent ideological movements, such as the mediæval Crusades, the Moslem wars or the wars of Inquisition, have deliberately preached and provoked strife as the only means of securing the victory of the right faith. Of more immediate concern to our own generation is the Communist creed that the establishment of a classless society is impossible without a final struggle between 'Capitalism' and 'Socialism'. Pure Communist doctrine further stipulates that the overthrow of Capitalism cannot be secured without the use of force, i.e. violent revolutions and, if necessary, major international wars. In this respect, however, a split has occurred in recent years, between the 'classical' attitude, now notably represented by Communist China, and the 'revisionist' attitude of the Soviet Union, which acknowledges the possibility and indeed the desirability of 'peaceful co-existence' between Socialist and Capitalist systems. To what extent these differences in Communist doctrine represent genuine conflicts of theory rather than expressions of the stage of development reached respectively by the U.S.S.R. and Communist China will be discussed later. Orthodoxy means the acceptance of a mission to convert, if necessary, by force.

Of the ideological forces which have exercised deep and lasting influence on the shape of modern international society, three stand out in importance. The first is Christianity, the second the liberal and enlightened Humanitarianism of recent centuries, the third the idea of a classless Socialist society.

Christianity and International Order

Religious movements have more often than not been used as a cover for the pursuit of political or economic objectives. The influence of Christian principles, both as a general force in the minds of men and in the organized preaching of the Christian Churches of various denominations, has undoubtedly been a powerful factor in the history of Western civilizations. Christianity proper, as distinct from Christian ethics, which are widely accepted in modern society, has, however, been hampered in its attitude to world events and politics by two conflicting trends. On the one hand, Christians have, at different times and with different emphasis, realized the impossibility of establishing a divine order in this world. The early history of Christianity in particular was deeply marked by this pessimism and the 'other-worldliness' of Christianity. St. Augustine's *De Civitate Dei*, written between A.D. 412 and 427, expressed this trend in its most radical form. Writing at a time of profound political and social chaos and the disintegration of the Roman Empire, St. Augustine divorces political institutions and the 'city of this world' entirely from the divine purpose, the 'City of God'. They are to him institutions of sin from which men can find redemption only by the grace of God. This trend prevailed throughout the confused period of the Dark Ages until the Catholic Church, firmly established and powerfully organized as the guiding spiritual power of Europe, led by masterful popes and brilliant thinkers, proceeded to link the Kingdom of God with the kingdom of this world. In the writings of St. Thomas Aquinas the divine order finds expression in laws of Nature as interpreted by the Church. These the State must obey, although it is left latitude in matters of expediency and utility. After centuries of confusion, the modern Catholic Church has, since the Encyclicals of Pope Leo XIII, reverted to scholastic doctrines and striven to formulate the laws of God in the social and political setting of the modern world. By this it has planted its feet firmly on the earth, but it has also descended into the arena of politics, and it constantly faces the dilemma of taking sides in the political and social struggle while professing to be the mouthpiece of God, Christianity and eternal truth. The political and social postulates of the Church, as reformulated by modern popes, will be summarized in a later chapter.[1] Suffice it to say here that Christianity, as a force working in the minds and consciences of men, can only find imperfect expression in any Church which is at the same time a powerful social and economic organization controlling a vast hierarchy of servants, properties and institutions in many countries.

[1] Ch. 3.

The other Christian Churches have faced different dilemmas. If, like (formerly) the Protestant Church in Germany or the Anglican Church in England, they are linked with throne and government, they have almost invariably become the defenders of the established order, and champions of their particular nation when at war. If the Catholic Church can take a supra-national attitude in wars but is deeply committed on the religious, political and social issues, the Protestant Churches face the difficult task of blessing the war in which their country is involved without denying their Christian principles. Yet it seems impossible to reconcile the pure spirit of Christianity with bloodshed and victory in battle. A few years ago a representative committee of Western Church leaders published a report on atomic warfare in which the majority gave cautious support to the use of atomic bombs in defence against aggression and oppressive regimes. In recent years the Churches, led by such men as the late Archbishop Temple, have tried to lessen this dilemma by supporting international organizations like the League of Nations and the United Nations Organization, and by sponsoring the establishment of an international police force in the place of national armies. No matter, however, what line Christians adopt, political or social action can never be but a pale and impure reflection of Christian principles.

There is yet another reason why the Christian religion as such cannot hope to be the sole instrument of world order. As the world shrinks and the conflicts as well as the links between the nations become world-wide, the problem of a meeting-ground between the civilizations of the Occident and the Orient assumes increasing importance. But the peoples of the Orient overwhelmingly practise religions entirely different from Christianity—such as Islam, Hinduism, Buddhism and Confucianism. As Northrop[1] and others have shown, the achievement of harmonious relations between the nations of the Orient and Occident will depend on the acceptance of common principles of behaviour which will not destroy the diversity of religions and cultures. The alternative would be an attempt of the Occident to convert the peoples of the Orient to Christianity by force. This would mean violence, bloodshed and suppression, as in the days of the forced Christianization of pagans in Europe under Charlemagne, the mediæval Crusades or the religious conquest campaigns of

[1] *The Meeting of East and West*, 1946.

the Moslems in Europe and India. It is a condition of international collaboration that the ethics of the different religions should encourage, or at least permit, their followers to participate in the building of international law. It is essential that Christians should join hands with Jews, Hindus, Buddhists or Confucians in the pursuit of peace and practical tasks of international collaboration, not that they should do so under the inspiration or compulsion of the same faith.

It is, in short, a condition of a successful international order not based on force or conquest that certain principles of action, such as the establishment of an international security force or an international Bill of Rights, or the international distribution of foodstuffs, should be agreed, but that the source of inspiration, which to one may be the Christian faith, to another the all-pervading goodness of Buddha and to a third an ethical and atheistic rationalism, should be left out of the realm of practical political action. To do otherwise would be likely to lead to a new era of religious and Messianic wars of conquest.

Humanitarianism

Non-theological cosmopolitan humanitarianism has been a very powerful force in recent international developments. Just as social and political reform in nineteenth-century Britain owes as much or more to the liberal humanitarian and non-theological doctrines of Bentham, Mill and the Fabians, as to the Christian inspiration of Shaftesbury, Kingsley or Florence Nightingale, so the modern movement towards international law and collaboration derives mainly from rationalist, liberal and Social-Democratic thought, although great Christians such as Archbishop Temple have done much to link international order with Christian principles. From the rationalist philosophers of the late eighteenth century to modern liberal and Social-Democratic humanitarian philosophy, this trend of thought takes up and modernizes the teaching of the Stoic philosophers of the third and fourth centuries B.C. It accepts the Christian values of the fundamental equality of man, regardless of race and nationality, and it postulates the peaceful organization of international society. It regards war as both objectionable and irrational. It is the combination of a strong ethical feeling with the belief in the inevitable progress of mankind, from the senseless use of destructive instincts to the rational use of its higher mental powers, which has given this trend of thinking such strength, especially between the end of the eighteenth and the beginning of the twentieth century. And it is the return to darker and more elemental instincts in our own time which has dealt a terrible blow to this liberal and enlightened movement towards a saner international order. Its most practical expression has been the establishment of a system of international law, in particular of peaceful methods of settlement of international disputes and the adoption of rules ensuring a more humane conduct of war. Above all, humanitarian influence has been the most powerful supporter of the international organization of mankind, through the League of Nations, the United Nations Organization and specialized international agencies.

Marxism

The idea of a classless and equalitarian society as such is only a new version of an old dream. The special power of Marxism derives from two other factors: its scientific or quasi-scientific foundation on an economic and political theory, and perhaps even more the fascination of 'inevitability'. At a time when the bleaker aspects of the Industrial Revolution and the misery of millions of exploited workers had become obvious, a theory which had its roots in the exploitation of the masses by the controllers of capital had an effect far stronger than it would have had in an earlier or a later period. By its use of the 'dialectic' method, which portrays one movement in world history as logically and inevitably flowing from another, it gave, and still gives, great strength to its followers, who believe that they are not only fighting for a better society, but that they are the executors of an inevitable movement of history.

Another element of strength in the Marxist attitude is its fundamental optimism. While the orthodox Marxist accepts struggle, revolution, bloodshed and strife as necessary means to a desirable end, the goal is bright: a world busily engaged, without distinctions of class, race, religion or wealth, in the promotion of the common welfare, and endowed with potentially unlimited powers for the achievement of paradise on earth. In this Marxism contrasts with other determinist philosophies, especially with those of modern comparative historians who see modern civilization doomed to perish in a remorseless cycle of rise and decline. The best known representative of this school is the German, Oswald Spengler, who, in a widely read work published after the First World War,[1] deduced from the comparison of a number of different civilizations the laws of their rise, prosperity and decline, and forecast for our Western civilizations the inevitable decline symbolized by the growth of cities and standardized societies which had lost the vitality of creative growth, and the rise of Cæsarean dictators. This has been developed, with a characteristic mixture of idealism and nihilism, by another German, Juenger, who visualizes the standardized, skilled and obedient 'worker' as the instrument of such Cæsarean society. The English historian, Toynbee, in a much more restrained and widely based comparison of the known civilizations of history,[2] has some difficulty in avoiding a similar conclusion. But he does allow for two factors neglected by Spengler. In the first place, he is aware that it is easy for later generations to survey the cycles of growth and decline, but that it is extremely difficult to measure accurately the stage at which one's own civilization has arrived. In the second place, he allows for freedom of human action, which may or may not avert a threatening catastrophe, and he places his hope in the Christian spirit of universality.

Relativist Ideologies

We have so far discussed ideas of man and international society based on a definite philosophy. The formulation of international policies is, however, possible from a relativist, and even sceptical, point of view. Many students of contemporary politics and international affairs postulate either a complete world-State, a world federation or a less ambitious form of world-wide international organization simply as a condition of the survival of civilized man. They see political institutions, such as tribal organizations, feudalism and, above all, the era of the national State, as forms of political organization sufficient in certain conditions but inadequate in others. They argue that the development of modern communications, the destructiveness of modern weapons, the growing inequality between big Powers and small Powers, and many other factors, make a world-wide international organization indispensable, whether or not it is inherently desirable. Even nationalist

[1] *The Decline of the Occident.*
[2] *A Study of History*, Vol. I.

politicians and statesmen may arrive at similar conclusions. Before the last war, for example, Winston Churchill supported a powerful and effective League of Nations because he saw, quite rightly, that such a League, under British leadership, would be the only means of holding down forces threatening Britain as well as democracy in general. Similarly, Machiavelli, more than four centuries ago, thought that contemporary Italy needed a prince who would be strong, cruel, crafty and perfidious, because he saw no other way of bringing about national unity in Italy. To Machiavelli, the realist, the achievement of a national State in Italy was, in 1516, when he published *The Prince*, as urgent a necessity as the achievement of an effective international authority is to many modern statesmen and thinkers. In both cases it is the question of a practical alternative to chaos. Usually, of course, practical and idealistic arguments are mixed. Most of the practical internationalists are likely to have a background of Christian, humanitarian or Socialist ideologies.

Individual and National Standards of Conduct

For a proper appreciation of the respective parts of ideals and power politics in international affairs, we should, however, bear two further factors in mind. The first is that in the present state of international relations the share of power politics in the conduct of nations is very much greater than it is in the conduct of individuals within a nation. People in a mass usually behave much worse than the same people taken as individuals. Conscience, habit and fear make the average individual conform to standards which he easily rejects when acting in a group. He may be ambitious, jealous and cruel in his mind, but the standards of ethics and law prevalent in the community prevent him from giving full vent to these instincts. In a group his identity and his individual responsibility are lost. He is apt to indulge in mass hysteria, or he has not the courage to resist leaders who, more often than not, appeal to passion rather than to reason. When the group is a nation-State dealing with other nation-States, the standards of national conduct are lowered by a second factor: patriotic loyalties are, for the overwhelming majority of contemporary mankind, far stronger than any sense of international community. In the name of patriotism, standards of conduct are sanctioned which would be greatly repugnant in any other relationship. It is despicable to boast about one's individual bravery, honesty, cleverness or strength, but all nations claim particular excellence in such accomplishments for themselves. The Nazi myth of Nordic superiority, or the Russian attempts of a few years ago to prove that every single modern invention or scientific discovery, from aeroplanes and television to Mendelian laws, has really been made by Russians are particularly grotesque examples of a tendency from which no nation is free. It is an interesting commentary on national psychology that these claims have given way to a much more balanced outlook with the attainment of incontestable scientific and technological eminence by Russia.

Closely connected with this question of loyalties is the problem of means and ends. The citizen within a modern State may desire great wealth or a powerful position, in government or business. But he must seek to attain them within the limits of law, enforceable by law courts, police, and the standards of public opinion. But the right to make war, as the ultimate end by which a nation achieves its objectives, is still the basic principle of international law. Recent attempts to limit the legality of war will be discussed later. The basic rule governing relations between nations is still that the end justifies almost any means, and the end itself is not controlled by an authority higher than the nation-State.

The great majority of vital world events, then, are determined by a blend of ideological and power motivations which sometimes reinforce and sometimes weaken each other. In former centuries religious conflicts were prominent causes of war. In modern times the unifying tie of national loyalty is usually stronger than divergencies between Catholics, Protestants and Jews, although the creation of the Jewish State in Palestine links a religious with a national loyalty. Religious factors as a cause of international conflict are now more likely to be important in the Eastern world. The conflicts between Hindus and Moslems in India, between Arabs and Jews in Palestine or between Greek Orthodox Christians and Turkish Moslems in Cyprus have recently proved to be forces capable of splitting or making nations.

In the last world war the defence of personal and national liberty and of democratic society was a vital factor. But at the same time the necessity for Britain to fight once more a Power threatening to dominate the Continent of Europe was bound to bring her into the war. In the present conflict between Soviet Russia and the

United States rival political and social ideologies are as vital as the conflicting power ambitions of different groups of people and the dictates of national self-preservation. In the emancipation of modern India the religious inspiration of Gandhi was as important a factor as the spread of nationalism in the Far East and the wish of the rising industrial and merchant classes in India to secure control of Indian resources and to destroy the original British monopoly of the Indian market. In the person of Gandhi himself the shrewd and ruthless statesman and the saint were inextricably mixed. Again, in the British withdrawal from India a wise liberalism has combined with the strategic interests imposed upon a Power which is no longer physically capable of controlling a vast empire scattered throughout the world. A study of international problems which ignores any one of these factors and elevates ideology, personal power or class domination into the single determinant of world developments over-simplifies, and thereby falsifies, as much as a study of human nature which only knows sex instinct or hunger on the one hand, or selfless devotion and love on the other.

Limits of Power Politics

The first of the modern 'realists', Machiavelli, taught (in 1516) that a prince ought not to be concerned with ethics but only with the best way of achieving his ends. To do so, he had to be both a fox and a lion; to use the cunning of the one and the strength of the other. Machiavelli went out of his way to praise the actions of Cesare Borgia, who had broken countless promises, murdered his friends, ransacked cities and is believed to have murdered his brother and seduced his sister. He died in battle, having escaped from a Spanish prison, exiled, miserable and despised. A similar fate recently overtook Hitler and Mussolini, both of whom regarded Machiavelli's *Prince* as a bible of politics. This should help us to understand the limits of power politics. First of all, the unbridled exercise of power and the use of every and any means to achieve it usually induce an attitude of mind which the Greeks called *hubris*, the intoxication with success which makes men forget the limits of human power, and almost invariably precedes their downfall. This happened to Napoleon and Hitler when they invaded Russia and challenged the world to be their enemies. Connected with this is, secondly, the revulsion of feeling which cruelty, craftiness and an insatiable lust for power almost invariably arouse. The master Machiavellians, such as Hitler, calculated that swift and merciless action would make them sufficiently secure to be able either to smother or defy such reactions. Given another ten years of rule, the Nazi regime might have succeeded in exterminating Jews and Poles altogether, and in so enfeebling the Russians, the French and other nations as to break their power of organized resistance. But it lost the race against time. The very mercilessness of Hitler's campaign of conquest and extermination aroused the fierce resistance of the suffering nations and races, and it also stirred the slumbering democracies into action. It thus defeated its own purpose. Thirdly, the last war showed again that people will fight and die for the preservation of liberties, for their Christian, democratic, Socialist or Communist faith, even though the ideals for which they fight fade and become polluted once victory has been achieved.

The modern statesman, and anyone who takes a responsible part in the conduct of international relations, will constantly have to balance these various factors. The Christian may hope that the spirit of brotherhood will eliminate the present conflicts between Soviet Russia and the West, but the statesman cannot take this as a guide to action. He will have to balance the people's longing for peace against their fear of suppression; the passion for liberty against the fickleness of democracy and the escapism of the majority; the aggressive policy of a Government against its state of military preparedness; the opportunities which technical superiority, such as the possession of the atom bomb, may offer for a swift victory of surprise, against the deep ethical revulsion which a preventive war would produce among the masses.

Lessons of the Allied Occupation of Germany

How extremely difficult the blending of ideological and power factors is in practice has been tellingly demonstrated by the results of the post-war occupation of Germany and the war trials of her leading statesmen and generals. In scale and magnitude this occupation exceeded anything previously known. The victorious Allies set out not only to exercise complete control — permeating all aspects of public and private life — over a highly developed nation-State; they also attempted simultaneously to secure themselves against any further political, military and economic threat from Germany, and to convert a nation impregnated with a continuous tradition of aggressive militarism and political cynicism to higher and different ethical standards: the worship of peace instead of war, the substitution of a democratic for an authoritarian faith, the replacement of pagan by Christian ideals. At the same time the trial of political and military leaders was to set a new landmark in international law and morality. For the first time, individuals particularly responsible for the preparation of aggressive war and the organization of inhuman methods of warfare were indicted as criminals. International law, instead of vaguely committing States, was to become a matter of immediate and binding concern to the individual.

There is, of course, a certain connection between the security and the ideological aspects of the Occupation. A genuinely pacific and contented nation constitutes no threat to others. Yet it is essential for the student of international affairs, as it was for the statesmen, soldiers and administrators making and executing the plans, to distinguish between these two aspects. For it is the uncertain vacillation between the one and the other that has largely contributed to what is now commonly acknowledged to be the failure of a great and vital experiment in international relations. The deeper causes of this failure were apparent very soon after the beginning of the Occupation. They may be traced to the futility of an attempt to preach ideals and moral values without regard to the human and psychological factors and to power considerations which, on the side both of victors and vanquished, were certain to nullify this preaching. These weaknesses were greatly accentuated in the case of Germany, where, as distinct from Japan, not one but four Powers were in control. Their mutual conflicts and suspicions soon made a mockery of their professed ideals in the eyes of the demoralized and cynical Germans.

The ambitious and comprehensive programme with which the Allies entered Germany was mainly concerned with power factors in so far as it aimed at the complete demilitarization of Germany, and planned to limit German productive capacity in vital industries such as steel, machine tools or chemical products, while entirely prohibiting the manufacture of certain materials of particular military value. Moral and ideological purposes predominated in the attempt to purge German life completely of Nazi ideology and organization, and to re-model the political as well as the cultural and educational life of the nation on the lines of a pacific democracy. An immense apparatus of thought, organization and manpower was put into the service of these tasks. The economic disarmament programme was not agreed among the Allies until a year after the start of the Occupation. It was a highly complex document, setting precise maximum limits of production for Germany's vital industries. But at the time of its completion the original objectives of the Occupation had already largely shifted. Both the magnitude of Germany's economic collapse and the growing discord between the Allies led to an almost immediate revision of the plan. As time went by, economic rehabilitation increasingly displaced economic disarmament as an objective, and Western Germany eventually became one of the largest recipients of American Marshall Aid. On the political side, the complexity of de-Nazification was greatly under-estimated. If ten or twenty thousand easily identifiable political, military and industrial leaders of the Nazi regime had been dealt with by swift and summary jurisdiction — as happened, at the risk of some injustices, to Fascist rulers in Italy and the Collaborationists in France — more would have been achieved than by the elaborate method of sifting many millions of Germans who had belonged, however inconspicuously and under pressure, to some kind of Nazi organization. Long before the process was complete, original zeal had cooled down and German stupefaction had given way to growing resentment. In the end it was the American Military Government, the main champion of all-embracing de-Nazification, which took the lead in restoring more and more industrialists, managers and administrators tainted with Nazi affiliations to responsible positions, for the sake of Germany's recovery — now America's main objective. The Americans also took the lead in substituting for the totalitarian regime of Nazi Germany and Japan parliamentary democracies closely modelled on the American Constitution. But they did much to damage the effect of this rule when they prevented democratically elected parliaments from implementing vital decisions where they conflicted with the social policies of the American Military Government (for example, on the socialization of the steel, coal and chemical industries, whose owners had been dispossessed and arrested as part of the original de-Nazification programme). The

British came up increasingly against the difficulty of rebuilding Germany in accordance with democratic principles without also reviving, by British effort and sacrifice, the export capacity of Britain's greatest industrial competitor. While teams of devoted educational reformers and political idealists worked for the spiritual conversion of the Germans, all these grim realities increasingly thwarted their efforts. But the greatest single factor which weakened this gigantic effort at re-education was the growing disunity among the Allies themselves. Their conflicts and suspicions, the vast divergencies in their interpretations of democracy, the comparison of their theories with their behaviour in practice — all these confirmed to the majority of cynical or indifferent Germans that the Machiavellian theories of their Nazi rulers were correct, and that only the master, not the system, had changed. A similar unfortunate mixture of power politics and ideology marred the moral effects of the trials of German and Japanese war criminals. The objective was a revolutionary departure in international law which, in view of the unprecedented crimes committed by the Axis Powers — fresh as they were in people's memories — might well have succeeded. International law, in the absence of an international law-giver, has to develop through periodic jumps of this kind. But the objective was marred, first, by the gross psychological mistake of making representatives of the four victorious Powers the sole judges, and, secondly, by extending the scope of the trials much too far. They included, for example, indictment for the bombing of undefended cities at a time when the bombing of German cities and the dropping of atom bombs on Japan were freshest in people's memories. The main judgment on the German war criminals was rendered in October 1946, that on the Japanese war criminals over two years later.

It was inevitable that power politics as well as moral purposes should influence Occupation policy. But the way in which the two were constantly mixed up proved fatal. International tribunals which did not represent the family of nations in general, but only the victors, could not hope to impress the vanquished as genuine agencies of a superior international law. The preaching of the spiritual values of democracy and peace could not succeed where the teachers constantly accused each other of undemocratic and aggressive behaviour.

All this does not show that ideologies and moral values are

only a farce. It does show that it is essential to know where the one starts and the other stops.

Some Conclusions

From the tangled skein of conflicting forces and motives which have been briefly portrayed in this chapter a few simple conclusions emerge.

The first and most fundamental principle is the moral necessity to accept freedom of choice and a sense of individual responsibility in the future of mankind. The historian may well regard political developments as conditioned by laws of growth and decline, or record helplessness in the face of circumstances. But the essential factor in such development has always been human behaviour, and only the conviction that we are enchained by the events of the past can compel us to believe in the inevitability of developments in our own time. The Marxist belief in the dialectic necessity of the conflict between Capitalist and Socialist forces, and the rise of the classless society, is no longer tenable. Already Marxism has proved wrong in such predictions as the progressive growth of misery in the working population of industrial societies, or the supremacy of international class solidarity over national loyalties, while the evolution of Soviet Russia since Stalin scarcely encourages hope in the predicted 'withering' of the State, even in the final stage of Communism. And the Marxist position is ambiguous in so far as its exponents do everything in their power to hasten the process of history by their own action. They pretend that history is predetermined until the dictatorship of the proletariat shall have achieved the classless society. Then dialectic development suddenly and magically ceases: the classless society is permanent. All further progress becomes the result of the free and creative development of human powers. We may be sure that the future development of international affairs will not be the result of forces beyond human control, but of a struggle between conflicting values and policies in which everybody has a part, however small.

The second conclusion is that the struggle for power is not the only motivating force in politics and world affairs. So far, the ideological forces which have led from lawlessness to civilized society and a high degree of individual morality in national affairs are still relatively weak in international relations, and some reasons for this have been outlined in this chapter. But this is not an absolute or necessary state of affairs.

Politics is the art of the possible. It has been shown that the pursuit of ideals in international affairs is not only a matter of faith, but also of practical necessity. But it is equally true that in a world composed of many nations, each consisting of many millions of individuals, the pursuit of ideals totally unrelated to physical and sociological possibilities is a matter for the dreamer, but not for the statesman and the citizen actively concerned in the shape of things to come. This must greatly condition our attitude towards such matters as the achievement of world federation or a world-State.

It is supremely important, but also dangerously easy, to have general guiding principles and ideas: of a classless society, of a world-State, of an international police force or of the settlement of disputes between nations by an international court of justice. The test of statesmanship is the attainment of such goals in the face of often seemingly insuperable obstacles, of national loyalties, of conflicting ambitions and power politics, of vested interests and, last but not least, of apathy and ignorance. The uncompromising idealist is only too apt either to proclaim his faith without any regard to practical means and needs, or to plunge into despair when obstacles pile up. The necessity for ideologies to compromise with the welter of mental and material obstacles also presents, however, chances of positive achievement, if properly used. The aim of Communism today is the overthrow of Capitalism and political democracies which stand in the way of the establishment of a world-wide Communist society. But Communist dogma accepts the necessity of strategic withdrawals and compromises, and it constantly revises its policies in the light of changing movements and forces in the international field. On the other hand, the liberal and Social-Democratic ideal is the establishment of a rule of international law by an effective authority, under whose protection the nations can live in peace and preserve the variety of their social, political and cultural heritage. But in the face of a threat by an aggressive Power and ideology, whether from the extreme Right or from the extreme Left, this ideal may have to be temporarily sacrificed in favour of similar, but more compact and practical, associations, such as the European Communities and the Atlantic Pact. This means compromise and retrenchment on both sides, and with it the possibility of prolonged and constructive periods of peace. It is not a peace that springs from a harmony of purpose, but it is still capable of preserving and developing the world for the day when such harmony may be obtainable. It is as easy to sacrifice ideals under the pressure of strategy, expediency and self-preservation as it is for political ideals to perish for the lack of practical means of execution. The only proper course — and it is a hard one — is to be inflexible in one's ultimate values but elastic and adaptable in the choice of means. This demands constant alertness. When in 1935 Mussolini's Italy invaded a helpless Abyssinia, the moribund machinery of the League of Nations was revived and remedied almost overnight by the strength of public opinion and the swift action of all its organs. The physical possibilities of denying vital supplies of oil, coal and steel to an aggressor State, singularly dependent on the import of these raw materials, or of stopping Italy's troop transports through the Suez Canal, by the joint action of the British, French and other Mediterranean navies, were never before or after present in such fortunate combination. It is one of the great tragedies of modern history that the weakness and vacillations of a British Cabinet in which Neville Chamberlain was the dominating figure, the corruption of the French Premier Laval and the pressure of oil and other business interests combined to deprive the League of this uniquc opportunity. From this moment it was doomed, and the Fascist dictators felt safe in supporting the series of aggressive actions which ended in the Second World War.

Again, European unity has been preached for many years. It failed to come about by democratic action between the two world wars. It nearly succeeded when Hitler forcibly unified the Continent of Europe. At present there may be another chance of coming nearer to it by the economic and political co-ordination of the States of Western Europe, though such union is of course limited by the split between the Soviet bloc of nations and the Western democracies.

The intelligent study of international affairs is thus not simply a study of international ideas. It means a study of the whole network of forces which guide the nations, and a constant alertness of mind which does not lose sight of the ultimate goal behind the infinite variety of ways which may lead towards it.

One final consideration should give encouragement — recent history has supplied abundant evidence to destroy the myth of the infallibility of the mighty. For generations, while Britain had world supremacy, Europeans were brought up in the belief that British policy was as cunning as it was far-seeing, that a few master minds at Whitehall controlled the world's destinies according to a master plan thought out far ahead. The English themselves, however, know, and the world at large has long begun to realize, that the British usually stumble from decision to decision, shunning master plans, and feeling their way by a mixture of self-interest, ideals and common sense. The British, like any other people, have had to bow to the force of economic conditions, of military power, public opinion or sheer misfortune. Again, Hitler, at the height of his greatest triumphs, persuaded not only himself but a large part of the world of his infallible instinct and his mystic inspiration for doing the right thing. The Nuremberg trials and much other evidence have since brought to light the hesitations, the internal struggles and massive blunders of Hitler, as well as of his generals and politicians. After the last war the doings of Soviet Russia acquired a similar aura of certainty and infallible determination. But it is now abundantly clear that Stalin and his successors have time and again been compelled by changing pressures or their own misjudgments to experiment with alternative policies. Whatever the Allied Military Government of Germany may have failed to achieve, it has shown not only the vacillations of democracy, but those of Soviet Communism, which has constantly wavered between ruthless destruction and reconstruction of Germany under Communist control. The belief in the infallibility of well-organized power greatly contributes to the feeling of helplessness which the common man increasingly has towards world events. It is salutary, and indeed essential, to be aware that the men and groups which seem to control events are themselves subject to fears, contradictions and doubts.

It is both the privilege and the burden of the student of international affairs in a democratic country to attempt an objective analysis of world events without thereby becoming indifferent or cynical. This is an increasingly difficult task. It means, above all, the capacity of keeping one's mind clear of muddled emotions, without losing one's sense of values. The challenge to this kind of approach is increasingly grave, and it comes from without as well as from within. Modern totalitarian philosophy, whether Fascist or Communist, demands, if necessary, the deliberate perversion of truth and facts for the sake of political objectives. In his book *Mein Kampf*, which was compulsory reading for every German youth, Hitler said that a lie had only to be big enough and to be repeated often enough to be effective, and the whole vast propaganda machine of the Nazi regime was devoted to this purpose. Atrocities by Czechs, Poles, Jews were invented as part of the preparation for war. Until recently the Soviet propaganda machine has sought to whip up a similar atmosphere of hostility against the Western Powers. But we cannot take a more objective study of politics for granted in a democracy. Perhaps the best illustration of the force of emotionalism in public opinion has been the attitude towards certain foreign nations in recent years. In both world wars the theory that the German nation was eternally and incurably aggressive gained much popularity, but only a few years later Russia became the main enemy, and no less a statesman than Winston Churchill has spoken of the 'Mongolian hordes' which again threaten Western civilization. At the same time, the Germans, ruthlessly demilitarized only a few years ago as unfit to be trusted with an army, were urged by Western statesmen to rearm and defend Western Europe against Communist aggression. Films picturing Japanese atrocities in the last war were withdrawn so as not to arouse the resentment of the Japanese, who are now indispensable, and the only major pro-Western State in the Far East, which is increasingly under the shadow of Communist China. All this would be easier to accept, as a strictly realistic adjustment of policies to new dangers, if the outstanding conflict of the moment were not usually distorted by wildly emotional and pseudo-scientific generalizations about national character. It has also been a frequent experience to find the same people violently anti-German, anti-Russian, anti-Jewish or anti-Communist in rapid succession. The reason is not any genuine change of facts or convictions, but a mentality which rushes into violent passion as an easy explanation for the existence of forces that it would be much more difficult to analyse soberly. It is perhaps the supreme challenge to modern democracy that it must preserve the quality of objectivity and detachment without thereby becoming incapable of action.

CHAPTER 2

NATIONALISM AND SUPRA-NATIONAL MOVEMENTS IN OUR TIME

MANY students of politics assert that the problem of nationalism, and the barriers it puts up against an effective international order, is the key problem of our time, around which everything else revolves. This is an over-simplification. The conflicting political and social ideologies of our time, the organization of modern society which allows the concentration of unprecedented power in a few hands, the threat of over-population in some and under-population in other parts of the world, to mention but a few other problems, are no less crucial. The failure of so many efforts to establish a better international order is not altogether unconnected with the 'one-track' mind which can see only one problem and one solution. But it remains true that the inability of contemporary society to replace the national State by higher legal and moral authority is the greatest single obstacle to international progress. The national State still claims political and legal sovereignty, including the right to solve conflicts with other nations by war; it claims the loyalties of its citizens to an extent ultimately incompatible with allegiance to humanity at large, and it means a host of economic, social and cultural frontiers which, in a world which desperately needs understanding among the ordinary citizens of different nations, strangles the free flow and interchange of ideas as well as of persons and goods.

Elements of Nationalism

What do we mean by nationalism? And what is the cause of its extraordinary strength and resilience? The strength of national sovereignty today rests on a combination of two elements, the ideology of nationalism, and the organizing and coercive power of the modern State, which moulds national groups into an effective legal, political and social organization. There is no single and universal definition of nationalism. The unifying factor may be race, language, territory, religion, economic interests or a common tradition. In the classical definition of Renan:[1]

> 'A nation is a soul, a spiritual principle. Two things, which are really only one, go to make up this soul or spiritual principle. . . . The one is the possession in common of a rich heritage of memories. And the other is actual agreement, desire to live together, and the will to continue to make the most of the joint inheritance. The existence of a nation is a daily plebiscite, just as that of the individual is a continual affirmation of life.'

A glance at the background of different modern nations shows how diverse the strands of nationalism are. The main unifying factor in the Arab nations of the Middle East and in Pakistan is the Moslem religion, with its combination of faith, rituals and historical associations. But the four million Swiss, whose small State, surrounded by powerful neighbours, has survived centuries of European wars, are almost evenly divided into Protestants and Catholics, and three main different racial elements, German, French and Italian. Modern Britain comprises four main racial elements, the English, the Scots, the Welsh and the Irish, divided not only by racial differences but also by a chequered history and centuries of hostility. The main unifying factor here has been the centralizing organization of a modern State which the Norman conquerors began to build in 1066. Its pillars were a strong monarchy, national law courts, a central system of tax-gathering and the rudimentary elements of a permanent Civil Service and a national army. In course of time common political institutions and economic interests provided stronger links. The United States of America and the Soviet Union both comprise a multitude of different racial elements, held together in Russia by centuries of a strong centralized rule, and in the United States by a combination of ideological, geographical and economic conditions. Nor is the unity of a nation a static factor. It may be broken up by sheer force, by social cleavages or by other disintegrating factors. Religious and racial elements have combined to split a once-united India into two national States: a Hindu India and a Moslem Pakistan. One of the strongest of modern national States, Germany, has in effect been replaced by two States, completely

[1] *What is a Nation?*, 1882.

different in economic and social organization and outlook, as a result of the last war, the Allied occupation and the split between Soviet Russia and the Western Powers.

There is not a single modern State where all elements of national unity are combined. Sometimes, as in the case of Britain or France, the advent of a strong government has moulded inarticulate national elements into a modern nation-State. In other cases, as in those of Germany and Italy, strong forces of nationalism have eventually produced a State which has given them political expression. On the whole, it is in the countries in which an efficient State organization combines with a strong national tradition that the national State is most durable. If in Great Britain the continuity of government, geographical factors and a growing heritage of political traditions have gradually overcome old enmities and racial differences, in Germany the desire to overcome the political impotence of a country divided into hundreds of principalities and States eventually brought a strong State into being; it is this background which partly explains the aggressive and militaristic record of this new State. The differences between Great Britain and the Republic of Eire over the future of Northern Ireland result from their divergent interpretations of nationality. The British view is that the six northern counties form a separate State, predominantly Protestant as distinct from the Catholic south, that they differ from the south in their historic and economic associations and are on these grounds entitled to determine their own destiny. As long as the six counties vote in favour of their continued association with the United Kingdom, the British Parliament has no justification to interfere with it. The Eire Government argues that the whole of Ireland forms one nation by virtue of its geographical unity, that this unity had been artificially disturbed by the British creation of the United Kingdom in 1800, and that the future of Ireland should therefore be determined by a majority decision of all Irish. This would presuppose a British Act of Parliament altering the structure of the United Kingdom.

Tensions between Nationalism and State Power

This difficulty of squaring the main elements which make for national cohesion and unity with the minimum conditions of an effective and viable State accounts for one of the most intractable and recurrent problems of modern nationalism, and in particular for the unrest which disturbed the newly established national States in Europe after the First World War. President Wilson's 'Fourteen Points' programme strongly emphasized the right of national self-determination, and the Peace Treaties of 1919 attempted to put this principle into practice. But what resulted were almost invariably new States in which several national groups had to combine. Mostly these groups were as antagonistic to each other, on grounds of race, religion or political traditions, as they had been to their one-time Germanic rulers. Poland, after an eclipse of one and a half centuries, arose again as a national State, but it never solved the problem of its Ukrainian minority in the east and its German minority in the west. Poland finally had to cede her Ukrainian territories to the Soviet Union, but received a large slice of eastern Germany in exchange. A gigantic new minority problem now arose which Poland attempted to solve by the wholesale expulsion of millions of Germans and the resettlement of that area by Poles. Czechoslovakia was formed in 1919 of two dominant elements — Czechs and Slovaks, with the Czechs generally in control — and a German minority of nearly three million. As subsequent history showed, geographical and economic conditions made an inclusion of this territory, settled by people of German race, inevitable. But it eventually accelerated the disruption of Czechoslovakia, despite the relatively enlightened minority policy of the Czechoslovak republic. German and Slovak grievances were skilfully exploited by Nazi Germany when she started on her Continental conquests. Under the ignominious Munich Settlement of 1938, Czechoslovakia was coerced into agreeing to the cession of the Sudeten area. Henceforth the State was indefensible and Germany achieved the domination of the Danubian basin which is the key to the control of central and south-eastern Europe. Yugoslavia, Hungary and Roumania faced similar national racial and religious tensions between their different component national elements. The only State that emerged from the ruins of the Austro-Hungarian Empire without a mixture of nationalities was German-speaking Austria, but this was also the least viable of all the States. About a third of its population lived in the one-time capital, Vienna, which the rest of a country of six million people could not support. Consequently Austrians of all parties sought a political union with Germany, which was brought about by force through the Nazi conquest of Austria, and dissolved by the victors after the defeat of Germany.

The very strength of national traditions and antagonisms may therefore be an element of weakness in modern States. Wherever national groups live together close and intermingled, as they do all over Europe, there is a danger of disruption unless and until all these various national groups can be fused in a higher and wider political unit.

The Rise of the National State

Nationalism as an ideology is much older than the national State, and is likely to survive it. The modern national State is the expression of a certain phase in history. It is nothing absolute or God-given, but an institution inherently neither better nor worse than a tribal community, a city-State or a world-State. It has dominated the European scene for only a few centuries. The main reason why so many national groups during that time formed themselves into modern States is due largely to economic and social conditions, most of which are rapidly losing their validity and significance. Perhaps the most decisive single factor has been the alliance between rulers and the rising economic classes which desired larger markets as well as greater political power. In the history of the national State the influence of the middle classes has been outstanding. They were free from the older ties of feudalism; they wanted secure and unified national markets for manufacture and commerce and, last but not least, they provided the main ideological and intellectual support for nationalism. The national State, as it came to dominate Europe in the nineteenth century, radiating from there to other parts of the world, was almost universally characterized by this combination of factors: a strong State government, a prosperous and articulate middle class, whose commercial and intellectual elements combined in the development of a nationalist ideology, and a liberal economic system which combined a growing measure of political liberties with the predominance and the strong legal protection of private property and free enterprise.

But today the economic, social and ideological factors are very different from what they were a century ago.

Today it is only in the relatively undeveloped countries of Asia and Africa — where the masses of the peasantry are as yet too illiterate or too depressed to be politically articulate — that the middle classes are the main force behind nationalist movements. Under the influence of Western ideals of education it is industrialists, professors, journalists, lawyers, who are mainly responsible for the new nationalism of the Arab States as well as of India or Pakistan. In the Indian Congress big industrial and commercial interests have been the main power behind the scenes, but intellectuals like Gandhi, Jinnah, Sukarno, Nehru, Nyerere, Nkrumah, became the main articulate voice of Asian or African nationalism in politics and in administration. In the more highly developed States of Europe, the cradle of nationalism, the social basis of nationalism has, however, shifted decisively. In the democratic States the same liberal tradition which combined with nationalism in the nineteenth century for the liberation of suppressed or dependent peoples from alien domination, has now moved on to the demand for wider international forms of political, social and economic organization. Those statesmen and intellectuals who carry on the liberal rather than the nationalist tradition of the nineteenth century are now the champions of the United Nations, of peaceful international collaboration and the recognition of the unity of mankind above races and nations. But those — and it is a large number — who absorbed the aggressive nationalism rather than the enlightened liberalism of the national movements of the nineteenth century, have become champions of the absolute State. In lending the power of their pen and dialectic ability to the justification of any aggressive action of their own State, they have sacrificed the genuine ideology of nationalism, which wants national groups to live side by side in freedom and independence. They have become tools of imperialism and tyranny. As such they are useful and important to the modern dictators. Hitler, Mussolini, Franco, Stalin made good use of the ability of lawyers, political scientists, economists to justify any aggressive action or internal purge in the name of a higher cause. Yet in the modern totalitarian State the intellectual middle class is deliberately debased and ousted from its former position of leadership. The tradition of intellectual and spiritual independence is intolerable to modern totalitarian governments. As both German and Soviet experience shows, this applies not only to theories of international law or of the respective economic merits of Capitalism and Socialism; it extends to the subjects and styles of musical compositions and to theories of genetics. Complete subservience is in these States the condition of a precarious survival. Ultimately this must lead to the extinction of the middle classes as they dominated nineteenth-century nationalism.

The commercial and industrial middle classes are similarly divided. Economic developments have led to increasing supranational alignments, to international cartels for the production of raw materials, such as rubber, tin or tea, to international production and market agreements in the chemical, steel and oil industries. The modern totalitarian State cannot tolerate such autonomy. It will either suppress it by complete Socialism, as has been done in the Communist States; or it will turn industrial and commercial leaders into powerful but junior partners in aggressive imperialist enterprises. In this way Hitler used the German chemical, steel and other concerns as agents of German economic control over conquered Europe. But ideologically the modern dictator seeks mainly the support of the 'common man'. The term 'National Socialism' was cleverly chosen, but far less true of the Nazi regime than of present-day Communist Governments. The alliance of fervent nationalism with Socialist ideology is a characteristic feature of the latest phase in European nationalism. The strong internationalist tradition of the organized working class in such countries as Germany and France made it very difficult for the Fascist regimes to win their positive support. They had therefore to rely far more on the lower strata of the middle class as well as a floating element of adventurers. It is modern Communist Governments which can appeal far more successfully to a combination of nationalism and Socialism, and as formal national independence has now been won by most national groups in Europe, the main emphasis is on social and economic liberation from 'Western imperialism' and its henchmen — that is, capitalists, landowners and the independent professions. There was an inherent contradiction between this appeal to nationalist sentiment and the ruthless subordination of the policies and interests of the smaller Communist nations to the dictates of the Kremlin. One of the most significant developments of recent years has been the beginning of the emancipation of Communist countries, in various parts of the world, from automatic subordination to Soviet policy. Much of this was stimulated by the decisive lead taken by

Communist China, in its increasingly sharp ideological battle with the Soviet Union. Communist China, with an estimated population of 750 million, the world's most populous State, and in terms of history and military, industrial and scientific potential one of the world's giants, was of course never a henchman of the Soviet Union in the same sense as the smaller States of South-east Europe. China's recent split with the Soviet Union has however helped to strengthen, at least for the time being, the combination of Communist ideology and nationalist appeal, especially in the eyes of the Asian States, for which Communist China's independent line can combine the appeals of revolutionary Communism, nationalist liberation and racial affinity.

In Europe the Communist States of South-east Europe, notably Poland, Hungary and Roumania, have also cautiously begun to assert national policies and interests in a relatively greater degree of independence from Soviet direction. The nationalist tide which today dominates the emergence of many peoples, especially in Africa, from colonial status to independence, thus infiltrates even the older States. It runs counter to the voluntary, or enforced, internationalizing tendencies of supra-national unions or associations. This leads to the consideration of what is probably the greatest problem and dilemma of our time: the conflict between the still powerful, and in many ways newly inflamed, passions of nationalism, and the political, economic and military realities which have made the national sovereign State an anachronism of the past.

The Decline of the National State

Superficially, nationalism seems to have gathered new strength and to have been raised to a new pitch of intensity. In India it has been not the only, but the principal force in the splitting of a country into two new States. In Palestine it has led to the creation of a new Jewish State in the face of immense difficulties, both physical and political. The gradual dissolution of the British Empire is largely due to strong nationalist forces. In Latin America, in India and the Middle East, in the Pacific and in the Far East, in Africa and the West Indies, nationalist movements were inspired by the campaign for liberation from European political and economic domination. National sovereignty, even without the artificial boundaries drawn by the colonizers, becomes the symbol of liberty. And even in the most firmly established national States, with many centuries of continuous unity behind them, nationalist movements have recently revived. In Great Britain, for example, Welsh and Scottish nationalism are more vocal and active than ever, though only a few fanatics go to the extent of demanding separate States. Nationalism has already led Southern Ireland to complete independence, and it is the main force behind Eire's campaign for union with Northern Ireland, which is still part of the United Kingdom. After nearly two centuries of political union with English-speaking Canada, Quebec nationalism is fiercer than ever, demanding far-reaching autonomy for French-speaking Quebec, or even a separate State. Communist States, too, pay great attention to the problem of nationalism where they contain a number of different national groups. Under the leadership of Stalin, himself a Georgian, the political totalitarianism of the Soviet Union was tempered by a federal system in which the numerous national groupings of Russia are represented by federal States, autonomous republics or less fully developed national units. Tito's Yugoslavia is similarly divided into six States, representing different nationalities. It is true that the iron rule of the Communist Party, and the effective concentration of political, military and economic power in the hands of the rulers, allow this nationalism only very limited outlet. But its effect on the revival of cultural, social and religious autonomy is considerable, quite apart from its international propaganda value.

Yet it would be an illusion to believe that the national State is now experiencing a 'second youth' or reaching its full maturity. Up to a point, the revival of nationalism is quite genuine and easily explained. In Europe, it is largely a reaction to the very brutality of the German invasion and the deliberate attempt of the Nazi regime to stamp out, by murder, starvation and degradation, the proud and old-established nations of Europe, especially those of Slavonic race. It is not surprising that the reaction of Russians, Poles, Yugoslavs, Czechs, Jews and others should have been a fierce reassertion of their national identity. Poland and Czechoslovakia have even gone to the extreme length of expelling millions of Germans, who had for centuries been established in their countries. To that extent nationalism is simply a natural reaction to suppression and exploitation, comparable to the way in which German nationalism was inflamed by the Napoleonic occupation between 1806 and 1812. In the colonies of Asia and Africa national independence was the immediate goal to be reached in the campaign for liberation from Western domination.

But the main symbol of the national State has been its legal and political sovereignty: that is, the absence of any control by a higher international authority; or, to put it in political terms, the power to wage war as the supreme means of settling international differences. This sovereignty can survive only as long as it is the expression of underlying political, economic and military power realities. There have always been big States and small States, powerful and weak States; but not until our present time have the disparity of military and economic power, and the inability of all except a few States to regulate their affairs in real as distinct from nominal independence, been so blatant as at present. The First World War showed already the difficulties of the smaller States of Europe in maintaining neutrality. The Second World War overwhelmed all the smaller States, and in Europe left only a few small countries, such as Sweden, Switzerland and Eire, in a state of precarious neutrality. The post-war period has shown even more clearly the hollowness of national sovereignty. The same States which proclaimed national independence more loudly than ever are compelled to seek wider international alignments. The Communist States of south-eastern Europe may fiercely proclaim their national sovereignty, but the reality behind it is the defence pacts with the Soviet Union and such supra-national organizations as the Cominform, or the Council for Mutual Economic Aid, which co-ordinates their economic programmes. The great majority of the new Asian and African States depend on massive foreign economic aid for their development, and on political and military support from one of the big Powers for their survival as nations. The Western States, too, must forgo national isolation for the protection of the United States of America. Its political and military expression is the Atlantic Pact, which seeks to coordinate the political and military action of the member-States. Without full American participation these would be as fatally weakened as the Eastern European bloc would be without the participation of Soviet Russia. The stark reality behind these developments is that instead of some 120 'sovereign' States which still make up the political map of the world, only a few 'super States' — of which there are at present only three — the Soviet Union,

Communist China and the United States — or equivalent closely integrated associations of other nations, enjoy the attributes of real sovereignty. This does not, of course, mean that everything that happens in the world will be directly controlled or dictated by Moscow, Washington or Peking. As we shall see later,[1] this 'bipolar' interpretation of international politics is increasingly outdated. But in a world in which wars of conquest and suppression are still the greatest single danger to independence and liberty, national sovereignty cannot survive the growing inequality of power between the States. The disparity of manpower, but even more of industrial and technical resources, has, in the age of air warfare and long-distance technical weapons, multiplied a hundredfold the inequality between great and small Powers. A hundred years ago States like Holland, Belgium or Spain still had chances of defending themselves successfully against a foreign invasion. Today these chances no longer exist. The conquest of Belgium and Holland was, in the last war, a matter of days: in the future it may be a matter of hours. National sovereignty means, in the last resort, war potential. The inequalities of space, manpower and productive resources have destroyed it for all but a very few nations. For all their weaknesses, such organizations as the United Nations, the North Atlantic Treaty, the Warsaw Pact, the Organization for Economic Co-operation and Development, the Organization of American States, and the various functional agencies of the United Nations are a recognition of mid-twentieth-century realities, while de Gaulle's attempt to restore the seventeenth-century grandeur of a nationalist France is, for all its tactical successes, an anachronism.

Alternatives to Nationalism

While nationalism is more vociferous than ever, the world has in fact steadily moved away from the age of national States and national sovereignty, though, as so often, the legal symbols of a former era survive. It remains to consider some of the main alternatives to national sovereignty.

Imperialism

The first possibility is that of international conquest by a single Power, followed by the establishment of a universal international

[1] Below, Ch. 4.

order under the control of that Power. For the western European and Mediterranean area this has once been accomplished — by the Roman Empire. Conquest was followed by consolidation and the gradual introduction of a universal system of law and administration, far superior to anything else known in the ancient world, and absorbing the best which the law and culture of other civilizations had to offer. Even then the period in which a fairly stable peace and order prevailed covers a span of less than two centuries, and it was frequently disturbed by violence and disorder. In modern times universal rule by conquest has been attempted again, first by France under Napoleon Bonaparte, and more recently by Nazi Germany and Fascist Japan. All of them succeeded in plunging continents into bloodshed and chaos, but in the end they only stirred up the very forces of national resistance which they attempted to exterminate.

In modern times imperial conquest is usually the result of the perversion of nationalism. Most nations, having attained preponderant political and physical strength over their neighbours and a chance of successful conquest, have turned from genuine nationalism to imperialism. France, Germany, Russia, to name but a few, have in turn moved from national consolidation to imperial expansion. Marxist doctrine, as developed especially by Lenin[1] and Hobson,[2] has analysed another form of imperialism: that achieved by the economic control of weaker and undeveloped peoples through States under the influence of highly developed Capitalism. This theory is summed up in the following passage:

> 'The system prevailing in all developed countries for the production and distribution of wealth has reached a stage in which its productive powers are held in leash by its inequalities of distribution; the excessive share that goes to profits, rents and other surpluses impelling a chronic endeavour to oversave in the sense of trying to provide an increased productive power without a corresponding outlet in the purchase of consumable goods. This drive towards oversaving is gradually checked by the inability of such saving to find any profitable use in the provision of more plant and other capital. But it also seeks to utilise political power for outlets in external markets, and as

[1] *Imperialism, The Highest Stage of Capitalism.*

[2] *Imperialism*, 3rd ed., 1938.

foreign independent markets are closed or restricted, the drive to the acquisition of colonies, protectorates and other areas of imperial development becomes a more urgent and conscious national policy.'[1]

As pointed out in the first chapter, this type of imperialism has in the past mainly affected colonial populations, or other peoples who had not yet developed modern national States, such as the Chinese in 1900. But it has also been shown that this economic imperialism has been relatively inactive and unsuccessful in any attempt to dominate fully developed national States. It has tended far more to operate through alignment with identical economic interests in such other States, and in modern times the political power of the State achieves increasing preponderance over, and utilizes its economic interests in, its own service. The modern and most dangerous type of imperialism is in fact the combination of political and economic conquest, of which the Nazi regime has given a devastating example. Its domination of the Continent of Europe meant not only the suppression of the national, political and social independence of the conquered nations, but also their integration in an economic empire. The German steel, chemical and other industrial concerns became the industrial rulers of the Continent, acting for their own benefit as well as being agents and instruments of Hitler's empire.

Imperialism is ultimately destructive of nationalism in a twofold sense. The conquered nations may be weakened, disrupted or extinguished by sheer force. A few years of Nazi rule in Europe have shown in ghastly clarity that another ten years might well have meant the literal extinction of Poles, Czechs and other nations, not to speak of the wholesale murder of Jews all over Europe. But where this modern and militaristic imperialism fails to achieve its object, it only stimulates the nationalism of the oppressed peoples to a new fever of intensity, while it corrupts the conqueror. The Nazi regime had to train master rulers of Europe who would be as ruthless towards their own countrymen as towards other peoples. The systematic training for domination, and the ruthless suppression of groups objectionable on national, religious or social grounds, are ultimately destructive of nationalism. In his private conversations, which were published in a most in-

[1] Hobson, *op. cit.*, p. xii.

structive book by a one-time associate and later opponent,[1] Hitler voiced his utter contempt for nationalism. This was amply confirmed when the Nazi leaders in defeat, early in 1945, destroyed bridges, communications, buildings, deliberately increasing the misery of the German people. They did it in the spirit which had bred contempt for their own people almost as much as for others once they had ceased to be useful instruments of conquest.

The Communist pattern of conquest is more subtle. The experience of the nations of eastern Europe since the war shows clearly that close association with the Soviet Empire threatened genuine political and economic sovereignty. They were forced to establish Communist Governments which would toe the line of Soviet foreign policy and must comply with an economic master plan. But in two respects the Soviet regime is less destructive of genuine nationalism than the Nazi regime. First it has no philosophy of discrimination between races and nations (although in recent years there have been many allegations of a revival of anti-Semitism). While all its national groups are held together under an iron political discipline, they have equality among themselves. Soviet political and military leaders include Poles, Armenians, Georgians, Jews, as well as Russians. Soviet policy actively encourages national groupings, provided they keep away from the political and economic field. Secondly, the Soviet regime has powerful groups of ideological followers in most countries, and is therefore able to administer Communist government through nationals of the different countries. In other words, the Soviet system undermines the national sovereign State no less than the Nazi regime, but it leaves far more scope to cultural and ideological nationalism. On this basis, the Communist satellites of the Soviet Union have been able, in recent years, to strive for greater political freedom of movement.

The United States is at present the only other Power capable of achieving world rule, although, in 10 years from now, China might be an even more powerful contender for world empire. It is unlikely that either could achieve it without a gigantic and terribly destructive battle with the other. If after such a struggle mankind were still capable of producing any organized society, a universal law could be established. The world would be free for the introduction of one political system, one economic plan, one

[1] Rauschning, *Hitler Speaks*.

social philosophy. This could not be achieved except by war and violence of unprecedented magnitude, and by the suppression of both national and personal liberties.

Regional Associations

The second alternative is that of a small number of more limited but more compact regional associations of nations, constituting in their mutual relations a balance of power similar to the uneasy balance maintained among nations in the past era of national sovereignty. The most significant international developments at present point in this direction. The tendency is towards several worlds instead of one world, as it was postulated by the leading Allied statesmen during the last war, and as it underlies the conception of the United Nations. The Soviet Union is the dominant partner in an association of Communist nations which is underpinned by military assistance treaties, common economic development plans, and above all tight political control through Governments which take their directions from the Kremlin. The United States of America is the leading and most powerful member of a group of nations pledged by the Atlantic Treaty to mutual assistance against aggression. Within the two major groups of nations led by the Soviet Union and the United States of America, there might still be smaller and more compact associations. The European Economic Community links six West European States in a customs union which may be the prelude to federation. The greatest problem of these regional associations is the same which made the former balance of power so precarious. The balancc is unstable, and likely to be upset by relatively small changes. A change of government in any of the States concerned, or the invention of a superior weapon by one side, can disturb it overnight. Nor do groups of nations formed in this fashion usually correspond to geographic, economic or other organic needs. In Europe, for example, the dividing line goes right through the middle of a resentful Germany. Closely integrated regional blocs simply create groups of States, instead of large numbers of single States which are no longer viable as units of political power, but they can hardly produce more than periods of prolonged truce.

Political and economic factors are closely intertwined in the movement towards more closely knit and mutually exclusive associations of nations. The Soviet bloc has a political origin; but in order to cement it the economic systems of the nations forming part of it are developed under a common plan. Trade relations between the nations within the group are encouraged to the utmost, but trade between the group and outside nations is regarded either as a necessary evil — for example in so far as British or American machinery is needed for industrial development — or as a means of political pressure. Tempting export possibilities might, for example, be promised to an Iceland glutted with codfish, or to a Western Germany faced with mass unemployment, as a price for political concessions.

Outside the Soviet world, the ideology of free and non-political trade persists at least in theory. In practice, however, the divergencies of national policies, but above all the chronic shortage of 'hard currencies', which threatens the vast majority of nations, work against free international exchange and in favour of close regional groupings or other discriminating associations.

There are, to be sure, certain contradictory tendencies. In recent years, and, in particular, since the easing of the most critical post-war shortages of goods and dollars in the European countries, there has been a certain movement towards a relatively freer general international trade, symbolized in the General Agreement on Tariffs and Trade (GATT) of 1948. In this Agreement, over sixty nations, the principal trading nations of the world, outside the Communist bloc, have agreed on certain principles of non-discrimination, based on the 'most-favoured-nation clause' in their mutual trade. Although a number of States from the Latin American region, as well as from South-east Asia and Japan, are members of this Convention, its core is formed by the Anglo-American group of nations, and the nations of Western Europe. Enough exceptions have been worked into this multinational Agreement to permit considerable scope to national, fiscal and economic policies. Moreover, it must be judged in the light not only of the complete abstention of the Communist group of nations (except for the purely formal membership of Czechoslovakia, who joined before she became a Communist State), but also of the far more closely knit European associations, and especially of the recent European Economic Community, which to a large extent re-emphasize the regional political integration principle, as against a wider free-trading international society of nations.[1]

Federalism as a Solution?

In the late thirties and early forties the idea of federal union between groups of nations, or even all the States of the world, claimed an excessive share of the attention paid to the improvement of international relations. The realistic experiences of recent years have helped to put the problem of federal union in its proper place. Federalism is a form of constitutional organization which, in a number of cases, has successfully united groups of States without depriving them entirely of their separate identity and self-government. The usual pattern of federation has been the transfer to the Federal Government of certain powers of overwhelming national concern: notably defence, foreign affairs, customs, and a varying number of legislative powers. Some federal constitutions, like those of the United States and Australia, give specifically enumerated powers to the Federation, while the residue remains with the States. Other federal constitutions, like that of Canada, do the reverse. This has made little difference to a problem which is producing increasing strains and stresses in all federal States: how to cope with the vastly increased minimum functions of government, its acknowledged task to develop national resources and social services, or to maintain full employment, within the rigid framework of existing federal constitutions. Tensions and jealousies are strong even in well-established Federations; it was the Provinces of Canada which unsuccessfully applied to the Privy Council to invalidate a Federal Statute abolishing appeals from Canadian courts to the Privy Council. Most of the Australian States bitterly opposed the Federal Government in its attempts to unify taxation or to nationalize banking. Yet overwhelming common interests and traditions, geographical, racial, economic or military, cement the existing Federations. Without such a minimum of common interests and traditions, federal government cannot operate successfully. We need not waste any words on plans for a world federation: the idea of linking in a federal union such States as Argentina, France, India, Spain, with Soviet Russia and the U.S.A., with all their divergencies of numbers, political systems, economic

[1] On some of these aspects, see further below, pp. 199 *et seq.*

standards and social development, is not worth serious discussion. The plan to link more closely existing associations, such as a Western Union, in a federal State is more serious. But the foregoing discussion has shown how difficult it would be to put into practice. Recent federations have been established with some prospect of success where, as in West Germany, they revive former constitutional forms and regional patterns, or where, as in the Soviet Union or in Yugoslavia, the federal form means little more than regional cultural autonomy. It is easy to proclaim a federal constitution where the fundamental rights of the citizen are not enforceable, and where a dictatorial central government and the all-pervading control of a single party, Communist or Fascist, ensure uniformity in all essential matters of government. But a Federation of Western Europe would have to operate against a background of dozens of different national traditions and systems of government, as well as a great diversity of social beliefs. In these circumstances, a federal constitution may eventually be obtained, but the proper approach to it is not another spate of blueprint constitutions, but the more painful way of securing the habit of co-ordination in the vital fields of military and economic planning, and of common discussion of matters of political controversy. One of the few fortunate developments of recent international politics is a healthy distrust of panaceas. The magic of federalism is one of them.

Universal International Law

Lastly, international order may be achieved through the voluntary merger of national sovereignties and the establishment of an international rule of law. This is the only method by which anything better than a temporary peace can be established without the unilateral sacrifice of national and personal liberties. Its achievement remains the paramount task of our generation, and the aspiration of all who do not believe in the superiority of any one nation or race, in the necessity of an international dictatorship, whether of the Fascist or the Communist pattern, or the inability of men to rise to loyalties higher than the national State. Unfortunately, the certainty that without the replacement of national by supra-national sovereignty the civilized survival of mankind is unlikely, offers no guarantee of its being achieved in time. This will depend on the relative strength of conflicting policies and ideals. It is just as likely that the world may find the peace of the grave which follows from universal conquest by one Power, as that it may dissolve into sheer chaos and barbarism, as a result of even more destructive wars and social revolutions.

Collective Security and the United Nations

There are three main lines along which an attempt to achieve international authority and the rule of law is being pursued. The first is the principle of collective security — that is, the guarantee of the peace, security and territorial integrity of any one State by all. Its main point is the promise of automatic assistance in the event of aggression. This is the basic principle underlying both the League of Nations Covenant and the United Nations Charter. The former of these two organizations was decisively weakened by its lack of universality, since its members did not at any time include more than five out of the seven great Powers. More fatal still was the lack of determination of the member-States to put the full weight of their power and their convictions behind the enforcement of the Covenant. The supreme opportunity offered and missed by the League of Nations when Italy invaded Abyssinia has been analysed in the first chapter.

The United Nations Organization — though originally based on the victorious Allies of the last world war and on the neutral countries not tainted by open partisanship for the vanquished — has, in recent years, become much more universal. Two of the three Axis Powers — Italy and Japan — have been admitted to membership, as have a host of new States, produced by the turbulent move towards national independence and statehood, which has swept over the Middle East, Asia and Africa. As a result of this — still continuing — development, the United Nations today approaches a membership of one hundred and twenty, including most of the major Powers and practically all the smaller States, old and new. But while, numerically, the vast majority of existing States are today members of the United Nations, the continued absence, due to post-war tensions, of two of the world's major Powers, prevents it from being a universal organization, or even a universal debating chamber of mankind. That Germany is not a member is a consequence of the partition of that country into two antagonistic States, which are closely linked with the Western and Soviet group of nations respectively.

While the Soviet Union, which, like every other permanent member of the Security Council, has a veto power over admissions of new members, would probably agree to the admission of West Germany, provided the Western Powers agree to the admission of East Germany, the latter have hitherto refused to recognize, or contemplate admission to the United Nations, of East Germany A mutual veto power, therefore, keeps the whole of Germany out. China is a founder member of the United Nations. But it is represented by the Government of Chiang Kai-shek, controlling eight million Taiwanese and two million mainland Chinese, while the Government of mainland China, controlling seven hundred and fifty million Chinese, remains outside, owing to the determined opposition of the United States, and the reluctance of other States to openly break with the United States over this question.

The absence of these two major Powers — apart from that of some smaller States, such as Vietnam and Korea, which are equally kept outside by partition and the Great Power conflict — increases the disproportionate weight enjoyed in the General Assembly of the United Nations by the smaller States, many of them new, weak and inexperienced in international affairs. This lack of balance has been increased by certain developments unintended by the framers of the United Nations Charter.

The basic principle of the Charter is an attempt to balance the principle of equality of representation of all States, big or small, with the acknowledgment of inequality in political, economic and military responsibilities and power. The Charter places the principal executive power in matters affecting the peace of the world in the hands of the Security Council, in which the permanent members, the 'Big Five', have predominance by virtue of their veto power in all matters of substance (as distinct from procedure). By contrast, the General Assembly, in which each member has one vote, regardless of size or importance, has only the power of 'recommendations', except for matters of internal United Nations organization. But under the pressure of post-war tensions, the reality of the United Nations structure is today very different. One of the 'Big Five', China, continues to be represented by a Government which, in effect, controls a weak country of ten million people. Dependent as it is on the support of the West, it sides with the free Western members of the Security Council. But the opposition of the fifth, the Soviet Union, in most major questions of policy, has been sufficient to paralyse the Security Council as the effective executive organ of the United Nations, and as the custodian of international peace and security.[1] This has not only weakened the general role of the United Nations as a guardian of international peace and security, but it has also served to shift, within the United Nations itself, the major weight from the Security Council to the General Assembly. Any decisions of importance that have been taken in recent years, in particular the United Nations resolution on the Franco-British-Israeli intervention in the Suez Canal dispute of 1956, following the nationalization of the Suez Canal by Nasser's Egypt, have emanated from the General Assembly. Its 'recommendations' have tended to acquire the force of 'decisions', and in the Suez Canal case, the Assembly resolution actually produced the United Nations Emergency Force (UNEF), which acts to this day as a buffer force in the contentious Gaza strip. But in the General Assembly, even though major resolutions have to be taken by a two-thirds majority, the balance is increasingly shifting in favour of the fast-growing number of smaller States. While formerly the West, and pro-Western States, such as the Latin American Republics, tended to be over-represented, today the trend is in the other direction. Many of the newly created States, carrying a legacy of resentment against Western political or economic domination, tend to side with the Soviet bloc or vote according to their immediate interests, which, at this time, often have no more unifying force than common resentment against the West. The result is frequently either a series of compromise resolutions, signifying little, such as successive resolutions on the Cyprus question or the national control over natural resources, or unpredictable attitudes which tend to shift the weight of political decisions outside the United Nations altogether. Of the major international conflicts of

[1] In the Korea conflict of 1950, action by the Security Council was possible only because the Soviet Union at that time boycotted Security Council proceedings in protest against the non-seating of Communist China. By a doubtful, but not unprecedented, practice, abstention or absence was not counted as equivalent to a veto, so that the Council could obtain the necessary majority for United Nations action in Korea. The Soviet Union has since been careful not to repeat a similar tactical mistake. In the Congo situation the U.S.S.R. supported the Security Council resolution of June 1960, but later was increasingly at odds with the Western Powers.

recent years, the Trieste issue in 1954, the Cyprus issue in 1959, the Austrian Peace Treaty of 1955, in which the four major Powers were directly involved, the Laos neutralization and, above all, the Cuba conflict of 1962 — were all settled by direct negotiation outside the United Nations, even though they were subsequently confirmed by that Organization. The United Nations has however been able to intervene as such in some recent international conflicts, and thus to fulfil at least to some extent the functions envisaged for it in the creation of the Charter. A few years after the, already mentioned, intervention of UNEF, created by resolution of the General Assembly as an order force, insulating the hostile forces of Egypt and Israel from each other in the Gaza strip, the United Nations intervened decisively — and in this case with the actual use of military force — in the Congo conflict (1960–62). The origin of this intervention lay in the *de facto* secession of the rich province of Katanga from the newly created republic of the Congo. In the opinion of the late Secretary-General Hammarskjöld, this situation created a threat for international peace and security that demanded U.N. attention. By a series of resolutions — the first, after years of paralysis, passed by the Security Council, and the later ones by the General Assembly — a joint force, composed for the greater part of African and Indian contingents, was established, under United Nations command. The fact that the international aspects of the Congo situation were mingled with a civil war situation created unique and delicate problems for the United Nations. After prolonged resistance on the part of the Tshombe Government of Katanga Province, which had at least moral support from Belgian- and British-controlled financial interests, the United Nations finally crushed the resistance of Katanga and was instrumental in bringing about the reunification of the Congo Republic. This action of the United Nations, while outwardly successful, raised however two major problems, both of which in different ways posed a potentially grave threat to the cohesion of the United Nations. In the first place, several Western Powers, notably Belgium, Britain and France, tended to regard the U.N. action as essentially an intervention in a civil war, and thus as an action outside the proper province of the United Nations. Even though the general peacekeeping mandate of the United Nations, as formulated in Article 1 of the Charter, may in special situations justify intervention in a civil war situation which would not be legal for any individual State or a group of States, the great majority of States are likely to resist any further attempt of the United Nations to take action which is instrumental in bringing about the victory of one party in a civil war. In the second place, the divergence of views — on the legitimacy and propriety of the U.N. action — was reflected in the refusal of several Powers, notably the U.S.S.R. and France, to pay their share of the assessment made by the General Assembly, under Article 17, for the expenses of the operation. The conflict was aggravated when an advisory opinion of the International Court of Justice, of July 1962, by a majority of nine votes to five, affirmed the power of the Assembly to make such compulsory assessments, in the exercise of its general concurrent responsibilities for the maintenance of peace. Despite the express approval of this opinion by a General Assembly resolution, the U.S.S.R. and France persisted in their refusal to pay their share and thus exposed themselves to the danger — which will become acute for the U.S.S.R. in the 1964 Session and for France in the 1965 Session — of being deprived of voting power in the Assembly, under Article 19 (arrears for at least two full years). Since the United States is determined to press for such action and the U.S.S.R. and France have shown no sign of yielding, there looms the danger of an irreparable split, including even the possible withdrawal of these powers from the United Nations. Such a contingency, coupled with the absence of Communist China, would fatally cripple the United Nations as an organization purporting to represent all mankind. The blow would be all the worse as, contrary to the earlier post-war period, the U.S.S.R. has in recent years more actively pursued its professed principles of co-existence, both within and without the United Nations. The latter would by such a split lose its most valuable function: the role of an international debating forum and a natural meeting ground for the nations' representatives from all over the world, as a focus of opportunities for the exchange of views, compromises and settlements by informal arrangements as much as by formal resolutions.

Even if this acute crisis can be avoided, another danger to the function and ability of the United Nations cannot be by-passed: as the number of politically and economically weak new member-States increases, the major and middle Powers in the United Nations may find themselves increasingly outvoted in the Assembly by a combination of States, whose political and financial responsibilities bear no relation to their voting power. In the absence of procedural reforms, the result may be an effective, though not a formal, withdrawal of the major Powers from the United Nations, since beyond a certain point they will not be willing to have their actions determined by such a combination.

Thus the future of the United Nations, and of its role in world affairs, appear uncertain at this time. In certain respects, notably through the more active role of the Secretary-General and the peacekeeping operations of the Organization, as well as by the continuing need for a universal forum for the nations of the world, the United Nations has, in recent years, become a more important factor in world affairs than in the first decade following its creation. On the other hand, the continuing absence of the world's largest State, the increasing weight, within the General Assembly, of shifting combinations of many small, weak and inexperienced new nations, and deep divisions between the major Powers as to the propriety and extent of the United Nations peacekeeping operations, threaten its survival at the very time when its stature and importance in international affairs has increased.

The split between the major Powers of the world, i.e. between the Soviet Union and Communist China on the one side, and the Western coalition on the other side, has also prevented progress on the most crucial issues of international security: the international control of military forces and of nuclear weapons.

A successful system of collective security does not necessarily presuppose a complete abandonment of national independence or individuality. It does, however, require the submission of the individual national will to collective decisions made in accordance with the Charter, and in order to be effective it requires the international control of military forces and vital weapons, which is certainly not possible without a severe restriction of national sovereignty. If any of the big Powers commits an act of aggression, no effective action can be taken against it under the Charter. These shortcomings might have been overcome to some extent by the establishment of certain vital international control agencies. Serious but unsuccessful attempts have been made to establish two such agencies: an international military force and an international organization for the control of atomic energy. The former failed mainly because Russia would not agree to the granting of a right of passage or of bases in national territories to an international force in which she would have to share control with the other big Powers, under the authority of the United Nations.

Underlying this inability to agree on a measure of international control over armed forces, which inevitably requires some abandonment of national, territorial and organizational sovereignty, is the very atmosphere of hostility and suspicion that such control is meant to destroy. This has led to an even more dangerous impasse: the vital question of limitation and control of nuclear weapons. The perfection of A-bombs, H-bombs, and the massive use of intercontinental missiles with nuclear warheads, by both the United States and the Soviet Union, with some other Powers following close behind, has pushed the destructiveness of a modern war between major Powers to a degree where the traditional purposes of war — the survival of a viable victor — appears impossible. After years of abortive negotiations, the Western Powers and the Soviet Union have not yet been able to agree on a mutually acceptable system of international supervision over the production of nuclear weapons or other arms, the size and location of armed forces, or any other aspects of the armaments race. The U.S.S.R. continues to object to any international control carried out on its own territory, while the West objects to any 'nuclear-free' zones or similar schemes in Central Europe. In July 1963 the United States and the Soviet Union finally agreed on a ban on nuclear testing (except for underground tests), but this came at a time when both sides had carried out many tests for years and had achieved an apparent capacity of 'over-kill', which made the continuation of testing less urgent. This, as well as certain economic motivations which have recently induced both the United States and the U.S.S.R. to halt the continuous growth in their armaments budgets, and the further build-up of nuclear arsenals, provide at best periods of breathing space rather than the prelude to permanent international co-operation in the field of armaments. Even if the West and the U.S.S.R. should succeed in arriving at more durable agreements and a measure of common institutional arrangements, the absence of the potentially largest military power of the earth, Communist China, greatly reduces the value of any such arrangements for the maintenance of peace.

Within the Western world, de Gaulle's France remains aloof from any such international arrangements, intent on carrying out its own national armaments policy.

Thus the development towards some measure of supra-national order, at least in the vital spheres affecting the survival of mankind, continues to be caught in the vicious circle which has controlled world politics since the end of the last world war: while the relations between the major contending groups of Powers are dominated by mutual fear and suspicion, even modest joint-control schemes, inside or outside the United Nations, cannot be brought about. Yet the creation and operation of any such scheme, even an initially modest one, would itself be a decisive step towards the weakening and eventual dissipation of this mutual distrust. While it lasts, such international order as governs the world at present will be essentially based on a balance of power and fear.

How and when it will be possible to break out of this vicious circle, it is impossible to predict. There is a possibility that the imminence of a universal catastrophe would bring about advances not possible without such extreme pressure. But it is surely an illusion to believe that fear, and the terror of modern nuclear war, are in themselves agents of international integration. The lack of institutions implementing international law and authority is not the cause of present world tensions, but a symbol of conflicts that reach far deeper. Hence, it seems utopian to attempt to overcome the deep political, social and psychological tensions of our time by constitutional blueprints, however elaborately and carefully constructed. Such a blueprint has recently been suggested, as a result of extensive studies of the revision of the United Nations Charter.[1] Its most important proposals are the weighting of votes in the United Nations General Assembly, in eight categories, graded according to the population of the member-States (ranging from thirty representatives for each of the four nations numbering over 140 million to one representative for two nations numbering less than 0·5 million). Also proposed is the complete abolition of national military forces, and the substitution of an international police force, composed of a standing force of professionals, with a reserve force standing by. For the process of judicial settlement and conciliation, the International Court of Justice, equipped with

[1] Clark and Sohn, *World Peace through World Law* (1958), 2nd ed., 1960.

greatly enlarged authority over the decision of international legal disputes, would be supplemented by a World Equity Tribunal, to deal with disputes which might threaten peace but are not of an exclusively legal nature. World development would be fostered by a World Development Authority, and a United Nations revenue system would be created to finance these various activities. The General Assembly, as revised, would have power to make binding decisions on matters affecting the peace of the world by 'special majorities', while the present Security Council is to be replaced by an Executive Council composed of representatives chosen by the General Assembly itself.

The basic weakness of this imaginative scheme is that voting adjustments and other institutional changes will not eliminate the deep political and social tensions which today basically divide the major as well as many minor States from each other. Indeed, the authors give no other justification for the practicability of this scheme than the overwhelming destructiveness of modern nuclear war. Fear of such universal destruction may, indeed, deter the major Powers of the world from going to war with each other. But this is a very different thing from united action in an international organization equipped with far-reaching powers over essential questions of national existence. The important advances made in this direction by smaller, closely knit groups of nations such as the six member-States of the West European Communities will be analysed later.

International Justice and Bills of Rights

A second approach emphasizes the peaceful settlement of international disputes through submission to an international court or international arbitration, and this has recently been coupled with attempts to lay down an international Bill for human rights, enforceable before an international court. Both attempts meet the same obstacle. A nation which is not prepared to restrict its sovereignty, or to abdicate the national right to make wars, in favour of collective security, will not submit any major disputes with other nations to an international forum, whether it is a law court proper, an equity tribunal or a court of arbitration. A Bill of human rights presupposes a measure of agreement on basic values which it is quite impossible to achieve between nations deeply divided in their political and social ideology. This is borne out by the failure of the Permanent Court of International Justice, established under the League Covenant, and the even greater failure of the present International Court of Justice under the United Nations Charter to attract any but relatively minor disputes before their forum.[1] Little more is achieved by such high-sounding proclamations as the Universal Declaration of Human Rights, which was one of the very few positive achievements of the United Nations General Assembly in December 1948. This Declaration, in thirty Articles, lays down human rights ranging from the equality of human beings to freedom of speech and worship, personal security, equality before the law, freedom of movement between countries, the right to own property, freedom of

[1] Considering the absence of any permanent international judicial organ until less than forty years ago, the achievement of the International Court is, indeed, important — as has recently been shown by Sir Hersh Lauterpacht's *The Development of International Law by the International Court* (1958). But compared with the need, for contemporary international society, to have major international conflicts submitted to adjudication rather than the clash of competing national Powers, the role of the Court has so far been very small. Only States whose friendly relations were above question have submitted to it certain questions of relatively major significance (such as the Fisheries dispute between Great Britain and Norway, involving the limits of Norway's territorial jurisdiction over its coastline). After the chastening experience of the Corfu Channel case, where Albania simply disregarded the judgment given against it, the Court has been careful to reject jurisdiction unless both parties had clearly agreed to it. This put many disputes of major international legal as well as political significance, such as the Iranian Oil dispute of 1952, out of its reach. The South American States, which dispute certain British territorial rights in the Antarctic region, have adamantly refused to submit the dispute to the Court. The so-called 'optional clause', under which a considerable number of States have agreed to submit certain disputes of a legal character to the jurisdiction of the Court, has been so much hedged about with reservations that its practical significance has been almost nil.

The Court has exercised considerably greater influence through its advisory opinions, which it can render at the request of the General Assembly. Thus, by the opinion establishing the international legal personality of the United Nations, and its right to demand compensation for injuries done to its servants (Bernadotte case), or the opinion which denied the General Assembly the right to set aside awards given by the United Nations Administrative Tribunal, the Court has considerably strengthened and developed international law. But this cannot blind us to the fact that the nations of the world are still overwhelmingly reluctant to entrust the decision of major conflicts to an international organ, be it called International Court of Justice or World Equity Tribunal.

association, the right to work and an adequate standard of living. But it does not establish any agencies capable of enforcing these rights, or entitle individuals to submit grievances to the international court. The interpretation and execution of these rights are left to the individual nations, which differ most widely in their views and standards. The adoption of such a resolution is deceptive. The more general the phrases used, the easier is the adoption of obligations which express little more than moral aspirations. One will equally find all nations condemning wars of aggression, or professing to adhere to 'democracy'. A code of human rights can only be the crowning achievement of a community held together by common values and ways of living. It comes at the end, not at the beginning.

It is not, therefore, surprising that the Covenants on Human Rights, which were drafted in the United Nations, as a practical implementation of the principles of the Universal Declaration — even though they differ substantially in content from the former — have little prospect of adoption. By contrast, the European States joined in the Council of Europe in 1954 set up the European Court of Human Rights as well as the European Commission of Human Rights, with power to decide over violations of the Code of Human Rights agreed upon between the members of the Council, at the request of one of the member-States or, in certain cases, of groups or individuals belonging to any of these States. In implementation of these arrangements, the Commission has rendered hundreds of decisions, the great majority of which have rejected the complaints, while a small number went forward to the European Court. Until now the Court has rendered preliminary decisions in only two cases, and it remains to be seen what impact this revolutionary advance in the international organization and protection of human rights will have on the development of international law and relations. Whatever the answer to this question may be, it is clear that the achievement of international judicial institutions must be built upon a minimum of common standards and values, not presently existent among the nations of the world as a whole.

Functional Collaboration between Nations

Lastly, disillusionment about the progress of general international organizations such as the League of Nations and the

United Nations Organization, let alone world federations or world parliaments, has led to increasing emphasis on the 'functional' aspect of international collaboration: co-operation of nations in specialized tasks, such as the fighting of illness and starvation, international labour conventions, or the advancement of education. In many ways this has been the most promising development of international collaboration. The Food and Agriculture Organization, for example, has done great work in the fighting of cattle disease and agricultural pests in various parts of the world; the World Health Organization has quickly and effectively distributed sera to fight cholera and other diseases; the International Bank for Reconstruction and Development has given considerable financial help towards the reconstruction and development of many countries (its loans have approached $1,000 million annually in recent years); the International Labour Organization has achieved important agreements on international labour standards, and in UNESCO, nations behind the 'iron curtain', such as Czechoslovakia and Hungary, still collaborate with Western nations in tasks of international cultural and social interests. But the possibilities of this approach must not be overrated. They will touch no more than the fringe of international tensions as long as the nations disagree on fundamentals. Where 'functional' international collaboration touches matters of national economic or social policy, it comes up even more acutely against the basic political difficulties which have impeded the progress of the United Nations Organization. Apart from the general suspicion which prevented the Soviet Union from accepting the majority proposal on the control of atomic energy, she feared that the ownership, management and inspection of plants splitting fissionable materials, as well as of their further uses, would involve a far-reaching interference with her national economy. Again, an International Labour Convention standardizing basic wages and conditions of labour, at least among the main industrial nations of the world, is most urgently needed. Once again the lower wages of German as compared with American, or of Japanese as compared with Australian, workers threaten to produce a dangerous competition for exports. Yet an international agreement on these matters — especially if it were to include the Communist nations — would cut deep into problems of State planning, social policy and other highly controversial political questions. Even the relatively unpolitical plan of the Food and Agriculture Organization — which does not include Soviet Russia — to establish itself as a clearing-house and trustee for the equitable international distribution of vital foodstuffs, and in particular the transfer of surplus commodities to deficit areas, was rejected by the United States because of internal policy considerations. The Economic Commission for Europe, a United Nations agency, has achieved some success because its Eastern and Western members still have considerable interest in the exchange of goods, and in particular of Western capital equipment for Eastern foodstuffs and raw materials. But political tension and strategic considerations greatly impede the flow of trade. A plan of the International Labour Office to establish an International Migration Council to organize and administer migration between Europe and other continents was rejected by the United States because some satellite Communist States are still (inactive) members of the I.L.O., and American Congress will not vote funds for any organization which might benefit a Communist State. On the other hand, certain functional organizations with strictly limited though important objectives have achieved significant success. The International Refugee Organization (I.R.O.) has successfully settled over two million Europeans, mainly displaced persons in Germany, in overseas countries. A good example of an international functional agency with executive powers is the Wheat Council, set up under the International Wheat Agreement of 1949, signed by over forty nations. This agreement could only be concluded at a time when the wheat-producing countries were faced with the prospects of an unsaleable surplus of wheat, while the importing countries were still interested in a stable and moderate wheat price for a definite period of years. The International Wheat Council, set up under the Agreement, has power to make binding decisions by a majority vote, and it can exclude an offending member from the benefits of the agreement. The International Civil Aviation Organization and the World Health Organization also have certain technical regulatory powers. Most international organizations have only advisory functions. They generally consist of a periodical conference of national delegates, who are appointed by the member governments, and a permanent executive which is genuinely international in composition and character. But even where such international agreements as a labour convention or a food distribution scheme have been duly passed by the international organization concerned, they are still subject to the separate approval of every one of the member nations. The main hope for the success of these organizations lies in the gradual strengthening of their permanent international staffs, and in the impression which continuity and solidarity of their work may make upon the nations in due course. The greatest chance for a co-ordinated effort of the specialized agencies of the United Nations may lie in the organization of technical assistance for backward areas. Following President Truman's call, in his inaugural address of January 20, 1949, the Economic and Social Council of the United Nations, in association with the executive heads of the functional international agencies, has developed a programme of international technical assistance to underdeveloped areas in which the Soviet Union participates. It covers expert advice on soil conservation, seeds, fertilizers, methods of cultivation, fighting of stock diseases, as well as assistance in the improvement of administration, health and education. The scale of such assistance ultimately depends on the financial support given to it by the United States and other major members of the United Nations. But there are strong reasons of world strategy which make such assistance a matter of great political as well as humanitarian importance to the Western Powers. And the highly developed national sensitiveness of the States in need makes international organizations far more suitable agencies of assistance than individual Powers, such as the United States.

The functional approach is thus no miracle solution, but it affords an important means of by-passing the propagandist atmosphere of political international assemblies, and of bringing the nations together in practical tasks of mutual interest and benefit.

For the purpose of bringing the nations together it has one other advantage. A less than universal organization of nations in the political and military field cannot but be in opposition to the wider objective of world-wide security by collective guarantee. A close military and political alignment of any group of nations invariably provokes a counter-move. As we have seen, this is inevitable in the present condition of the world, but it shifts the maintenance of peace from an organic system of world-wide mutual assistance to a system of balance of power. But functional collaboration on a less than universal scale, while obviously less good than a world-wide organization, can fulfil the same objective. UNESCO, the World Health Organization, the International Wheat Council or the International Bank for Reconstruction and Development, are not diverted from their basic task by bringing together the United States and India, Mexico or Turkey, even if the Soviet group stays outside. The main objective — namely, to put in a common pool the material and spiritual resources of different nations and to bring their peoples together in the pursuit of common tasks — remains the same. If the abstention of Soviet Russia and her satellites is a fatal blow to collective security or the control of atomic weapons, it is only regrettable in the case of the International Wheat Council or the World Bank.

The Future of Nationalism

What, in conclusion, is the future of nationalism likely to be? The era of genuine national sovereignty is over. It is also reasonably certain that there will not be in the foreseeable future a world State or a world Federation in which existing nationalities are fused and extinguished. Nor would the world be any happier with the elimination of the diversities of national cultures, achievements and traditions without which Western civilization would not exist. Most probably the blending of national and supranational allegiances will proceed in different forms in the Eastern and Western associations of nations which are taking shape. The Soviet bloc will almost certainly extend the multi-national organization of the Soviet Union to other nations associated with it. This means that existing national groups will retain their identity and obtain some administrative and cultural autonomy. They will keep their distinctive national traditions and languages, their literature and theatre, and to some extent different legal systems. The multi-national system is easy to work where there is no danger of such nationalism reaching out towards military, political or economic sovereignty. In the multi-national States of the Soviet pattern, such as the Soviet Union or Yugoslavia, economic and political control is firmly anchored at the centre, and the monopoly power of the Communist Party ensures that movements of independence will not go too far. The main problem for any association of Western democracies will be how to maintain the national diversities of its constituent members without the iron control of a one-party system and of totalitarian government.

This is a far more difficult task. It is likely that the Western approach will be 'functional' rather than 'organic'. Supra-national loyalties may develop around joint military organization and staff work, the possibility of which was so well demonstrated during the last war in the combination of British and American forces under General Eisenhower. They may crystallize around a joint economic council whose task must be the gradual integration of the production and the finances of the participating nations. If the nations concerned should agree to a common Bill of Rights enforceable before a common international court, this will mean a gradual adjustment of standards of justice and civilization. Above all, the free flow and exchange of people and ideas will not extinguish national identity or pride, but give a better sense of perspective and counter the poisonous but fashionable doctrine of the moral superiority of any one nation over all others.

A single concrete achievement, such as the pooling of West European steel and coal resources under a joint, supra-national Authority (as achieved in the European Coal and Steel Community), or a convention which will adjust labour standards and thus eliminate one source of international cut-throat competition, or the abolition of passports between a number of countries, is worth many blueprint constitutions, federal or otherwise.

CHAPTER 3

THE MAIN POLITICAL MOVEMENTS OF OUR TIME AND THE INTERNATIONAL SITUATION

MILLIONS of men and women have died and suffered for their political ideals. Even if often enough a skilful use of ideology cloaks the power lust of a few individuals or small groups of men who thus induce the common man to sacrifice his life, possessions and happiness for what he conceives to be a worthy cause, this does not diminish the force of ideological issues. But it is all the more compelling for the student of international affairs to distinguish between genuine and fake currency in ideologies.

The main organized political movements of our time, in their effect on the policies of States, on international ideologies and the issues of war and peace in general, can hardly be understood without an analysis of certain sociological developments which affect them all.

The Authoritarian Trend of Modern Society

As recently as half a century ago, most philosophers and politicians would have described the movement of Western civilization as one from authoritarian to liberal government. Between the seventeenth and nineteenth centuries Western society in particular, inspired by French and British thinkers of the seventeenth and eighteenth centuries, and led by the evolution of the British political system, clearly moved towards the emancipation of the individual from the absolutist government of former centuries. This expressed itself in many ways: through the widening of parliamentary representation, the growth of freedom of speech, of the Press, of worship. No less powerful was the movement for economic freedom from State trading monopolies and the restrictive effect of small markets and nationalist economic policies. Theoretically, this freedom applied to everybody; for it went together with an increasingly humanitarian and cosmopolitan conception of mankind, a conception which led to religious tolerance, the emancipation of Jews, the abolition of slavery and the growth of international law. But in practice the social and economic conditions limited effective freedom to a section of society. The main influence in the State gradually passed from the older privileged classes, the nobility and the clergy, to the industrial, commercial and intellectual middle classes. But the 'common man' still remained the object, not the subject, of politics. The French Revolution of 1789 accelerated the social and political emancipation in Europe of the middle class, but it also set in train movements for the further emancipation of the people. In the nineteenth-century France and, through French influence, the newly developing United States of America, were the spearheads of political democracy; in Britain the older conception of a not fully democratic liberalism continued to prevail, although it was increasingly undermined by the extension of the franchise, by the gradual abolition of property qualifications, and later by the granting of voting rights to women. But it is the social aspect of democratic ideology which is responsible for the most recent developments. The Industrial Revolution greatly deepened the cleavage between the economically privileged and the economically underprivileged, and at a time when the ideologies of political democracy, human rights and international equality were steadily advancing, this social cleavage lent increased force to the call for a social as well as a political democracy. This call was taken up from two different sides, which have already been referred to in the first chapter. On one side humanitarian reformers — men like Shaftesbury, Owen, Bentham, Mill — demanded social justice, whether from religious, ethical or utilitarian motives. On the other side, Marxism demanded the revolutionary replacement of the Capitalist order of society, which is regarded as the bulwark of the middle classes, by the Socialist order of society, the order of the proletariat, the 'common man'.

But whereas political and social ideologies overwhelmingly moved in the direction of an ever-increasing extension of liberty and democracy, other social factors, equally resulting from the growth of the modern industrial society, point in an entirely opposite direction. The growth of industry has led in all highly developed industrialized countries to the gradual depopulation of the country and the congregation of vast masses of people in cities. Outside Europe and the United States, this is only beginning to touch the fringe of societies which are still dominated by a peasant economy. But in Europe and the United States, and to some extent in present-day Russia, this movement is proceeding at a rapidly increasing pace. Its main social effect is the diminution or disappearance of the older village communities, and the growth of amorphous cities. In Europe, history and tradition are retarding the speed of this movement. But where, as in Australia, a modern society is built up in a vacant continent, this is far more obvious. The majority of the people congregate in a few sprawling cities, while the farming community is small, scattered and ranks as an industry rather than as a social community. Education has become far more universal, but it has not meant that the majority of people think or act independently, following their own judgment and conscience. The vast majority of the people can now read and write, they can be useful members of a modern military or industrial army, but universal elementary education has also made them far more subject than ever to the Press, the radio, the film, the organized political mass meeting. In conjunction with modern weapons and means of communication these pillars of urbanized society immeasurably increase the power of the rulers over the masses. Never have so few exercised so much power over so many as the rulers of Nazi Germany, Soviet Russia or Communist China. But the growth of power in the hands of the Executive, while subject to parliamentary and other checks, is hardly less marked in the democracies. It is significant that in the last few decades leading political and social thinkers of different countries have studied the growth of a new 'élite', a new oligarchy of rulers dominating the masses. The sociological studies of the Frenchman Sorel, the Italian Pareto, the Spaniard Ortega y Gasset, the Germans Spengler and Juenger or the American Mills, find their counterpart in Aldous Huxley's picture of a completely mechanized and standardized *Brave New World*, or in George Orwell's Oceania of *1984*. Together with the superficial trend towards democracy and the greater participation of the people in political and international affairs, the technical means by which small groups of people can guide and rule the masses have grown immensely, in quantity and quality.

The Social-Welfare State

Another result of the increasing complexity of society, which is reinforced by the ever-widening call for greater social equality and justice, is the necessity for more and more government. The trend towards the planned society and the social-welfare State is today world-wide. Outwardly one of the main battle-cries today is that between 'liberty' and 'planning'. But the differences between parties are far less wide than these slogans suggest. A State of many millions living closely together in big cities demands more regulation than a society of a few hundred thousand scattered in village communities. And in an age in which the 'common man' has not only voting rights, but is also called time and again to sacrifice life, health and property in war, he will not look quietly at the gross inequalities of wealth and power which the early capitalism of the nineteenth century produced. In all countries, regardless of their political complexion, people demand more and more security against unemployment through State assistance, public works, subsidies and other means; they demand social services such as health and pensions insurance; they demand free public education and a reduction in the grossest inequalities of wealth by graded taxation. Nor will they tolerate slum dwellings or insanitary factories. What is left of an unregulated capitalist society is further reduced by the threat or actual conduct of war which has overshadowed contemporary Western society for the last fifty years. Such a situation compels the Government to take charge of defence, and defence today includes not only armies, navies and air forces, but scientific research, industrial priorities, the direction of labour and a host of other matters deeply affecting the life of society.

All these currents of modern thought and social development operate today in varying mixture in the main political movements of our time. It is not simply a matter of liberty versus authority, or democracy versus dictatorship. If the American political system claims to be the expression of democracy, so does the Soviet system. The one regards political freedom as essential, the other considers the abolition of private economic power as the most fundamental condition of democracy. Liberals of the old school decry the increasing control of the State as a threat to individual freedom. But Socialists regard a universal free State education, or national health services, as essential conditions of a free and full development of personality which mere equality of political rights cannot guarantee. Trade unionism started as a measure of collective self-defence of the underprivileged working class against the exploitation of Capitalism, but in the more developed industrial countries it has now reached the stage in which the individual worker is left less and less freedom. In practice, if not in theory, he must join the union or he will lose his livelihood.

The Major Political Movements of our Time

Five major political movements compete today for supremacy and the allegiance of men. There are, first, Communist movements, which dominate the Soviet group of nations and are powerful in many other countries. There are, secondly, the Social-Democratic Labour movements, which outside the Soviet bloc still represent the majority of the organized Labour movements and many other independent progressive elements. There is, thirdly, capitalist democracy mainly represented by the United States. There is, fourthly, Fascist authoritarianism, which, despite the defeat of the Axis Powers, is far from being an extinguished force. And, lastly, the Catholic Church represents a powerful international political and social force.

Many other political forces and organizations act today as a ferment rather than as organized movements of major international significance. The various Christian Churches other than the Catholic Church, for example, have powerful influence on international policy, but they are scattered and diverse in their effect. On the other hand, non-Christian religious movements like Hinduism or Buddhism may have made or unmade States, unified or divided nations, but they are of no major account as international ideological movements. Islam, however, is now becoming a powerful ferment in the political movements of the Middle East and Africa. It may be that the blend of Western political ideologies with Eastern civilization and conditions may produce new and different political philosophies, an Indian nationalism or a distinctive Chinese Communism. But this it is too early to judge. So far Western ideologies have been imposed upon alien civilizations which may absorb, adapt or ultimately reject them. Finally, Liberalism and Conservatism are still very powerful ferments of political thought, but they are, as will be shown, increasingly absorbed in the political movements analysed in this chapter.

International Communism

The Socialist movement has for some time been split into two wings, the Radical Communist and the moderate Social-Democrat wing. The conflict between these two has dominated the history of the Socialist movement.

Modern Communists claim to be heirs to the Marxist theory as originally laid down in the Communist Manifesto of Marx and Engels. Marxism regards the control of the means of production as the key not only to economic but to political power in the State. It regards the State itself as an instrument of coercion, created by the controllers of Capitalist society in their own interest. It demands the transfer of the means of production into the hands of the community, following upon a period of growing concentration of capital in increasingly monopolistic enterprises. The chosen instrument for the transfer of the means of production into the hands of the community is the proletariat, which has to exercise a temporary dictatorship in order to achieve a classless society. Once the transfer has been achieved, the State — that is to say, the instrument of coercion — will no longer be necessary. It will 'wither away'. Communism is an international movement, and in its original form postulates world-wide revolution. The distinction between nations and States is replaced by the distinction between classes. As in feudal society knights and peasants of different countries were closer to each other than the different classes of one nation, so the proletarians of different nations are linked by the community of their class interests. No ties of sentiment or loyalty link them with the Capitalists of their own nation.

The modern leaders of Communist Revolution, men like Lenin, Stalin, Mao Tse-tung, Krushchev, have, however, had to think in terms of practical action, of tactics as well as principle. The revolution had to start somewhere. It was in Russia, where the great majority were illiterate and politically passive peasants, that the disorganization of war, the corruption of the Czarist regime and the dynamic energy of a highly disciplined and resolute group of men led by Lenin combined to produce the great opportunity in

1917. Originally the Soviet leaders expected similar revolutions to take place in Germany and Central Europe, spreading from there farther throughout the world. When this expectation failed, the heirs of Lenin disagreed. Trotsky still regarded the task of immediate world revolution as paramount. Stalin wanted to consolidate the revolution in one State, making it the heart and pivot of further action. Krushchev and Mao, each seeking to adapt Communist ideology to the national interests and policies of their respective countries, arrived at so starkly differing conclusions that a split between the two major leaders of Communism became inevitable.[1]

Communist theory contributes the main long-term objectives which have been briefly described in the first chapter. More important, however, than the distant aim of a classless society are two other attributes of Communist doctrine. First, the Messianic character of the Communist message has produced the highly disciplined and devoted groups of Communist leaders all over the world who have time and again proved their readiness to sacrifice everything to their faith. It accounted for Communist leadership in many of the resistance movements during the last war, when, for a while, Communist and nationalist policies were at one in opposing the Nazis. It now accounts for the disciplined efficiency of the Vietcong guerrillas in the struggle between North and South Vietnam. Secondly, the conviction that the advent of world revolution is a matter of dialectic necessity gives to the Communist élite the self-assuredness which the followers of less radical movements often lack because they see human history as a conflict of beliefs and values, none of which can claim the monopoly of truth or of scientific necessity.

Russian Imperialism and Communist Ideology

The emergence of a powerful Soviet Russia has profoundly modified the character of international Communism. In the first place, Communism has had to be reconciled with the nationalist aspirations of Russia and the power politics of its leaders, who have shown no desire whatsoever to let the State 'wither away'. It may be that Brezhnev and the other members of the Politburo, which is the effective government of Russia, still believe in the eventual attainment of a classless international society.

[1] See further below, pp. 71 *et seq.*

But even if for them the advance and strengthening of Soviet Russia were to be only a stepping-stone to the eventual objective of world-wide classless and stateless Communism, the attainment of this goal would take many more decades. Meanwhile a new generation of Soviet citizens has been taught obedience and loyalty to the Soviet Union. The unity and greatness of Soviet Russia are identified with the progress of world Communism. In Russia itself this new nationalist turn of Communist government has on the whole strengthened the authority of the Government. The Soviet rulers still claim to be the heirs of Marx and Lenin, but obedience does not for Soviet citizens produce the same conflict between an international ideology and patriotism as in other countries. Moscow regards itself as the centre of a world-wide movement, but Soviet power politics are indistinguishable from those of other States, except that the use of an international ideology, with organized support in many countries, provides a most powerful weapon of expansion. Foreign nations are conquered not by armed force — except in the very last resort — but by the encouragement of the Communist élite, which, once in power, is made subservient to the policy-makers of Moscow. The tactics have varied with opportunity. In the case of ex-enemy States like Hungary and Roumania, Soviet Russia could use the military prerogatives of a victor to set up the desired regime. In Allied States like Czechoslovakia the tactics had to be different. The proximity of the Soviet army supplied the necessary support for internal political manœuvres ending in a Communist *coup d'état* in February 1948. Both arms support and economic assistance (through aid and trade) have been used to bind Castro's Cuba to Russia, in a situation of weakness created by the United States' economic boycott of Cuba.

The international agencies of Soviet Communism have been adapted to these changes in strategy. The original Comintern, founded in 1919, was still an expression of earlier Marxist teaching, the nucleus of a genuine international Communist movement. It steadily lost in importance until it was dissolved by Stalin in 1942. Its place is now taken by the Cominform in the political, and the Comecon in the economic, field. They are supplemented in the military field by a series of military pacts between Soviet Russia and other European Communist States, ostensibly directed against German aggression or any State which 'directly or indirectly' associates itself with German aggression. The Cominform, centred at Bucharest but directed from Moscow, is under the close supervision of the Kremlin. It consists of the representatives of most Communist parties elsewhere. This means that its directions have immediate effect in countries with Communist Governments. It is not an instrument of internationalism, but an agency ensuring the utmost co-ordination of policies by as large as possible a group of States. The Comecon similarly directs a programme of 'mutual economic aid' in which the economic development plans of Communist States are co-ordinated with those of Soviet Russia and an attempt is made to co-ordinate the economic aid to, and trade with, the underdeveloped countries.

The Dilemma of non-Russian Communists

This policy is not necessarily and completely disadvantageous to the smaller States. Whereas Nazi Germany considered the Slavonic States of Europe as racially inferior, and economically not worthy of high industrial development, Soviet policy encourages the industrialization of satellite States in so far as this is compatible with her own interests. There are ambitious industrial programmes for Czechoslovakia, Poland, Hungary, within the framework of the Council for Mutual Economic Assistance, while Yugoslavia has made important industrial progress on her own. Nevertheless it is inevitable that sooner or later Communists outside Russia have to choose between conflicting loyalties. They must either decide to subordinate the political, social and economic development of their country to a policy laid down in Moscow, and pretend that this is necessarily in accordance with the national interests of their own country, or they must risk conflict with the Kremlin. Until recently, Communist leaders everywhere chose the former course, or were 'liquidated' in time, with the significant exception of Tito in Yugoslavia. As long as Communist leaders can concentrate on fighting 'Western imperialism' internationally, and social oppression within their country, they may disguise their dilemma. They can expropriate Western oil interests in Roumania, abolish Western shipping rights on the Danube, and liquidate their own landowners and middle classes. Such actions can postpone but not eliminate the dilemma of Communist policy. It is shown by the frequent *volte-face* of Communist foreign policy, such as its overnight change of front in the last world war, after Russia had been invaded by Germany. Recent examples are even more revealing. German Communists constantly clamour for German unity and national sovereignty whenever it is a question of opposing a West German State under Western auspices or an international control of the Ruhr in which Russia does not participate. But at the same time they have had to approve the annexation of a large part of eastern Germany by Poland — which is more acutely felt by the majority of Germans — because Russia officially backs Polish claims to this area. On the other hand, French Communists under the Fourth Republic agreed with the right-wing parties in France in demanding a restriction of German sovereignty and her permanent demilitarization and international supervision. Communists have always been champions of the liberation of colonial peoples from Western imperialism, whether in the United Nations or elsewhere, but a few years ago Italian Communists posed as champions of the restoration of Italian colonies, in opposition to British and American plans for either British or international trusteeship. On the other hand, Greek Communists, after the quarrel between Stalin and Tito, suddenly had to advocate a Greater Macedonia which would mean the cession of parts of Greece to a new federal State. As has been pointed out in the previous chapter, the championship of nationalism is today passing from the middle classes to the radical left; but in order to carry conviction the new Communist nationalism must be consistent. The first open revolt within the Communist camp was started by Tito, one of the very few Communist rulers who came to power without Russian assistance. He found that he could no longer square subservience to Russian policy with his own ambitions and plans for the development of Yugoslavia. These dilemmas are more damaging to Communism in relatively developed and politically articulate States than in others. The Communist parties have lost heavily in Western Germany, Austria, Holland, Sweden, Norway, not to speak of Britain, where they hardly count as a political as distinct from an industrial force. They have still considerable strength in France and Italy, two highly industrialized and politically developed countries. But Communist success there has been in almost exact proportion to the weakness of unstable coalition governments, and to the degree of prevailing economic chaos and distress.

Communism in Western Europe is not so much a religion for the dispossessed as an outlet for economic and social grievances.

This leads to the second point. In four decades of Communist government, Soviet Russia has developed a powerful State machine, the pillars of which are the one-party system, a small and powerful ruling group that includes the military leaders, and central economic planning. To some extent this is a continuation of the Russian tradition. A country so vast and diffuse, peopled by so many nations of different characteristics, may need stronger government than most other countries. But the 'élite' character of Communist government goes deeper than national particularities, as shown by the more recent organization of Communist China. What in original Marxist doctrine appeared as a necessary but temporary technique, namely the imposition of social revolution by a trained élite on the masses, has become a permanent aspect of Communist rule. In the course of time the split between the radical Communist and the moderate Social-Democratic group of the Socialist movement has deepened. It has been caused by the growing prosperity as well as the political and social advances of the organized working class in the leading industrial countries. This has steadily reduced the gulf between rich and poor, exploiters and exploited. Wherever the organized working-class movement, and Socialist opinion in general, has had a strong influence on the government of the country, Communism has remained relatively weak. Its prospects are all the more powerful in undeveloped countries, where a small group of politically articulate leaders can easily impose a new form of government upon illiterate and impoverished masses. And Communist leaders in these countries have been able to use either a growing nationalism, as in Indonesia, or the corruption of a decadent and unscrupulous ruling class, as in China. In such cases Communist leaders can not only more easily apply the technique of revolution, but they can also appear as genuine benefactors of the people. Contrary to original Marxist prognosis, Communism has today greater prospects in the undeveloped and mainly agrarian countries of the Middle and Far East, of Africa and Latin America, than in the more industrialized and developed countries of Europe and North America. There is more than accident in the present contrast between Communist defeats in Europe and Communist victories in Asia. The issue becomes most acute in countries like

India, where a relatively high degree of political and industrial development contrasts with the destitution and backwardness of the vast majority of the people. The speed of economic development and of social reform, especially in the redistribution of land, may decide which way India will go.

Russia, China and the Split in Communist Ideology

One of the most important international developments of recent years has been the gradual disruption of the monolithic aspects of Communist ideology. Stalin's Russia had already gone a long way in adapting the teachings of Marx and Lenin to the needs of a strongly nationalist, bureaucratically governed and economically and socially developing State which had to survive and co-exist in a predominantly non-Communist world. But as long as Soviet Russia remained the undisputed leader of contemporary Communist ideology, without serious rival and able to impose its own views and policies on the Communist satellite States of Europe, Soviet interpretations of Communist ideology could not be seriously challenged from within the camp of Communism. This situation was bound to change with the emergence to world stature of another major Communist State. At no time did Mao Tse-tung and the other Communist Chinese leaders consider themselves to be, personally and nationally, satellites of the Soviet Union. Ideologically, they were among the original students and disciples of Marx and Lenin. Nationally, they were always conscious of being members of one of the oldest and, through many periods of history, most powerful nations of the world. Their sense of independence was immensely strengthened by the fact that they conquered China through their own efforts, without major assistance and, at times, against the advice of the Soviet leaders. But for several years after the victory of the Communists over Chiang Kai-shek, Communist China could not afford to display too much political and ideological independence. They were strongly dependent on Soviet supplies and technical assistance in the development of their infant industries. They needed solidarity with their powerful neighbour against the hostility of the United States, which has a military pact of defensive alliance with Chiang Kai-shek.

A number of factors have contributed to the change of posture which has gone far to destroy the monolithic structure of

Communism, and which shows today two rival ideologies and two rival political leaders in the struggle for allegiance by Communists all over the world. Economic considerations alone would have counselled against any open or semi-open conflict between China and the U.S.S.R. After the fiasco of the 'great leap forward', by which the Chinese leaders thought that they could, through ruthlessly regimented communes, by-pass many years of development and push both agricultural and industrial production forward at a greatly accelerated pace, it became clear that they would for many more years depend on Soviet technical, scientific and economic assistance. It is political considerations that prevailed over economic caution. It is impossible for the outsider to say in what proportions personal ambitions, rivalries and animosities contributed to the growing split. Mao Tse-tung, a veteran of Communist revolution, may well have considered Krushchev as a relative upstart. Be that as it may, the split between the rival Communist leaders and nations became more definite, as Krushchev developed the theory of 'co-existence' of Communist with capitalist countries, not as a temporary expedient but as a more permanent pattern of life. The Chinese theoreticians do not have too much difficulty in showing that this is hardly in accordance with the classical Communist doctrine, for which accommodation with capitalism can at best be a temporary phase, and for which the ultimate revolutionary struggle appears as inevitable. But it is doubtful whether Mao Tse-tung and his associates would have proclaimed these differences of ideology, at the risk, and even with the deliberate intent, of provoking a conflict with the Soviet Union, had it not been for considerations of national policy and international strategy. The first major factor in these considerations is the difference in the phases of social and economic development reached by the U.S.S.R. and Communist China respectively. The former is gradually passing from a phase of underdevelopment, revolutionary discipline and national privation, to that of a highly developed and relatively satisfied society, in which the desire to preserve what has been worked for increasingly prevails over the ruthless drive of the early revolutionary phase. Communist China is still in that earlier phase, when rigid ideology is an important weapon in the control over the minds and bodies of the masses, which must be inspired to unflagging effort. From this first difference of position follows the second major divergence: the desire of a relatively static and sophisticated Soviet Union to find ways of accommodation with the non-Communist world, as an alternative to an all-destructive nuclear war. By contrast, Communist China judges the need for revolutionary fervour and undiminished hostility to the 'capitalist' world as exceeding in importance the possible destruction of thermonuclear war. The ruthlessness of Communist ideology helps in the consideration that, in the case of such a war, China might somehow survive even with hundreds of millions of its people dead, whereas the rest of the world might have been virtually wiped out or ceased to exist as organized communities. But perhaps the decisive consideration is the belief that the greatest chance of Communist victories today lies in the underprivileged and underdeveloped countries of Asia and Africa — and of some parts of Latin America. To the dissatisfied and exploited millions of peasants and unemployed or half-starved city dwellers of these continents, the appeal of a collectivized, egalitarian and ruthlessly anti-capitalist Communist China is greater than that of a semi-bourgeois Russia in which there are considerable differences of status and wealth, and an educated class, whose aspirations — both materially and intellectually — are closer to those of the Western than of the Communist world. Added to this are racial aspects. Increasingly, Communist China exploits the fact that the Russians are basically Europeans and white, whereas they, like the struggling peoples of Asia and Africa, are not white.

As the ideological split deepens, old national rivalries and conflicts revive, e.g. over the control of border areas such as Sinkiang or southern Siberia.

While so far the older authority and prestige of the Soviet Union has succeeded in keeping the allegiance of the majority of the Communist parties in other countries, there are many signs that, at least in Asia, the Chinese Communists are gaining ideologically and politically. Be that as it may, Communism no longer presents one face, but at least two rival interpretations and images. This has also contributed to loosening the tight hold that until recently the Soviet Union could exercise over the satellite Communist States of South-east Europe. Not only tiny Albania — which has consistently been in the Chinese camp — but such states as Hungary and Roumania, not to speak of Yugoslavia, which has followed an independent line since 1948, assert with increasing boldness their own interpretations of Communist ideology dictated by considerations of national development and national interests.[1] There is today a decisive difference between the original doctrine of revolutionary Communism and the contemporary practice of Communism, which shows increasing diversity.[2]

Thus there is little in common between the Yugoslav and the Chinese conceptions of Communism, although both States profess to adhere to Communist ideology. Yugoslavia has not only abandoned the collectivization of farming — in a realistic recognition of the almost universal failure of communization in agriculture — but also developed a system of decentralized planning and management in industry. Under the Yugoslav system, only general planning powers are left with the central authorities, while the individual enterprises are given far-reaching autonomy of decision and management, including reinvestment, expansion and use of profits.

In a much more limited way, and against the background of a vastly bigger and more complex system, the Soviet Union has also attempted to transfer a degree of autonomy and decision-making from the centre to the major enterprise units and regions. By contrast, Communist China has gone to very great lengths in both centralized planning and the rigid collectivization of agriculture, through the so-called 'commune'. Under the Chinese system, the collective entirely supplants the individual farmer as the unit responsible not only for production, prices, trade, but also for the social and personal conditions of life within the commune.

Thus, modern Communism, while still united in its emphasis on State planning and the principle of State ownership of major industrial enterprises, is beginning to show as much diversity in the organization of relations between State, group and individual as the different forms of democracy.

[1] This tendency was reinforced by the publication and endorsement by the powerful Communist Party of Italy, in August 1964, of Togliatti's Testament calling for a 'polycentric' conception allowing national autonomy and diversity to Communist movements. This polycentrism and the growing sense of national independence found further expression when almost all the Communist parties of Eastern as well as Western Europe voiced their alarm over the summary dismissal of Krushchev in October 1964.

[2] See further on 'co-existence', below, pp. 134 *et seq.*

New Methods of Aggression and International Law

Communist ideology and strategy affect the whole structure of international relations and law by creating new concepts and methods of aggression. Both in the right of a State to make war, and in the provisions for collective security embodied in the League of Nations Covenant and the United Nations Charter, international law assumes that war arises from organized physical violence between two or more States. On this basis only can the Covenant and the Charter conceive of sanctions against wars of aggression without defining it. In practice it has not usually been difficult to find out when one nation attacked another without provocation. There could be no doubt about the unprovoked attacks by Japan on China in 1931 and 1937, and on the United States in 1941, by Mussolini's Italy on Abyssinia in 1935, and by Hitler's Germany on Poland in 1939. The difficulty in all these situations was not that of determining aggression, but the inability or unwillingness of the other nations to act. The Nazi State undermined these conceptions to some extent by appealing to the racial and ideological solidarity of nationals of other States in defiance of their duties as citizens. But it is Communism under the direction of Soviet Russia which applies this method as a primary weapon. It is difficult for a system of international law based on different assumptions to find an effective answer. The North Atlantic Treaty of 1949 is the first major international document to recognize the problem.[1] According to its Article IV, the parties will consult together whenever in the opinion of any of them the territorial integrity, political independence or security of any of the parties is threatened. It acknowledges the emergence of a new type of aggression much less tangible and easy to define, which is illustrated by the *coup d'état* in Czechoslovakia in February 1948.[2] A Communist minority of Cabinet Ministers, among them the Minister controlling the police, forced the resignation of the non-Communist Ministers, set up a new government and compelled President Beneš, who died soon after, to give his consent.

[1] See further below, p. 125.

[2] The formula is repeated in the Security treaty of 1951, between the United States, Australia and New Zealand, and in the South-East Asia treaty of 1954. It was anticipated in a more elaborate formula in Article 6 of the Inter-American Treaty of Reciprocal Assistance of Sept. 2, 1947.

Later elections were held under the control of the new, completely Communist Government on the 'people's front' model. This was on the face of it an internal Czech affair against which international law offers no remedy. Yet the Czech Communist leaders were leading members of the Cominform which is controlled by Moscow, and the proximity of Soviet Russia gave the Czech Communists strength and confidence. Is this a case of intervention by a foreign Power? Generally the U.S.S.R. has been successful in avoiding open intervention, even in the Berlin uprising of 1953, which was suppressed by the East German government. She did suppress by military force the Hungarian revolution of 1956, which threatened the survival of the satellite Empire, in the certainty that the West would not intervene. But the widespread political repercussions of this brutal action are likely to have counselled further caution. The difficulty of the problem is indicated by the vagueness of the above-quoted clause of the North Atlantic Treaty and the failure of the so-called 'Eisenhower doctrine' to prevent further revolutionary changes in the Middle East. It illustrates the increasing preponderance of social and ideological over physical warfare. Whether or not the parties under the Atlantic Treaty will take action in the case of any further successful Communist revolt is likely to depend mainly on questions of strategy and the balance of forces. The advent of a Communist Government in France or Italy, for example, would greatly threaten the whole structure of Western strategy. Yet it would be very difficult to justify armed action against a change of government even if it did not come by strictly constitutional means. Foreign interference in internal changes is always apt to rouse national resentment, unless it is itself an answer to foreign intervention. No doubt the United States would immediately withdraw all economic assistance and trade from a Communist country. But, as the experience of American economic boycott of Castro's Cuba has shown, most boycotts cannot be universally effective, and the affected country can obtain vital supplies from alternative sources. Moreover, experience shows that economic sanctions do not induce a change of policy. On the contrary, they would provide Communists with welcome proof of the aggressiveness of Western capitalism. In this difficulty of disentangling internal changes from outside influence lies the real danger of international conflict, especially in areas where the opposing power groups both have vital interests at stake.

Social Democracy

The split between the forces of the Second and Third International goes back to the end of the nineteenth century, although Communist parties as such did not come into existence until 1917. On the European Continent, which has been far more subject to Marxist influence than the Anglo-American world, a 'revisionist' Socialist wing, led by Bernstein, Jaurès and others, reflected the growing strength of the Trade Union movement in industry, and of the Socialist Party in Parliament. It believed in the victory of Socialism through evolution and gradualism. The main objectives of Socialism remained substantially unaltered. But strategy came to differ more and more decisively from that of the radical Marxists. In revolutionary Russia, a similar split divided Mensheviks and Bolsheviks. On the other hand, the British Labour movement, supported on the industrial side by the Trade Union movement and on the political side by the Fabian Society, never adopted Marxism as its theoretical basis. Its great spiritual inspiration was the religious and ethical humanitarianism of the nineteenth century, the Radical Liberalism of thinkers like T. H. Green and Hobhouse, the idealistic Socialism of men like Owen and Morris. The Fabians preached the attainment of Socialism through political and social reform. Today the difference between Continental and British Social Democracy has greatly lost in importance, while their common opposition to Communism has grown into a fundamental issue of political philosophy. In the period preceding the Second World War, when Fascist and Nazi aggression was the main menace to other nations, including Soviet Russia, Communists under the direction of the Comintern for a while advocated 'popular fronts' — that is, alliances of all progressive parties. This was a tactical move widely supported by progressives of all kinds, but concealing the deep conflict between Communist and Social-Democratic forces. Present-day coalitions between Communists and Socialists in the countries of Eastern Europe are only a thin disguise for Communist rule. In all of them, the Socialist Party has within a few years been either extinguished or become a complete tool of Communist policy. The writings both of Lenin and Stalin are permeated by contempt and hatred for the Social-Democratic faith, because of its belief that Socialism can be attained without violence and by parliamentary means — that is to say, by compromise with the ruling classes. And today Social Democracy is the main competitor for the allegiance of the progressives, and in particular of the organized working class. Reference has already been made to the decline of Communist strength in the more advanced countries of Europe — in North America it hardly counts at all as a serious force — as compared with its rapid and in part triumphant advance in parts of Asia. The reason for the relative strength of Social Democracy in Europe is that, in some countries at least, it has reached the stage of actual government and achievement of a Socialist programme. As the Trade Union movement as well as the political representation of Labour grew in stature and influence, especially during the last war, the belief of Social Democracy became more firmly established that Socialism could and should be achieved in partnership with, and not in opposition to, political liberty. That liberty which in the early days of the Industrial Revolution was a sham for the average worker has now acquired meaning and reality. The attainment of Socialism by evolutionary and parliamentary means has become possible. Some smaller States, notably the Scandinavian countries, have for some years been governed by Social-Democratic parties, either alone or as the dominating party of a coalition. This has led to a vast development of public enterprise and social services. In Britain a Labour Government was, from 1945 to 1951, able to carry out, through its parliamentary majority, a programme of partial Socialism which was an implementation of years of theoretical and practical preparation. Its most important feature has been a series of gigantic experiments in public enterprise — affecting coal, electricity, gas, transport and steel — and the introduction of comprehensive national insurance schemes and health services. Except for the denationalization of the steel industry, these changes have not been reversed by the Conservative Government. Their economic success is a matter of controversy, although the socialization of the coal, electric and gas industries is almost universally accepted as a necessary step towards modernization and greater productivity. But the answer to the question of whether partial socialization has destroyed political liberty can now be given with some confidence. In the critical years of post-war tension political liberty in Social-Democratic Britain was far less threatened than in the anti-

Socialist United States. But the greater the practical achievements of Social Democracy, the bitterer will be the cleavage between Communism and Social Democracy.

It is, however, only in relatively few cases that a Social-Democratic Government has been able to govern singly and to carry out a Socialist programme by parliamentary means. In most countries, such as pre-Nazi Germany or present-day Western Germany, Japan, France and Italy, Social Democrats are either in opposition or have to form Coalition Governments with other parties. This forces them either to sacrifice their belief in political liberty by an alliance with Communists, or to sacrifice Socialism by an alliance with Liberals or Conservatives. In this dilemma the Social-Democratic parties in all these countries are being gravely weakened. Moreover, the main objectives of moderate Socialism have been achieved in many advanced countries, such as Sweden, Britain or Australia. Outside Communism, there is little popular support for wholesale socialization of industry or agriculture. On the other hand, conservative parties have largely accepted comprehensive social services, the democratization of education and even the nationalization of certain basic industries (such as coal, electricity and transport in Britain). This has taken the ideological fervour out of Social Democracy.

Fascism

The history of the now defunct regimes of Nazi Germany, Fascist Italy and Imperial Japan permits a fairly clear and final analysis of Fascism, the modern form of Right-wing authoritarian government. But Fascism is far from being a matter of history. It survives today quite openly in Franco Spain and several Latin American States, and, in a modified form, in Portugal, Vietnam and other States. It is also likely that the authoritarian governments headed by generals, which, in 1958, swept aside weak and inefficient parliamentary systems in Burma, Pakistan, and the Sudan, are not merely transitory. With very few exceptions, the new African States — among them Ghana and Tanganyika — have abandoned democracy and established one-party forms of government.[1]

[1] It will be all the more interesting to watch the outcome of the removal of General Abboud's military government by a civilian coalition in the Sudan (November 1964).

Fascist authoritarianism shares with modern Communism many methods and tactics of government. Soviet Communism was in this respect the acknowledged teacher of the German National-Socialists. They differ, however, in their ultimate aims.

Fascism demands one-party government and the absence of free political controversy not only as a means but as an end. It believes openly in the difference between rulers and ruled, and in the right of an élite to govern the masses. It despises liberalism, freedom of speech and of association. It openly worships the State as a permanent instrument of realizing the people's destiny. It differs decisively from Communism in rejecting the international equality of men, races and peoples, even as an ultimate goal. This difference between Communism and Fascism has some effect upon present-day international politics, as has been shown in the preceding chapter. But they differ above all in their social foundations. The Fascist regimes of Germany, Italy and Japan did not choose open revolution but a pseudo-constitutional *coup d'état* in which they were supported by the military and the propertied classes. The technique was suppression of the Communist Party, followed by the intimidation of other parties, and the exercise of emergency powers which were used to destroy the democratic constitutions. No modern mass movement can afford openly to despise the masses. But whereas for Communism the proletariat is the chosen instrument, Fascism cultivates the common man only because he supplies modern military and industrial manpower.

The ultimate vision of Fascism is that of a hierarchical society, in which small groups of leaders, ruthless and freed from any restraint of morality, rule over the masses which they use but despise. The ultimate vision of Communism is that of a free society which, after the abolition of the private ownership of capital and the development of the full potentialities of the common people, will benefit all mankind.

The actual methods of Fascism and Communism are however much closer to each other than their ultimate aims. Both have totally abolished the separation of powers within the State by which a democratic legislature and an independent judiciary restrain the executive government and afford protection to the citizen. Fascist governments tend to abolish parliaments altogether, whereas Communist systems maintain the machinery of parliament through annual meetings and discussions, but without any genuine freedom of dissent and opposition. There is only one party, and the restriction in the choice of candidates makes it certain that there can be no genuine opposition. The judiciary is, under both systems, trained according to political principles and subject to political control. It is told to put community interests first, and judicial decisions are open to Government criticism whenever they tend to interfere with the Government policy of the day. The secret police, with unspecified and practically unlimited powers, acts as deterrent to any genuine diversity and freedom of opinion within the community. Recent experience has shown that this common aspect of Fascist and Communist regimes often overshadows the diversity of their ultimate aims. The complete subordination of the individual to Government policy, backed by the secret police and made secure by the abolition of an independent judiciary, is the most important link between modern Communism and modern Fascism. Just as on the Communist side the U.S.S.R. and Yugoslavia are experimenting with a limited relaxation of mental and economic regimentation, so Franco's Fascist Spain is under strong pressure from workers and liberal elements — encouraged by the more liberal attitude of the Church since John XXIII — to mitigate the rigours of Fascism. But it is doubtful whether either form of totalitarianism can go far in any direction without destroying its very foundation.

A detailed study of Fascism would have to distinguish between different types of Fascist government. Italian Fascism, for example, differed in some respects from German National-Socialism. It had originally no race theory or anti-Semitism. Mussolini adopted it only towards the end of his career, when he was increasingly under German pressure. Italian and Spanish Fascism, both influenced by modern Catholic doctrines of state, especially Pope Pius XI's approval of the corporative state in the Encyclical '*Quadragesimo Anno*' (1931), laid more emphasis on the corporate organization of industry, whereas German National-Socialism saw labour relations as a neo-feudal relation between leaders and followers. Italy retained through the period of the Fascist regime a senate whose members, appointed for life, maintained a certain right of criticism which the much more thoroughly disciplined Nazi State would not have tolerated. Yet in their impact on international relations these differences are insignificant as compared with the ideas and principles of action which they share: their belief in leadership, their contempt for the masses, their worship of war, their disregard of international law, their belief in power as the sole arbiter of international action, their contempt for political democracy and individual liberty, their claim to total physical and mental education of the people in preference to any ties of religion, personal conscience, family loyalties or political convictions.

The social policy of Fascism is outwardly very different from that of Communism. It does not purport to abolish the existing ruling classes, militarists, industrialists or bureaucrats. It secures their alliance, and in return it gives them power and wealth.[1] The Nazi regime gained the support of the German military aristocracy by promising them big armies and the prospect of vast wars of aggression. It gained the support of the industrialists by giving them a vast and profitable programme of war production and promising them an international economic empire. It gained the support of most of the Civil Service by appealing to its tradition of loyalty to any Government, but even more by destroying its security of tenure. Whereas Communism maintains a powerful Trade Union movement, Fascism utterly destroys it. In its place employers and employees are organized in corporations under the strict control of the State and the Fascist Party. No genuine independence is left to either, but the employees are worse off because they have lost any right to collective organization and because — as under the Nazi law of 1934 — they are turned into 'followers' of the management, instead of facing it as independents or equals. Yet the Trade Union movement in a Communist State has no real independence either. Management and employees form separate organizations, but both must follow the policy of the State, of which the Communist Party is the sole guardian. Strikes, lock-outs or any other spontaneous collective action holding up production are unthinkable under either system.

It is only logical that both systems of government should aim at obtaining the greatest possible mental control of all their citizens by training them from childhood onwards in the prescribed ideology, in discipline, military efficiency and obedience. It follows equally that science and research of any form become aspects of State policy. The Nazis sponsored special Germanic theories

[1] Of the surviving Fascist regimes, Franco's Spain exemplifies this social policy most clearly.

not only of anthropology and biology, of law and economics, but also of mathematics and physics. And the Lysenko controversy in Soviet Russia has shown that genetic theories of the mutability of plant characteristics are also considered as an eminently political matter, in which the State Government took a decisive part, by removing from office and apparently 'liquidating' an eminent Russian scientist who had doubted that the hereditary characteristics of a plant could be altered by grafting and other experiments — that is, by the power of human action directed to a social purpose.[1]

The aims of Fascism and Communism are still divergent enough to attract different types of people and different strata of society. If faced with a choice which they detest, Conservatives will be more sympathetic towards Fascism and Progressives towards Communism. But behind the ominous similarity of their methods and government looms one of the great dangers of our generation: the development of the thoroughly efficient State in which an all-powerful small minority of determined leaders use modern technique, science and administration for the complete exploitation and domination of the masses.

Conservative Democracy

It is no longer possible to define democracy in general. Various types of democracy have developed into very different forms of society. Modern British or Swedish democracy is in some ways much closer to the State Socialism of Soviet Russia than to the economic system of the United States. But in matters of personal and political freedom it is the other way round. As has been pointed out before, it may be that the threat of war will drive all States into the orbits of either the U.S.A. or Soviet Russia. This would be likely to bring about their gradual domination by two rival forms of government. Meanwhile the American version of democracy requires separate analysis, not only because of the pre-eminent importance of the United States in present-day world politics, but also because of its particular contribution to the ideologies of political democracy and private enterprise.

The United States' constitutional and political system is deeply

[1] Since Stalin's death, there have been increasing signs of a change in the official attitude towards science and welcome evidence of a willingness to discuss scientific problems objectively.

influenced by these two aspects. The new State, established under the ideological impact of the philosophies of Rousseau, Locke and Paine, soon became a haven of refuge for many of the most active and courageous citizens of Europe, who fled from political, religious or racial persecution. The outlook and experience of those who shaped the American political system in its formative stage reinforced the political and personal freedoms which are written into the American Constitution. But at the same time the unexplored and immensely rich continent offered unlimited scope for private pioneering. There seemed endless opportunities for the farmer as well as for the industrial worker or the organizer of business, transport and industry. As long as this phase lasted it was understandable that State control was regarded as an evil to be minimized as far as possible, and this tendency was reinforced by the federal structure of the United States. Where a Federal Government and a number of State Governments have divided competences and powers and a law court has the ultimate decision, the result is inevitably a weakening of government in general. This has been the experience of all democratic federations. States will often oppose the exercise of any particular powers by the Federation even if they are not able to use the power themselves.

The fundamental freedoms are embodied in the first ten Amendments of the American Constitution, the so-called Bill of Rights. They cover freedom of religion and speech, of the Press and of assembly. They include personal security from unwarranted arrest and search, and a legislative prohibition to deprive anybody 'of life, liberty or property without due process of law'. It is this clause which was built up by the jurisdiction of the Supreme Court of the United States into a powerful legal bastion of private property. Between the middle of the nineteenth century and the middle of the 1930's the Court interpreted this clause so as to make even modest social legislation unconstitutional: a ten-hour working day as much as a Minimum Wages Act or legislation making collective bargaining compulsory in industry. Under the cover of such judicial interpretation, modern American democracy has moved far away from the conception of its founders and of the Constitution of 1776. While private business was shielded from Government interference, powerful monopolistic corporations came to control such vital commodities as oil, steel, chemicals, rail transport and other basic industries. At the same time the United States ceased to be a country of unlimited economic possibilities. As industrialism grew there were periodic crises, culminating in the disastrous depression of 1929–33, which has deeply influenced further American developments. The country experienced the problems of mass unemployment, of sudden over-production, and the social evils of slum cities and industrialization. It has since steadily moved away from the constitutional idea of a country of free and equal pioneers abhorring Government control as well as big business. The sweeping language of the Constitution masks a conflict of philosophy which has accompanied the United States throughout her history and is today arising in a new form. One trend of American political thinking, most clearly expressed by Alexander Hamilton, has stood for the unhindered development of big business, industry and finance, and for the removal of constitutional, social and humanitarian obstacles to the industrial and commercial development of the United States. The other, expressed by Jefferson, has stood for an equalitarian and static rural society, the most widespread sharing of ownership of land and the nation's resources and for a balanced life rather than feverish industrial development. In the early days the former party supported federalism, the latter party supported the paternal society of the southern States. The Civil War decided this issue clearly in favour of federalism, and it displaced the slave labourer, who belongs to an estate, by the labour contract which means mobility and which modern industrial society demands. But the deeper conflict between these political and social ideologies persists, although the fronts have shifted. Modern big business and industry are now generally distrustful of strong federal powers because they can operate more effectively through the State legislatures or because they oppose the social and equalitarian tendencies of modern federal legislatures. The Jefferson ideology has been revived in a new form, first through the older Roosevelt's 'Square Deal' and his anti-trust legislation, and above all through the younger Roosevelt's 'New Deal', which has laid the foundations for the American social service State. Social justice now means better standards of labour, a guaranteed income for the farmer, unemployment insurance and the conservation of national resources rather than the preservation of rural society. But it rests on a continuity of philosophy, the strength of which was revealed in the successive victories of President Roosevelt against the bitter hostility of industry and business and of the vast majority of the Press, and more recently in the electoral victory of Roosevelt's successor Truman. Nor did the two successive Republican governments of President Eisenhower bring any major change of direction. There was greater friendliness to business, more suspicion of organized labour and a definite reluctance to use federal resources for the development of national services and resources (power, transport, education). But there has been no major reversal. As a result of these various influences, the United States of today is moving rapidly closer to the social-welfare ideology which it theoretically still abhors. Enormous Government subsidies are paid annually to farmers, to railway, road and air transport, to shipping and to other industries. The range of unemployment assistance pensions and other social services increases steadily. Public enterprises, e.g. the Tennessee Valley Authority, however much derided, are now a permanent part of the national economy. Modern military preparations include an important sector of industry and scientific research. A large part of the modern research on nuclear fission and the utilization of atomic power must remain a Government monopoly and a Government secret because of its military implications. Above all, the Government is now expected to fight an economic depression by vast schemes of public works and other relief measures. The Employment Act, 1946, set up a Council of Economic Advisers to the President which makes periodic reports. On the basis of these reports, the President prepares an Economic Report to Congress, which analyses it through a joint Committee of both Houses. This Act openly recognizes governmental responsibility for the economic condition of the nation. This responsibility of government, not only for the economic and social conditions, but for the basic development and purposes of the nation, was emphasized in the late President Kennedy's 'New Frontier', an approach which is being continued in President Johnson's programme. Responsibility for the balanced economic productivity of the nation, for employment — threatened by the spread of automation even in times of economic prosperity — for the conservation of the nation's natural resources and recreational facilities, for the channelling of at least some of the nation's enormous wealth into the abolition of slums, the improvement of educational, medical and communication facilities, for a far more vigorous development of the nation's cultural and scientific potential, these and many other tasks are emphasized as a continuing responsibility of government. Yet, at the time of writing, the opposite philosophy, one that wishes not so much to restore an utterly fictitious system of unassisted private enterprise as to demolish as many public controls and responsibilities as possible, that seeks to reduce though not to abolish social services and altogether deny the primary responsibility of government for the social and economic life of the nation, has become vociferous and solidly organized. Its most articulate spokesman is Senator Goldwater, the Republican presidential nominee of 1964. In the presidential election of November 1964, however, Goldwater was decisively defeated by President Johnson. But over 25 million Americans voted for him, and while for many of these traditional loyalty to the Republican party was the reason, a high proportion certainly endorsed the Goldwater philosophy.

The Catholic Church

Since Christianity became organized in an international Church, and Christian doctrine, under the influence of the mediæval Catholic thinkers, substituted for the earlier 'other-worldly' and pessimistic attitude the doctrine that the Church was the instrument and guardian of the law of God on earth, the Catholic Church has become a powerful international influence. Despite many periods of weakness and decay, the continuity of its organization has lasted for about a thousand years. It is the authoritative interpreter of a form of Christian religion which has the allegiance of hundreds of millions dispersed among all the nations of the Western Hemisphere. It is also a closely knit hierarchical organization whose head, supported by the College of Cardinals, commands the loyalties and obedience of a vast international hierarchy of priests, from archbishops down to the village priest in Ireland, Spain, Peru or Austria.

The Catholic Church has taken a definite stand on vital political and social questions of contemporary society, especially since the Encyclical Letters issued by Pope Leo XIII at the end of the nineteenth century. Since then the influence of the Catholic Church, although unsupported by the organized power of a State and by military forces, has probably been superior to that of any single State in the world.

The political teaching and the international policy of the Catholic Church reflect the attempt to reconcile Christian principles with the political and social interests of a worldly organization.

The application of Christian principles has meant that the Catholic Church is hostile to extreme nationalism and to racial discrimination. It recognizes the fundamental equality of all men, and it is the predominant influence of the Catholic Church which has helped to solve racial problems in South America, where the conquering Spaniards and Portuguese have mingled freely with the native peoples. It opposes Fascist doctrines of racial persecution and discrimination. It condemns war and supports the peaceful settling of international disputes.

The Church, building on scholastic doctrine, also supports individual freedom of worship, of the family, of association and of property. Its particular insistence on the right of private property, as a God-given institution, has, however, generally led the Catholic Church into the Conservative camp. This has been reinforced by the fact that, in some strongholds of Catholicism like Spain and Italy, the Catholic Church is itself a very large landowner and controller of industrial enterprises. The Church does not defend unqualified freedom of speech, as distinct from freedom of worship. It has therefore taken a definite stand in civil wars of international implication, such as the Mexican disorders of 1937, and above all the Spanish Civil War of 1936–39. In the first case it has opposed the revolution; in the second it has supported it, defending its own interests rather than any principles of international law or of divine justice.

Another important aspect of Catholic doctrine is hostility to social revolution. It demands obedience to authority — which again is reflected by the structure of its own organization — but it also demands social justice in the individual relations of employers and employees. The Church therefore supports social legislation, but rejects any class conflict, and with it any kind of social uprising. Pope Pius XI openly blessed the corporate system of Fascist Italy — that is to say, a system by which employers and employees were compulsorily organized by the State, without any autonomous right of collective bargaining, strike or lock-out. Obviously such a policy supports the existing social order, in particular where it is conservative and a defender of private property. Within this general policy there is, however, some latitude.

Catholic policy in Spain is generally reactionary and pro-Fascist. But in Germany, before the Nazi regime, a powerful Catholic Trade Union movement and a Catholic Centre Party were closer to Social Democracy than to Conservatism. In Australia the strong Irish influence in the working class makes it impossible for the Catholic Church to be strongly Conservative in politics. Not only in the evolution of its religious and social doctrines, but also in its attitude towards non-Catholic Christian Churches and non-Christian religious faiths, the Catholic Church is at present in a process of evolution, whose dimensions and importance cannot yet be fully assessed. Under the surface, many members, both of the Catholic hierarchy and lay workers, have for years been sceptical of the rigidity and autocracy of the Church's government, of many aspects of the Catholic religious services, and of such vitally important social doctrines as the rigid opposition to birth control. It was Pope John XXIII who, in less than five eventful and momentous years of Papal reign, initiated an openness and mobility in the outlook and doctrine of the Church which his successor, Pope Paul VI, appears to be intent to continue and develop. Two successive Ecumenical Councils have begun the immense work of modernizing the spirit and language of the Catholic liturgy. Above all, the two Encyclicals of Pope John XXIII, '*Mater et Magistra*' (1961) and '*Pacem in Terris*' (1962), have initiated a far-reaching revision of the official Catholic doctrine, both in its social and international outlook. Without abandoning the natural law system and the Thomistic foundation of the doctrine of the Church, the first of these Encyclicals is far more open-minded than its predecessors, in its acknowledgment of the legitimacy of public enterprise and public property, as possible expressions of social responsibility. It is far less exclusively dedicated to the emphasis on private property as a natural right. It emphasizes strongly the need for a just distribution of property and an adequate status (as distinct from mere protection) of the working class. The second Encyclical stresses not only the basic human rights, including 'the natural right to free initiative in the economic field and the right to work', but also the growing unity of the world, the need for close collaboration, the right to independence of all peoples and the duty, on the part of the economically developed nations, to come to the aid of those which are in the process of development — an appeal already made in the previous Encyclical. The entire Encyclical is permeated by the stress on the paramount need for men and nations of all kinds to work together in the pursuit of common order and peace, and by a spirit of tolerance with regard not only to the relations of Catholic groups and individuals with those of other faiths, but also between states adhering to Christian principles and other states. In implementation of this philosophy, Pope John XXIII initiated certain moves towards better contacts with the surviving Church organizations and the governments of some Communist States, a move that was symbolized by the visit of Premier Krushchev's son-in-law to Rome. Since the death of John XXIII, this tentative move towards 'co-existence' has not made any further progress. On the other hand, Paul VI has vigorously pursued this spirit of reconciliation and closer contact with non-Catholic Christian religions, and he has symbolized the new openness of outlook, in his historic pilgrimage to the Holy Land, at Christmas 1963, during which he met not only with various heads of the Greek Orthodox Church, but also with Arab and Israeli political rulers.

It is at least possible that this new open-mindedness of the Catholic Church, and the urgent concern with elementary problems of human life and peace, expressed in the last Encyclicals and the actions of John XXIII and Paul VI, may in due course also modify some of the surviving legal and social doctrines of the Church, notably in the field of birth control.[1]

In the field of international relations, the present attitude of the Catholic Church has become more flexible, less one-sidedly concentrated on anti-Communism and the support of conservative political regimes, and more intent on supporting moves that will help mankind to survive and attain a modicum of international order and security. The Church will no doubt in most questions continue to side with the policies of the West. But if the present approach is maintained and developed, the Catholic Church is more likely than before to play an independent and powerful role in the assuaging of international conflicts.

[1] In the discussions of the Ecumenical Council on 'The Church and the Modern World', in October 1964, there was a remarkable degree of support, even by many of the most senior delegates, for a revision of Church doctrine, both on grounds of principle (effect of the population explosion on human dignity) and of realism (discrepancy between theory and practice in the lives of Catholics). See further below, pp. 321 *et seq.*

CHAPTER 4

CONFLICT AND CO-OPERATION IN POST-WAR WORLD POLITICS

Major Trends in Post-War International Relations

THE pattern of international relations, since the end of the Second World War, has been dominated by three major trends, which have to a large extent been in conflict with each other: the first is the increasing erosion and insufficiency of the national State, as the repository of effective military, political and economic power, and the corresponding concentration of power in the few super-States tending to function as leaders of a wider grouping of States. The second, completely contradictory, trend has been the emergence of a multitude of new national States, from colonial status or a state of semi-dependence, aspiring to all the attributes of national sovereignty, but lacking in most cases the effective minimum conditions of national power to a far greater extent than the older States.[1] The third major trend is the overwhelming significance, for the first fifteen years following the Second World War, of the 'Cold War' between the Communist States and movements led by the Soviet Union, and the anti-Communist coalition led by the United States. How far this 'bipolar' division of the world into two opposite camps, coupled with the concentration of nuclear power in the hands of the two leaders of the antagonistic coalitions, is still the controlling factor in international politics, will be discussed later in this chapter.

Relations between Russia and the Western Powers since the Bolshevik Revolution

Until the Communist Revolution of 1917, the relations between Russia and the other Powers followed the normal pattern of power politics. Though weakened by the backwardness of her industrial development, the illiteracy and poverty of the great

[1] See above, pp. 26 *et seq.*

majority of her peoples, and the corruption and inefficiency of her Government, Czarist Russia was one of the Great Powers of Europe. She joined Britain, the Austro-Hungarian Empire and Prussia in the fight against Napoleonic France, and after the conquest of Napoleon formed the so-called Holy Alliance: a three-Power agreement designed to preserve the existing monarchical order and to suppress the rising forces of liberalism. In the successive partitions of Poland, Russia shared the spoils with the Habsburg Empire and Prussia. In her conflicts with Turkey and Japan, she looked mainly for outlets to the open sea, a policy which any other Power of comparable size, without an outlet to the open sea, would have pursued. On the other hand, Russia was invaded by Poles and Swedes in the seventeenth century and by the French in the nineteenth.

The Bolshevik Revolution of 1917 first introduced the conflict of social philosophies as a major factor in modern international relations. From the beginning, the Bolshevist leaders, inspired by Lenin's writings, proclaimed international social revolution as a legitimate objective leading to world Communism. Russia's former allies, on the other hand, saw in the Communist Revolution a threat to their existing political and social freedom, and between 1917 and 1920 they actively supported the White Russian anti-Soviet forces in an unsuccessful attempt to suppress the Communist Revolution. Naturally Allied intervention coloured the first phase of the relations between Communist Russia and the Western democracies. Having abandoned the first hopes of early world revolution, the Soviet Union gradually established normal diplomatic relations with neighbour States, such as the newly emancipated State of Finland and the Baltic republics. In 1921 Great Britain made the first commercial agreement with the Soviet Government. The cautious acceptance of the Soviet Union in the family of nations may be dated from April 1922, when she was invited to an economic conference of the European Powers at Geneva. The most significant event of this Conference was the conclusion of the Rapallo treaty of friendship between the two outcasts, defeated Germany and revolutionary Russia. Although relations between Soviet Russia and the Western Powers continued to be unhappy for some years, especially while the Conservatives were in power in Britain, recognition of the Soviet Union could not be permanently delayed. The regime had obviously come to stay. Moreover, the victory of Stalin over Trotsky in 1925 emphasized the intention of Soviet Russia to consolidate her own position as a Socialist State in a non-Socialist world and to postpone world revolution. This introduced a phase of better, though far from cordial, relations between Soviet Russia and the other Powers. The United States did not legally recognize the new Government until 1933, but during the period between 1925 and 1933 a series of commercial agreements were accompanied not only by Soviet purchases of vast amounts of industrial equipment in the Western countries, but also by the employment of a considerable number of foreign engineers and technicians.

The next phase — which lasted until the Munich Settlement of October 1, 1938 — saw the growing industrial development and self-confidence of Soviet Russia, marked by the gradual elimination of foreigners from employment and the ruthless consolidation of Stalin's power by successive purges of Soviet leaders. Internationally, however, the emergence of Nazi Germany, with her violent anti-Communist propaganda and her plan for the conquest of eastern Europe, created a new and formidable threat to Soviet Russia. This led to a few years of apparently genuine attempts of Soviet foreign policy, guided by Litvinov, to establish a system of collective security with the Western democracies against Nazi aggression. During the same period Communists everywhere encouraged the formation of 'popular fronts' — that is, anti-Fascist coalitions of all progressive parties from centre to extreme left. This policy was not necessarily in conflict with the ultimate programme of Communist world revolution, which allows for many changes of tactics. Unfortunately, the readiness of the Soviet Union to collaborate in a system of collective security, expressed by her entry into the League of Nations in 1933, coincided with a most discreditable period in the policy of the Western Powers. Collective security lost its last chance when the members of the League, under the influence of Chamberlain and Laval, failed to take effective measures against Mussolini's invasion of Abyssinia. The policies of Soviet Russia and the Western Powers clashed again in the Spanish Civil War of 1936–39, and in particular in the Munich Settlement of October 1938, by which Britain and France forced Czechoslovakia to surrender the Sudeten territory to Hitler.

Soviet Russia's reaction to the Munich Settlement was a policy of accommodation with Nazi Germany. She entirely abandoned collaboration with the Western Powers, and during 1939 concluded important commercial and non-aggression treaties with Nazi Germany, followed by the partition of Poland between Nazi Germany and Soviet Russia in September 1939.

This policy found a dramatic end in the German invasion of Russia on June 22, 1941. The Allied Powers, on the initiative of Winston Churchill, immediately accepted Soviet Russia as an ally. The remaining war years, until the conclusion of the Yalta and Potsdam Agreements in 1945, were marked by outward friendship and collaboration, which did not, however, at any stage lead to an intimate association comparable with that of the United States and Britain. Soviet Russia resented the repeated postponement of the invasion of Western Europe by the Allies. She felt that she had to bear the brunt of devastation, gigantic human sacrifices and military resistance, while the Western Allies conducted only limited warfare. Russian propaganda minimized or concealed the very substantial supplies of war materials sent at great risk during these years. It also minimized Allied operations, their sea and air war, the North Africa campaign, and ultimately the Allied assault on German-held Western Europe in June 1944. It completely ignored that the brunt of effort and sacrifices in the war with Japan was borne by American and Commonwealth forces, while Russia's last-minute intervention secured for her at practically no cost the control of Manchuria, Sakhalin, Northern Korea and other sweeping gains. There were occasional conferences between the political leaders and a limited number of diplomatic and military contacts, but there was no true co-ordination, in particular in the vital field of the conquest and control of Germany. The Soviet and the Western forces operated on the whole independently of each other.

Up to the end of the last war, the relations between Soviet Russia and the West were characterized by distrust and expediency rather than the assumption of inevitable and irreconcilable conflict. Economic and political contacts were relatively superficial and limited. The war alliance and the post-war situation which it produced brought far closer contacts and common responsibilities. This was bound to lead either to more collaboration or sharper conflict.

The Agreements of Yalta and Potsdam laid down the principles of Allied war policy, and especially those governing the occupation of Germany and Japan. For the first time, Soviet Russia and the Western Powers were engaged in joint international tasks of outstanding importance. In particular it was the first time that Soviet Russia and the United States were in close and continuous contact. Until the Second World War there had been few contacts and conflicts between these two giants of the modern world. The relative military and strategic position of the two Powers has been likened to that of an elephant and a whale. The continental power of the one is opposed to the oceanic power of the other. As long as the interests of both States were mainly confined to their own territories, the possibilities of conflict were remote. Differences of social and political systems do not by themselves lead to war.

But both Powers emerged from the Second World War with world-wide interests and responsibilities which clashed most acutely in Germany and Japan.

Post-War Clashes in Germany and Japan

Post-war Germany offered a supreme and unique test case for the question how far the divergent strategies and political systems of the Great Powers could be reconciled. Some of the general objectives of Allied occupation have been outlined in the first chapter.[1]

At first there was at least a degree of unanimity on the destruction of Germany's military and political structure. All military organizations were dissolved, and major political leaders were tried by joint Allied tribunals. The State of Prussia was dismembered and the strong central power of a totalitarian Germany was replaced by a number of smaller States, each with its own government. The Powers soon clashed over the positive alternative. To Soviet Russia the democratization of Germany meant, above all, drastic social change. It meant the splitting up of the large estates and redistribution among smallholders who were gradually compelled to combine into co-operatives; it meant the socialization of major industries and the elimination of former German business and industrial leaders. At first Soviet Russia seemed to

[1] See above, pp. 17 *et seq.*

agree with the Western Powers on the meaning of political democracy. A number of political parties representing the major shades of opinion were admitted. But soon the Soviet military government sponsored the formation of a 'Socialist Unity Party', which was nothing but the Communist Party with the addition of some fellow-travellers. After the establishment of the new party, the Social-Democratic Party was outlawed, and only two smaller parties were left in existence, which had no chance of forming a government by themselves. Following the general pattern of Communist-controlled States, all the key posts of government, trade unions, industrial management and education were filled by Communists, and the Soviet-occupied Zone of Germany became in effect a one-party State, aligning itself completely with Soviet policy, denouncing the Western Powers and professing the same principles as Communist States throughout the world.

The three Western Zones originally differed considerably from each other as well as from the Eastern Zone. The French were much closer to the Russians in their intention to take the greatest possible amount of reparations out of Germany and to keep her permanently weakened. The Americans and the British, on the other hand, were more concerned with getting their Zones on a working basis again, so as to reduce the heavy burden of support which fell upon them in order to maintain a minimum standard of living. Gradually, however, the growing antagonism between Russia and the Western Powers brought the Western Zones closer together, and West Germany represents today a vastly different picture from East Germany. The concept of democracy which has prevailed in Western Germany is mainly that of the Americans. It means parliamentary democracy, with a great measure of freedom of speech and opinion accompanied by a conservative social policy and a definite bias against Socialism. If the Russian interpretation of re-education for democracy has meant a one-party State which closely resembles the Nazi regime, with its one-party monopoly, the power of the secret police, the political conception of justice and many other features, the Western interpretation resulted in reliance upon some of the most important pillars of the Nazi regime, viz. industrial and business leaders as well as high civil servants who were closely associated with the Nazi empire. As late as 1963 and 1964, German trials of war criminals showed that some of those responsibly associated with the mass extermination of Jews or Slavs were holding high office under the Bonn Republic.

The clash of policies would have developed on very similar lines in Japan, except for the entirely different pattern of Allied military government. In Japan, the United States alone was in executive control; it exercised this control over a unified Japan, and through a Japanese Government. The Emperor continues to be the head of the State, thus linking the old and the new Japan. Soviet Russia, as well as the other Allied Powers, has been confined to an advisory role, which has become increasingly ineffective. General MacArthur remodelled the new Japan according to his own ideas, which were those of a conservative American who believed in democracy. The problems and dangers of occupation policy were not very different from those which have arisen in Germany: demilitarization increasingly gave way to the desire to preserve and rebuild Japan as a bulwark against Communism and Russia.[1]

Ideological Aspects of the Conflict

Official spokesmen on both sides describe the conflict between the Powers in ideological terms. 'Democracy' and 'dictatorship', 'free enterprise' and 'Socialism', 'liberty' and 'tyranny', 'capitalist imperialism' and 'people's democracy' are opposed as irreconcilable.

In the eyes of the majority of Americans, the political and social system of Soviet Russia is objectionable, both as a Socialist system and as a form of totalitarian government which rejects parliamentary democracy and suppresses the fundamental liberties of the individual. To Communists, American democracy is a sham, an instrument of the wealthy and of aggression against 'people's democracies'. Yet such a conflict of values is not in itself a cause for war, or even acute political tension. Among the States which receive American aid are Nationalist China, South Korea, South Vietnam and Spain, whose Governments are much nearer to Fascism than to Democracy. Few of the Central and South American Republics or of the new African States, with all of which the United States and Great Britain maintain cordial, or

[1] See further below, pp. 234 *et seq.*

at least correct relations, are genuine democracies. Close international integration, in the form of a world-State, a world federation or an international code of human rights, would certainly demand a greater conformity of political and social values. But in the world of today this is a distant aspiration.

The particular menace which the United States and other democracies feel to come from the Soviet political system results from a different fact: the avowed international character of Communist ideology, and the deliberate use of Communist movements outside Russia as allies in a struggle which aims at internal social change, but — as proved by the history of the Communist movements in the last forty years — invariably aids and abets the foreign policy of the Soviet Government. Soviet Russia is thus seen as the nerve-centre of a world-wide confederation of forces affecting the internal stability of every State professing a different political system. This American fear was greatly stimulated by the conduct of a spy trial in Canada in 1946, which revealed an organized system of Soviet espionage aiming to obtain the secret of the atom bomb. Since then anti-Communist hysteria in the United States has sometimes risen to dangerous proportions. But it is only since the coupling of internal party politics and social tension with the policies of a foreign Government that the social and political system of Soviet Russia became the direct enemy of American policy. Soviet Russia appeared not only as the centre of a world-wide Communist movement — though increasingly challenged by Communist China — but she is also, since the end of the Second World War, the most powerful State in Europe, as well as a very important Asiatic Power. At the same time the United States has acquired responsibilities in Germany and Japan, which involve her directly in the political affairs both of Europe and Asia. Each direct or indirect expansion of the Soviet Union is therefore seen by the United States not only as a further victory of Communism, which threatens the American way of life, but also as the expansion of a State which might ultimately threaten the national integrity and security of the United States, either through direct armed attack or through the control of vital outlying bases and points of support. The reality of this threat was brought home to Americans when, in October 1962, Russian missiles, bombers and troops entered a friendly Cuba in both offensive and defensive military preparations against the

United States. In both respects Nazi Germany constituted a similar but less formidable danger. Nazi policy included the deliberate attempt to foster disloyal and subversive activities among the many people of German descent in foreign States, and it did not shrink from the most unscrupulous threats, including reprisals against relatives living in Germany, in order to obtain such collaboration. But the use by the Soviet Union of Communist sympathizers in other States is a much more formidable weapon than that available to Nazi Germany, for reasons which have been outlined in a previous chapter.[1]

Through the eyes of the Soviet Union the world looks, however, very different. The Soviet leaders remember the years when Allied forces actively intervened against the Socialist Revolution by supporting Czarist and reactionary elements. They remember the betrayal of collective security over Abyssinia, and the sacrifice of Czechoslovakia to Nazi Germany, due in large part to the reluctance of Conservative circles in Britain and France to collaborate with Russia against Nazi Germany. Soviet Russia still acutely feels the immense losses — estimated at between twenty and thirty million military and civilian casualties — which she suffered in the last war, and the devastation of her most important industrial regions, especially in the Ukraine. Soviet citizens rightly think that of all the Allied nations they have suffered most, though Soviet propaganda deliberately exaggerates the Soviet part in the Allied victory and underplays the Allied effort, especially in the conquest of Western Europe and Japan. Lastly, Soviet Russia sees in the undoubted resurgence of nationalist and reactionary industrial leaders in Western Germany and Japan a sign of both aggressive and reactionary Western policy, designed to gather all anti-Russian and anti-Communist elements in the struggle against Soviet Russia. Suspicion is reinforced by the Marxist thesis, already referred to earlier in this book, that monopoly Capitalism is driven to aggression and war by economic causes, namely by the threat of unemployment and the search of capitalists for new markets in order to compensate for a domestic slump. This is the official Soviet explanation for the vast economic assistance given by the United States to the nations of Western Europe, of the Mediterranean area and the Far East.

[1] Ch. 3, pp. 66, 80.

Moves and Counter-Moves since the War

After a brief and uneasy interlude of limited collaboration in the early stages of the occupation of Germany and Japan and in the formative stage of the United Nations Organization, the policy of both the United States and Soviet Russia came to be dominated by mutual fear and distrust. The rest of the world has been increasingly drawn into the struggle, but it has also watched with growing uneasiness the difficulty of drawing a proper line between defensive and aggressive measures, between ideological warfare and the naked struggle for power.

The first major expression of this policy of distrust was the struggle over the constitution of the United Nations, and in particular of the Security Council. The Soviet and United States delegates were the principal but not the only supporters of the view that only unanimity of the Great Powers could ensure peace. The veto right, as a corollary to the burden of responsibility devolving upon the Great Powers, was expressly defended in a joint statement by the four sponsoring Powers of the San Francisco Conference which debated the Charter. The practical result—namely, the inability of the Security Council to take effective action, for example, to impose sanctions, without the concurrence of all the permanent members—would not have prevented a satisfactory functioning of the Council given fundamental unanimity of the Powers. But the exercise of the veto by Soviet Russia became almost automatic with the deepening of the split between herself and the other permanent members. An International Military Force, international control of atomic energy, or of food distribution, all became for Russia organizations by which a hostile majority could exercise control over Soviet actions.

Soon after the conclusion of the Second World War, Soviet policy gave practical expression to its lack of confidence in the United Nations by concluding a series of military defence pacts with her neighbour States in eastern and south-eastern Europe, as and when they turned Communist under direct or indirect Soviet pressure. A network of such pacts now links Soviet Russia and Poland, Czechoslovakia, Hungary, Bulgaria and Roumania, while corresponding pacts with Yugoslavia have been denounced by the other Communist States after the feud with Tito. All these treaties provide, in identical terms, for mutual assistance in the case of aggression by Germany or 'any Power directly or indirectly associated' with Germany.[1] In almost any controversial issue, such as atomic energy control, the trials of religious leaders in Hungary and Bulgaria, the admission of new members, or trusteeship and colonial problems, the Communist member-States customarily vote with Soviet Russia, whose position is reinforced by the granting of separate status to two of her constituent republics, White Russia and the Ukraine. Another practical expression of this policy is the new Danube Convention of 1948, which, with the votes of Soviet Russia and the Communist Danubian Powers, terminated the control of the Western Powers which they had exercised by virtue of a Convention of 1921. Finally, the East German Republic, in terms of political, social and economic development, has become one of the Eastern group of Soviet-dominated States. The Warsaw Pact of 1955 — allegedly a reply to West Germany's admission to NATO — was nothing but a formalization of a situation that had existed for years.

The Western reaction to this policy of political and military regionalism started considerably later. Until late in 1946 the policy of the Western Powers was dominated by the desire to maintain Four-Power unity in the United Nations as well as in the Military Government of Germany and Austria, and to develop international collaboration and reconstruction on a world-wide and non-discriminatory basis. Cautious moves towards a closer integration of the Western Zones of Germany began in September 1946. The first post-war reconstruction agency — the United Nations Relief and Rehabilitation Administration, to which the United States made the biggest contribution — sent supplies impartially to the Ukraine, Poland, Yugoslavia and Italy, as well as to Western Powers. Increasing Western despondency about a lasting agreement with Russia, whether in Germany, Japan or elsewhere, did not lead to any concerted international countermove until Secretary Marshall's Harvard speech of June 5, 1947, initiated a new phase of Western policy.

[1] This thin disguise of the main objective of the Pacts — which are aimed at the Western Powers — pays lip service to Art. 107 of the United Nations Charter, which permits action against enemies of the signatories during the Second World War.

The Western Counter-Offensive

The Western response, under United States leadership, has three different though closely connected aspects: economic, political and military. The economic counter-offensive was the first to get under way. It is even now by far the most fully developed of the three. The common objective has been the creation of an association of nations able to resist further economic, political and military Soviet penetration in Europe.

This objective has involved a more serious attempt than ever made before to overcome the barriers of national sovereignty, historical differences and ideological conflicts between the nations of Europe outside the Soviet camp. The common values which could hold these nations together have been sought in the principles of political democracy, individual freedom and respect for the rule of law in international affairs.

But three basic weaknesses have hampered the execution of this plan: first, the line which now divides Soviet and anti-Soviet nations in Europe has greatly increased the difficulties of European economic integration, as well as the dependence of Western Europe on the economic assistance of the United States. Secondly, strategic and tactical considerations have weakened the ideological core of the counter-offensive, as they have compelled the inclusion of some States, not because of their adhesion to the values of democracy and liberty, but because of their strategic and military importance. Lastly, the counter-offensive has taken a definite form only in Europe. The power conflict, however, is world-wide. Western moves in the Far East have been contradictory and uncertain, largely because of the collapse of the Nationalist regime in China. Even a successful counter-offensive in Europe may therefore only mean a diversion of pressure and the shifting of the main area of the conflict to Asia.

The Revolution of United States Foreign Policy

The European tensions and emergencies forced upon the United States a fundamental and dramatic revision of her foreign policy. The change has been breathtaking in speed and dimension.

For a brief period following the end of the last war the United States tried to return to 'normalcy'. Lend-Lease aid to Britain was terminated abruptly; pressure was brought upon Britain to agree to the free convertibility of sterling into dollars, a move which brought Britain to the brink of economic disaster. The immense military machine built up during the Second World War was dismantled while the people of the United States, for a brief period, prepared to resume a life of peace, business and greater plenty. It has already been shown how the responsibilities assumed by the United States in the United Nations, in Europe and the Far East, made this policy unreal and impossible. The advance of Soviet influence in Europe, and the sharpening of tension over Germany, compelled the United States to begin with a revision of its policy in Europe, as the war-shattered nations of Western Europe could not by their own strength recover sufficiently to offer economic, moral and military resistance to further Soviet expansion.

The United States reversed her policy with characteristic swiftness. Her own responsibilities and enlightened self-interest dictated a policy of active participation in the recovery of Europe.

The historic turning point can be dated to June 5, 1947, when the U.S. Secretary of State, General Marshall, outlined the objectives of a European Recovery Plan, commonly known as Marshall Aid. His speech reveals a decisive revision in American thinking on international affairs, but also shows the problems which the new phase in American policy left unsolved.

'It is logical that the United States should do whatever it is able to do to assist in the return of normal economic health in the world without which there can be no political stability and no assured peace. Our policy is directed not against any country or doctrine but against hunger, poverty, desperation and chaos. Its purpose should be the revival of a working economy in the world so as to permit the emergence of political and social conditions in which free institutions can exist. Such assistance, I am convinced, must not be on a piecemeal basis as various crises develop. Any assistance that this Government may render in the future should provide a cure rather than a mere palliative.

'It is already evident that, before the United States Government can proceed much farther in its efforts to alleviate the situation and help start the European world on its way to recovery, there must be some agreement among the countries of Europe as to the requirements of the situation and the part those countries themselves will take in order to give proper effect to whatever action might be undertaken by this Government. It would not be fitting for this Government to draw up unilaterally a programme designed to place Europe on its feet economically. That is the business of the Europeans. The initiative, I think, must come from Europe. The role of this country should consist of friendly aid in the drafting of a European programme and of later support of such a programme so far as it may be practical for us to do so. The programme should be a joint one, agreed to by a number of, if not all, European nations.'

The invitation was extended to the Soviet Union and other States of Eastern Europe, Communist or non-Communist. The Soviet Union rejected the entire plan in so far as it was aimed at a joint European programme instead of giving economic assistance to the participating nations singly. This was in accordance with the recent insistence of Soviet policy on 'national sovereignty', which is one means of perpetuating the division between the Communist and non-Communist parts of Europe. Subsequently Czechoslovakia — at that time not yet Communist-controlled — withdrew, under Soviet pressure, her original acceptance of the invitation to participate in the plan. This shattered the idea of a joint European economic plan. The nations in both Eastern and Western Europe have since struggled to overcome some of the consequences of this partition by a series of bilateral treaties.

The Marshall Aid Programme thus had to be limited to seventeen nations of Western and North-western Europe.[1] It could not achieve what was, in its original conception, at least a possible objective: the healing of the split between Communist and non-Communist Europe through economic assistance and collaboration. It marked, instead, the first phase in the beginning process of defensive consolidation of the Western democracies.

Europe's Recovery

When the Marshall Plan programme officially came to an end in June 1952 it had achieved triumphantly what it had set out to

[1] Austria, Belgium and Luxembourg, Denmark, France, Greece, Iceland, Ireland, Italy, the Netherlands, Norway, Portugal, Sweden, Turkey, the United Kingdom, Western Germany, Trieste.

do. After four years of operation, all the participating nations were well set on the road towards recovery and greater economic independence. Since the end of the Marshall Plan, economic aid as such to Europe was steadily reduced and finally terminated in 1954. Certain indirect aid, in the form of United States defence expenditure and so-called offshore purchases connected with the rearmament programme under the North Atlantic Treaty, continues, and the economic significance of this form of aid for the balance of payments as well as the balance of trade of the West European countries is not to be underestimated. Yet the further economic progress of Europe, which the Marshall Plan programme set in motion, has continued steadily.

The impetus to economic recovery and continued progress in Western Europe provided by the Marshall Plan has continued in the years since its termination to an extent that probably far exceeds the most sanguine expectations of its proponents. The annual rates of increase in the output of goods and services in the area as a whole have exceeded those in the United States, and by early 1959 the concern with the excessive strength of the dollar and with ways of closing the international 'dollar gap' had been replaced by worry over the ability of the United States to compete with Western Europe in third markets and even by alarm over the rate at which the gold stock of the United States was being depleted by gold purchases of countries in Western Europe.

The industrial production index of nine Western European countries combined — Austria, Belgium, Denmark, France, West Germany, Italy, the Netherlands, Sweden, and the United Kingdom, accounting for 90 per cent of Western Europe's industrial production — was 132 in 1958, compared to 100 in 1953. The increase in growth rate was particularly noteworthy in the case of France. France's industrial production index reached 154 in 1958 from 100 in 1953, which was the highest rate during the period of any of the nine countries, and represented a considerable stepping up of industrial output compared to its slower progress in 1950–54. The increase in industrial output continued to be marked in the case of West Germany (from 100 in 1953 to 151 in 1958), and in Italy (from 100 in 1953 to 141 in 1958). The United Kingdom showing, on the other hand, continued to be poor (from 100 in 1953 to 115 in 1958) compared to that of the other major countries.

The rate of increase in industrial output in Western Europe was even greater in 1959 and 1960. Since 1960, however, the rise has generally been less dramatic, except for Italy, whose industrial output in 1962 was 153, compared to 100 in 1958; while the United Kingdom has continued to progress at a lower rate (114 in 1962, compared to 100 in 1958). France and Western Germany (132 and 131, respectively, in 1962, compared to 100 in 1958) continued to show large gains.

In 1963, all four major industrial countries of Western Europe registered further substantial increases in national production over 1962 (7·2% for France, 5·7% for Britain, 5·2% for Italy, and 4% for West Germany).[1]

Progress in agricultural output in Western Europe is equally impressive. The increase in agricultural production compared to pre-war has been about twice as great as the increase in population, permitting appreciable improvements in per capita consumption, particularly of foodstuffs of greatest nutritive value such as meat and milk.

Although expansion in Europe during the last decade has been accompanied by considerable price stability, wage and price rises during the last year or so have become a major concern of most Western European Governments. This concern was expressed by an increase in the British bank rate decreed in February 1964, and by the grant of a combined stand-by credit of $1 billion, by a consortium of Western central banks and the International Monetary Fund in March 1964, to enable Italy to carry out an anti-inflationary programme.

The gold and foreign exchange holdings of Western Europe more than doubled between the low point at the end of 1948 in the difficult early post-war years and the end of 1958, when they amounted to more than $17 billion. Most countries shared in this improvement, but it was particularly marked for some countries, such as West Germany, which alone accounted for more than half of the increase. By the end of 1962 the reserves of Western Europe had risen substantially once again, amounting to $28 billion. The largest increases in the most recent years were registered by France. In 1963 and 1964, Germany's already large reserves, after a period of stabilization, showed further gains.

Although the balance of payments position of Western Europe

[1] Source: *The Economist*, Feb. 1, 1964.

continued to be helped by military expenditures of the United States Government, these have ceased to have the critical role they played in the early days of the Marshall Plan in the balancing of Western Europe's international accounts.

Evidence of the more solid and independent economic situation of Western Europe is provided by the relaxation of import restrictions and exchange controls that took place during the fifties.

The effect of all this has not only been a drastic improvement in the average standard of living of West Europeans, but also a corresponding increase in self-confidence and a sense of independence. In the last few years the European allies of the United States have shown more and more signs of independent thinking in matters of world politics, and they have been correspondingly more critical of American leadership.[1] But it should never be forgotten that Europe's recovery would have been indefinitely retarded — and indeed might never have happened — except for the great and statesmanlike series of American actions that culminated in the Marshall Plan. After the immense strains, disruptions and undermining influences of the last world war, the countries of Western Europe were in danger of physical and moral disintegration. Without the kind of assistance which the United States gave them — an assistance that was generous and, despite many temptations, refrained from dictating to the assistant nations what they ought to do and how they ought to behave — there would be a very different Europe today.

Economic Aid and International Trade as Policy Problems

In its new role as a world Power the United States faces a dilemma which did not exist when Britain exercised comparable supremacy in the nineteenth century. The United States is the world's biggest producer and also its biggest creditor. If, like Britain in the nineteenth century, the United States could balance its financial supremacy by a dependence on imports of raw materials and finished products from overseas, an international economic equilibrium would quickly be restored. This, however, is unlikely to happen. With the exception of a few raw materials, the United States can produce practically everything she needs. Her industrial and agricultural capacity is steadily expanding; both industrial and farming interests are far too powerful to per-

[1] See further below, pp. 138 *et seq.*

mit any major reversal of United States economic policy, despite many enlightened reports by economists and others who believe that a more liberal import policy will in the long run benefit both the United States and Europe.

In the last few years, some corrective influences have tended to lessen the excessive dependence of other countries on either American trade or American aid. They have, however, been almost entirely confined to Western Europe. Indeed, the recovery of industrialized Western Europe, catching up on the immense lead of the United States, has tended to widen the gap between the highly developed industrial and commercial nations of the West and the underdeveloped, over-populated and impoverished countries of Asia, Latin America and Africa. Virtually all the new States which have gained independence since the end of the war have a yawning gap between their minimum aspirations and their actual economic condition. The situation of the majority of the new African States is perhaps even worse than that of the, mainly Asian, States which acquired independence during the first post-war period. In Africa, the transition from primitive rural economies to the aspirations of modern States was even more sudden. In addition, the 20 nations of Latin America — long politically independent — have only in recent years joined the newer nations in an increasingly insistent claim for economic and social development. The Latin American claims are of course of particular urgency to the United States, for geographical, political and economic reasons.

The continued crisis of most of the underdeveloped countries of the world, outside the Communist sphere of control, has emphasized the second challenge to United States policy, which would be far less urgent and powerful, if the United States were not in the dilemma that has just been described: of being both the world's leading financial power and industrial producer. This challenge is the need to assist the many underdeveloped countries of the world in the struggle for survival, and the race between production and increasing populations, which most of them are trying to win by the improvement of agricultural, and the development of industrial, production. Some of the problems of these countries will be discussed later in this book. At this point, only the challenge to United States policy needs emphasis. The role forced upon the United States as much the most powerful leader of a world-wide coalition in the competition with the Communist powers, and the inability of the United States, for the reasons just outlined, to open its doors without restriction to imports of foodstuffs, raw materials and industrial products from the rest of the world, forces it to support a large number of tottering States fighting for their survival, by powerful financial and other forms of economic aid. Only Europe has now ceased to receive such aid — except indirectly through the local expenditures of United States military establishments. On the other hand, the needs of the rest of the world have become ever more pressing. The answer of the United States to this challenge has been the development of a massive and continuing economic aid programme which has taken a variety of forms. In recent years the total amount of annual aid dispensed from various official U.S. sources has been well in excess of three billion dollars. A relatively small proportion of this (averaging about two hundred million dollars a year) goes to United States contributions to the multilateral agencies, i.e. the International Bank for Reconstruction and Development, and to its two affiliated agencies, the International Finance Corporation and the International Development Association. Of the remainder, substantial amounts go into development grants, investment guarantees and commodity assistance — the latter mainly under Public Law 480 which provides for local currency sales and grants of surplus agricultural commodities. But by far the greatest proportion goes into development lending. The administration of this huge programme is now essentially in the hands of two public agencies: First, the U.S. Export–Import Bank, a government-owned corporation which was constituted before the last war in order to finance exports, but has developed into a major agency for development aid, primarily for Latin America. Second, the Agency for International Development (AID), a semi-autonomous public agency within the State Department, which administers capital grants, development and other long-term loans and technical assistance. To these essentially financial aid institutions there must now be added the Peace Corps, established under the Kennedy Administration, a rapidly growing organization of volunteers trained to work in a variety of functions, mainly educational and technical, in underdeveloped countries which request their aid. Corresponding to the world-wide responsibilities of the United States in the political field, the economic aid programme is also on a world-wide basis. It is relatively modest in Africa, where the newly independent countries still receive their principal assistance from the former colonial powers, i.e. Britain and France. But United States aid is of massive proportions and indispensable, for example, to India, who receives about half of its foreign aid from the United States. This is justified, in the eyes of the U.S. Government, though not necessarily of Congress, by the key role attributed by United States policy to the maintenance of India as a non-Communist democracy in Asia. Increased emphasis has been placed in recent years on aid to Latin America, especially since the initiation of the Alliance for Progress by President Kennedy in 1961, a programme which aims at a total investment of some twenty billion dollars over a decade in the economic development of Latin American countries, and the creation of the Inter-American Development Bank.[1]

But the very magnitude and diversity of the United States aid efforts makes it particularly sensitive to domestic criticism which has grown from year to year, and now threatens to undermine the whole conception of the aid programme. To the majority of the members of the United States Congress — whose principal preoccupations are domestic — the foreign responsibilities and commitments of the United States are at best a burdensome necessity to be tolerated reluctantly. The aversion to foreign aid is increased by two considerations: one is the obvious temptation to eliminate, or at least substantially reduce, the international balance of payments deficit of the United States by a drastic curtailment of foreign aid. The second consideration, which tends to reinforce the first, is uncertainty or downright scepticism about the long-term efficacy of the programme. On this latter question the views are deeply split according to the outlook of the observer. Those who instinctively regard the foreign responsibilities and burdens of the United States with distrust, are also generally the same who will tolerate foreign aid at most if it is demonstrably and quickly shown to redound to the political advantage of the United States. To these politicians the acid tests are a firm political and military commitment to the Western Alliance and, where the Alliance is split, to the policy of the United States; and the

[1] See further below, pp. 313 *et seq.*

development or maintenance of as undiluted a system of private enterprise as possible. In both respects, the majority of aided countries are deficient. Practically all of them adhere to some kind of planned economy, with more or less pronounced socialist features. The obvious reasons for such a policy, namely, the general deficiency of responsible private venture capital (both domestic and foreign) and the paramount need to establish priorities in the development of economies that are generally deficient in basic resources, foreign currency and trained manpower, escape this type of politician. For him the simple test is the failure to live up to the American ideal of free enterprise, undisturbed by any questions as to the extent to which the United States itself still adheres to this ideal, and how far it is applicable to the development of countries gaining their independence in completely different circumstances and at a different period of history. Nor is there compensation in any firm political or military adhesion to the United States. Overwhelmingly, the developing countries wish to concentrate on their own affairs and outside the entanglements of the Cold War. With this goes a readiness to accept aid from any side — World Bank, United States or the Soviet Union — which will offer it on acceptable terms. And although some of the developing countries, notably India under the impact of Chinese threats, have somewhat modified their political stand and veered cautiously towards the West, a major Asian member of the Western Alliance, Pakistan, has more than compensated for this change of orientation by establishing closer links with Communist China and expressing increased reservations and criticisms about the Western Alliance.

To the minority of American politicians and other leaders of public opinion who have a longer vision, continuing foreign aid is both a political and humanitarian necessity which may bear fruit in the long run by avoiding violent left-wing or right-wing revolutions springing from poverty and despair, and which may also ultimately benefit the United States politically precisely because she has not insisted on a political *quid pro quo*. But since these long-term hopes are less tangible and spring from a far more subtle conception of international strategy than that of the isolationists and nationalists, it is very much on the defensive at a time when Argentina, Brazil or Peru cancel the contracts of American oil enterprises or other utilities, or when Egypt or

Indonesia — which also receive substantial American aid — engage in military threats against Israel or Malaysia. It is quite possible that at a time of exceptional exasperation or internal economic difficulties, the isolationist ideas will gain the upper hand and support, in Government and Congress, a policy which will combine a general scepticism about aid to developing countries with a tough and aggressive policy towards any state labelled as 'Communist'. This kind of criticism has recently been reinforced by the strictures of international-minded politicians (such as Senators Fulbright, Morse and Proxmire) who have attacked the economic and political wastefulness of the Aid Programme, and in particular its apparent failure to stimulate political and social reforms. These critics have pointed to the weakness and corruption of regimes in Asia and Latin America, which are able to maintain themselves in power through American financial support. A coalition between conservative and liberal critics might deal a fatal blow to the whole foreign aid policy.

Return to Isolationism?

That there are very many Americans who yearn for the days when the United States could turn its back on the wars of Europe and other continents, is obvious and understandable. But today the fortress America covers the whole globe. A change of government in Vietnam concerns it as much as a revolution in Argentina, let alone a crisis in Berlin. There may be, and there have been, considerable changes in the emphasis of American foreign policy on the European and the Asian fronts. Especially since the rise of Communist China as a world Power, the fear of a Communist advance in Asia tends to outweigh the fear of a Soviet advance in Europe. By tradition and sentiment a right-wing Republican Congress tends to place more emphasis on a tough American policy in Asia. But the two basic facts of contemporary American policy — vulnerability to atomic attack, from the sea and via the Arctic, and the world-wide character of its involvements — cannot be basically affected by party politics or prejudices.

Although the new foreign policy of the United States was initiated in the Roosevelt era, it is not the product of the whim of one man or one party. It is the result of basic changes in the world balance of power, of a combination of circumstances which limit the freedom of action of the United States as much as that of any other country. In the first place, the technical character of modern war has changed to such an extent that the American continent is far from invulnerable. It is well within the range of long-range bombers, pilotless projectiles, submarine attacks and of airborne attacks from the Arctic North. And even if the United States decided to limit its international commitments, it is unlikely that Soviet Russia would take a similar view of the American position. More important, however, is the inability of the United States to disentangle herself from European affairs without drastic repercussions on her global position. The conquest of Western Europe by Soviet Russia, by military force or internal revolutions, would vitally affect the world balance of power and release immense additional strength for a more aggressive Communist policy in Asia. Moreover, it would destroy the one sound and substantial line of defence established by the Western democracies. In Europe, resistance to Russian expansion commands the voluntary support of the majority of the peoples which are still free to decide. In Asia, the policy of resistance to Communist expansion is almost entirely dependent on the extent of military and economic support given by the West.[1]

On the other hand, American foreign policy is largely determined and contained by two factors which no modern democracy, however powerful, can disregard: one is the fundamental aversion of the nation to any war which is not clearly and demonstrably defensive. The other is the necessity for the United States to find a common policy with her principal allies. Both these factors have time and again served to correct any tendencies towards reckless adventures in international politics.

During the first Eisenhower administration Secretary of State Dulles and other political and military leaders made certain foreign-policy statements which deeply alarmed America's allies. Prominent among them were the promise that the policy of 'liberation' would replace one of mere 'containment', which had characterized the Truman–Acheson administration. The other was the announcement that henceforth American counter-measures against Communist advance would be in the nature of 'massive retaliation'. It was evident that a policy of liberation of the Communist-controlled peoples of Europe and Asia could

[1] See further below, pp. 276 *et seq.*

be implemented only by a war which neither the people of the United States nor those of her allies would support. Again, the policy of 'massive retaliation' by atomic weapons in substitution for land and naval forces was soon felt to be morally objectionable if it meant that the West would take the initiative in atomic warfare, and impractical if applied to the vast land masses of a scarcely industrialized Asia, where such forms of warfare would be singularly ineffective. Therefore, it was with great concern that America's allies watched, in 1955 and again in 1958, the apparent determination of the United States to risk world war over the attempt of Communist China to drive the forces of Chiang Kai-shek from two small islands off the mainland of China, Quemoy and Matsu. These small islands are held by the Nationalist Chinese Government, now confined to the control of Taiwan (Formosa), as a matter of accident rather than of design. The civil war, in which the Communist forces had driven the forces of Chiang Kai-shek from the mainland, happened to be temporarily stabilized at that point largely through the intervention of the United States. Geographically, they must be considered as part of the mainland, and they have been compared with the situation of Staten Island in relation to the mainland of the American continent. It is unlikely that any Government in control of the mainland will, more than temporarily, abandon its claim to the control of such offshore islands. United States policy was dictated by the determination to back the Government of Chiang Kai-shek as the only remaining Chinese bulwark against Communist control. American firmness, and present superiority in naval and air strength, have halted the threat for the time being. But it can only be a matter of time until Communist China, rapidly gaining in industrial and military strength, will renew the attempt, perhaps at a time when the resources of the United States are otherwise engaged. Allied backing for United States policy has been far more definite, in the critical and dangerous Berlin situations of 1948, 1958 and 1961, as well as in the Cuba crisis of October 1962. The situation of Berlin as an enclave in potentially hostile, Communist-controlled territory is one which none of the Western allies can welcome. After the collapse of Four-Power government in Germany in 1947, a strong case could — and perhaps should — have been made for a Western evacuation of Berlin, in anticipation of the division of Germany, since

Berlin was then losing its expected role as the capital of a united Germany. However, it is much too late for such a policy. At this time the abandonment of West Berlin would fatally damage the Western position in the Cold War and destroy the confidence of millions who have placed their faith in the constancy of such a policy. Hence any threat of force against the status of West Berlin has to be met with counterforce, as successive American Presidents, from Truman to Johnson, have reaffirmed with the full backing of their Allies.[1] In the case of Cuba, the initiative and aggression was clearly on the side of Cuba and the Soviet Union, and the response of the United States an essentially defensive one. Whether the unanimous support of her allies would have withstood the test of the 'quarantine', which included the search of ships destined for Cuba on the high seas, is not so certain. Fortunately, however, this question was not put to the test. On the whole, support for American foreign policy, inside the Western Alliance and to a large extent even outside the Alliance, will be strong as long as the purposes of American action are essentially defensive. But offensive or other interventionist actions, such as a war over the offshore islands of China, or armed intervention in Cuba, would leave the United States isolated and possibly destroy the Western Alliance altogether.

The clamour of American internal politics make it often difficult to appreciate the relative consistency of contemporary United States policy. This does not mean that internal American politics or temporary changes of direction could not have a disastrous effect on the world situation. The result of presidential elections or a single Congressional resolution might be sufficient to shatter European confidence in American leadership, and to upset the delicate balance of forces in Europe. Yet a sober estimate of the tendencies and forces at work justifies the conclusion that in its main outline the foreign policy of the United States will not be affected by a change of leaders.

Whether or not the United States will retain her role as the leading Power in the non-Communist world is not as great and threatening an uncertainty as the question in which spirit this leadership will be exercised. United States foreign policy is more immediately influenced by internal politics than that of any other

[1] On the interlocked problems of the status of Berlin and the partition of Germany, see further below, pp. 171 *et seq.*, 361 *et seq.*

Power which in the past has held a comparable position. The leading world Powers of former centuries — Spain, France, Great Britain before the nineteenth century — operated in the pre-democratic era, when foreign policy was the prerogative of princes and Cabinets. When democracy penetrated British political life it did so gradually, and in a form which insured the stability of the Government in power. The United States Constitution, on the other hand, is based on an intricate balance of powers in which only rare coincidence gives the administration the unqualified support of Congress and a free hand in the conduct of foreign affairs. Not only does any foreign commitment require a two-thirds majority in the Senate, but every financial commitment, such as foreign economic aid, or the Mutual Security Programme, or American contributions to NATO or the United Nations, must obtain approval of the numerous committees of both Houses, and finally of Congress as a whole. In this process internal politics and lobby pressure become mixed up with considerations of world policy. Persons and groups neither experienced nor interested in world affairs can thus exercise a major influence on the foreign policies of the United States. In Presidential election years such internal influences are particularly strong. They create a double danger; one is that of vacillation, contrasting starkly with the concentration of power in the Communist bloc. Such vacillation and uncertainty are all the more dangerous, as the United States is the leader of a group of nations greatly differing in history, political structure, temperament and social development. It is not a monolithic bloc.

Such a situation underlines the second danger: the almost irresistible temptation to use military and economic power for the purposes of dictation. Since the United States was suddenly thrown into a position of world leadership for which she was not prepared, she has been singularly fortunate in her leaders. Political leaders such as Roosevelt, Truman, Acheson, Marshall, Eisenhower, Kennedy, Johnson and Rusk, have faced with courage and skill the task of using power with restraint. But when the temperature of the Cold War rises, the temptation increases to weld the anti-Communist front into a monolithic bloc. The most isolationist politicians in the United States are usually the most intolerant and the most conservative. They are responsible for the agitation to ignore any sober estimate of the social forces in Asia and to give the utmost backing to any anti-Communist Government, regardless of the measure of support it has in its own country, of its ideology, of its integrity — in short, of any factor other than force and strategy. Yet it is usually the same politicians who are loudest in their praise of the unique virtues of American democracy, and incapable of understanding that democracy is not a standard formula; that it means tolerance and diversity, and that to the nations of Europe and Asia, the American form of democracy and the American way of life are but one of the many possible ways of living democratically.

In any attempt to be tough with its Allies, to use its financial and military supremacy for dictation, the United States would, however, be certain to run a bad second to Soviet Russia or Communist China. The many factors which combine to make such a policy possible for the U.S.S.R.,[1] though decreasingly so, do not operate in the United States. Her policy would be torn between the desire to adhere to her tradition of freedom and the urge to use power. In the process America's allies would become increasingly distrustful and resentful. One of the great values of the United Nations and its affiliated agencies, but even more of NATO, is that it constantly compels the United States to seek agreement with her allies, by discussion and compromise. An equally heavy responsibility rests upon America's weaker allies. The dominant power of the day is never popular. The more it is needed, the less it is liked. The nations that today depend on the help of the United States — and on whose support the United States, in her own turn, depends for her international policy — are either old nations which, like Britain, France or Germany, are conscious of past greatness and power and have to adjust themselves to a new situation; or they are nations which, like India, have recently gained national independence, and are therefore particularly sensitive to dictation — most of all to the use of economic power for political purposes.

So far, the foreign policy of the United States has almost invariably risen far above the often appalling level of internal politics. The fate of the Western world largely depends on the continued supremacy and articulateness of those Americans who know that the internal politics of the United States — the lobby, the election tactics, the tendency to regard politics as an aspect of

[1] See above, pp. 66 *et seq.*

business, and public service as an inferior form of activity — are no longer America's own affair, and that if unchecked they can plunge the world into disaster.

United States policy will be increasingly compelled to give priority to its role and its responsibility as the leader of a world-wide alliance, over considerations of domestic policy. The recurrent crises over Quemoy, Vietnam, Berlin or the Middle East, each carrying a potential danger of another world war, pose, however, certain long-term problems which United States policy-makers have, with a very few exceptions, not so far been willing to face squarely. The intervention of the United States in the last two world wars — difficult and courageous as it was — was based on a position of immense industrial superiority, and a domestic invulnerability which permitted the development of this huge potential, while America's Western allies held the fort. This invulnerability has vanished in the age of hydrogen bombs and intercontinental missiles. Above all, the strength of the potential enemies of the United States — the Soviet Union and Communist China — is growing steadily, and already vastly greater than that of any other hostile coalition faced in the past. American moral and legal defence commitments embrace many States in Asia, which are politically, militarily and economically weak. For the first time in its history, the United States has to face the kind of problems to which its European allies have become accustomed during the present century. It cannot afford to dissipate strength in the defence of exposed and, in the last resort, expendable positions, with the risk that no strength may be left for the defence of vital positions. And it needs the support of its major allies, hardly less than they need the support of the United States. Firmness must be related to sustained strength, and the possibility of retreat at some points must be envisaged. Such an estimate must go beyond the counting of missiles and nuclear bases, and beyond the distribution of combat divisions (of which the Communist Powers have in any case a greater number). It implies an 'agonizing reappraisal' of economic and social policies, and of habits of life that have not in the past been seriously challenged by any actual or potential enemy.

The Challenge from the Soviet Union

Since Pearl Harbor, and in particular since the end of the last world war, the principal task of U.S. policy has been the adjustment of American thinking to new responsibilities; the replacement of an attitude of detachment and isolation from world entanglements, by the assumption of leadership in world-wide military and political alliances; the taking on of ever-growing responsibilities, by the world's richest nation, for the living standards, for the social and economic development of the many poor nations of the world; the recognition that the defeat of the Fascist Powers has not brought a united and harmonious striving of the world for peace and international order, but new, and perhaps more permanent divisions, in terms of power, aspirations, responsibilities. But, until very recently, the overwhelming majority of Americans have never conceived the challenge as directed to the foundations of their economic and social system. The superiority of the American economic system of 'free enterprise' over the planned and regimented economy of the Soviet Union, the permanent superiority of American science, technology and methods of industrial production, and of the whole vision of what Kenneth Galbraith has recently termed 'the affluent society', have been taken for granted by all but an unpopular and small minority. The progress of the U.S.S.R. in the development of nuclear energy, and, in particular, the speed with which she had achieved the manufacture of atom and hydrogen bombs, well in advance of American forecasts, caused no more than a small ripple in the calm sea of complacency. When the Soviet Union shot the first earth satellite into orbit late in 1957, deeper doubts began to assail the combination of politicians, business leaders and military men, who had not been moved by the warnings of a handful of dissenters. Since then, the process of reappraisal has widened. It has extended from the immediately pressing question of balance of military strength, and in particular of deterrent power in missiles and other nuclear weapons, to the adequacy of the American educational system and — though far from sufficiently — to the way of living which the great majority of Americans have tended to regard as the unique, and unquestionably beneficial and superior, contribution of their country to the progress of the world. Some of the most patent self-delusions have at last been abandoned by all but the most die-hard: that the planned socialist economy can never match a 'free' economy in efficiency and progress; that the immensely greater availability of all kinds of consumer goods to the American, as compared with the Soviet and other Communist people, is in itself a sign of superiority of the former over the latter system; that the absence of political freedom in the Communist world would sooner or later lead to the downfall of the regime. But the mental obstacles to a critical and searching reappraisal remain great. For the vast majority of American businessmen and politicians, the belief in the superiority of free private enterprise over any kind of planning or public control of the economy is a matter almost beyond reasoning; it is an article of faith. It has not been shaken by the undeniable fact that the United States economic system of today is a highly regulated one, and that business and industry is second to none in any other country, in demanding the intervention and protection of the State when it sees its interests threatened, by the very competition that it champions in theory. To name but a few examples: United States agriculture is largely protected from the fluctuations of supply and demand by a highly complex and costly system of price supports, Government purchases and the like; U.S. shipping competes with that of other countries only by virtue of heavy Government subsidies; the most important reservations in the General Agreement for Tariffs and Trade (GATT) were made in favour of American agricultural interests, thus detracting from the already greatly curtailed idea of relatively free international trade; whenever foreign imports, e.g. of Swiss watches or British bicycles, have tended to capture an American market, there has been pressure for increased tariffs or import quotas — often, though not always, successful. Domestic oil producers have successfully fought for the imposition of quotas, by Government regulation, on the import of cheaper oil from abroad. Government subsidies, import quotas, protective tariffs and the whole machinery of a semi-private economy are, of course, a familiar feature of many countries. But nowhere outside the U.S. are the facts so widely ignored in an appraisal of the real degree of 'freedom' and 'private enterprise'. Hence, the awakening to the real nature of the new Soviet challenge, the rise of an industrially more and more developed, technically progressive and generally well-trained and educated country, has been so tardy.

There is even some danger that the agonizing reappraisal that followed the belated recognition of Soviet scientific, technical and educational progress a few years ago, will once again give way to complacency. A report published by the Central Intelligence Agency at the end of 1963 estimated that contrary to previous years and earlier estimates, the recent growth rate in the national product of the Soviet Union had only been of the order of 2·4%, inferior to that of the United States. Unquestionably, the Soviet Union has faced serious economic difficulties, particularly in agriculture. A very bad wheat harvest in 1963, due predominantly to exceptional drought, forced her to make major purchases of wheat abroad, especially in Canada and the United States. The new programme of improving agricultural productivity by the massive production of chemical fertilizers compels the diversion of investment resources from other fields, including, to a modest extent, the military establishment. The economic problems of the Soviet Union also limit her ability to extend or improve the terms of her substantial aid to the developing countries. At a time when economic aid is under heavy attack in the United States and elsewhere in the West, this is a fortunate coincidence for the Western world. But while a corrective to the somewhat exaggerated views about Soviet productivity, scientific and technical progress, and the general level of education, which followed the shock of Russia's achievements in space science and technology, is appropriate, the opposite danger of mistaking temporary setbacks for general defeat would be infinitely greater. Contacts between the Western and the Communist world have now been sufficiently continuous, and the exchanges of visits between scientists, educators, artists and others sufficiently numerous, to attest to the achievements and progress of Soviet society, and especially to the growth of a substantial and sophisticated intelligentsia. Although at her present stage of development the economic policy of the Soviet Union must increasingly take note of higher and more sophisticated consumer demands, her growing productive capacity — including the high scientific and technological potential of her people — remains geared to national goals, and to a priority of essential over non-essential products and services. A mere comparison of gross national product figures can thus be very misleading. Above all, it totally conceals the fact that the figures for production in the United States — an economy geared to the satisfaction of consumer demands, regardless of their value to the life of the nation, and to services which are richly rewarding in the affluent society of conspicuous consumption — are not necessarily related to the capability of survival. The State-directed economy of Russia and China means many scarcities, constraints and lack of consumer choice — though this is now conspicuously less so in such countries as Russia or Hungary than even some years ago. It does, however, mean that the economy is directed towards *essential* production. The need for the United States and its allies to put first things first may be no less urgent, but it is not yet recognized as such. Meanwhile, millions of dollars are spent annually on the retooling of automobile factories for more and more extravagant models, and for the advertising of luxury consumer products. Yet there remain not only considerable regions of poverty, especially in the South, and in many of the major cities; funds are lacking for the adequate development of schools, housing, roads and other basic public services. It would be insulting to the United States to suggest that the funds for such vital services are not there. They cannot, however, be redirected from the demands of conspicuous consumption to public services, as long as the political and economic leaders of the nation refuse to awaken their nation to the urgency of the situation. Nor is it sufficient to deplore inadequacy of schools, of scientific or linguistic training, or of slum-clearance schemes. As long as the question: 'Production of What, and For What Purposes?' cannot be asked, even short spurts to boost a missiles programme cannot disguise the basic problem. The relative growth of the strength of the Communist opponents of the United States rests not on a short-term lead in satellites or missiles; it rests on their use of resources, of materials and manpower, for major national goals, such as basic industries, irrigation and educational facilities, at a time when year after year federal school aid appropriations fail to pass Congress, and golden toothpicks are advertised for 'the man who has everything'.[1]

[1] The Congressional approval in 1964 of the President's programme for 'war on poverty' in depressed areas, urban renewal, conservation and substantial federal aid to higher education indicates at least some awareness of these issues. The Civil Rights legislation of 1964 poses gigantic problems of housing and educational reforms needed to match formal legal equality with social and economic opportunities for the Negro population.

The favourite American answer has usually been that the abandonment of free consumer choice means the loss of freedom and the advent of totalitarianism. As has been pointed out earlier in this book, the experience of such countries as the Scandinavian States or post-war Britain shows that the survival of political and spiritual freedom is not threatened by economic priorities and social planning. It would be more gravely threatened by a combination of military, political and business leaders who would tend to preserve the existing system of business by a tougher policy towards labour and social services, and, in the process, curtail freedom of expression. While the possibility of such a development cannot be entirely dismissed, there are more hopeful alternatives.

Within less than twenty years the United States has transformed itself from a tradition of over a century and a half of isolationism and the largely uncontrolled competition for wealth, into the leader of the world's democracies, assuming heavy military, economic and moral obligations. It is not too much to hope that the new and even graver challenge which comes from the attainment by America's greatest opponent of industrial and scientific maturity will also be met before it is too late. This certainly does not mean the socialization of the American economy. It does mean the need to put first things first, to redirect, by taxes, by public allocations on the federal, State and local government levels, some of the nation's immense wealth and productive capacity, away from a self-perpetuating machinery of production of increasingly redundant consumer goods, to the essential requisites of a nation that wants to survive and grow in a tough world, under a mortal challenge from rivals.

The reason why President Kennedy made such a deep impact upon the people in the Western world and elsewhere, despite the tragic shortness of his less than three years in office, was his awareness of both these aspects of contemporary American policy: the internal as well as the external challenge. Throughout the brief period of his Presidency, Kennedy laboured to make his own nation as well as the rest of the world understand that power and restraint were inevitably linked; that the world-wide implications of the use of power, in the nuclear age, were far too momentous to tolerate the methods of the turn of the century, or even of a generation after that; that talk of 'an all-out fight against Communism' and of 'total victory' ignored the continuous and subtle nature of a challenge that will last for many years, and in which the alternative to total destruction is the use of power with flexibility, as well as restraint. But Kennedy also saw the equal importance of the domestic challenge — in its interrelatedness with the international situation; the dilemma of a nation that stands for anti-colonialism and the right to national and individual freedom, regardless of race or religion, while still reluctant to grant such equality and freedom to its own Negro citizens; the incongruity of preaching social and economic reform to other countries, while tolerating slums, overcrowded schools and inadequate public health facilities in the richest country of the world; the inescapable need for a qualitatively improved and quantitatively widened system of education in the United States, able to meet the challenge not only from the education-conscious Communist powers but from the pressing demands of contemporary social and technological conditions; the inescapable governmental responsibility for the conservation and development of national resources. President Johnson is seeking to maintain and develop all these principles. They are strongly challenged by powerful conservative forces in the country. They aim at the reduction of governmental responsibility in every field except the military establishment — in matters of taxation, education, social welfare, conservation of resources, urban renewals, economic aid to developing countries; they include even a demand for the handing over of a public enterprise, the Tennessee Valley Authority — which has rescued an entire region from floods, erosion and stagnation — to private enterprise. In the field of foreign policy they reject the blend of power and restraint applied by Republican as well as Democratic Presidents, and demand 'total victory' against Communism. While the decisive defeat of Senator Goldwater, a strong protagonist of the 'total victory' philosophy, in the presidential elections of November 1964, indicates a rejection of this approach by a strong majority, millions of Americans will continue to endorse it, even without some major international upheaval that might heighten Cold War tensions again.

The North Atlantic Treaty[1]

The military association of the member-States of the Council of Europe, with the addition of Iceland and Portugal, and the omission of the Irish Republic, is the third major move in the Western counter-offensive. The North Atlantic Treaty joins the two American Powers of Canada and the United States with a group of European States. Such is the shift in the balance of power that a defensive alliance of West European Powers alone could not hope to restore the balance of military power against the Soviet Union and its allied States. Only the full participation of these two non-European States, immune from a sudden attack of overwhelming land forces, and equipped with almost all the raw material and industrial resources demanded by modern war, could have this effect. The most important clause of the Treaty is its Article 5, by which the parties declare that they will regard an attack on one of them[2] as an attack on all, and that, if an armed attack occurs, each of them will assist the party attacked by such action as it deems necessary, including the use of armed force. As distinct from the Brussels Pact of 1948, the Atlantic Treaty imposes no automatic obligation of military assistance or action against armed aggression. An isolationist Senate could still prevent the United States from entering a war provoked by an attack upon Western Europe. This, however, should not give cause for undue alarm. It is not legal obligations, but the logic of her present world position, that has led the United States to lay out enormous sums for the recovery of Europe and to develop a military and strategic programme completely contrary to her traditional policy of neutrality. The strongest guarantee for American intervention, in the case of armed attack on Western Europe, is not her signature to the Treaty, but the presence of United States occupation forces in Europe. The vague and uncertain Article 4, which obliges the parties to consult together when, in the opinion of any of them, the territorial integrity, political independence or security of any of the parties is threatened, has been discussed in another connection.[3]

[1] The text is reprinted below, pp. 391 *et seq.*

[2] This includes an attack on the occupation forces of any of the parties in Europe (Art. 6).

[3] Above, pp. 74 *et seq.*

Like the military pacts of the U.S.S.R. with the Communist States of Eastern Europe, the North Atlantic Treaty protests its fidelity to existing international organizations by specific reference to the 'inherent rights of individual or collective self-defence, if an armed attack occurs against a member of the United Nations, until the Security Council has taken the measures necessary to maintain international peace and security' (Article 51, U.N. Charter). In accordance with Article 51, the parties also undertake to report any such measures immediately to the Security Council. A Treaty which is clearly defensive is not contrary to the Charter. Yet, like the Soviet Treaties, the North Atlantic Treaty owes its existence to the tacit assumption that the Security Council will be unable to act effectively. As the Treaty has been provoked by the fear of further advances of Soviet Russia, who is a permanent member of the Security Council, it would be absurd to regard the Treaty as a supplement rather than a substitute for the paralysed security organization of the United Nations.

A military counter-alliance, based on the assumption of a world-wide conflict between two groups of Powers, is under even stronger compulsion to sacrifice ideological to strategic considerations, than the political and economic moves analysed earlier in this chapter. Although the North Atlantic Treaty is as eloquent as the Statute of the Council of Europe on the objective of safeguarding 'the freedom, common heritage and civilization founded on the principles of democracy, individual liberty and the rule of law', the inclusion of Portugal, an authoritarian though non-aggressive State, means a sacrifice of ideological to strategic considerations. On the other hand, a number of commentators have doubted whether the military alliance of a number of States strung across all Europe, and difficult to weld into a strategic or military front, is a factor of strength or of weakness. Above all, it is the omissions rather than the inclusions which bring out the dilemma of the present situation. So far, the difficulty even for the most robust anti-Communists to describe Franco's Spain as a defender of democracy and individual liberty has prevented the inclusion of Spain, although this is partly offset by bilateral agreements between the United States and Spain which give the former certain rights to use Spanish military bases in return for extensive economic assistance. Spain is obviously in a strategic key position, and military pressure for her inclusion in the Treaty is very strong. If danger of war became imminent, these military considerations would undoubtedly prevail. The remnants of peacetime political ideology would disappear.

Strategic considerations have also diluted the geographical conception of the 'North Atlantic' area. Italy became a member of the alliance soon after its formation. In 1951, both Greece and Turkey, which have for some time received great amounts of American military equipment, as well as the assistance of British and American military advisers, joined the Pact. These two States are regarded as vital bastions against a Russian advance into the Mediterranean. They are not, of course, Atlantic Powers. Again, an attack on Yugoslavia would almost certainly lead to intervention by the NATO Powers, although Yugoslavia is not a member. A Defence Treaty between Britain, Turkey, Pakistan, and Iran (Central Treaty Organization) creates another defence link with NATO. The Atlantic Treaty may or may not be effective as an emergency dam against a flood threatening to overwhelm Europe. But, unaided by a network of other regional arrangements, it may only serve to divert the flood. Some observations on the Asian position will be made in a later chapter. For Europe, the Mediterranean area and the countries of the Middle and Near East are obviously of vital importance in any future major conflict. The Suez Canal still remains an indispensable link between Europe, India and the South-west Pacific. Above all, the most important oil resources outside America and Russia are concentrated in that region.[1] In the present unsettled state of that whole area, it is impracticable to extend the alliance either to a number of Arab States which are militarily weak, socially and economically backward, and divided among themselves, or to Israel, which is surrounded by hostile or suspicious Arab States. But a struggle for control in the Mediterranean would be inevitable, with or without the definite alignment of the States in that area.

The scope and influence of the North Atlantic Treaty Organization have been greatly widened — and possibly altered — by the inclusion of West Germany. The merits of German rearmament, and the effect of West Germany's inclusion in the West European and North Atlantic organizations on the political conflict

[1] See below, p. 182.

between East and West, will be discussed elsewhere in this book.[1] Basically, West Germany shares more history, traditions and cultural background with the other NATO Powers than some of the other recent members, such as Turkey.

The whole-hearted participation of West Germany in NATO is however countered by the increasing lukewarmness and even partial defection of France. Soon after he returned to power in 1958 de Gaulle indicated the trend of French policy, by withdrawing the French Mediterranean fleet from NATO control. The successful termination of the Algerian war, with its heavy commitment of French forces, released important elements of the army for other duties, but they were not returned to NATO control. Only two French divisions are under NATO command, while the remaining forces are under national control. Moreover, de Gaulle has insisted on the development of a national French nuclear force, which will be quite independent of any NATO control. During the last period of the Adenauer regime in Germany, de Gaulle strove mightily to achieve close Franco-German military collaboration, in derogation of NATO control. In this attempt he has probably failed, since neither German public opinion nor the new leadership of West Germany appears to have any enthusiasm for a Franco-German military entente, an attitude for which the rest of the world can be profoundly grateful. This does not however affect General de Gaulle's basic conception, which is dominated by the idea of French national grandeur and the consequent contempt for international or supra-national associations, except perhaps those in which France would play a clearly dominant role. It is difficult to say how far he would push this attitude in the case of acute conflict — it has to be remembered that in the Cuban crisis of 1962, France unconditionally supported the U.S. reaction. But the defiant nationalism of de Gaulle's France which expresses itself in a multitude of ways[2] imparts an element of uncertainty into the NATO organization which without France would be fatally weakened.

Given the deplorable division of Europe, the association of the United States and Canada with both Britain and the democracies of Europe provides the widest and, potentially, the most powerful association of nations united by common purposes and values. In

[1] See below, pp. 164 *et seq.* [2] See below, pp. 159 *et seq.*

this organization the United States is not in the position of a benefactor whose munificence is interrupted by periodic irritation. She is herself a member, sharing rights and duties, and compelled to observe the rules of the organization. The participation of a State so much more powerful and wealthy than the other members has its dangers. But the dangers are far outweighed by the advantages of joint responsibility. The membership of Britain creates a link with the British Commonwealth of Nations and thus builds a bridge to the non-European world. This link is further reinforced by the defence treaty between the United States, Australia and New Zealand.

So far the practical significance of NATO rests overwhelmingly on the collective defence force directed by a Supreme Headquarters under the command of an American General. Defence today is the primary preoccupation of the Western world, and the joint army, navy and air force which is formed by contingents from all the participating nations is the real backbone of NATO. But the cohesion of these forces is inversely proportional to the fear of attack from the Soviet bloc. As this fear weakens, nationalist conflicts within NATO are given freer rein, as shown by the temporary withdrawal of Greek and Turkish forces from NATO control in the summer of 1964, during their bitter conflict over Cyprus. Its organization has been strengthened by the establishment of a permanent staff under a Secretary-General and of a permanent high-level Executive Committee.

NATO faces many unsolved problems. Reference has already been made to the problem of the scope of its membership.

One of the purposes of the North Atlantic Treaty is the encouragement of economic collaboration between any or all of the members. Article 2 of the Treaty lays down that the parties 'will seek to eliminate conflict in their international economic policies and will encourage economic collaboration between any or all of them'. After more than ten years of operation of the Treaty, little has happened to translate these aspirations into reality. The abolition or reduction of customs duties between the member-States, for example, has never been seriously considered. Such a move — which would have to be ratified by the parliaments of all the States concerned — would meet with the customary resistance of the United States Congress to any substantial lessening in the protection of its national industries. It would, moreover, conflict with the specific commitments and privileges that the Commonwealth members of the North Atlantic Treaty Organization enjoy, and are pledged to observe, as members of the British Commonwealth. Further, all NATO members are also parties to the so-called GATT agreements — which aim at a cautious liberalization of international trade — with which any specific privileges that some of the parties to this treaty would accord to each other would scarcely be compatible. Again, it might be conceivable and desirable that the NATO members should work out a common migration and labour policy. Not even tentative moves have been made in this direction. Nor have there been signs of a joint currency policy between countries which are divided between the dollar and sterling areas. Even in the field that is most immediately linked with the primary military task of NATO, the co-ordination of productive and other economic resources has remained within strict limits. The budgetary and other obligations of the NATO Powers are determined from year to year by a conference of the government representatives, which must decide by unanimous agreement. After many discussions, some progress has been made in the direction of standardization of weapons. A standard rifle and a standard calibre for small weapons have been agreed upon although France, in line with her general nationalist policy, decided, in 1964, to use a French-made rifle. But nothing approaching a joint production plan which would lead to a common industrial policy has been established. A certain degree of co-ordination of the productive resources of NATO countries has been achieved. Thus certain types of British tanks and Italian jet fighters have been ordered on the basis of technical merit, and in the face of opposition from the representatives of the national forces. West Germany has balanced the heavy cost of American and British military forces stationed in Germany by placing substantial orders for military equipment in both the United States and Britain. On the whole, however, it is likely that Article 2 of the North Atlantic Treaty will remain one of the high-sounding but practically meaningless provisions in which international treaties abound. There is, on the other hand, no reason why the NATO Powers should not go much farther than they have so far done in the development of common social, legal and cultural institutions. Linked as they are by common values, traditions and interests, they could extend to each other's citizens social benefits, educational and travel privileges, much in the way in which the Members of the Council of Europe have done it for some years. Nor would the establishment of a common court of justice for the protection of certain basic rights within the NATO countries be impracticable. It would be a far more realistic attempt to implement a basic charter of human rights than would at present be possible on a world-wide scale.

The form and scope of NATO will be determined by rapidly changing pressures. Yet certain fundamental principles should not be lost sight of. The first is that the moral strength of the Organization rests on the idea of a community of nations which have a common background of civilization and institutions, which think and act in similar ways. An indiscriminate dilution of the Organization would destroy this purpose. The second is that NATO can never be an exclusive international association. Because it links the United States and Canada with both Britain and the leading nations of Western Europe, it should facilitate and encourage close collaboration with other international associations, in particular with the British Commonwealth on the one hand, and purely European organizations, such as the European Economic Community, on the other hand. The precise relationship of these various developing associations is bound to be complex and fluctuating, but fundamentally it reflects a sound reality of contemporary world politics. A universal and all-embracing organization of all, or even a large number of nations is not capable of effective action in the present state of international society. Different associations are required for different purposes. The British Commonwealth of Nations represents ties and interests quite different from those of NATO, or the European Community. Yet they cannot live or work in isolation, or in competition with each other. The North Atlantic Community, the British Commonwealth of Nations and a more closely integrated democratic Europe can exist side by side, but they must work together.

Accomplishments and Deficiencies of Western Strategy

The price which mankind has to pay for its failure to establish a universal pattern of law and society is heavy. In the absence of such organization, the fact that the two strongest States are on opposite sides serves to maintain, however precariously, a measure of peace and freedom for the majority of nations. Either the unchallenged supremacy of one Power, or the association for world dominion of both, would destroy the vestiges of independence and political balance. But the new alignment has been established at very great cost. For both sides it means the consolidation of dividing lines which run counter to many natural ties of history, geography and economic resources. For the Western Powers it creates a further problem which does not exist for the Communist group: that of balancing the preservation of national independence, political democracy and individual liberty against the strategic necessity, in a conflict of power, to muster all available forces against the main danger. So far, the States which form the nucleus of the Western Coalition, and whose preservation has been the main objective of the counter-offensive, have retained their liberty and their distinctive ways of life. The price paid is a considerable weakening of their striking power. Lastly, the alternative to world-wide collective security is a world-wide chain of alliances and counter-alliances. But the difficulties increase with the magnitude of the task. The main assumption underlying the North Atlantic Treaty is the expectation that the certainty of a war with the United States and other Powers will prevent Russian aggression. But for a number of reasons, commitments and obligations cannot be equally definite in other parts of the world, and this increases the danger of conflict developing anywhere through the exploitation of 'soft spots'.

Yet it is not necessary to take an entirely negative and pessimistic view of present developments.

The position may perhaps be summed up in three broad conclusions: first, the contest between the two great powerful coalitions is still a major but no longer the controlling factor of contemporary world politics. Second, the nature of the contest is such that it means constant strife and tension in all fields of social and political life, but not necessarily war. Third, if a major war can be avoided, the effects of the conflict are not altogether destructive, but may, in a roundabout and strenuous way, help the progress of mankind.

It is unfortunately true that the bipolar power conflict has dominated almost every political, economic or ideological development since the war. It has reduced the function of the United Nations to that of the organized forum of world opinion and of a mediator in conflicts between minor Powers. It has prevented the establishment of an international military force in accordance with the terms of the United Nations Charter, and of an effective machinery for the international control of atomic energy. It has turned what was meant to be a pattern of international government centred around the collaboration of the big Powers, in the administration and reorganization of Germany and Japan, into a continuous source of discord between the Powers, and a secondary effect of this has been the gradual remilitarization of Germany and Japan. The conflict has also prevented the organic and harmonious evolution of new patterns of supra-national organization. In Europe it has led to the tearing apart of the organic unity of the Continent. In Asia it prevents the flow of Western capital equipment and technical experience to any area within the Communist sphere. Above all, the conflict keeps the larger portion of mankind in a state of fear, insecurity and privation, while immensely adding to the burden of States exhausted by the last war.

But there are some counter-balancing factors. In the first place, the very magnitude of the catastrophe, which a war involving the major part of mankind and all the destructive agencies of modern science on both sides would unleash, has prevented several very explosive situations from developing into war. The recurrent conflicts between the big Powers over the control of Berlin offer a good example. Both sides have applied the greatest possible pressure and resources at their disposal, short of war. Soviet Russia has so far been very careful not to let pressure, conflict and the fomenting of discord, in Berlin, Laos or Cuba, develop into open war. The Korean war of 1950–52 did not become a worldwide war, nor have militant statements on either side led to actual hostilities between the United States and China. Common sense and a sense of moral responsibility have prevented a small but at one time very powerful section of American public opinion from pushing the nation and the world into a preventive atom-bomb war against Russia or China. Despite their division over almost every major issue, the great Powers continue their active membership of the United Nations. They do so less because they expect agreement over major issues than because they are aware of the collective influence of world opinion organized in the United Nations. Finally, the great Powers are becoming increasingly aware of the immense burdens and responsibilities of a major war. All this enables small Powers to exercise a greater influence and freedom of action than would otherwise be possible.

Nevertheless, the danger of war is constant and real; a relatively small shift in the balance of power, such as intervention in Cyprus, a revolution in India or the development of a new weapon, may provide the spark which causes the explosion. Whether this is likely to happen will depend largely on the effect of the concentration of too much power in too few hands.

The defensive character of the Western Coalition follows not so much from the text of the various treaties as from the strategic situation of the Western Powers, which could at best hope to hold some essential line until American aid becomes effective. Aggression would be suicide. Communist propaganda can do little more than reiterate the stale thesis that Capitalism must sooner or later want war. It is a thesis which had some force fifty years ago, but completely ignores the vital changes in the relation of economic forces and State power.

How great the danger of aggression from the Communist Front will be depends on the degree to which power will blind the rulers of Soviet Russia or Communist China. The concentration of too much power in too few hands has as corrupting an effect in Soviet Russia as it has had elsewhere. But there is much evidence to show that the technique of the Kremlin differs from that of Hitler or Mussolini. Because Communist dogma believes in the dialectic of ideas and has elaborated the technique of infiltration, propaganda and subversion, it gives a correspondingly more subordinate significance to sheer military force. The belief in the contradictions of Capitalism and in the inevitable progress of Communism has certainly not led Soviet Russia or any other Communist movement to watch passively for the inevitable, but it strengthens their faith in the power of economic depression, of unemployment and other social factors to produce the desired change. And if the Nazi regime, in its last phases, clearly revealed its fundamental nihilism, its love of destruction, the Soviet regime has not so far shown similar tendencies, and it would certainly have to pervert the Communist dogma completely to do so. In short, there is some reason to believe that the 'cold war' is not a necessary preparatory phase for a 'hot war', but a new technique of conflict.

The New Phase in Soviet Strategy

The ubiquitous and elastic character of the Cold War was underlined by the more subtle and dynamic strategy adopted by Stalin's successor, Nikita Krushchev. In a sense, Stalin made things simple for the West. His was the mind of a cunning but limited, stubborn and, in world affairs, inexperienced Georgian peasant. After the war, Stalin's policy was to exploit ruthlessly the greatly increased military power of the Soviet Union, but to withdraw at any serious threat of a major war. It was to expand and fortify the Soviet position wherever possible and never voluntarily to let go of anything once held. Internal subversion was helpful and necessary, but it succeeded nowhere where it was not backed by overwhelming Soviet power, as in central and south-eastern Europe. In the one case in which the national leader of a small nation had the courage and the prestige to resist, that of Yugoslavia, the Stalin answer was abuse but no action. When it became evident, soon after the end of the war, that Four-Power control of Germany would not work, the Stalin policy was to consolidate the Soviet hold over that part of Germany which was in its immediate grasp. And from the end of the war to the present time, Soviet propaganda often talked about German reunification, but it never did anything seriously to shake the belief of the great majority of Germans that the U.S.S.R. would not agree to re-unification on acceptable terms. Soviet action, as distinct from words, was designed to turn Eastern Germany into another solid and reliable Soviet satellite.

In the post-Stalin era, until October 1964 dominated by Krushchev, Soviet strategy has become more flexible. It alternates between toughness and conciliatory gestures, but it generally prefers, far more skilfully than under Stalin, the exploitation of political turbulence or weakness in another country, to blunt military threats or actions. Soviet strategy has generally profited from the fact that Communist movements elsewhere tend to follow the Kremlin line, though much less automatically than some years ago. Again, most of the nationalist movements, especially in the Middle Eastern area, have tended to look with greater sympathy on the Communist countries, as compared with the West. It has often been sufficient for the Soviet Union to express its sympathy, in words and actions, with nationalist anti-Western movements. On occasion, as in the Lebanon troubles of 1958, it was left to the United States to provide a show of direct military intervention. The Soviet Union exploited, for example, the refusal by the World Bank and the United States to finance Nasser's Aswan Dam project by granting Egypt a substantial loan, while it pandered to Arab anti-Israel sentiment by increasing hostility to Israel and the supply of arms and equipment to the United Arab Republic and to other Arab States — thus making them dependent on further supplies and military instruction from the Soviet Union. In 1963, the Soviet Union concluded a military assistance agreement with Somalia, one of the recently created African States, which claims areas from both Ethiopia and Kenya and, with the help of Soviet arms, could create much trouble in Africa. Soviet policy may find it increasingly difficult to back simultaneously pro-Communist and anti-Communist nationalist movements which are in conflict with each other. A change of front and tactics is, however, far easier for a State in which policy is determined by a small group of men at the top, who need not fear public discussion or internal opposition. A survey of Soviet actions in the last few years seems to show that the Kremlin will react, with force and ruthless suppression, to any immediate physical threat to the security of its East European Communist empire. This is shown by the suppression of the Hungarian revolt in 1956, and the determined activity displayed by the Soviet Union in protecting the stability of the East German Communist regime. Outside this immediate sphere of control, Soviet policy has generally preferred to exploit its advantages as a power not tainted by past political or economic colonialism, and increasingly able to detach from its growing industrial and technical arsenal sufficient capital, machinery and men to give substantial economic assistance to underdeveloped countries. A notable — and nearly catastrophic — exception from this policy was the intent to create an advanced base for Soviet forces and strategy in Cuba, through the supply and placement of Soviet intermediate missiles and support troops in Cuba, the United States' southern neighbour, and a state that, under Castro, is ideologically firmly in the Communist camp. It is likely however that the firm response of the United States, and the consequent withdrawal of the missiles and of the bulk of the troops sent by the Soviet Union, will have counselled further caution. Such a trend will be supported by the harvest failure of 1963 and other economic pressures, which strongly favour at least a standstill, if not a substantial reduction, in military expenditures. Since the peaceful solution of the Cuba crisis of October 1962, the main accent has been on co-existence, on the denunciation of war as a possible instrument of policy in our time, and a generally relaxed tone in the negotiations with, and comments on, the United States. This attitude is symbolized by a few agreements, of which the best known is the ban on all, except underground, nuclear tests by a treaty concluded in July 1963; an agreement not to use space vehicles for military purposes; co-operation in certain technical and meteorological matters, such as weather observation, exchange of data, continuation of the modest, but nevertheless important, cultural exchange arrangements and a consular treaty. Further, and more far-reaching, agreements are periodically proposed by both sides in the Cold War; a controlled agreement on the manufacture and location of nuclear weapons; gradual steps towards disarmament; an agreed status of West Berlin; joint explorations in outer space. The viewpoints and interests of the two major antagonists remain far too opposed to make any substantial progress likely in the near future. Sudden and overwhelming pressures on one side or the other, such as the intensification of the tensions between the Soviet Union and Communist China, would probably produce a major change of attitude and a substantial acceleration and extension of agreements between the U.S.S.R. and the U.S.A. Meanwhile, the most characteristic aspect of the co-existence is a tacit understanding that the many sharp conflicts between the strongest Powers of the world, which persist in many areas of the world, should not be allowed to develop into war; that it may be possible as well as inevitable to continue for a long time with situations that neither side finds satisfactory but neither wishes to disturb by unilateral action, at the risk of world war.[1]

[1] As this book goes to press (November 1964), the removal of Krushchev indicates the end of a phase and a possible change in Soviet policy. But the appointment of two long-time associates of Krushchev, Leonid Brezhnev and Alexei Kosygin, to the posts of Party Secretary and Premier, as well as the inherent problems of Russia's situation, indicate continuation of the general lines of Krushchev's policy. It is likely, however, that both the Soviet and the Chinese leadership will attempt to assuage the bitterness of the Sino-Soviet conflict which had reached breaking-point at the end of the Krushchev

The Decline of 'Bipolarism'

Previous editions of this book have challenged the validity of the 'bipolar' theory by pointing to the growing importance of a third world power, Communist China, and the influence of the many medium and small States on the balance of power between the giants.

Events since the publication of the last edition (1960) have reinforced the trend away from bipolarism to such an extent that this approach to world politics can no longer be regarded as even basically correct. A number of factors have contributed to a far-reaching reorientation of world politics. First, Communist China has, despite severe economic setbacks, emerged more and more clearly as the third major world power, a power that only awaits the further progress of its industrial and scientific potential to play a dominant role in world politics. The independence of its position and role in world affairs has been underlined by its ideological and political split with the Soviet Union. China has become a rival leader of Communist-nationalist revolutionary forces throughout the world, and is assuming, at least in Asia, a role superior in political and military influence to that of the Soviet Union. This has been a major reason for the attempts made by the two leaders of the hostile coalitions of the Cold War to find a measure of accommodation and perhaps even limited co-operation, i.e. a tendency not to let the Cold War antagonism be any longer the dominant force of contemporary world politics. The Cuba crisis of 1962 dramatically underlined for both the U.S. and U.S.S.R. the catastrophic dangers of direct confrontation.

Today the control of overwhelming destructive power is a major factor of restraint, as long as such power is in reasonable balance between potential antagonists and as long as it is controlled by men of wisdom and restraint. Both the Soviet Union and the United States have, however, some additional motivations in de-emphasizing the bipolar orientation of the Cold War. For the Soviet Union the most important reason for seeking at least a lessening of acute tension with the Western world is the increasing threat from Communist China, not only as a rival

---

era. But the muting of open hostility cannot dispose of the basic national and international rivalries and of the many divergent interests of the two Communist giants.

leader of Communist forces, but as a potential enemy in the old-fashioned nationalist sense, i.e. as a neighbouring state of potentially equal or even superior power which may claim disputed frontier territories, and which has already indicated dissatisfaction with the acquisition by Russia in past periods of 'imperialism' of territories alleged to properly belong to China. A war on two fronts is a calamity that any Power has traditionally sought to avoid. The strategic and international considerations are reinforced by economic troubles, i.e. by the shortcomings of successive harvests, the need to concentrate resources on agriculture rather than on military expenditures and the growing demands of an increasingly articulate and sophisticated Soviet public for more consumer goods.

It is partly as a result of the split between the Communist giants, but also for other reasons, that the European satellites of the U.S.S.R. show increasing independence in their political and economic policies. Poland, Hungary and Roumania seek more economic and cultural relations with the West, and Roumania may even join an international organization as incompatible with Communist economics as GATT. At the same time these States increasingly resist the integration of their economies with countries under Soviet control.

On the American side, there are equally powerful, though different, factors counselling a modification of the 'Cold War' orientation. Since the end of the last world war and notably since the formation of NATO, the bulk of the Western world and less directly, the Latin American world, have accepted and followed the political as well as the economic leadership of the United States. But in recent years the emergence of new 'sovereign' states, especially in Africa, without any such definite orientation, has been powerfully reinforced by the increasing independence and diversity of movements and policies among America's Western allies and followers. Economically all the states of Western Europe have not only fully recovered from the physical and economic exhaustion of the Second World War and its aftermath, but they have gone forward to impressive and continuing increases in their productive capacity, their general welfare and their international economic associations. This is particularly true of West Germany and France, although this has led them to different political conclusions. Far and away the most important breach in the Western Alliance is the partial defection of France under de Gaulle, who has repudiated the leadership of the United States and reduced France's participation in NATO to minor proportions.[1]

The near-open defection of France from the Western Alliance has not so far been followed by any of the other members of the Coalition. But even America's most stalwart allies — such as Britain, West Germany or Canada — regard their partnership association with the United States as one implying a far greater degree of equality, and of independence of movement. Thus Canada several years ago recognized Communist China and it has sold substantial quantities of wheat and of certain other products to China, regardless of and preceding the more recent U.S. sales of wheat to the Soviet Union. Canada's tendency towards independence is increased by the growing nationalistic resentment against U.S. economic control over many of Canada's major industries and natural resources, and the revival of Quebec nationalism which has an isolationist, and certainly an anti-United States, orientation. West Germany has, under the leadership of Erhard and Schroeder, strengthened her political ties to the United States, which had become precarious in the last years of Chancellor Adenauer's close entente with de Gaulle's France. But not only in matters regarding the particularly sensitive and potentially explosive question of German reunification and policy over Berlin, but also in many other international questions, Germany asserts the right of consultation and independent action, to a far greater extent than before. Britain is more than any other partner of the United States likely to remain in line on major policy questions. But major divergencies have arisen out of the refusal of Britain to go along with the United States' anti-Communist trade and economic policies. Thus Britain is readier, with far fewer restrictions than the United States, to increase trade with the Communist bloc, including Communist China, and she recently weakened the U.S. economic boycott of Cuba by selling that country a large number of buses.

The new fluidity of the international power and diplomatic situation resulting from the above-mentioned factors is immensely increased by the growing quantitative and qualitative influence of the many smaller States which previously either did

[1] See further above, p. 127 and below, p. 162.

not assert an independent policy or did not exist as independent political units. This goes far beyond the policy of so-called 'neutralism', previously formulated by such States as Yugoslavia, India or Egypt, all of which for different reasons wished to assert their independence of the opposing factions in the Cold War. It is not of course surprising that the many new States emerging in Asia and more recently in Africa from previous colonial subjection to the British, French, Belgian or Dutch empires, should assert independent positions in international policy questions, inside and outside the United Nations. It is perhaps more remarkable that the nations of Latin America, which have traditionally been under the political and economic shadow of the United States, have become more and more independent, sometimes to the point of acute conflict with the United States. An entirely new factor entered international politics when Cuba, the closest neighbour of the United States, became in 1962 the spearhead of a Communist strategic move against the United States. And while in the case of Cuba it is the United States who has taken the initiative in the rupture of diplomatic and economic relations, it is the small republic of Panama, created in 1903 under United States auspices, after its secession from Colombia, which temporarily broke off diplomatic relations with its giant neighbour, over the refusal of the latter to commit itself in advance to a revision of the Panama Canal Treaty. Less extreme tensions have arisen from the nationalization or cancellation of concessions of American and other Western-owned enterprises in Argentina, Brazil or Peru.

Such is today the collective and individual independence of action on the part of the smaller Powers that many of them can afford to antagonize the United States politically, while expecting the continuation of economic aid from the very same country and from international institutions in which the United States plays a leading role. Thus Panama coupled her rupture of diplomatic relations with the United States with the expression of the expectation that economic aid and U.S. Peace Corps work would continue. It is entirely possible that countries such as Argentina, Indonesia, Panama and others, which take strong political actions in opposition to the United States, in the expectation that this will not affect economic aid, might overplay their hand. Public and Congressional opinion in the United States is becoming increasingly hostile to the whole concept of a moral and political obligation to grant economic assistance to the underdeveloped world, and it may be driven to actions as irrational and destructive of healthy international co-operation as those that count on continued United States assistance, regardless of their own political posture. But this new international power situation is explained by factors far transcending in importance the whims or immaturities of this or that nation and its leaders: its basic factor is the fundamental change in the significance of power in international relations. In the days of Lord Palmerston, Great Britain could threaten military action against Greece because of an alleged injustice done to a shady British subject called Don Pacifico. In 1964 the United States did not consider any military reprisal against the high-handed action of a 27-year-old military adventurer of the tiny island of Zanzibar, who arrested at gunpoint an American diplomat and several American newsmen. Militarily, one or two naval units of the U.S. fleet could have coerced the island into submission. But politically, the ability to use military power becomes inversely proportionate to the magnitude of such power. This is due not only to the fear of countermoves by another major military power, and the consequent dangers of a major, even nuclear, war. It is equally due to the fierce opposition that any military move by a vastly superior against a small, especially an ex-colonial, State would produce in the now preponderant number of medium or smaller Powers in Asia, Africa or Latin America. Overwhelming military power, as it is today possessed by the United States and the Soviet Union, is — fortunately for the peace of the world — an inhibiting factor, which calls for restraint, not for arrogance. And consequently, in direct confrontations, as in the delicate Berlin situation or in Cuba, the major Powers have tended to refrain from extreme exploitations of a tactical advantage. But by the same token, many of the small Powers, uninhibited by the awesome burden of the responsibility of power, act with impunity and even irresponsibility, because they know that the major military powers will go to extreme lengths in not letting local or specialized conflicts develop into a major conflagration. This is not a healthy situation, since it is based on a stark discrepancy between responsibility and political action. As will be discussed further in other sections, the consequences may be an increasing tendency on the part of the major Powers to settle important affairs outside the United Nations, where the medium and smaller Powers have a disproportionately large influence, or even a growing trend towards joint action by the big Powers outside the United Nations in the way in which they were supposed to have acted as a joint policeman of the world, in the original conception of the United Nations Charter. Such fluidity and impunity of movement would immediately disappear in the case of actual war, when the lines would be firmly drawn and when real military and economic power would be decisive. But since such a development would almost certainly spell catastrophe in the conditions of modern war, it is not likely to occur. Meanwhile, the smaller States can engage in local or limited hostilities, in the calculation that the major Powers will do everything not to let such conflicts develop to world-wide proportions.

Nuclear Weapons and World Peace

Previous predictions that the destructiveness of modern war would be a guarantee of peace have proved wrong. The last two world wars have shown how the scale of physical destruction as well as the scope of modern warfare has steadily expanded. In the last world war civilian populations were almost as much the target of enemy attacks as the armed forces. On the other hand, the civilians took a very much more active part in the defence of their countries than ever before. The legal concept of 'military objectives' melted away with the increasing concentration of attacks by both sides on cities, communications and the morale of the civilian population. Bombing from the air, inevitably more indiscriminate than war on land or on the seas, greatly widened the physical scope of warfare. At the same time unprecedented attention was given to moral and psychological warfare. Everything was subordinated to the attempt to subdue the enemy militarily, economically and morally. But the likelihood that this would happen did not prevent war in 1939. Has the advent of nuclear warfare altered the prospects? Have the terror and destructiveness of modern weapons at last reached a scale which might act as an effective deterrent against major wars? This is, in fact, the thesis which has been put forward in recent years not by pacifists or wishful thinkers but by military experts with great experience and responsibility in modern war. Modern atom bombs have many times the destructiveness of the atom bomb that destroyed the

Japanese city of Hiroshima in 1945. The hydrogen bomb has many times the destructiveness of the atom bomb. It is estimated that about twelve of them could virtually destroy Great Britain's industry and cities. To the destructiveness of hydrogen bombs delivered by air must be added the prospects of accurately guided long-range missiles with nuclear warheads, and the ghastly possibilities of bacteriological warfare which might destroy a major part of the food production of any country. There is some argument as to the extent to which civil defence is possible against major attacks of this sort. There is also some doubt as to how effectively automatic defence weapons intercepting enemy bombers could become. But there is hardly any doubt among scientists or military experts that the minimum scale of destruction of any major war would completely dwarf the destruction achieved in the last stages of the previous world war, when entire cities were laid in ruins.

From such a state of affairs follow three possible courses of action: one would be the unleashing of a war of aggression by any one Power because its government is convinced of its ability to deal a decisive knock-out blow before the other side has had a chance to bring its countervailing power into operation. In the present stage of preparedness, in both the Communist and the anti-Communist camps, such an action could only be characterized as madness. But as recent history has shown, sheer madness can determine the fate of nations. Hitler's megalomania was coupled with a nihilism that contemplated total destruction with sadistic satisfaction. As has been pointed out earlier in this book, there is little indication that the Soviet leaders, trained in an essentially rationalistic and, at least in its original inspiration, humanistic faith, have similar visions. The record to date shows clearly that Communist leaders look upon military power as a necessary policy weapon, but not as an end in itself.

A war arising from sheer megalomania, over-confidence or madness cannot, unfortunately, be excluded from the realm of possibilities. Far more actual, however, is the danger of a major war arising from an originally limited engagement from which neither side feels able to withdraw. In 1955 and again in 1958 such a danger became clearly apparent when the United States and Communist China took up adamant and irreconcilable positions over the defence of some small islands off the mainland of

China. While, for the time being, Communist China is not pressing the challenge, such situations might arise again, especially in the disputed and important areas of South-east Asia. It may not be possible to achieve again the relative restraint of the Korean war. An action intended to be limited on both sides may spread until the major Powers of the world become involved. The difficulty of containing a conflict in which the chief antagonists of the Cold War have important interests at stake forms the chief objection to the theory of 'limited war' which has been much discussed in recent years, especially in the United States. In large part, this discussion has been a salutary reaction to the official United States policy of placing increasing reliance on the major nuclear deterrent, at the expense of conventional forces. Exclusive or predominant reliance on nuclear deterrents would mean that there would be little, if any, room for manoeuvre between the alternatives of a mutual war of total destruction and surrender. It is also true that, on several recent occasions, such as the war in Vietnam, the interventions by Britain and France in the Suez Canal crisis, and above all, the Korean war, hostilities have stopped short of the use of nuclear weapons in an all-out effort at total destruction of the enemy. But then the objectives of these conflicts were also limited, and in no case were the two leaders of the antagonistic coalitions, the United States and the Soviet Union, both directly engaged. In a conflict over Berlin and Germany, where they would face each other directly, there would also be initial reluctance to use nuclear bombs. But not only is the borderline between 'tactical' and 'strategic' nuclear weapons somewhat fluid. It is also unlikely that either of the two Powers would watch the loss of a major position without resorting to the most effective weapons at its disposal. And here the greater dilemma faces the West, which is inferior to the Communist bloc in conventional forces. It is the recognition of the incalculable dangers arising from escalation, the spread of an originally 'limited' war, that has so far induced the major Powers to move with great circumspection in the use of even limited force lest the fire spread beyond control.

A much-discussed possibility, and one which emotionally appeals most to a great majority of mankind, would be the abolition of nuclear weapons, coupled with a system of international control and inspection. The outlawing of nuclear weapons and destruction of existing stocks have been persistently proposed by the Soviet Union, at least until recently, and it is explained by the obvious desire of a Power then inferior in such weapons to eliminate the advantage of its opponents. Such an agreement, unsupported by an international control system, would have left the Western Powers at the mercy of the Communist Powers. But even if an effective system of control and inspection could be devised, the limitation of disarmament to nuclear weapons would pose great problems to the Western Powers. For a variety of reasons, they are bound to remain vastly inferior to the Communist bloc in the potential strength of land armies. The restraints which the power of mutual destruction by nuclear weapons imposes on the potential belligerents today would be eliminated by a temptation for the Power that is stronger in conventional weapons to use that superiority. It has, therefore, been rightly argued by Sir John Slessor and others that an agreement on the part of the West to outlaw nuclear weapons would be an act of suicide. An effective agreement supported by international control on disarmament in general would, of course, be a different matter. The reduction of armament to a level which would leave neither side at the mercy or crushing superiority of the other, but retain, on a far lower level of armaments, enough equality or deterrent power to make such a war unlikely, would be welcomed for psychological and economic as well as political reasons. The major Powers have met periodically to discuss ways of disarmament. It is, however, very unlikely that any effective disarmament system can be devised without an adequate international control system which is really part of the wider problem of international security. Both the problem of an international military force and of an international control of atomic energy were amply debated in the first few years of the United Nations. Neither an international military force — for which the United Nations Charter specifically provides — nor an international control agency over atomic energy materialized. The reason is basically the same which has accounted for the persistent use of the veto power by the Soviet Union, and the consequent paralysis of the Security Council: the inability of the great Powers to agree and trust each other in major matters of policy. It is difficult to see how such trust and collaboration could be achieved in the field of nuclear and other military weapons and organizations if it has been impossible to attain it in other spheres. So much are weapons and military forces linked up with the general industrial production of a country that no effective control system can be devised which does not entail far-reaching powers of inspection over industrial production. This the Soviet Union has consistently refused to accord to an organization in which potentially hostile Powers are represented. There remains, for the time being, the paradox of the major Powers developing all conceivable nuclear weapons to the utmost pitch of perfection and destructiveness, in the hope and belief that the very magnitude of destructiveness stored up in this fashion may prevent a third world war and the likely destruction of modern civilization. And if the thesis *si vis pacem, para bellum* has proved fallacious before in history, the world has never before faced a situation where a few days of full-scale warfare would end civilized life for generations. Nor is it paradoxical that, at the very height of mutual scientific and military operations for an almost inconceivably destructive war, the major Powers should be found more ready than before to get together, in order to find ways of reducing tensions, cautiously and step by step, by collaboration in certain spheres, such as the peaceful use of atomic energy or the joint exploration of outer space, by the removal of some at least of the trade barriers which have split the world economically as well as politically into two separate armed camps, by a formal agreement not to press national claims in the Antarctic and by the encouragement of official and unofficial contacts between politicians, scientists, educators and others. On the other hand, the danger of a dissemination of nuclear weapons among a growing number of nations increases year by year. The detonation of China's first atomic bomb, in October 1964, immediately provoked pressure in India to develop her nuclear research for military purposes. Both Germanies, Egypt and Israel are, among other States, capable of developing nuclear bombs, and might be tempted to do so by international tensions. The speed of nuclear weapons immensely increases the danger of a world war started by a local or regional conflict.

Progress in a Divided World

A world dominated by political and ideological strife is an uncomfortable world, constantly living in danger of annihilation.

But it is not a static world. The strife between the big Powers has already produced some overdue moves for the unification of Europe. It has done more than decades of propaganda to awaken the United States to the responsibilities of the world's greatest economic Power. It accelerates the industrial development of backward areas and impoverished peoples; but, above all, the fear of Communism is compelling the democracies to shake off lethargy and self-complacency. They must respond to the Soviet challenge by more than mere physical or military countermeasures. Political franchise, voting rights, parliamentary democracy are essential conditions of genuine democractic society, but they are no longer recognized as sufficient by the great majority of modern men and nations. Sheer physical force can, of course, bring a nation into the one or the other camp and ignore the free choice of the peoples. This has happened to Czechoslovakia and other States of Central and Eastern Europe. But outside this sphere, in Eastern Europe, and even more in Asia, the struggle goes on. Ultimately the strength of the Communist appeal, whether in France, Italy, India or Latin America, will depend on which side has more to offer in the way of good and honest government, of economic development, of social justice and a worthwhile life. But no less important will be the ability to inspire the articulate minorities which will lead the millions of Europe, Asia, Africa and direct their growing restiveness into one or the other channel. The Marshall Aid Plan, development aid outside Europe and the beginnings of an economic and political West European Union are among the positive and constructive answers which democracy has been compelled to give to the Communist challenge. Whether India or Burma will lean towards the Western camp or sink into a condition which favours Communist penetration will largely depend on the soundness of economic development schemes and the improvement of the status of the peasant. The challenge is present everywhere, in the work of UNESCO, in the vast economic aid now going to Africa, Asia and Latin America from the United States direct as well as from various United Nations agencies, in the kind of technical and scientific assistance now offered to many countries by both the U.S.S.R. and the Western Powers, or in the joint ventures in which various highly industrialized countries — the U.S.S.R. as well as the United States, Britain or Germany — participate together with Asian governments in the development of oil wells, steel mills or fertilizer plants. There is no present chance of the bipolar conflict giving way to genuine international collaboration, but there is a chance of the mutual fear of war leading the conflict into the political, social and economic rather than the military sphere.

The avoidance of war, or of a purely destructive struggle for power, presents a tremendous challenge to the Western democracies, and in particular to the United States, whose leadership is not the only but the most important single condition for the survival of the Western democratic world. The Communist group of States led by Soviet Russia have the advantage not only of singleness of purpose, but also of the initial superiority of striking power, which all totalitarian systems enjoy. A few men can direct vast masses into action, and concentrate all available resources swiftly. The many concealed weaknesses inherent in the excessive concentration of power, in the destruction of freedom and the brutality of conquest, become apparent only gradually, perhaps in time to bring ultimate defeat, but not in time to avert war. Similar purposeful and sustained leadership is infinitely more difficult to achieve in the Western democracies. The emergence of the United States from isolation and neutrality to world leadership has been the work of a small far-seeing minority. They have been able to obtain the unstable and shifting support of public opinion by thc exploitation of a number of varying tactical opportunities: the nakedness of Nazi aggression, the Japanese attack on Pearl Harbor, the fear of Communism. But the internal pressures and forces bitterly opposing this policy are very strong. There is the tradition of isolationism, and of aversion to American entanglement in European conflicts. There are recurring rebellions against what appear to the uninformed observer unending American gifts to lazy and disunited foreigners, at the expense of the American taxpayer. There is strong pressure from various well-organized interests, in particular the numerous protected American industries, against the liberalization of American economic policy, without which many other countries cannot pay their way. These different policies do not add up to any logical or consistent total. Sometimes, hysterical accusations against the alleged failure of the American Government to fight Communism and Soviet Russia everywhere, go together with accusations that it is wasting money on Western Europe, or failing to take any positive steps to end the Cold War with Russia. The combined effect of these attacks, however, is constantly threatening the precarious unity and consistency of Western policy. President Roosevelt laid the foundations in educating American public opinion to accept the new responsibilities of the United States as a defender of liberty against tyranny, and as the world's wealthiest nation, which has to distribute its wealth. When Roosevelt's vision of post-war unity of the anti-Fascist coalition faded, Truman, Marshall and Acheson accepted the fact of the split between the Communist and the democratic world, and laid the foundations for a new American policy, designed to buttress the tottering democratic front through political, economic and military assistance. The foundation of this policy is that any agreement with Russia and the Communist front must be based on strength, not weakness; that the building up of this strength is a matter of constant and unflagging efforts on behalf of the United States to give economic and political assistance to all nations fighting for their independence from Soviet domination. This means the surviving Western democracies in the first place, but it also includes Tito's Yugoslavia, or those Asian or African nations which are not yet irrevocably within the Communist camp. It is however essential for the leaders of all the Western nations, and particularly for those of the United States, to be aware of the fluidity of the international conflict and the balance of power configuration. President Kennedy, during his tragically short tenure of office, made some important, though tentative, moves towards a greater flexibility of American policy. Although he was compelled to lead his nation — and with it, most of the rest of the world — nearer to the brink of a third world war than any other leader, when confronted with a direct Soviet threat in Cuba, in October 1962, he was increasingly aware that 'Cold War' policy might no longer be the only, or even the principal, guiding factor in United States policy. Aware of the changes that both external pressures (mainly from Communist China) and internal developments (rising consumer demands and the growth of a new educated class moving for greater freedom of expression and communication) were putting on Soviet policy and leadership, he used the advantage gained by the United States through the Cuba confrontation to move towards limited areas of agreement and generally reduce the climate of the tension at a time when the Soviet leadership seemed responsive. Partial results were the Nuclear Test Ban Treaty of 1963, certain agreements on limited co-operation in outer space and the consular treaty of 1964. More important perhaps was the beginning of a tacit mutual understanding that the interests of both the United States and the Soviet Union might require a lessening of their tension, in view of pressures from other quarters and in other directions. Among very urgent preoccupations for the United States are the growing restlessness and potential hostility of a number of its Latin American neighbours, and the increasingly complex task of holding the Western Alliance together, let alone develop it, in the face of reduced threats from outside and the growing independence of America's European partners, notably of de Gaulle's France. For both the United States and the Soviet Union, the giant shadow of an increasingly independent Communist China poses new problems. What for the Soviet Union is a potential but direct threat from her giant neighbour, inducing stronger efforts to reduce tensions with the West, poses for the United States anew the question of the costly and frustrating maintenance of military, economic and political efforts to sustain tottering anti-Communist regimes in many parts of Asia. While the United States is far too deeply engaged in South Vietnam, in Thailand, South Korea and Taiwan, to abandon support, it is conceivable that long term strategy might compel a concentration of effort and resources, that efforts to contain Communist China in the Asian region, might become increasingly unmanageable short of another world war, and that that United States might have to concentrate its military, political and economic efforts on the improvement of its ties within the American hemisphere and Western Europe. And it is by no means impossible that the Soviet Union might find itself in an intermediate position between an increasingly threatening Communist China and a less hostile but still antagonistic Western, Atlantic Alliance. Quite apart from illusions of French grandeur, it is a realization of the shift in the international configuration that may have induced General de Gaulle to give diplomatic recognition to Communist China and to work for a neutralization of South-east Asia. Such a policy is of course unacceptable to the United States, as long as it is determined to resist Chinese pressure everywhere in Asia, and hopeful of achieving this end. If such expectations vanish — as well they might — the policy of neutralization might become a prelude to a gradual withdrawal of Western political and military influence from Asia. The Orwellian vision of three major empires, Oceania, Eurasia and Eastasia, might approximate reality even before 1984. But there are obviously too many uncertainties in the policies of the major actors, notably in the direction of United States policy, Soviet policy and the extent of West European integration, to make any definite predictions. The only certainty is the continuity of a challenge that requires constant reorientation of political thinking. This, despite a few extravagant statements about 'liberation' or 'massive retaliation', has been the policy of successive U.S. governments.

There is, finally, a less dramatic but ultimately more deadly danger. In trying to meet the Communist challenge, the Western Powers have already had to depart considerably from the idea of a democratic front of Powers united in their basic beliefs and values. They have already had to urge rearmament on their former enemies, Germany and Japan — whose lasting disarmament was one of the major objectives of the Second World War. They have accepted Franco's Spain as half an ally. Every intensification of the Cold War would reduce the ideological elements and emphasize the struggle for power.

Already the degree to which new inventions and scientific research determine modern warfare is visibly impeding freedom and research and thought in the Western democracies. The danger of regimentation of intellectual and spiritual life is increased in proportion to the intensity of the anti-Soviet and anti-Communist crusade. Under the label of anti-Communist activities, independent progressive thought and the freedom of political discussion have been endangered. With that, the only real safeguard against the tendency towards mass regimentation, which is inherent in the development of modern society, becomes progressively weaker. There is a definite danger that the conflict between the two groups of Powers, thinly masked by such formulas as democracy versus dictatorship, or liberty versus the slave State, may produce an increasing likeness, that on either side a small hierarchy of military, scientific, industrial and political leaders may exercise an increasingly absolute control over the public and private life of the community. In such a society, as George Orwell has trenchantly put it,[1] the object of power is power.

[1] *1984*, by George Orwell (1949).

PART II — REGIONAL ASPECTS OF WORLD POLITICS

CHAPTER 5

POLICY PROBLEMS IN EUROPE AND THE NEAR EAST

THE growing fluidity of the international situation has increased the importance of the policies and problems of the Western allies of the United States, and of other European States which have no clear alignment in the power conflict.

British Problems

With a population of about fifty-two million, the United Kingdom is the second most populous European State outside Soviet Russia (exceeded only by the population of West Germany). The importance of Britain rests, however, mainly on her intense industrialization, on the social and political cohesion which generally makes her a far more powerful international force than suggested by her size, on her still considerable naval and air power, on the moral prestige of her centuries of political experience and international leadership, on her still important position as the centre of the British Commonwealth of Nations.[1]

Modern British policy in Europe is faced with two great problems. The first results from Britain's inability to preserve the traditional policy of 'balance of power' without definite commitments. The other results from her ideological position between the totalitarian State Socialism of Soviet Russia and the 'free enterprise' democracy of the U.S.A. In former centuries Britain could afford to follow a policy of interested aloofness from European affairs. She was powerful and geographically safe enough to look with detachment upon the Continent as long as it was not dominated by one Power. Her policy consequently was to be distrustful of, and if necessary hostile to, the strongest Continental Power, by supporting the weaker side. This policy was threatened by the emergence of modern Germany as a Power able singly to

[1] Cf. below, Ch. 7.

defeat the Continent outside Russia. In the last two wars Britain had to join a world-wide coalition of nations in order to break this predominance. The present emergence of Russia as by far the strongest European Power, and the weakening of Britain's military and economic position in the world, have brought the policy of relative detachment to final collapse. Britain cannot afford to act at the last minute. She must form alliances and associations with other nations to restore a reasonable balance of power in post-war Europe. No association without the active participation of the United States can achieve this position. It is a change of historic importance from which Britain cannot retreat. It means the choice of allies, which is not made easier by her own social and political evolution.

Britain has been gradually and reluctantly forced by post-war developments to give up hope, first, of genuine inter-Allied collaboration, and, secondly, of preserving a non-committal and neutral attitude in the antagonism between the Soviet Union and the United States. Opposed to the totalitarian government of Soviet Russia, but also differing strongly from American political and social philosophy, she has come to consider post-war Russia as a far greater danger to her national and ideological independence than the United States. This has led to some acute dilemmas, as in West Germany, where Britain has been a reluctant follower of United States policy. But on the whole there can be no doubt that the combination of political freedom and social progress, which is contemporary Britain's main aim, would be in far greater jeopardy from close association with Soviet Russia than with the United States. When a Conservative Government is in power in Great Britain, American suspicions of British sympathies for Socialism, or appeasement of Communism, tend to be less acute than when Labour governs. Yet recent experience has shown that social and international facts dominate the position of Britain far more than conflicts of political philosophy, party polemics or the differences in approach and personality between Churchill and Attlee, Macmillan and Gaitskell, Home and Wilson. The foundations of a Welfare State are firmly laid. Nor can the policy of Conservative and Labour Governments differ materially on such matters as Britain's chronic shortage of raw materials, her dependence on a large volume of exports, the threat to the stability of sterling, or on British policy in Europe, the Middle

East or the Far East. The dominating fact is the reduced economic and military power of Britain, which makes her increasingly dependent on American assistance and dictates caution in meeting breaches of international treaties or vital threats to British interests, of which the expropriation of the Anglo-Iranian Oil Company and the Egyptian nationalization of the Suez Canal Zone are recent examples. Even half a century ago Britain would have answered such threats by forceful and, if necessary, military action, but today Britain must either accept humiliations in dealing with all but the most extreme threats, or seek closer international associations. The abortive and humiliating Franco-British military intervention in the Suez Canal crisis of 1956 showed that no such action is now feasible, against the opposition of the super-Powers and world opinion. Britain can no longer stand alone and detached. She cannot join the Soviet group without abandoning her fundamental political beliefs. She must therefore seek closer associations in a three-cornered relationship with the U.S.A., the non-Communist nations of Europe, and the non-European members of the British Commonwealth of Nations. As will be shown in a subsequent chapter,[1] the British Commonwealth of Nations is still very much a reality, though not as a military Power. In a shrinking Europe menaced by swift and overwhelming aggression, the close association of Britain with what remains of Europe outside the Soviet sphere is an absolute necessity. But, unlike the Soviet bloc, the nations of Western Europe retain their distinct identity and a great diversity of political and social systems. Moreover, the power conflict has divided Europe in such a manner that the nations with which Britain can and must seek closer association cannot form a strong enough and self-sufficient military and economic entity. In the last few years the number of voices, both in continental Europe and in Great Britain, which have pleaded for a more independent British–European policy, has greatly increased. Several factors have strengthened such tendencies: the inevitable distrust of the overwhelming power of the United States, benevolent and indispensable though it may be, is particularly strong in countries that feel themselves displaced from centuries of supremacy. The more conciliatory tone of Soviet foreign policy since Stalin's death has strengthened the belief in many

[1] Below, Ch. 7.

quarters that the Cold War, even a relatively mild Cold War, is not an inevitable necessity of present-day politics, but one that can be mitigated by patient negotiations and mutual concessions. These feelings are particularly strong in British Labour circles but by no means confined to them. Added to this is the deep-seated distrust of German rearmament and of the increasingly powerful military role of West Germany's twelve divisions in NATO. To all this must be added the ever-growing fear of the annihilating effect of modern war on any highly industrialized country.

Yet the policy which, in any decisive test, has, of necessity, prevailed so far and determined the direction of British politics is based on the sober insight that Western Europe, even including Great Britain, is neither economically nor militarily a match for the monolithic pressure of the Communist bloc, unless it is firmly associated with the United States and Canada. On the need for such firm and lasting association, there is not much disagreement between the Conservative, Labour and Liberal parties. There is, however, considerable internal disagreement on the extent to which Britain should maintain and develop an independent military posture, especially through the maintenance of a national nuclear force, or depend entirely on the superior resources of the United States, largely through NATO, and in part through a cherished but fading special privileged association between Britain and the United States, which dates back to the days of close military and scientific collaboration during the war. At this time Conservative policy leans towards the maintenance of an independent force, while official Labour policy seems committed to its abandonment. While the Conservative Government gave halting and tentative support to the American proposal for a mixed surface fleet under NATO auspices, equipped with Polaris missiles, military leaders doubt both the military wisdom of a highly vulnerable surface missile fleet, and the possibility of a truly joint operation of this American-controlled weapon. Their belief that a decision to use it — which would inevitably mean a nuclear holocaust — will ultimately have to be made by the President of the United States, and that total reliance on this operation by any other Power would therefore render such power dependent on an American decision, is reinforced by the political opposition of the Labour Government — led by Harold Wilson — to any scheme designed to give West Germany a share in nuclear weapons.

Economically, the dependence of Britain on American support, which was extremely strong in the first decade following the last world war and the exhaustion of Britain's resources, has considerably lessened. But Britain continues to be plagued by periodic balance of payments crises provoked by the gap between the import demands of a rising standard of living and the relatively slow rise of Britain's exports. Britain, comparable in her dependence on growing exports to West Germany and Japan, has been less successful than either of these two countries in meeting the challenge. Sterling remains one of the two major world currencies. The gap between the recurrent weaknesses of the Sterling Area, and the formerly overwhelming strength of the American dollar has greatly narrowed since the series of annual deficits in the American balance of payments, caused largely by the massive size of American expenditures for military establishments and economic aid in other parts of the world. At the same time, a number of agreements between the Central Banks of the major Western financial powers, by which they hold certain amounts of each others' currencies in reserve, for use in emergencies that might arise in the one or the other system, has lessened the danger of sudden slumps of sterling, as of other major currencies, as they have periodically occurred in former times.[1]

The major unsolved problem of Britain's international associations remains her relation to continental Western Europe. When the first of the Western European communities, the Coal and Steel Community, was established in 1951, all its members were extremely anxious for Britain to join. Neither Conservative nor Labour leaders in Britain rose to this challenge. Traditional British aloofness from close political ties with the Continent was reinforced by erroneous doubts about the viability of the new Community. When the Coal and Steel Community, and after an uncertain interval of several years, the new Economic Community developed an unexpected speed of progress and sense of cohesion, large segments of British political and economic leaderships and of public opinion became aware, a decade after the original invita-

[1] The importance of these arrangements was dramatically illustrated when in November 1964 the Central Banks of eleven Western countries provided a $3 billion stand-by credit for Britain to counter a run on the pound caused by lack of confidence in her economic position.

tion, of the necessity for a full association of Britain with the Communities. This was not a party matter. Both the Conservative and Labour parties were deeply split between supporters and opponents of such a move, as were the economic and social organizations of Britain. British industrialists in their great majority favoured a move for membership in the Communities, because of the growing strength of the European Common Market and the increased opportunities for export and investment for a Britain that would be inside, not outside, a common European tariff wall. The agricultural interests were almost unanimously opposed, because of the threat from the competition of Continental agriculture, without tariff protection. Organized labour was divided and on the whole sceptical. The main problem was the impact of British membership of the European Communities upon her political and economic relations with the Commonwealth. Australia, Canada and New Zealand, although claiming for themselves the full privileges of national determination of their trade and economic relations with other countries, protested against the possible threat to their traditional exports to Britain, from an abolition of the preferential Ottawa tariff agreed upon in 1931. Important segments of British public opinion — cutting across party lines — protested against the further weakening of Commonwealth ties for the sake of what seemed to them a politically risky association with Continental Europe. The Conservative Macmillan Government decided however in favour of an application by Britain for admission to the Common Market. This application was qualified by considerable reservations, a request for lengthy periods of transition, and the gradual reduction of preferential tariffs for the Commonwealth. Nor had the constitutional and legal implications of a full association of Britain with the European Economic Community been worked out, especially in the event of a political confederation. But steady progress was being made towards the elimination of these various obstacles, by continued negotiations between Britain and the members of the Community, when on January 14, 1963, General de Gaulle delivered the famous speech by which France — whose consent to the admission of a new member is required by the EEC Treaty — flatly barred Britain's application for membership. His principal ground was the alleged unreadiness of Britain to accept the political and constitutional implications of an integrated Western Europe. The real motivations of a man whose resentment against '*les Anglo-Saxons*' can be gathered from his memoirs as well as from many recent actions, and whose devotion to a fully integrated European community is conspicuously absent, may have been of a very different nature. Since de Gaulle's speech, British membership of the European Community has, for the time being, ceased to be a question of practical policy. At least as long as de Gaulle remains in charge of French policy it is very unlikely that either British public opinion could be rallied again in sufficient strength to support a British move for membership, or that the European Community could assume the initiative for such a move. Instead, Britain has reverted to the policies of looser collaboration, expressed in a variety of associations and policies: she is a founder member of the European Free Trade Association (EFTA), an association of Britain and six other European States outside the Community, which among themselves have achieved a far-reaching liberalization of conditions of trade; she is a full and active member of the Organization for European Co-operation and Development (O.E.C.D.) which includes not only a much wider circle of West European States, but also Canada and the United States, and most recently, Japan. She is actively pursuing friendly political and economic relations with the five members of the European Communities other than France, relations notably strengthened since the replacement of Chancellor Adenauer by Ludwig Erhard. While Britain's economic relations with the Common Market remain strong and have indeed expanded in the last few years, her main efforts will now inevitably be directed towards a more general liberalization of trade conditions through the forthcoming negotiations for a revision of the General Agreement on Tariffs and Trade (GATT) and the co-ordination of Atlantic economic policies through O.E.C.D.

The Nationalist Policies of de Gaulle's France

Ever since a united Germany, emerging under the leadership of Bismarck from the victorious war of Prussia against France in 1870, became a national state of great military and economic power, after centuries of division among hundreds of princes and cities, France suffered a steady decline from her position as the leading Continental power. A new Germany overtook France in terms of population, military power and industrial potential.

In two world wars started by Germany, France suffered severely, and she would have succumbed except for the support of an international coalition backed by Britain and the United States, and in the last world war, also by Russia. While France has retained her position as one of the major Western States and as a permanent member of the Security Council of the United Nations, her effective power has been greatly reduced. Until recently a continuous decline in military power was accompanied by a very low birth-rate, leading to an almost stationary population, and by a lag in industrial productivity which caused constant crises of trade and payment balances in this naturally rich country. The weakness of France was accentuated by deep political divisions. After the war a number of conflicting political forces emerged which tended to form six political groups of approximately equal strength, resulting in shifting and weak coalitions which accounted for an extraordinary and debilitating turnover of governments. Between the powerful Communist party on the left, and various Conservative right-wing groups, as well as the Gaullist party on the right, the main pillars of the Fourth Republic were the Socialists, the Radical Socialists and the Christian Democrats. None of these groups of the middle was able to govern singly, or in a stable coalition, for any length of time. At the same time, France was beset by colonial problems which dwarfed those of Britain. Much later than Great Britain, France recognized the need to transform her colonial empire into a looser association which would take account of the nationalist aspirations of the colonies. One irrevocable result of this tardiness was the loss of French Indo-China (now divided into mutually hostile Communist and anti-Communist factions in Vietnam and Laos) after years of costly and unsuccessful warfare which ended in a truce in 1954. But France retained a major empire in Africa.

The African colonies of France were closely linked to her, through economic dependence, military association and the educational and cultural orientation of the African leaders of these colonies. The attainment of full French citizenship for her African subjects remained the goal as well as the limit of the French concessions to the growing nationalism of her colonies.

The return to power of General de Gaulle, France's wartime resistance leader, in January 1958, after more than twelve years of political retirement, was essentially the result of the inability of the Fourth Republic to combine parliamentary democracy and freedom of political expression with the minimum strength and continuity of government necessary to maintain and develop

France's position. In her international policies, France had, through the efforts of Robert Schuman and Jean Monnet, engineered the birth of the European Communities. She was an important and loyal member of the NATO Alliance, acknowledging the military, political and economic leadership of the United States. The former protectorates of Morocco and Tunisia had been granted independence, but the rebellion of Algeria, constitutionally a department of Metropolitan France, showed no signs of solution after five years of warfare between the French and the Arab rebels. During the first few years of de Gaulle's regime, his principal preoccupation was the internal constitutional reform which drastically reduced the functions of Parliament and correspondingly increased the power of the Executive. The President of the Republic, formerly essentially a figurehead, became the effective head of Government, who under a recent constitutional amendment will be directly elected by the people. A drastic weakening of the powers of Parliament, the semi-totalitarian methods of placing the control over the essential media of communication into the hands of the Government and the economic stability and progress of France under de Gaulle — whether attributable to his Government or not — have all contributed to produce during the last six years a degree of stability and continuity in French politics not known for generations. The French currency — for decades one of the weakest of the major currencies — is now one of the strongest, and the gold and foreign exchange reserves of France have risen dramatically. Industrial production and exports have steadily gained, both within the European Common Market and with the world at large. Internationally de Gaulle's principal preoccupation during the first few years was the liquidation of the Algerian rebellion. His first major international action was the grant of independence to the African colonies of France, within a French Commonwealth association that now closely resembles the older pattern of the British Commonwealth of Nations. This dramatic transformation was achieved quickly, peacefully and with a continuing close association of the new states with France, due, in large measure, to the extraordinary economic dependence of these ex-colonies on France. While some of the younger leaders of the French-speaking African states show impatience with this exclusive French association, and move towards a greater degree of independence, there is little sign of any other than an evolutionary process, which may weaken but not destroy the continuing close ties of independent French-speaking Africa with France. African resentment may, however, have been strengthened by France's military intervention in Gabon, in February 1964, reversing a successful *coup d'état* and restoring a deposed ruler. Relations with Morocco and in particular, with Tunisia, which were greatly troubled by bloodshed over the continuing control of the naval harbour of Bizerte, have improved in recent years. There remain important though greatly reduced elements of French settlers and teachers in both these former Protectorates, and France grants some economic assistance to both of them. The Algerian conflict was far more difficult to liquidate. To have settled it, by the pursuit of Algerian independence at the cost of a complete break with the French *colons* and with the powerful group of French military leaders who bitterly opposed Algerian independence, is de Gaulle's major achievement. The Socialist-oriented, independent Algeria, which emerged from the Treaty of Evian of 1962, maintains relatively friendly relations with France, despite unsolved disputes over the control of the increasingly important oil resources of the Sahara desert, explored and administered by France but claimed by Algeria as being within her territorial sovereignty. By and large the liquidation of France's colonial problems in Africa has immensely strengthened her liberty and power of action in other arenas of the world theatre. In retrospect, it becomes abundantly clear that one of the principal motives in de Gaulle's policy of speedy independence for all the remaining African possessions was the desire to reassert a stronger French position and independence of action in the Western world. Here France has, under his ruthless leadership, moved towards a position of increasing independence from, and even antagonism to, the policies of the NATO Alliance, and in particular of the United States. Several years ago de Gaulle took the French Mediterranean Fleet out of the NATO command, thus weakening France's military participation in that organization. The barring of Britain's application for membership in the European Economic Community struck not only at Britain but at United States policy which, under the Kennedy administration, had evolved the 'grand design' of a strengthened NATO Alliance, with the European nucleus being formed by a strong European Community, including Britain. Angered by an American–British monopoly of nuclear weapons within the Western Alliance, de Gaulle decided to develop an independent French nuclear force, a policy which he shows no signs whatsoever of abandoning. Recently he has acted in open opposition to United States policy in several key areas outside Europe. His offer of military and other aid to Cambodia, at a time when Cambodia's relations with the United States are strained, has been accepted by Prince Sihanouk, its volatile ruler. In Vietnam — which like Cambodia was formerly a French colony — France has advocated a policy of unification and eventual neutralization, i.e. a cessation of the conflict between South Vietnam and Communist-controlled North Vietnam, in which the United States is heavily engaged in support of South Vietnam. The recognition of Communist China is in direct opposition to the continuing refusal of the United States to bestow any measure of full official status upon one of the most powerful states of the world. It also indicates a conviction shared by many outside France, that the growing fluidity of the international situation makes the maintenance of Cold War ideology and policy correspondingly futile. But French policy within Europe and the Atlantic Alliance remains the cornerstone of de Gaulle's ambitions. Here his intense nationalism, his almost pathological preoccupation with the glory and grandeur of France as the leading power of Europe and one of the leading powers of the world, has involved him in contradictions which may yet destroy the basic aims of his policy. His hostility to a close association of Britain with Europe, as expressed in his speech of January 14, 1963, has led him to rely more heavily on the associations of Continental Western Europe, despite his strong aversion to any political entity which would in any way derogate from national sovereignty. At least such an integration of Western Europe would be acceptable to de Gaulle only if the undisputed supremacy of France were assured. Since none of the other five members is willing to accede to such a position, de Gaulle has striven to seek a close and exclusive association with Western Germany. While Adenauer, for whom a close Franco-German entente formed the supreme goal of his political life, was Chancellor, de Gaulle was largely successful in the implementation of this objective. In 1962 he succeeded in bringing about the conclusion of a Franco-German Treaty which provided *inter alia* for a close political, military and cultural collaboration. But this treaty — which was probably never warmly endorsed by the majority of Germans — has limited value, since the new political leaders of West Germany have reaffirmed, not only West

Germany's firm association with NATO and in particular with the United States, but also the necessity of associating Britain with the policies and aims of Western Europe. While boldly progressive in the rapid emancipation of France's African colonies and protectorates, de Gaulle's policy with regard to Europe and the Atlantic Alliance is reactionary. It is based on the belief that France can regain a position of national power and sovereignty comparable to that of former centuries. Until now its effect has been mainly destructive. It has decisively weakened the movement towards West European integration and the Atlantic Alliance. France has refused to sign the Nuclear Test Ban Treaty of 1963 and is hostile to any further moves for agreements with the Soviet Union. This is based not so much on hostility to the U.S.S.R. but on the belief that the latter will be compelled by her conflict with Communist China and by her economic weaknesses to seek an accommodation with the West, without any need for moves on the part of the latter.

Thus France under de Gaulle, while stabler and more influential as a nation than for decades, has contributed more than any other member of the Western Alliance to a drastic modification of the pattern of international politics that dominated until a few years ago.

Germany's Key Position

Because of her central position, the clash between Soviet and Western policies, and her potential importance as an ally for either side, Germany has once again become a key problem of world politics. In effect, Germany must now be regarded as divided. The Eastern State, with a population of some 17 millions, is politically, militarily and economically an integral part of the Soviet group. But having lost to Poland its most important agricultural area, which accounted for about 13 per cent of Germany's pre-war agricultural production, and having only slowly recovered from the wholesale dismantling of machinery for reparations, East Germany (the D.D.R.) — more properly called 'Central Germany' — is vastly inferior to West Germany in size or importance. The Federal Republic of Germany (Deutsche Bundesrepublik) has a population of over 57 million people — larger than that of France. Its steel production has overtaken that of France, and the coal production of the Ruhr exceeds half the total coal output of Britain. The many heavy, medium and light industries, as well as the immense concentration of scientific research and technical skill accumulated in that area, are once again playing an important part in world affairs. The original Allied purpose of eliminating Germany as a political and economic Power has long given way to one of deliberate reconstruction. The motive has been twofold: on the one hand, the sheer financial and administrative burden of occupation compelled the Western Allies to help their zones towards greater self-reliance and self-sufficiency; on the other hand, the growing conflict with Russia pushed the objective of reparations and de-industrialization into the background, and increasingly substituted for it the objective of a new and strong partner in a Western coalition. The international tensions of the last few years have greatly accelerated the economic and political revival of West Germany and left the original objectives of military occupation and control as an awkward legacy to be liquidated as painlessly and gracefully as possible. As a result both of the natural vitality of the Germans and of the decisive reversal in Allied post-war policies, West Germany has, politically and economically, forged ahead with increasing momentum, rebuilding her shattered cities, as well as her industrial production, and becoming once again a powerful exporter of finished industrial products on the world market. The *de facto* partition of Germany, which has left most of the agricultural area under Communist control, has increased West Germany's dependence on imports of foodstuffs and other raw materials, and therefore made the struggle for exports of industrial products an even more vital concern than before. In a world which, owing to the post-war scarcity of consumer goods, to such sudden crises as the Korean war and the growing needs and aspirations of the many underdeveloped countries, has, on the whole, been willing to absorb any increased industrial production, this problem has not so far been too critical. West Germany, together with other major European exporters, mainly Great Britain and the smaller Western countries, has steadily increased her exports of automobiles, photographic articles, chemical and steel products, electro-technical products, and others. In recent years she has become an important source of economic aid to underdeveloped countries, through long-term loans, technical assistance and government-backed investment guarantees and export credit insurance designed to help investment and trade with the developing countries. The West German mark is now one of the world's strongest currencies. The competition between countries which are at the same time trying to form closer political links with each other has not yet become deadly. It might become so when conditions alter. Politically, West Germany has regained full sovereignty. With the ratification of the Paris and Bonn Agreements of 1952 and 1954, the remnants of the prerogatives of Germany's conquerors disappeared. Foreign armed forces remain stationed on West German territory, no longer as part of the prerogatives of the occupying Powers, but by virtue of a free agreement between the Federal Republic of West Germany and the other Powers concerned, with whom she is now linked in the NATO Alliance. In the same way, the West German Republic has committed itself to certain restrictions in the field of military production and armaments.[1] In 1949 West Germany joined the Council of Europe. More important was her association, as one of the three major partners, with the European Coal and Steel Community in 1952, and subsequently with Euratom and the European Community. Her twelve divisions are by far the strongest contingent of NATO's land forces, thus adding military strength to West Germany's industrial and political power. While the split between the U.S.S.R. and the West over the status of East Germany has so far prevented German membership in the United Nations, West Germany is an influential member of the World Bank, the International Monetary Fund, and other special United Nations Agencies.

Yet a state of uncertainty and uneasiness about the future of Germany lurks under the surface of bustling activity and high prosperity. The causes for this state of uncertainty and uneasiness, at the very time when Western Germany has obtained a status of free and equal association with the West, and a degree of political and economic power undreamt of fifteen years ago, may be

[1] West Germany's increasing desire to participate in the nuclear weapons of NATO without an open violation of her solemn renunciation of nuclear weapons is the principal reason for the American multilateral nuclear Polaris-equipped naval project (MLF). West Germany is the only enthusiastic supporter of a plan which is bitterly attacked by the U.S.S.R., and viewed with great scepticism by Britain, France and other NATO allies, who fear Germany's growing military power and doubt that the control over the use of Polaris missiles can be shared between ten or more nations.

briefly summarized as follows: first, and most widespread, is the growing strength of German sentiment for the reunification of the two divided Germanies. It is not weakened — though it is frustrated — by the realization that with every year that the Cold War continues, the partition hardens and reunification by peaceful means recedes further. The sentiment for reunification is more powerful in East Germany, where reunification must appear to a great majority of the people as the one way out of permanent and enforced association with the Communist world. The ties of blood, language, institutions, law and traditions which led to the reunification of Germany in 1870, after centuries of division into many states, principalities and cities, are strong and natural. In the present condition of Germany, the general urge for reunification is not, however, supported with equal strength by all sections of opinion. Catholicism is much stronger in West Germany, where, even after the influx of millions of mainly Protestant refugees from the East, it comprises half the total population. The dominant Government party, the Christian Democratic Party, is overwhelmingly Catholic in orientation, and the influence of the clergy is strong. Old ties of religion, civilization, politics and law with Western Europe make the majority of Catholics in West Germany look with greater fervour upon an association that would bring West Germany together with the predominantly Latin and Catholic nations of Western Europe and reaffirm the ties of a Christian civilization. The same circles look upon the reunion with a fundamentally different Protestant part of Germany with considerably greater coolness (a coolness that cannot, however, be acknowledged publicly). On the other hand, the Protestant Church, as well as the Social Democratic Party, which counts the bulk of the organized working class among its adherents, have their main strength in East Germany and Berlin, and their relative position in a reunited Germany would be stronger than it is in a divided Germany. Faced with the stark alternative of subjection to Communist influence or a firm association with the West, the Social Democrats would however prefer the latter, especially if they were faced with such a decision as a Government rather than as an Opposition party.

Another section — only potentially important — would prefer a Germany poised between the Eastern and Western blocs, uncommitted to either and able to pursue a policy of balance guided by her own national interests. This attitude recalls the policies of Bismarck, who consolidated the strength of a newly reunited Germany in a skilful balance-of-power strategy between East and West. All too many forget that under Bismarck's lesser successors this policy quickly collapsed and soon led to the catastrophe of the First World War. Many Ruhr industrialists look eagerly to East European markets which a political agreement with the Soviet group might open up. Undoubtedly an economic depression in the Western world would greatly strengthen pressure in that direction.

There is a small, presently unimportant, but potentially influential group which does not believe in any balancing policy for Germany and thinks of another German–Russian alignment. The combined power of such a coalition — which was a distinct possibility until Hitler's supreme act of insanity, the invasion of the Soviet Union in 1941 — would be overwhelming. Certain military leaders and geopoliticians, in Germany as well as in Russia, have always favoured such a consolidation of the greatest single land and power coalition of Europe, one which would bring together an overwhelming potential of military, industrial and population strength. Conflicting ideologies do not deter these circles, and, at any rate, extreme nationalist and extreme Communist ideology have more points of contact than more moderate political opinions.

Pacifist sentiment, powerful in the first decade following Germany's defeat, has receded under the impact of continuing rearmament and close association with the Western Alliance. But it has not — at least not yet — given way to a widespread revival of militarism. The present generation of Germans has seen physical destruction, political collapse and moral disintegration overwhelm Germany in a way which no previous generation of modern Germans has witnessed. For the first time in modern German history a majority of the young generation, students, workers, church movements and others, have looked for an alternative to the ideology of militant nationalism and the worship of military glory. They found it mostly in the ideal of European unity and a new era of Franco-German relations. Much of this enthusiasm has waned, but no significant alternative has emerged. Meanwhile, Germans continue to concentrate on the immediate tasks of economic expansion. The contemporary visitor to West Germany cannot fail to be impressed by the apparent absence of the militarist outlook, and the revival of the type of non-political German that used to be regarded as characteristic before the reunification of the German Reich. Yet there is deep uncertainty as to what change in this atmosphere actual German rearmament might bring. Whether rearmament will revive slumbering instincts, nobody knows. Future German developments will be decisively influenced by Soviet policy. For several years, Soviet propaganda hammered the scheme of German reunification, with the obvious purpose of strengthening West German opposition to Adenauer's pro-Western policy. It was always very doubful whether the Soviet Union would agree to free all-German elections, at the risk of losing control over East Germany. When West Germany joined NATO and the Western Union in 1955, the Soviet line changed. It now favours the existence of two separate German States, and the Soviet Union has established diplomatic relations with West Germany. It wishes to postpone the whole issue of German reunification until an all-European security system has been established and NATO has been dissolved. In short, present Soviet policy prefers continued partition to a united, anti-Communist Germany, unless such a reunited Germany renounced membership of NATO and became at least 'neutralist'. Western policy has no reason either to press for reunification, which would recreate a more powerful Germany with a doubtful attitude towards continued Western associations, but the Western Powers have been forced into advocacy of German reunification by the need to support the political leaders of West Germany, who — whatever their personal views may be — must reflect the strong pro-unification sentiment in their country. All this creates a highly complex psychological and political situation, a chess game in which both players seek to conceal their moves.

With every year that passes, the association of West Germany with Western Europe and the North Atlantic Community becomes more firmly established — in terms of political community, military links, trade relations and cultural contacts. On the other side, the East German Republic becomes more firmly integrated with the Communist bloc, in which its political and industrial importance has increased considerably during recent years. It is now highly unlikely that any West German Government would take West Germany out of the European Communities, or sever the links with NATO, except under a radical reorganization of the whole European security system — which could only be the result of successful negotiations with the Soviet Union. It is equally unlikely that the Soviet Union, especially after the Hungarian experience of 1956, would abandon control over East Germany — whose Communist Government, though certainly not based on the free will of its people, is nevertheless the effective government of the country — like a multitude of undemocratic and objectionable governments elsewhere in the world. In the post-Stalin era, the Soviet Union has increasingly tended to recognize this reality by abandoning its former attempts to force West Germany out of its Western associations, but demanding in return the recognition of East Germany. Between the two separate German States, Berlin continues to occupy a difficult and potentially explosive position. After the unsuccessful attempt to throw the West out of Berlin, and absorb the city into East Germany, made in the blockade of 1948, Soviet policy has reluctantly come to concede the continued existence of an anti-Communist West Berlin, with over two and a quarter million inhabitants, and an outpost of non-Communist ideology and ways of life, which has been bolstered by the vast inflow of aid from the West German Republic and from public and private United States assistance. Krushchev repeatedly proposed an international guarantee for the status of West Berlin, which might be backed by the presence of a United Nations force. But the Soviet Union wishes to couple such a recognition of the status of West Berlin not only with the formal recognition of East Germany, but with the recognition of East Berlin as the capital of that state. It is conceivable that West Germany and the other Western powers might consider an international guarantee of the status of the city of Berlin — comprising both West and East Berlin — as a third unit, forming part neither of West nor of East Germany. But the West has never acknowledged the permanence of the partition of Berlin — any more than that of Germany as a whole. In 1961 the East German Government, with the backing of the Soviet Union, moved unilaterally to emphasize the partition between East and West Berlin, by erecting the notorious wall which makes any movement between the two parts of the city impossible, except at the risk of death, or by permission of the authorities — hitherto granted once in 1963 and once in 1964, for the visits of

West Berliners to friends and relatives in East Berlin. Although the primary motive for this brutal act of truncation was unquestionably the continued outflow of skilled professionals, scholars, technicians, workers and others vital to the East German economy, it has physically underlined the partition between the Communist and the anti-Communist parts of Germany. But whereas the border between West and East Germany is geographically one that is not essentially different from the frontiers drawn, more or less artificially, between dozens of other national States, the partition of Berlin cuts right across a city as a living and organic unit. It symbolizes with particular brutality the uneasy situation of a world which cannot solve its political and ideological conflicts with co-operation or unity but hesitates to push them to the point of war, which in contemporary conditions would almost certainly mean universal annihilation.

The belief that the partition of Europe and Germany into two different political and economic worlds is a more than transitory fact has the logic of reality behind it. While the Western Powers cannot now abandon the protection of West Berlin, which, during and after the Soviet blockade of 1948, they helped to survive and develop into an impressive bastion of Western freedom, they can hardly indefinitely refuse to recognize the reality of the partition without attempting to alter the present status. Indeed, in terms of consular and trade relations, of civilian passport controls, of calculations in the political and military balance of power, the partition of Germany has come to be accepted as one of the major political changes of our generation. It is admitted by the West German Government as a fact — except for formal recognition, the denial of which is meant to symbolize the continuing aspiration of German reunification. But short of a war which would immediately assume world-wide proportions, and therefore submerge the issue of German unification in a far greater holocaust, Soviet Russia will not abandon political control over East Germany, except in return for the neutralization of Germany or other concessions unacceptable to West Germany and the Western Powers. On the other hand, the West does not propose to alter the present state of affairs by force; indeed, it showed its unwillingness to do so when, in 1953, it did not help the people of East Berlin whose revolt was crushed by Russian and East German forces. Nor can the West seriously expect the Soviet Union to agree to reunification on terms which might imply the accession of a reunited Germany to NATO, and thus a major advance of Western military bases towards the Soviet frontiers. It is unrealistic to count on a policy which even a weaker Russia — or indeed any Power in a similar position — would not countenance. The policy of West Germany seems inconsistent in both pursuing the firm integration of West Germany with Western Europe, and denying the political reality of East Germany. In practical terms, a gradual increase of mutual contacts as between two States and Governments might indeed be more promising than the present policy of total non-recognition. The West, like the Soviet bloc, has increasingly accepted the vision of a world divided into two ideologically and politically divided blocs, which, faced with the alternative of total destruction, might seek a 'live-and-let-live' agreement. Such a co-existence allows for a measure of diplomatic, economic and cultural relations, but it is entirely different from the intimate community of interests and values on which alone a political union, or any effective international authority, can be based. It is only in regard to Germany that the West refuses to acknowledge this development, largely because the United States dares not contradict the policy of a West German Government, which, itself, must constantly demonstrate its concern with German reunification. From this results a situation fraught with ambiguities and danger.[1]

The Austrian Peace Treaty

The Austrian Peace Treaty, concluded in May 1955 between the Republic of Austria and the four major Allies of the last war, was the first major international treaty on which the four erstwhile Allies were able to agree, after years of an unbroken record of dissension and tension, sometimes threatening to lead to the brink of war. The reasons for the agreement over Austria are not, however, to be sought in a sudden advent of goodwill and harmonious co-operation, as many hoped for in the darkest days of the war and the earliest days of the United Nations. The Austrian Peace Treaty had been drafted in 1949, but the U.S.S.R. was not at that time willing to forgo any immediate advantage, such as the stationing of her troops in a part of Austria, and its capital,

[1] On the legal and diplomatic status of Germany, see further below, p. 361.

Vienna. This was characteristic Stalin policy. Present Soviet policy is more subtle. The creation, by international treaty, of the Austrian Republic as an independent, uncommitted, moderately armed State, which will not enter into any alliances, is seen as a model that Germany, and perhaps other States in Europe, might follow.

The treaty provides for the recognition of Austria as a 'sovereign, independent and democratic State' and contains an undertaking by the Allied Powers to respect the independence and territorial integrity of Austria. Austria undertakes not to seek directly or indirectly any political or economic union with Germany, or to tolerate any organizations that would favour such a movement. This obligation implies an undertaking not to join an organization such as NATO. An interesting feature of the treaty is the specific undertaking given by Austria to guarantee the fundamental freedoms and human rights without discrimination of race, sex, language or religion, as well as to maintain a democratic government based on secret and universal suffrage. Austria is permitted to have national Armed Forces, but has undertaken to exclude from them former German nationals and anybody associated with National-Socialist organizations of a number of enumerated categories. Austria — like Germany in the Paris treaties discussed above — also promises not to manufacture certain categories of weapons, such as atomic arms or other major weapons 'adaptable now or in the future to mass destruction'.

In return for sovereignty and independence, Austria has had to undertake heavy financial commitments to the Soviet Union. This is a concession to the U.S.S.R.'s constantly maintained claim that many industrial assets in Austria — which had been annexed by Hitler in 1938 — were really German assets and therefore liable to reparations. After the war the Soviet Union had taken complete control of the important Austrian oil-fields and extracted oil to the value of nearly $300 million. In return for the Soviet Union's relinquishment of direct control over the Austrian assets — such as oil-wells, Danubian shipping, etc. — Austria undertook to deliver $150 million worth of goods to Russia in the following six years, as well as 10 million tons of oil during the following ten years. She also agreed to buy back the Soviet-controlled Danubian steamship company for a 'reasonable compensation'. These obligations, as well as the new burden of national Armed Forces and the loss of revenue from the expenditure of the occupation forces, would have been an unbearable burden a few years ago, but thanks to American and World Bank aid and the industry and ingenuity of her people, Austria has made a spectacular economic recovery, expanding her industrial production and export trade, as well as improving her agriculture. Whether Austria can maintain herself as another neutralized Switzerland, only the future can show. She is reasonably secure so long as the balance of power between East and West makes it inadvisable for either side to disturb this arrangement. On the other hand, the natural defences and impregnability of Austria — largely situated in the Danubian plain — cannot compare with those of mountainous Switzerland. Although Austria would almost certainly seek to join the European Economic Community if free to do so, strong Soviet opposition to such a move as incompatible with Austria's neutrality obligations has prevented her from doing so. But Austria is a member of the European Free Trade Association formed between Britain, the Scandinavian states, Austria, Switzerland and Portugal.

Italy and the East–West Conflict

Ever since, after centuries of division, she became a national State, Italy has been nearly, but not quite, one of the great Powers. Her poverty in good soil and raw materials, her chronic overpopulation and a national temperament which makes Italians less amenable to that military discipline and efficiency which has led Germany to power and disaster, have prevented Italy from being numbered among the leading Powers, and the Fascist era under Mussolini only served to reveal the discrepancy between ambition and reality.

The present world situation, however, has given Italy an international position of cardinal importance. Strategically, the participation of Italy — not an Atlantic Power — in the North Atlantic Treaty Organization is a vital factor in the defence of the Mediterranean area. Her present position makes it easier for both Yugoslavia and Greece, on the other side of the Adriatic, to resist Soviet pressure. At the same time, any change in the position of these two countries would weaken Italy's position.

An event which has greatly contributed to the easing of tension in this area is the settlement of the conflict between Italy and

Yugoslavia over the status of Trieste. The City of Trieste, the most important harbour of the Adriatic, with an overwhelmingly Italian population, became part of Italy in 1918, after the collapse of the Austro-Hungarian Empire. It was, however, surrounded by the Slavonic peoples of the newly created Yugoslavia. After the Second World War Tito's Yugoslav partisans temporarily occupied Trieste. Later, British and American forces jointly assumed the administration of the port of Trieste itself, while the surrounding territory came under Yugoslav administration. In 1954, after much patient preparatory work on the part of the British and Americans, and with a considerable degree of courageous compromising on the part of both Yugoslav and Italian leaders, a settlement was reached. The City of Trieste itself reverted to Italian administration, subject to a guarantee of Yugoslav rights to use the harbour. The surrounding territory with its overwhelmingly Yugoslav population became part of Yugoslavia. Allied military control ceased. So far this solution, which did not satisfy the extreme nationalist aspirations of either Italians or Yugoslavs, has worked excellently. It seems to confirm that the solution of such disputes is a matter of attitudes rather than of inherent conflicts. Whether and in what form Italians and Yugoslavs can live together, despite divided political allegiance, appears to depend predominantly on their, and their leaders', will to do so.

Italy is one of the three major members of the three European Communities which link the basic industries of France, Western Germany and Italy with those of the Benelux countries, and are designed to lay the foundations for a West European Confederation. The Community, the North Atlantic Treaty Organization, the Council of Europe and any other form of European consolidation would be greatly weakened by Italy's defection. Such a defection is, however, far from impossible. The Communist Party of Italy is the strongest Communist Party outside the Soviet bloc itself. While the generous grant of Marshall Aid, the influence of the Catholic Church and other factors have so far prevented the Communists from gaining an actual majority, they constantly receive new strength from Italy's deep-seated social troubles. These arise from a chronic unemployment problem, largely due to the disproportion between the high birth rate and the poverty of Italy's natural resources, but are reinforced by the stark contrasts between wealth and poverty, between industrialists and workers, between rich landowners and landless peasants, between the developing and increasingly prosperous North and the more stagnant and backward South.

Throughout Italy's post-war history, the Christian Democratic Party has been the dominant political force. Either singly, or in coalition with some weaker parties, it has controlled a succession of governments, which have favoured close association with the West through participation in the North Atlantic Treaty, the Council of Europe, and the West European Communities. Italy also received a generous share of Marshall Aid, which not only spurred its economic recovery but also led to strong aid and investment links with the West. The Western-oriented policy of the Christian Democratic Party — which bears much resemblance to its namesake in Western Germany — had the strong support of the Catholic Church whose influence, through the Vatican, is more direct in Italy than in any other country. But the Christian Democratic Party of Italy is, more strongly than its German counterpart, divided between a left and a right wing. The divisions between these two sectors of the Party became accentuated when recent elections weakened the controlling position of the party and forced it to seek associations with other political groups. Under Fanfani and the present Prime Minister, Moro, the decision was made to seek an 'opening to the left'. Early in 1964, a coalition was formed between the Christian Democratic Party, the moderately left Social Democratic Party led by Saragat and the more left-wing Socialist Party led by Nenni. The latter had for years been torn between an independent left-wing policy and association with the Communists, and a coalition with moderate Left and Centre Parties. The latter tendency prevailed after much discussion, although a segment of the Socialist Party refused to support this line. As there are also important elements in the Christian Democratic Party which strongly oppose the opening to the left and would prefer to associate the party with more conservative groups to the right, the future of this coalition is by no means assured. But as long as a more progressive outlook, both in matters of domestic and of foreign policy, apparently favoured by the late Pope John XXIII and the present Pope Paul VI, prevails in the Vatican, the Left–Centre coalition is less exposed to opposition from the Catholic Church which would have been more pronounced under the conservative leadership of Pope Pius XII and the ruling Catholic hierarchy. The present coalition government has expressed continued support for the NATO alliance and a basically pro-Western orientation. Italy remains a strong supporter of the European Communities and generally opposes, together with the other four members of the Communities, the strongly nationalist line of de Gaulle's France. Domestically, the present Government is pledged to support social reforms, including agrarian reform and the strengthening of public enterprise in the basic utilities. Under the previous Fanfani Government, the electricity undertakings of Italy were nationalized and thus enlarged the already very considerable segment of public enterprise in Italy. These are generally operated through State-controlled holding companies which comprise the exploitation and the operation of the major mineral resources and the shipping industry. Under the dynamic leadership of the late Enrico Mattei, the State-owned corporation which controls the oil and natural gas resources and operations of Italy (ENI) had already become a strongly independent and expansionist enterprise. By contracting with the Soviet Union for supplies of oil, by constructing refineries in Italy and abroad, and by entering into concession agreements with foreign states, such as Iran, Egypt and other Middle Eastern Governments, on terms more favourable to the concession-granting Governments than those customarily offered by the leading Western oil companies, the ENI had frequently clashed with the policies and interests of the latter.

The continuing strength of the Communist Party and the precariousness of the present moderately Left–Centre coalition creates an element of uncertainty in the future policy and orientation of Italy. On the other hand, Italy's industrial capacity and national wealth has dramatically increased in recent years, although it has also widened the gap between the affluent North and the poor South of Italy. To narrow this gap remains one of the principal tasks of any Italian Government. If it is solved by evolutionary means, including legislative and other social reforms, it is likely that Italy will stay in the Western camp.

South-east Europe and the Middle East

The importance of this area, as one of the major centres of international politics, has steadily increased in recent years. The two main reasons for this are the strategic importance of the area and the richness of its oil deposits, which, at a time when American and other oil resources (e.g. in Roumania) show signs of exhaustion, are increasingly important. At the same time, strong nationalist and, to some extent, mutually antagonistic movements in the Middle East, both in the Arab world and in Israel, have increased turbulence and uncertainty.

Strategically, the Communist bloc can exercise considerable pressure in the eastern Mediterranean, from the Black Sea and the Communist-controlled states of Hungary, Roumania and Bulgaria. The potentialities of this advance are greatly reduced as long as Yugoslavia remains on its independent course.

The Kremlin has always been aware of the strategic and political importance of Yugoslavia. Under the Stalin regime the Russian answer to Tito's independence was abuse, political warfare and the hope that pressure and threats would lead to a change in Yugoslavia's policy. Tito's Yugoslavia, being staunchly Communist in ideology, has always refused to join the West without reservations, although she has for some years accepted substantial military and industrial aid, especially from the United States.

Under Krushchev Soviet tactics towards Tito's Yugoslavia shifted repeatedly, indicating perhaps some uncertainty of purpose. Shortly after his accession to power, Krushchev went out of his way to make gestures of reconciliation towards Tito's Yugoslavia, acknowledging even quite freely errors of Stalinist policy, which led to the ostracism of Yugoslavia by the Communist bloc. This was followed by a period of renewed tension, largely caused by the Soviet Union's ruthless suppression of the Hungarian revolt of 1956, and her realization of the precariousness of her control over the Communist satellite States in south-eastern Europe. At that time, Tito's Yugoslavia, whose natural sympathies lay with the Hungarian rebels, appeared to the Kremlin to be more dangerous than ever, as the only example of a relatively weak State which, despite general adhesion to Communist ideology, had been able to steer an independent course. That it was able to do so, despite the hostility of the Soviet Union, was due to the fact that the Tito government alone among the Communist regimes of south-eastern Europe, had come to power through its own internal actions stemming from the partisan warfare of the Second World War, and not by the patronage of the Soviet Union. More recently, however, the growing tension between the Soviet Union and Communist China — which violently denounces the Tito regime in Yugoslavia as an extreme example of revisionist 'deviationism' — induced new, and more successful moves by the Kremlin to seek a reconciliation with Yugoslavia. In the general alignment of Communist governments and parties throughout the world, in the battle for allegiance between the Soviet Union and Communist China, Yugoslavia clearly sides with the Soviet Union. Socially, the main Yugoslav contribution has been the development of a relatively decentralized concept of Communism, an emphasis on co-operatives and autonomous management, within a central economic plan. Internationally, Tito has been a supporter of vigilant 'neutralism', i.e. an attitude of watchful and uncommitted independence, which has led him, for example, to establish fairly cordial relations with such States as Nasser's United Arab Republic and Nehru's India. Such policies are possible as long as the Cold War between the big Powers remains a matter of precarious balance and permits a great variety of manœuvres for position. Generally, the international position of Yugoslavia has been considerably strengthened in recent years. The policy of neutralism, i.e. one of independent manœuvre between the opposing blocs in the Cold War, has found many more adherents, especially among the newly independent States of Africa. At the same time, the temperature of the Cold War itself has somewhat abated, and a policy of maintaining friendly relations with both the Soviet Union and the United States is no longer regarded by the leaders of both these States with the stark hostility of former years.[1] Moreover, the greater independence of action, and in particular the modest strengthening of economic and cultural relations with the Western world, which now characterizes the policies of at least some of the Communist States of south-eastern Europe, and in particular of Yugoslavia's neighbours, Hungary and Roumania, has further decreased the political isolation of Yugoslavia. The hostility of Communist China is a fact of life which affects the whole of the Western world, and to a considerable extent the Soviet Union itself. Economically, the relative success of Yugoslavia's experimentation with a blend

[1] The repeated attempts made in the U.S. Congress to prohibit further aid to Yugoslavia and to Poland as Communist States, strongly opposed by the Eisenhower, Kennedy and Johnson Administrations, would upset this precarious balance. These attempts have only been narrowly defeated by the energetic opposition of the U.S. Government and the more far-sighted leaders of the Senate.

of centralized planning and decentralized autonomy of enterprise, and in particular her decision to abandon collective farming — generally the most conspicuous failure in the economic planning of other Communist states — has considerably improved Yugoslavia's agricultural output. Industrially, her progress has been sufficient to enable her to give considerable technical assistance to developing countries, especially in Africa.

In 1954 Yugoslavia concluded a pact of mutual assistance with Greece and Turkey — both of whom are members of NATO. But while relations between Yugoslavia and the two other parties have remained friendly, the pact never came to life, and it was almost entirely paralysed by the bitter conflict between Greece and Turkey over the future of the British-controlled island of Cyprus. For several years Greece strongly supported a movement for enosis, led for the Greek majority of the island by the Greek Orthodox Archbishop Makarios, while Turkey supported the claims of the Turkish population — approximately one-fifth of the total — to partition. While Britain steered uneasily between these two incompatible claims, relations between these two important Mediterranean members of the NATO alliance deteriorated, imperilling greatly the whole Western position in south-east Europe and the eastern Mediterranean. The Cyprus settlement of 1959, for some years, greatly alleviated a dangerous situation. Under the settlement, Greece abandoned her claim for the union of Cyprus with Greece, while Turkey dropped her claim for partition between the Greek and Turkish regions of a small island. Britain granted independence to Cyprus, and all three parties agreed on certain constitutional safeguards for the Turkish minority, and the right for Britain to maintain certain military bases on the island. But the hope that this settlement and the passage of time would gradually reduce the antagonism between the Greek majority and the Turkish minority, and develop instead a common feeling of allegiance to the new national State of Cyprus, has hitherto remained unfulfilled. At the end of 1963, violent clashes occurred again, reviving not only the old feuds on the island itself but creating new tensions between Greece and Turkey. The Makarios government openly proclaimed its wish to abrogate the treaty of 1959 and in particular the constitutional privileges of the Turkish minority. Violence on the island, and the danger of military intervention by Turkey and Greece — on opposite sides — became so great that, in March 1964, a United

Nations Peace Force, composed of Canadian, Irish and Scandinavian contingents, incorporating the British Forces and commanded by an Indian general, was established to prevent full-scale civil war and intervention by other Powers. While generally successful in their immediate objective, UN intervention can only be temporary and UN mediators have not so far been able to bridge the quite irreconcilable objectives of the Greek majority and the Turkish minority — each backed by their mother country — which in September 1964 were on the brink of war. A possible solution is union of Cyprus and Greece, against cession of some island to Turkey and a Turkish military base on Cyprus — but Makarios is cool to a union which would diminish his power. The Makarios government has support from the U.S.S.R. and Egypt, while the United States and Britain seek to mediate, apprehensive of war in the Mediterranean and the disruption of NATO.

The position is aggravated by signs of instability in both Greece and Turkey. Both are members of NATO, and both have received substantial economic aid from the United States, from Western Europe and from the World Bank. Recently, both States have become associated members of the European Economic Community, which will give them access to trade with the members of the Community on privileged terms and also opens up possibilities of economic aid by the European Investment Bank, an autonomous institution which forms part of the E.E.C. But in both countries internal political conditions have become unstable. Since the failure of the strong Communist-led attempt of the radical Left to take over control in 1947 — defeated with the strong help of Britain and the United States (Truman Doctrine) — Greece has remained firmly in the Western camp. Economically her position, though still greatly inferior to that of Western Europe, has considerably improved, mainly through the dramatic increase of the earnings of the tourist industry. After years of political instability a landslide victory of a middle-of-the-road party under Papandreou early in 1964 appeared to promise a period of internal stability.

Because of its strategic position at the eastern end of the Mediterranean, its strongly anti-Soviet orientation, the size of her population approaching thirty million, and a strong military tradition, Turkey has throughout the post-war era been a most important pillar of the Western Alliance in that part of the world.

Under the leadership of General Inönü, an associate of the founder of the new Turkey, Kemal Atatürk, Turkey made gradual progress towards a parliamentary democracy terminating in free elections which, in 1950, brought the opposition party under Menderes to power. The Menderes regime strongly favoured the numerically preponderant and traditionally oriented peasantry, and it engaged in reckless inflationary devices to support the precarious Turkish economy. This led to a dwindling of foreign aid from the World Bank and other Western sources. A military revolt brought the Republican Party back to power in 1960. Menderes and his political aides were executed after a lengthy and somewhat embarrassing trial, but Turkey never regained economic and political stability, and the most recent elections of 1963 gave greatly increased strength to the 'Justice Party' which, under a new name, essentially comprises the forces that supported the Menderes regime. Although General Inönü succeeded in forming a coalition government based on his own party, the internal situation in Turkey remains unstable, and the economic stability and development of a country that has a fast rising population remains uncertain. There is however little likelihood that any Turkish Government would basically change the pro-Western orientation of Turkey, a change which because of Turkey's strong military establishment, as well as because of her strategic position, would disastrously affect the whole south-eastern flank of the NATO alliance. The main reason for this likely continuity of Turkish foreign policy is the fear of Soviet expansion, which goes back to the nineteenth-century policies of Czarist Russia. The fears are increased by periodic Soviet attempts to strengthen the nationalist tendencies of the Kurds, who form one of the minority peoples of the Soviet Union, but also an important segment of the Turkish population.

In the perspective of world politics, the balance of power between the Communist and the anti-Communist forces is greatly influenced not only by the position of Turkey, but by that of the three States that flank the eastern and south-eastern borders of Turkey — Iran, Iraq and Syria. The whole of that region is vulnerable to Soviet influence, for two entirely disparate reasons. The first is economic: the region's immense oil resources — producing approximately one-quarter of the world's oil outside the Soviet bloc — and hitherto almost entirely operated and used by Western enterprise and for Western consumption — are indispensable to the European economy, while the Soviet Union and Roumania produce all the oil they need and have some to export. The U.S.S.R. is, therefore, in a position to manœuvre in that region without being touched in its vital economic nerves. The denial of oil resources in all or part of that region to the West, under Soviet influence, would be an immensely greater threat to Western interests and positions than the present position is to the Soviet Union. Until recently, the West derived some strength from the fact that only its own equipment, engineers and resources were able to sustain and develop oil production and refining in that region, and to produce incomes on which the Governments of such States as Iran, Iraq, Kuwait, Bahrein or Saudi Arabia are now vitally dependent. But here, as in many other fields, the tremendous industrial and technological advance of the Soviet Union has altered the picture. There is little question that Russian or Roumanian engineers and equipment could, today, take the place of Western machinery and skill, and ensure continuity of production. A more important safeguard for the West is the continuing dependence of the oil-producing States of this region on Western markets. For the very fact which makes the Soviet Union independent of oil imports also impairs its ability to take up the sales which might be denied to the West.

The second factor that tends to work in favour of the Soviet bloc is the ferment of nationalism. In all the parts of the world which have, in the past, experienced Western political or economic domination — i.e. much of Asia, the Middle East and almost all of Africa — nationalist movements almost inevitably express resentment against their former masters, even though they may no longer exercise effective control. This tends to make nationalist movements sympathetic towards the Soviet Union, and this tendency has been skilfully exploited in recent years by Communist identification with nationalist aspirations.

In the last few years, Soviet policy has sought to exploit all these factors. It has first concentrated on Nasser's Egypt, exploiting Egyptian hostility to Israel, regarded by the Egyptians and others as essentially a Western creation, and, in particular, Egyptian resentment against the Franco-British-Israeli attempt to resume military control over the Suez Canal in 1956. As a result, the military forces of Egypt — now called the United Arab Republic — have been increasingly equipped with Russian machinery and arms, on which they are now largely dependent. The Soviet Union also jumped into the breach left by the Western reluctance — both on the part of the United States and of the World Bank — to finance the Aswan Dam scheme, by a substantial loan and technical assistance to Nasser's Government. Undeterred by Nasser's hostility to internal Communist movements, Soviet policy has relied on the likelihood of inevitable continued tensions between Nasser on the one part, and Israel and the major Western Powers on the other part, while gradually increasing its military and technical hold on this desperately backward country.

Until 1958 a pro-Western regime kept Iraq, as a member of the Western-led Baghdad Pact (now renamed Central Treaty Organization), within the Western coalition. A nationalist revolution in the summer of 1958, led by General Kassim — now in turn deposed and executed — radically changed Iraq's political orientation. While rivalries between the Ba'athists and the pro-Nasser factions produced several changes of regime, since the overthrow of the Kassim government the trend is now towards a closer association with the Arab League and in particular with Nasser's Egypt. There is, however, little doubt about Iraq's anti-Western orientation, which means increasing pressure on the Western oil interests in Iraq, mainly the Iraq Petroleum Company, an enterprise owned and operated by a consortium of British and American companies. Already the company has been forced to abandon some of its concessions, refinery capacity and harbour rights. Full nationalization may only be a matter of time.

The neighbouring State of Iran also went through a period of violent anti-Western policy.

The Mossadegh Government in 1951 expropriated the immense installations of the Anglo-Iranian Company and denounced the concession under which it operated. After the dismissal of Mossadegh by the Shah, and after years of negotiation, a new settlement was reached by the new pro-Western Government of Iran and a consortium of Western companies (British, American, Dutch and French), which now operate the Abadan refineries under a complex agreement with the Iranian Government on the usual fifty-fifty basis of division of profits. Meanwhile an Italian State-owned oil company has obtained oil concessions under terms of profit-sharing even more favourable to Iran.

Iran remains a member of the Central Treaty Organization, and under the leadership of the Shah, is firmly pro-Western. But the social situation is precarious. Power and wealth are concentrated in a very small number of princes, landowners, generals and businessmen, while the peasants and labourers remain in a state of abject poverty, dependent legally and economically on absentee landlords.

In awareness of this explosive social situation, the Shah, with some support from the Army, initiated a bold scheme of land reform by which the large estates, including a high proportion of his own lands, are being redistributed among the landless peasants, who thus become independent farmers and receive support from the State with regard to the terms of payment and equipment for cultivation. The indications are that this bold move, despite the opposition of the ruling classes and property interests, has gained the Shah strong sympathy among the people of Iran. If this support succeeds in keeping him in power, the policy of Iran — which has also attempted recently to improve relations with the Soviet Union — is likely to remain basically pro-Western. Transcending in importance even the oil enterprises of Iran and Iraq, for both revenues and indispensable oil supplies, there is the now independent sheikhdom of Kuwait, producing at present over 7% of the world's oil outside the Soviet area. While Britain, and indeed the whole of the Western world, could afford the loss of supplies from any one of the major oil-producing States, such as Iran, Iraq, Kuwait or Saudi Arabia, the loss of any major part of the combined supplies from that area would be fatal to the economic life of Europe. Important new oil production has been developed by France in the Sahara, and by various Western oil companies, operating under concessions, in Libya. But the former are in the territory of the now independent Algeria, and the latter in the territory of another member of the Arab League. Thus Britain and Western Europe must look at the Middle Eastern tangle with even greater apprehension than the United States, whose immediate oil interests are strongest in Saudi Arabia, but who is not to anything like the same degree dependent for its survival on oil supplies from that area.[1]

[1] The U.S. Government has imposed restrictions on oil imports from the Middle East for the protection of domestic oil supplies which are considerably more expensive, but considered strategically vital.

While developments in that part of the world must be viewed by the West with deep apprehension, it is relatively powerless to arrest, let alone change, the course of events. Any direct political intervention would be likely to strengthen the already vehement anti-Western sentiments on the part of both nationalist and Communist elements. The Central Treaty Organization — in which Britain and, in effect, though not in name, the United States, are joined with Iran, Pakistan and Turkey in a defensive alliance — might become effective in the case of direct aggression. However, no means has as yet been found to provide an effective shield against what is somewhat vaguely called 'indirect' aggression, i.e. the undermining of a Government by infiltration and propaganda. And this is much the more important way in which anti-Western influences are spreading in the Middle East. It is almost impossible to determine the point at which external intervention can be distinguished from internal revolutionary developments. Hence the so-called Eisenhower doctrine propagated in 1957 was bound to remain ineffective. It is not possible for any outside Power to intervene in internal revolutions without incurring the odium of aggression. And in the more subtle play of manœuvre and counter-manœuvre for internal political influence, the West is handicapped by its past history and the present trend of nationalist feeling in that area. Its only, rather fragile, hope is that the rival influences of pro-Communist and nationalist (pro-Nasser) elements may to some extent neutralize each other, thus preventing the establishment of any one predominant anti-Western influence throughout the whole region.

The tense position in this area is increased by the corruption or instability of many of its governments. With the partial exception of Turkey and Israel, all the Middle Eastern States have conditions of stark contrast between great wealth and extreme poverty; government is usually in the hands of privileged cliques, and the standards of honesty and efficiency in the public services are generally very poor. Such conditions open up good prospects for Communist doctrine, or right-wing military dictatorship.

Thirteen Arab States[1] are joined in an Arab League, which is nominally a regional association for mutual political and military assistance, but whose effectiveness lags far behind its aspirations.

[1] Algeria, United Arab Republic (Egypt), Iraq, Kuwait, Lebanon, Libya, Morocco, Saudi Arabia, Tunisia, Syria, Sudan, Jordan, Yemen.

The economic efficiency and the standards of government of the Jewish State of Israel are far in advance of those of the Arab States, but the policy of unlimited immigration into a small and partly barren country creates great economic problems, and an almost inevitable pressure for an extension of boundaries. With incredible energy and resourcefulness, Israel has brought vast stretches of formerly arid desert into cultivation. In the face of Arab threats, Israel has developed a new seaport, Elath, at the entrance of the Gulf of Aqaba — which reduces her dependence on the Suez Canal, from which Egypt bars her — and proceeded energetically with the development of the arid stretches of the Negev. But the aridity of most of Israel's land, and the continuing growth of a population now approaching two and a half million, make further measures necessary. Intensive cultivation and industrial development have reduced the level of ground water, while more water resources are needed for the cultivation of the new areas. The only possible source for such additional water is the Jordan River which flows through Israel as well as through the hostile Arab States of Jordan, Lebanon and Syria. A few years ago Israel supported an American-sponsored scheme for the joint development and exploitation of the Jordan waters by Israel and the Arab States concerned, under an international authority somewhat modelled on the Tennessee Valley Authority. The Arab States refused to take part in such a scheme, since it would imply indirect recognition of the State of Israel. Israel then proceeded with a plan of its own, which involves the use of waters feeding the Jordan River on Israeli territory, through the now completed construction of pipes taking the waters from lake resources in the north of Israel to the Negev. Legally, this is unobjectionable, since the present state of the international law concerning international rivers permits each State to use whatever part of the river flows through its own territory at its own discretion, unless bilateral or multilateral international treaties provide for the joint use of resources. Since the Arab States have refused to participate in an international scheme, and since they themselves proceed with several dam and irrigation projects aiming at the utilization of Jordan tributaries in their respective territories, they can raise no legal objection to the Israel scheme, except on the ground that they do not recognize the existence of Israel as a legitimate entity. This cannot of course be accepted by Israel itself or by the majority of nations, including the entire West which recognizes Israel and her membership in the United Nations. There is no present sign of Arab preparations for military measures against Israel — which would of course be legally acts of aggression — and would be resisted to the utmost not only by Israel's efficient military forces, but presumably by the United States, France and other friendly Western Powers. Such action would also call for United Nations intervention. But in January 1964, the members of the Arab League met to consider counter-measures, apparently short of war. If and when the Arab neighbours of Israel should proceed with the various ambitious projects for the diversion of the waters of the Jordan and its tributaries within their own territories, which would drastically diminish the flow on Israel territory, a conflict would seem almost unavoidable. To Israel, water for the irrigation of its lands is a matter of life and death. On the other hand, enmity to Israel is the strongest link between the thirteen members of the Arab League which otherwise are divided by many feuds and rivalries. If they should ever succeed in overcoming these rivalries to the point of a joint military organization, whose efficiency and technical equipment would be aided by Soviet officers and engineers, as well as by individual German missile experts, their numerical superiority over an encircled Israel would be overwhelming. On the other hand, Israel would not be isolated. She has particularly close ties with France, which has supplied her with modern aircraft and other military equipment. She can count on strong though not unconditional support from the United States, whose policy has been to strike a balance between the pressures of its influential Jewish population and its enormous stakes in Middle Eastern Arab-owned oil. One of the most imaginative and successful moves of Israel, in its fight against encirclement and isolation, has been the use of the scientific, technical and agricultural know-how of a highly educated nation for technical assistance to the new countries of Africa, as well as to Burma and some Latin-American States. Israel's engineers and agricultural experts have been active and welcome in Ghana, Nigeria, Tanganyika, Ethiopia and other African countries. While these countries may not go to the length of opposing any Arab military action against Israel by military force, they have already exercised considerable influence in opposing or moderating anti-Israel resolutions in a number of

Pan-African meetings and institutions. Nevertheless, the conflict between Israel and the Arab States remains one of the most dangerous and explosive trouble-centres of the world.

On the other hand, two sources of conflict and bitterness in the Middle Eastern area, which were prominent a few years ago, have now abated. The abortive British-French-Israeli expedition of November 1956, designed to regain control of the Suez Canal, in response to Nasser's nationalization of the Suez Canal Company, ended with the withdrawal of the forces under strong pressure from the United Nations, led on this occasion by concurrent attitudes of the United States and the Soviet Union.

A negotiated settlement of the compensation payable by Egypt to the Suez Canal Company in which British and French shareholders predominate, and the subsequent resumption of diplomatic relations between Britain and France on the one side and Egypt on the other, have helped to push this lamentable episode into the background. On the other hand, a new source of conflict has been opened up through massive Egyptian military support for the revolutionary regime in Yemen, linked with attempts to undermine the British-sponsored South Arabian Federation and the important British base of Aden.

The granting of independence to Algeria, after years of bloody strife between France and the Algerian rebels, has, at least for the time being, removed another source of bitter tension, as has the restoration of friendly relations between France and Tunisia after a violent clash, a few years ago, over the continued French control of the Tunisian harbour of Bizerte. The most recent acts of violence in that area arose between two independent Arab states, the former French dependencies of Algeria and Morocco. Behind these local clashes there are unsolved disputes over the ownership of the oil-rich areas of the Sahara Desert. Control over the oil-producing areas, which have been developed by French capital and engineers, with recent moderate participation by other Western interests, is claimed both by Algeria and by Morocco.

From Turkey in the east to Morocco in the west, the Middle East area remains divided, turbulent and uncertain. It reflects all shades of opinion, from the strongly pro-Western stand of Turkey and Iran, through the vacillating neutralism of Egypt and other Arab countries, to the increasingly anti-Western sentiments of the Arab populations in Algeria or Iraq.

CHAPTER 6

PROBLEMS AND PROSPECTS OF EUROPEAN INTEGRATION

DECISIVE political changes — even those long overdue — seldom occur as the result of quiet and deliberate planning. They are far more often the product of emergency. The partial integration of Europe which we are witnessing is, in large part, the result of the unintended and unfortunate divisions of the post-war world. The idea of European unification, proceeding through various stages of confederation, has occupied statesmen and thinkers for many years, and prominently so since the end of the First World War. Disgust with the destructive and debilitating effects of centuries of war between the nations of Europe, combined with the awareness of the insufficiency of the national sovereign State, and the relative decline of European power, have reinforced the sense of a common European heritage. Yet the work and thought of such men as Aristide Briand or Count Coudenhove-Calerghi could not prevail against the continuing political divisions and rivalries, which were brought to a desperate climax with the rise of the Nazi regime in Germany and the Fascist regime in Italy. The Second World War saw once again the larger European nations fight each other — Germany against France, France against Italy, Britain and Russia against Germany, while the smaller European nations were helpless to avert invasion and humiliation. But Europe also experienced, for a few years, a kind of United Europe — even though it was the ghastly perversion of a Nazi-dominated Europe, controlled by German military men, politicians, industrial leaders, based on the idea of Nordic supremacy over the other peoples of Europe — and the enslavement or extermination of millions.

The Pan-European idea, i.e. the integration and eventual unification of the whole of Europe, from the Vistula and, perhaps, from the Urals, to Gibraltar, has been set back for an indefinite period by the post-war division of Europe. Even if a *modus vivendi*, some kind of peaceful co-existence, can be evolved between the Western-oriented and the Soviet-controlled parts of Europe, the gulf between their political, economic and cultural ways and ideals is far too vast to permit any form of integration. This very partition has, however, helped to push a group of Western nations closer towards integration than would ever have occurred in less troubled circumstances. Above all, France and Germany — at least the greater part of Germany represented by the present West German Republic — have, for the first time in centuries, substituted co-operation and even the partial integration of their institutions for enmity and war.

A number of post-war developments have combined to bring the nations of Western Europe closer together than at any previous period in their history, even though they have, at the same time, revealed the magnitude of the problems yet to be solved before Europe becomes truly united.

One powerful impetus came from the chaos and state of exhaustion in which the whole of Europe found itself after the last war, and the need for powerful and organized economic assistance, to which the United States responded with the historic Marshall Plan.[1] Out of the Marshall Plan arose the Organization for European Economic Co-operation (O.E.E.C.), which was originally concerned with the proper allocation of United States funds between the participating European nations. With the co-operation of a number of enlightened American administrators, the O.E.E.C. developed into a machinery of co-ordination of economic and financial policies and the liberalization of trade between seventeen European nations, and an organizational link between Great Britain and the nations of continental Western Europe. The European Payments Union, established in 1950, with the objective of aiding in the liberalization of trade through a clearing arrangement, was replaced in 1959 by the European Monetary Union, by which the twelve participating States, including Great Britain, West Germany, France and Italy, made their currencies fully convertible into each other. In December 1960 the O.E.E.C. was replaced by the Organization for Economic Co-operation and Development (O.E.C.D.). Its principal objective is the promotion of policies designed to assure continued economic growth and economic development among member

[1] See above, p. 103.

countries and in the world at large, and to work towards the expansion of world trade on a multilateral, non-discriminatory basis. The most important of the specialized bodies of the O.E.C.D. is the Development Assistance Committee (D.A.C.) which functions as a co-ordinating agency for the methods and policies pursued by the member-States in the field of development assistance. The D.A.C. has so far mainly functioned as a clearing and information centre, rather than as active co-ordinator of national aid policies. The principal difference in the membership of the O.E.C.D., as compared with the former O.E.E.C., is the accession of the United States and Canada as full members. In 1964 Japan also joined, so that all the important financial and economic States of the Atlantic Community, with the addition of Japan, are now in the organization.

Liberalization of trade, economic expansion and convertibility of currency were not, however, an adequate expression of the plans and ideals that emerged in continental Western Europe from the devastations of the last war and the political conflicts of the post-war world. It is unlikely that these ideas would have concretized to the extent they have without the growing pressure from the expanding and monolithically-controlled Communist bloc led by Moscow. But a more positive ideal had to be found. It was found partly in the new outlook of a post-war generation disillusioned with national grandeur and military conquest. For the first time in modern history, large sections of young Germans and Frenchmen came to think similarly, while the smaller States of Western Europe were only too conscious of the insufficiency of national sovereignties and rivalries. At the same time, three conservative, Catholic and Latin-oriented political leaders controlled the affairs of their respective countries — France, Italy and West Germany — for a sufficiently long period to give a powerful stimulus to West European integration. Adenauer of Germany, Robert Schuman (aided by Jean Monnet) of France, and De Gasperi of Italy understood each other and worked towards similar goals.

Ironically, the first important implementation of partial West European integration, the European Coal and Steel Community, was a constructive conversion of the old-fashioned idea of revenge. France, twice invaded by a more powerful Germany, had emerged from the last world war with the definite desire to keep the German industrial potential down by a permanent control of its basic industries, especially coal and steel. When political developments made the attainment of this goal increasingly impossible, the idea of a Coal and Steel Community, under joint control, gained ground. While the plan of restricting German output quickly receded, the idea of joint control by a supranational authority survived. The European Coal and Steel Community was established in 1952, and more than six years later it was joined by the European Atomic Energy Community and the European Economic Community. Before we turn to a description of the structure and purposes of these, in many ways revolutionary, new European institutions, we shall have to reflect on some of the basic obstacles that still bar the way towards fuller European integration.

Problems of Economic Integration

The decisive, and as yet largely unsolved, problem remains that of merging a number of national economic systems, each backed by national interests and traditions of centuries, into a bigger unit. In practice, such an economic integration would mean that France, for example, might have to close down some heavy industries if their products could be supplied better and more cheaply by Germany, while Britain might have to take timber from her housing programme so that France would have pitprops for her coalmines. It would mean that the British miner, the German farmer, the French steel-worker, the Belgian textile-worker and the Norwegian fisherman should see their own national economy and their personal interests as subordinate to the wider aim of European recovery, and that they should consequently submit to the restrictions of planning, and a direction of economic development to which most Europeans have submitted on a national, but not yet on an international, basis. Joint economic planning will be somewhat easier in regard to future industrial development rather than existing capacity. It is psychologically more feasible to limit the future expansion of steel production or oil refineries than to close down existing works and to dismiss or transfer workers.

Economic thinking and planning in European rather than national terms is in itself a difficult enough task. Its solution depends to a large extent on the pressure of events, on bold statesmanship and the firing of the imagination of at least the more active sections of the nations concerned. The accomplishment of this task is, however, made much more difficult by certain intractable facts. The Russian and Communist offensive was provisionally halted when it had penetrated and absorbed the major part of eastern and south-eastern Europe — that is to say, Europe's main producers and exporters of bread-grains, timber and other primary produce. It is on the whole the industrially more highly developed and densely populated but agriculturally deficient nations of Europe that have been left outside the Iron Curtain.

The political division has had far-reaching effects on the economic structure of both halves of a truncated Europe. The traditional pattern of exchange between the more industrialized West and the mainly agricultural East has been replaced by the conception of East and West as essentially separate, potentially competing and even hostile areas of industrial development and trade. There have been certain modest efforts to intensify economic relations between East and West,[1] but they have not so far been sufficient to reverse this general trend. The western part of Europe, of course, being under a far smaller degree of co-ordination and compulsion, has had to try as best it can to blend co-operation with competition — inevitable between highly industrialized countries producing and exporting similar products. The most significant change is the welding of the Communist countries of Eastern Europe into a mighty industrial and trading bloc.

The patterns of trade, both between the States of the Communist bloc and between the Communist and non-Communist States of Europe, strongly reflect the political constellation. Generally, the bulk of the trade of the Communist European states has been within the bloc, and the trade of Western Europe with the Communist States has been a very small proportion of the — much higher — volume of West European trade with the world (from 4 to 4·5% of the total international trade). But there are signs of significant changes in both groups. About two-thirds of the total exports and imports of the East European Communist States, including the Soviet Union, still are within the bloc organized in the Council for Mutual Economic Assistance

[1] See, for some recent trade figures, below, p. 371.

(C.M.E.A.).[1] The major change that has occurred in recent years has been the dramatic decline of their trade with Communist China, reflecting the political split between the Soviet Union and China. Between 1959 and 1961 imports of China from the Soviet Union declined by about two-thirds and the subsequent years have almost certainly brought a further sharp fall.

It is perhaps no less significant that within the European Communist bloc there has been a sharp rise of industrialization and a related diversification of export trade in some of the smaller states, most of all in Roumania. Roumanian exports of industrial equipment such as tractors, chemicals or oil refinery equipment have risen dramatically. Of the Communist-bloc group, it is Roumania that most strongly opposes the development of the Council for Mutual Economic Assistance (C.M.E.A.) into a tightly knit organization, which seeks to have the different members specialize in different lines of production and is generally dominated by the overwhelming weight of the U.S.S.R. The resistance to such specialization reflects the desire for greater political and economic independence which within the Communist bloc is most marked in the case of Roumania, but is notable in several other bloc countries.

There is a general desire on the part of the Soviet-bloc countries to expand their trade with Western Europe which doubled between 1955 and 1962, but it is limited by their ability to earn the foreign exchange needed for imports. The most important item of the exports of Communist Europe to the West is crude materials and mineral fuels. In the reverse direction it is mainly machinery. Despite the many political and economic limitations, there has been a continuous rise in East–West trade, and it is part of the change in the political scene that Britain, France and Italy have recently sought to expand their trade with Communist Europe.[2] By contrast, the trade of the United States with the Soviet bloc is still minimal (in 1962 exports from the U.S. to the

[1] In 1962, according to Soviet sources, the total foreign trade of the C.M.E.A. countries was 28,600 million roubles and reciprocal trade between them 18,500 million roubles. (*International Affairs*, No. 2, 1964, p. 68.)

[2] In September 1964 a British consortium gave a fifteen-year credit of £24 million — guaranteed by the Government — to the U.S.S.R. for the purchase of a polyester fibre plant. The following month the French and U.S.S.R. governments concluded a trade agreement which included the grant of 5–7-year credits for Soviet purchases.

Soviet bloc were $125·1 million out of a total export value of $19 billion 474·4 million). The West European trade with East Europe, while still under 5% of their total trade, is likely to rise continuously, thus emphasizing the growing divergencies in international policies between the U.S. and its allies (which are also reflected in their controversies over the trade embargo against Cuba). The trade agreement concluded in May 1964 between the United States and Roumania may, however, indicate a cautious shift in U.S. policy. American business interests are now strongly in favour of an expansion of trade with the Soviet bloc. Understandably, the U.S.S.R. bitterly attacks West European economic groupings, such as E.E.C. or EFTA; but its own association with the other Communist countries is even stronger, as it is based on State trading systems which regard trade largely as a matter of official policy and decision.

For the United States, export trade is altogether of far lesser significance than for the highly industrialized and export-dependent countries of Western Europe. Great Britain, France, West Germany, Belgium, the Netherlands, Sweden, all depend to a varying extent on a high level of exports and they are all actual or potential competitors. The vast spaces and needs of Communist Europe, including the Soviet Union, and the complementary character of the primary produce of Eastern Europe and the finished products of Western Europe, provide a strong incentive for expansion of trade relations, which is held back only by political obstacles. If and in so far as the economic relations between Communist and non-Communist Europe should continue to grow, they would tend to emphasize common European interests and correspondingly weaken the ties between Western Europe and the United States.

Political Problems of European Union

The political integration of Western Europe has, like its economic associations, been actively sponsored by the United States. In the American view the existing divisions of Europe are politically and economically outmoded, and militarily disastrous. But whereas the United States, as the chief provider, has been able to take a very active part in Western Europe's economic reconstruction, she can only be a very interested and anxious spectator in regard to political integration.

It is unnecessary to analyse in detail the rapidly changing pattern of Western Europe's political organization. Its official beginning was the Brussels Treaty of March 1948, between Britain, France and the three Benelux countries. The mutual defence obligations of this Pact have been almost totally submerged in the wider North Atlantic Treaty Organization. But in 1954 the Brussels Treaty became the nucleus of the Western European Union, an organization which has remained dormant but, after the rejection of Britain's move to join the European Economic Community, has occasionally been reactivated, since it joins Britain with the members of the E.E.C. The Council of Europe, established in London on May 5, 1949, was at first greeted with high hopes as a vital advance towards the union of Europe. It united the countries of the Brussels Pact with the three Scandinavian kingdoms, and with the Irish and Italian Republics. Greece, Turkey and Iceland joined later. West Germany became an associate and later a full member (1951). The declared purpose of the Statute is 'devotion to the spiritual and moral values which are the common heritage of their peoples, and the true source of individual freedom, political liberty and the rule of law, principles which form the basis of all genuine democracy'. Article 3 of the Statute states even more specifically that 'every member of the Council of Europe must accept the principles of the rule of law and of the enjoyment of all persons within its jurisdiction of human rights and fundamental freedoms'.

Of the two organs of the Council, the Committee of Ministers acts on behalf of the Council of Europe, as the Security Council acts on behalf of the United Nations. This Committee consists of the Ministers for Foreign Affairs of the member-States. Resolutions taken by the Committee have no automatically binding force on the member-States, though the participation of senior Ministers gives a fair prospect of their resolutions being seriously considered. The conception of the European Parliament has been watered down to that of a Deliberative Assembly, whose agenda is determined by the Committee of Ministers. The participating States elect their members according to a ratio laid down in the Statute and broadly proportionate to their population. While the method of appointment is left to the Governments of the member-States, the present Assembly does not only represent the Government of the day. The British delegation, for example, represents

Conservative, Labour and Liberals roughly in the proportion of their present strength in Parliament. Party divisions have often split the Council of Europe as much as national antagonisms.

The main political problem of the Council of Europe, and indeed of all projects of European Union, goes deeper. Not only theorists but also many practical politicians and statesmen regard the present situation as a unique opportunity for the complete political integration of the member-States of the Council of Europe, as a challenge, to the nations brought together by external pressure as much as a broad community of interests and ideas, to push aside at last the barriers of national sovereignty. This school of thought, powerful especially in the Benelux countries, demands a European Parliament which, at least in certain vital matters of common concern, would have overriding authority over the national legislatures. The other, more cautious school of thought, mainly supported by Britain and even more emphatically by Gaullist France, regards the establishment of a supra-national Parliament and Government at this stage as premature, and likely to discredit rather than foster the cause of inter-European collaboration. It favours the empirical and functional approach; agreement and joint action on specific matters of common concern, such as the abolition of passports, the mutual recognition of academic degrees, a Court of Human Rights which was established in 1958, specific labour conventions and so forth. The present Statute almost entirely embodies this approach.

Against this cautious approach, it may be said that emergencies demand boldness, and that eventual disruption may be the only alternative to complete union. Yet it is difficult to see how a genuine federal union, or any constitution which would make the Council of Europe the supreme legislature for the member-States, could operate successfully at this stage. Winston Churchill's dramatic offer for complete union with France, made in June 1940, under the threat of impending disaster, was never put to the test. For better or worse, the end of the war revived most of the different constitutional, political and social traditions of the nations of Europe. Some of them have been forced into the Soviet pattern; the others are all the more anxious to retain their individuality. It is one of the great burdens of democracy that it must achieve action and unity without destroying national individuality and the variety of political patterns.

The British two-party system, with alternating majority Governments, contrasts with the French autocratic (presidential) Constitution and other Continental systems of frequently changing coalition Governments. This divergence of social and economic policies is another obstacle. It has been considerably increased by the emergence of the Fifth French Republic under de Gaulle, with strong ambitions to regain France's stature as one of the world's major Powers.

A British Parliament with a Labour majority will hardly accept, for example, a decision of a European Parliament or Government drastically curtailing social services, or revising the income-tax systems. It is no more likely that French workers or industrialists would accept a decision to close down French steel mills.

The dramatic and unprecedented moves which, despite these obstacles, have taken place in the last few years to bring about a closer association of the nations of Western Europe and, to a much lesser extent, between Britain and Western Europe, have overwhelmingly been the result of specific functional needs and experiments rather than of comprehensive constitutional schemes. The Council of Europe and, especially, the annual meetings of its Assembly at Strasbourg can and do increase the habit of collaboration, of mutual understanding, of personal contact and the exchange of ideas. The Assembly has made important suggestions in a number of fields, ranging from a currency union to a European army. It can lay the foundations for European thinking, but the practical and immediate chances for a closer European integration rest on the gradual extension of functional experiments such as the European Communities or the integration of Western defence forces under NATO.

The European Communities[1]

The Treaty constituting the European Coal and Steel Community — popularly known as the Schuman Plan[2] — was a bold, far-reaching and original attempt to overcome the dilemma just traced: the need to balance the necessity of closer economic and political integration of Western Europe against the obvious

[1] The texts are reprinted (in part) below, pp. 425 *et seq.*

[2] The French Foreign Minister, Robert Schuman, proposed the Plan on behalf of the French Government on May 9, 1950.

impossibility of introducing at one stroke a supra-national government. The inspiration behind the Plan was the reluctant acceptance by France of the revival of German power, and the desire to substitute for yet another phase of Franco-German rivalries a common supra-national authority which would control the keys to economic power — coal and steel, to start with — instead of leaving them in the hands of national, potentially aggressive Governments. It was plainly impossible to create a supra-national political authority, for example, a council of ministers deciding by majority rule, since the Ministers of France and Germany and other countries continue to be responsible to their national parliaments. On the other hand, the creation of yet another advisory agency, such as the Food and Agriculture Organization or other United Nations agencies without executive power, or of committees of Ministers able to take action only on unanimous decisions or to make recommendations to their Governments, was rightly regarded as inadequate. The only alternative was to create an independent supra-national authority with powers of decision, and not directly responsible to any national government. But the discussion showed unwillingness on the part of several of the participating countries to entrust far-reaching power to a functional international authority without any link with the policies of the participating States. Again, it was felt that some quasi-parliamentary control organ over the activities of the newly created authority should be established. The product of all these considerations was the European Coal and Steel Community, an international legal entity with power to deal with governments, industries and other kinds of organization. The Community has four institutions: by far the most important of them is the High Authority, composed of nine members (not more than two from any one nation), of whom eight are designated by the member governments and the ninth elected by the other eight. The High Authority is instructed by the Treaty to 'neither solicit nor accept instructions from any government or from any organization' and to 'abstain from all conduct incompatible with the supra-national character of their functions'. The High Authority decides by a majority vote, and its decisions are binding on the parties. Attached to it is a Consultative Committee of no less than thirty and no more than fifty-one members, in which producers, workers, consumers and dealers are represented in equal numbers.

As the name suggests, its function is advisory, and not executive. The third institution is a quasi-parliamentary one called the Assembly — now a common organ of the three Communities — which meets once a year to discuss the report submitted by the High Authority. The Assembly reflects the differences in industrial importance of the participating countries. Germany, France and Italy have thirty-six delegates each, Belgium and the Netherlands fourteen each, and Luxembourg six. The functions of the Assembly are more than advisory. If, by a two-thirds majority, it adopts a motion of censure on the High Authority, its members must resign. In other words, the Assembly — which, with the establishment of the two newer Communities, Euratom and E.E.C., became a joint assembly for all three — has no legislative powers, but it has a controlling power comparable to that of the British Parliament over the Cabinet.

The member-States, as such, are represented by the Council, whose function it is to harmonize the policies of the High Authority and the participating governments. The Treaty enumerates the cases in which the concurrence of the Council, either by unanimous decision or majority vote, is required to make a decision of the High Authority effective. Finally, a court is created with the power to annul decisions of the High Authority on appeal from a member-State or from the Council, but it can annul such decisions only on the grounds of lack of legal competence or other violations of the Treaty; it has no control over the policies of the High Authority as such. Like the Assembly, the Court now serves the three Communities. Unlike the International Court of Justice which has no compulsory jurisdiction and suffers from the unwillingness of the member-States of the United Nations to submit vital disputes to it, the European Court of Justice, equipped with compulsory jurisdiction, has become an important organ of the Communities. It has been appealed to both by member-States, and by individual enterprises affected by the decisions of the executive authority. It has played an important part in the strengthening of the supra-national constitutional aspects of the Community, in their relation to national powers and policies. By virtue of a provision that allows the national courts of the member-States to refer certain disputes affecting the Community treaties to the European Court, it has ruled for example in a recent decision that certain Dutch fiscal tariffs were incompatible with the Treaty and therefore could be contested as invalid by direct action of the affected individual. It has also refused to interpret extensively the provisions that allow the member-States certain deviations from the common trade regulations of the Communities, in situations of emergency. Recently the Court has begun to interpret the very complex anti-trust provisions of the European Economic Community.

The E.C.S.C. Treaty provides a careful and delicate balance between international authority and national sovereignty. The economic and social provisions of the Treaty show an even more complex and delicate balance between these conflicting pulls. The main purpose of the High Authority is to exercise control over the coal and steel industries of the participating countries. It has power to forbid monopolies, agreements on production or price control or other restrictive devices; it can grant loans for investment programmes, borrow money and place levies on the production of coal and steel. It is to encourage technical and scientific progress, prevent discrimination in wages and social standards and, above all, forbid discrimination in prices as between the different participating nations. Like the typical American controlling authority, it does not operate itself, but supervises conditions of fair competition. Another function of the Authority is to promote actively the integration of the European steel and coal industry. Numerous concessions are made to national policies in the matter of wage regulations, agreements with third States or, in certain cases, price discrimination. One of the most progressive provisions of the Treaty is the unqualified prohibition of national discrimination in regard to employment in the coal and steel industries. The object is to produce a free flow of workers between the member-countries, which means a revolution in traditional immigration policies. The compromise which has resulted is complex enough. Thus, it is a fundamental object of the Treaty to secure equality in wages and social standards. Yet, a member-State is permitted to lower wages 'to re-establish its external equilibrium'.

Unlike a statute in a firmly established national legal system, an international treaty — and especially one of as revolutionary a character as the Treaty establishing the European Coal and Steel Community — constitutes essentially a framework of principles and policies, apt to be tested and modified by practice. To carve out of the national sovereignties of six States — which in many ways and for a long time had been political and economic rivals — control over important segments of basic industries, and to transfer them to a supra-national organ, was certainly a bold attempt. In some ways, it was more difficult than a constitutional change, which transfers major powers from individual States to a new Federal authority. For the new Community, with its limited supra-national powers, had to establish itself and to function within the remaining framework of separate States and sovereignties. After twelve years of effective operation, it can be said that the attempt has, on the whole, succeeded. Today, the Coal and Steel Community forms an accepted, though far from uncontroversial, part of the political and economic life of Western Europe, although it was essentially the work of small groups of political leaders in the different member-States, established in the face of scepticism or actual resistance of both industrial and labour leaders. The Community has certainly been successful in the establishment of a common market for coal and steel. Over the years, trade in coal and steel within the member-States has steadily increased, both absolutely and relatively to their trade with outside countries in these commodities. A major decline in the demand for coal since 1958, due largely to widespread displacement of coal by oil in Europe, has posed grave problems to the Community, which had the good fortune to operate, for the first five critical years of its existence, in economically favourable circumstances. Since 1962, steel production, threatened by increasing competition from abroad, has also remained relatively stagnant.

Transcending in importance the strict economic achievements is the political significance of the Community. To establish a Community, even with limited supra-national powers, between six States which, less than seven years before, had been on opposite sides in the most destructive war of history, was a daring experiment. But in the meantime much has happened to overcome the tragic memories, dividing especially France and the Low Countries from Germany, by an atmosphere of co-operation in a common cause. This is, of course, far more marked in the headquarters of the Community, at Luxembourg, where a permanent staff have, as in other international organizations, acquired an *esprit de corps*. This spirit of co-operation is far less marked in the executive offices of the participating industries, which tend, each from its own point of view, to regard the Community as favouring foreign over national interests. National policies also assert themselves through the Council.

The High Authority has only been moderately successful in its attempt to implement the anti-trust and anti-cartel provisions of the Treaty which forbid restrictive trade practices and undue concentrations of economic power. The German coal industry, heavily cartelized for over half a century, has been busy re-establishing its sales and price syndicates and it objects to being singled out for attention, while the nationalized and, therefore, of necessity, monopolistic French coal industry remains untouched. After years of negotiations between the High Authority and the German coal industry, an uneasy compromise was reached under which instead of a single wholesale syndicate for the entire Ruhr region, three, later reduced to two, syndicates were established, which are supposed to be in competition with each other. This is certainly a far cry from the probably highly theoretical conception of the Treaty which was inspired by American anti-trust ideas of free competition. Perhaps more ominous are the re-formations of several major steel cartels within the Community. Despite prolonged attempts on the part of the High Authority to stop excessive concentrations, mergers between major enterprises in France and Belgium on the one hand, and in Germany on the other, have established giant enterprises each accounting for a major share of the Community's steel production and leading the steel industry of the Community towards an oligopolistic structure rather than the Treaty ideal of free competition. In a report published in 1963 and looking back upon ten years of operation, the High Authority of the E.C.S.C. surveyed both the achievements and the failures of the Community, set against the aspirations of the Treaty. It stressed that the major objective in the creation of the E.C.S.C. had been political — a first step towards a United Europe — and that the E.C.S.C. had indeed been a driving force in the political evolution of Europe.[1] The report regards the implementation of the Coal and Steel Community's

[1] The sudden arrest and stagnation of this evolution towards political confederation in Western Europe, since de Gaulle's speech of January 1963 blocking Britain's proposed membership of the E.E.C., will be described below, in the analysis of the E.E.C. It is not due to any shortcomings of the E.C.S.C.

powers in the economic and social field as generally effective, particularly with regard to the guidance of investment and production, the community tax, the raising of funds and loans, the handling of scrap iron and generally with regard to problems of adaptation and redevelopment. In view of the severe and chronic coal crisis, the report deplores the blocking of the powers given to it by Article 58, to meet a 'manifest crisis'. The objective of closing down the antiquated and inefficient Belgian coal-mines was however eventually achieved by the use of the treaty provisions dealing with special unemployment allowances, and a generous interpretation of the treaty provisions on readaption and redevelopment aid in depressed areas. The report points to the severe restrictions imposed upon the E.C.S.C. by its inability to deal with matters of social policy, transport, trade, and above all, energy sources other than coal. Here the problems of the E.C.S.C. link with the problems of the two new Communities and the broader question of the future of the West European integration movement.

Euratom and the Economic Community

Although the Coal and Steel Community was designed to fulfil certain economic objectives, by the establishment of a common market in coal and steel, its primary motivation and objective was political. It was meant by its founders and promoters to be the first pillar of a future political West European Community which, in turn, would attract other States. If it had been left to itself, however, the Coal and Steel Community would have found itself in increasing isolation, vainly trying to maintain and strengthen a common market and policy in two important basic materials, while the member-States retained their political and economic sovereignty, for example, in regard to transport, electric power, labour and social services, and manufacturing industries using coal and steel. The isolation of the Coal and Steel Community reached its height with the collapse of the proposed European Defence Community in 1954. In 1956, however, new efforts were started by the Governments of the six member-States to enlarge the basis of the European Community. From it resulted, in 1958, two new Communities, one the European Atomic Energy Community and the other the European Economic Community. Structurally, they are close to the pattern of the Coal and Steel

Community. They, too, have an executive authority (called 'Commission', instead of 'High Authority'), and a Council of Ministers, while the Assembly and the Court of Justice have been merged so as to serve the three Communities jointly. The two new Communities are clearly designed as further pillars of a West European confederation. In many respects, they differ, however, in function and purpose, from the Coal and Steel Community as well as from each other. Euratom has potentially a most promising task. Unlike the Coal and Steel Community, this Authority is called upon to develop a new and nascent industry, through the pooling of material and scientific resources of all the member-States. For this purpose, the Atomic Energy Community is equipped with rights of ownership and powers of management. It has ownership in the 'special fissionable materials', i.e. such materials as enriched uranium in the isotopes 235 or 238, which furnish the basis for the various types of nuclear reactors. It may establish joint enterprises for undertakings 'of outstanding importance to the development of the nuclear industry in the Community'. In addition to these functions, there are extensive powers of investment, research, health protection and safety inspection. In most cases, however, the Commission — i.e. the executive, supra-national nucleus of the Community — is subject to the consent, or the final decision by the Council of Ministers, which represents the member-States as such.

So far, the actual scope and importance of the Atomic Energy Community has fallen far short of the expectations prevailing at the time of its creation. The major reason for this is the unexpected abundance of oil and natural gas supplies, from old and new sources. At a time when the acute anxieties caused by the uranium crisis of the early fifties and the Suez Canal troubles of 1956 had subsided, this led to a slackening of interest in the still costly production of nuclear fuel. At the same time a reaction against the extensive powers granted to the Community, in terms of ownership and management, set in under the leadership of a strongly nationalist France. The far-reaching powers and functions of the Community have therefore remained largely on paper. Its principal activity has been the pursuit of research and the establishment of several joint research centres and enterprises. Its main short-term aim is the development and improvement of the known reactor types best suited for industrial application. The Commission has expressed the hope that, in this way, it will make nuclear electricity available in Europe at prices competitive with those of the cheapest alternative energy sources by 1970.

It is the simultaneously established European Economic Community (E.E.C.) which has, to a far greater extent than the other two Communities, become the centre of the hopes and problems of European integration. In its general purposes the E.E.C. is an enlarged and generalized version of the E.C.S.C.; it aims at the establishment of a general common market, both for industry and agriculture. This is to be accomplished through the gradual establishment of a Customs union, the abolition of quantitative restrictions on trade and the establishment of a common customs tariff towards the outer world. Parallel with this, full freedom of movement across the frontiers of the member-States, of persons, services and capital is to be established. This, in turn, will imply a harmonization of labour conditions and social services, which is perhaps the most ambitious and most difficult of all the plans laid down in the Community Treaties. Eventually, the European Economic Community, aiming at a general common market, is to absorb the more limited and specific common market in coal and steel. The greatest drawback to economic integration is the concentration on *freedom of trade* without the corresponding unification of transport, energy and above all, taxes. Divergencies of national tax policies impede freedom of movement of capital, as divergent labour and social standards impede freedom of movement of labour. Hence, the decision taken by the Council of Ministers of February 1964 to work out a plan for the harmonization of taxes is a step of great significance.

In order to make this extremely ambitious programme acceptable to all the six original member-States of the Community, the supra-national powers of the Community, i.e. of its executive organ, the Nine-Member Commission, had to be greatly weakened, as compared with the powers of the High Authority in the E.C.S.C. In Article 155 of the E.E.C. Treaty, the functions of the Commission are defined as primarily those of applying the Treaty and formulating 'recommendations or opinions in matters which are the subject of this treaty, where the latter expressly so provides or where the Commission considers it necessary'. Its power of decision is limited and subject to the Council, i.e. the multinational organ of the Community composed of representatives of the member-States. This is the principal decision-making organ of the Community, which decides, depending on the subject at hand, unanimously, by qualified or by simple majority. Where a qualified majority is required, the three major members, France, Germany and Italy, have four votes each, Belgium and the Netherlands two votes each and Luxembourg one vote. Another retrograde step from the point of view of supra-national integration is the method of financing the Community. Whereas the E.C.S.C. finances itself by levies on the member industries and is thus independent of any national budget appropriations, the E.C.S.C. depends on the financial contributions of member-States fixed according to a scale laid down in the Treaty. Only for the future is it envisaged that this method of financing might be replaced by revenue accruing from a common customs tariff.

Despite the constitutional and economic limitations, the E.E.C., during the first five years of its effective operation, made dramatic progress, not only towards the accomplishment of the economic objectives of the Treaty, but also towards a closer integrated co-ordination of the policies of the partners, with the avowed aim of eventual political confederation. The establishment of the Common Market which, under Article VIII of the Treaty, was to be 'progressively established in the course of a transitional period of twelve years', proceeded in several respects ahead of schedule. A series of important tariff reductions were decreed, and corresponding, although more limited privileges, accorded to non-member-States. Freedom in the movement of capital and business enterprises was encouraged by the mutual recognition of companies in the member-States, by work towards common, or at least assimilated, laws in the fields of patents and trade-marks, company law, anti-trust and other fields. Above all there was general confidence within and outside the Community, that it was there to stay, that it was rapidly becoming an economically unified region, with dramatic increases in production and in trade, principally among the member-States, but also with the outer world.[1] One result of this universal confidence was a rush of investments from other countries within the Community. Hundreds of U.S.

[1] Trade within the Community increased by 19% in 1959, 25% in 1960, 15% in 1961 and 14% in 1962. In 1960 — the year of greatest confidence and expansion — sales of the Community to the United States increased by 24%, but hardly increased any further in 1962.

and British companies established subsidiaries, normally incorporated in Switzerland, but operating within the Community, in the expectation of growing markets and opportunities. Another result was the move for associated membership in the Community, not only of the former African colonies of France — for whose association provision was made in the Treaty — but also of other States strongly dependent on trade with the E.E.C. Greece and Turkey are now associate members, while negotiations are in progress with Israel and Nigeria. One constitutional effect of this development was the growing prestige of the supra-national body of the Community, i.e. the Commission, which as a permanent executive represented the supra-national rather than the national policies of the Community. Such was the general confidence in the development of the E.E.C. that a half-reluctant Britain — which had refused the urgent invitations of the Continental members to join the E.C.S.C. in 1951 — decided to apply for membership in the Community, despite the important impact of such membership on Britain's relations with the Commonwealth, the threat to its largely subsidized farming community and the aversion of many sectors of British public opinion and Parliament to close association of Britain with the Continent. Britain's application made it necessary for most of its partners in the European Free Trade Association to apply for membership as well.

The entire dynamism of the E.E.C. was arrested with dramatic suddenness by a speech of General de Gaulle, of January 14, 1963, by which on behalf of France he unconditionally rejected Britain's move for admission to the E.E.C., on the ground that she was, politically, psychologically and constitutionally, not ready for such an association. Since, under Article 237 of the Treaty, the unanimous vote of the Council is required for admission of any other European State as a member, France's decision was sufficient to defeat Britain's application. It also produced a profound psychological and political change within the Community itself. Although all the other five members were to varying degrees opposed to France's move, the defiant nationalist attitude of Gaullist France rekindled nationalist differences within the Community and made, for example, any further progress in the adjustment of agricultural prices within the E.E.C. far more difficult than in previous years. De Gaulle's appeal to the Community of Continental

European interests and aspirations, as against the essentially different and alien character of the 'Anglo-Saxons', has a particular irony, because it does not in any way imply any positive attitude towards political or constitutional integration. On the contrary, no single statesman has been more contemptuous of moves towards any diminution of national sovereignty within the E.E.C. than de Gaulle.

The Future of European Integration

The future of European integration remains uncertain. The E.E.C. has survived the acute threat of disintegration caused by France's policy, and recent agreements on the assimilation of agricultural prices and plans for tax assimilation are beginning to revive confidence. In July 1964 the Council of Ministers agreed to the merger of the executive authorities of the three Communities in a single consolidated Commission of fourteen members, to be followed by a merger of the Communities themselves (hopefully in 1966). French support for such an apparent strengthening of the supra-national body is probably due to the calculation that the merger will greatly weaken its most supra-national element, the E.C.S.C., following the emasculation of Euratom's supra-national powers some years ago. The merger decision is subject to ratification by the members' national Parliaments. The opposition to de Gaulle in France, composed of the major elements of the former Centre and moderate left- and moderate right-wing parties, is strongly critical of the extreme nationalism of Gaullist France, including its attitude towards European integration. But its influence remains in doubt. A change in French policy would presumably lead to an active revival of integration tendencies within the E.E.C., but a renewal of any British bid to join the Community is highly unlikely, and thus European integration would remain confined to a part of Western Europe. The intensity of any such developments is likely to be further influenced by the state of relationships between the Atlantic Alliance and the Soviet Union. The most tragic and dangerous aspect of the policy of de Gaulle's France is the revival of a narrow nationalism that the mature nations of Europe had gone further than any other nations to overcome in previous years. While the conviction of the insufficiency of national sovereignty may still prevail among the people of Europe, the faith in the progress of a great and dynamic pioneer experiment in Western Europe, which would show that nations, after hundreds of years of nationalism and conflict, could overcome their history, has been shattered, perhaps beyond repair.

The halt in the momentum of the development of the European Communities coincides with the end of a fifteen-year period in international politics, which was dominated by the Cold War. This meant that any political and economic alignments were controlled by the political and geographical division of Europe, which runs right through Germany. As discussed earlier, the position has now become much more fluid, with the growing independence of the European Communist States from the U.S.S.R. on the one side, and the diversity of politics within the NATO Alliance, on the other side, with France going farthest in the virtual denial of a Western policy based on the NATO concept. Some commentators, notably Walter Lippmann, who agrees with much of de Gaulle's thinking, believe that, in Europe, the desire for a greater European concept, including the reunification of Germany and the overrunning of the East–West schism, now increasingly displaces the acceptance of the Western Alliance and Cold War concept which means a *Western*, anti-Communist Europe aligned with the United States and Canada.

In this writer's opinion, this is looking far into the future. Co-existence is very different from co-operation, let alone integration. There is no realistic prospect of German reunification, which is the principal key to such a change. But the new fluidity of European politics may powerfully contribute to a conservative and static approach to the present structure and concept of West European integration and thus give support to the attitude of de Gaulle's France, though for different reasons.

CHAPTER 7

THE BRITISH COMMONWEALTH IN WORLD AFFAIRS

Historical and Political Factors

THE development of the British Empire and Commonwealth of Nations is a matter for the historian. A few salient facts are, however, essential to an understanding of the present structure and function of this unique international association. It has often been said that the British Empire has arisen by accident and not by design. This is a half-truth. It was inevitable that in the age of exploration, commerce and sea travel, a country of the particular geographical, economic and social structure of England should expand overseas. Nor has this expansion been entirely a private affair. Jamaica, for example, was conquered by an expedition sent by Oliver Cromwell, which laid the foundations for the West Indian Empire. Drake's aggressive expeditions were actively supported by Queen Elizabeth. But the most populous part of Britain's former colonial empire, India, was conquered, exploited and administered by a private company acting under Government charter, and it is only since the beginning of the nineteenth century that the Government gradually took over direct responsibility for India. The particular geographical structure of the British Empire — that world-wide and scattered medley of continents, islands and enclaves — is due to this combination of political, military and trading ventures of a seafaring nation. A glance at the map shows that an empire on which 'the sun never sets', which includes such scattered possessions as British Guiana, the Falkland Islands, Gibraltar and Hong Kong, could be regarded as an effective unit of power in world politics only as long as the British Navy had unchallenged supremacy and as long as the nations and races surrounding these possessions were objects rather than subjects of politics; in other words, as long as they had not yet begun to form national States of their own.

Another historical factor is of vital importance for the ideological significance of the British Commonwealth in the modern world. The Commonwealth includes countries predominantly populated by British stock as well as a large majority of non-white peoples. The former type — that is, most of the older Dominions — were colonized by emigrating British people. The latter were conquered. But the principle which, since the famous Durham Report on Canada of 1838, has led to the gradual emancipation of the British colonies towards a state of complete autonomy of government, has increasingly influenced and permeated British colonial policy in general. The goal of gradual education towards self-government became the keystone of the transformation of the British Empire into the Commonwealth. Its dominating trend over the last generation has been centrifugal, not centripetal. There has been an increasing tendency, first on the part of the colonies populated by British settlers, and later on the part of other colonies as they gained political consciousness, to become more independent of Britain politically and economically, and Britain has deliberately supported this development. Whereas all modern States are driven towards more and more centralized control over manpower, production and other aspects of community life, it has been the other way round in the British Empire. Since the Imperial Conferences of 1926 and 1930 the Dominions and Britain do not share either a common Parliament, a common government, common judicial institutions or even a permanent co-ordinating machinery in military, political or economic matters.

Until 1947 the full autonomous British Dominions consisted of countries entirely or predominantly populated by British people, and therefore linked with Britain through close ties of race, sentiment and tradition. Even this applied fully only to Australia and New Zealand, the two Dominions which are still closest to Britain in allegiance and policy. Southern Ireland, which had become a Dominion in 1922, broke away in 1937, despite her close proximity to Britain. Centuries of suppression, a new nationalism, racial and religious antagonisms were more powerful. In the next group, Canada has a strong French Catholic and, in many ways, anti-British minority.

In the Republic of South Africa, which became a Dominion after the conclusion of the Boer War, the ruling white minority of some three million people is, in approximately equal parts, composed of Boers (Afrikaners) and British, divided by many antagonisms. In the post-war era, the British element has greatly lost in influence. The Afrikaners have formed the Government for a number of years. Their strongly racialist 'apartheid' policy, which is in stark contrast to the emancipation of Africans on the rest of the Continent and the association of many of the new African States with the Commonwealth, led to a situation in which South Africa was compelled to leave the Commonwealth. For Britain and the other senior members, it was a question of choosing between the continued association of the former colonies and association with South Africa, based on a racial policy that Britain and the other older Dominions reject. Even acute conflict between South Africa and Britain is possible if South Africa presses her claim for the incorporation of the native Protectorates of Bechuanaland, Swaziland and Basutoland, at present governed from Whitehall. Britain cannot voluntarily surrender these Protectorates to a Government whose dominant policy is the reduction of coloured races to a status of political and economic inferiority.

The transformation of the British Empire into a Commonwealth of Nations composed of a growing number of independent States has proceeded at a greatly accelerated pace in recent years. Only widely scattered territories of minor size and development now constitute the shrinking colonial empire. By the end of 1964, all the major British possessions in Asia, Africa and Central America will have reached full independence. So far, only one of the former colonies, i.e. Burma, which obtained its independence in 1947, has chosen to leave the Commonwealth.

The unexpectedly rapid growth of the number of independent members of the Commonwealth, as well as the growing diversity in the racial background, the political orientation and the degree of kinship with Britain is, however, changing the structure and meaning of the Commonwealth.

The Present Structure of the Commonwealth

The nature of the Commonwealth has changed decisively in recent years. Racial or cultural kinship is no longer the predominant basis of Commonwealth relations. The majority of the independent members are now States, entirely non-European in race, religion and culture, nations not settled by emigrants of

British stock, but conquered and exploited as colonies. Given this change, it is remarkable that the Commonwealth should survive at all and that all but one of the former colonies should have chosen to retain any form of special association with the former colonial power. But inevitably, this transformation of the Commonwealth has greatly altered the nature of the ties that bind its various members in different continents, both to Britain and each other.

Even the one constitutional symbol, that formerly united the Dominions, the allegiance to the British Crown, has disappeared. While the Queen continues to be accepted as sovereign for the older Dominions of the Commonwealth, the newer Asian and African members have chosen the alternative status of republics, headed by a President of their own race and nationality, instead of a Governor-General. With this corresponds the status of their nationals as 'Commonwealth citizens' instead of 'British subjects'. The decision to permit this diversity of constitutional allegiances as not incompatible with membership of the Commonwealth, was itself a typically informal understanding reached at a conference of Commonwealth heads of government, and it is symbolic of the looseness and flexibility of contemporary Commonwealth ties. For most purposes, however, the nationals of any member of the Commonwealth are still regarded as having a general overall link of nationality. They are not treated as 'foreigners' in each other's territories. As the Commonwealth widens and its various members become more and more disparate, these links are, however, apt to weaken. Already some of the non-British member-States of the Commonwealth require visas from each others' citizens. Britain herself recently took a drastic step in the restriction of the traditional freedom of entry into Britain for all citizens of the Commonwealth and Empire, by establishing certain criteria of admission (guarantee of support or employment), designed to limit the immigration, especially of West Indians, whose influx into Britain began to create racial and social problems.

Second, the various parts of the Commonwealth are not linked by any general military alliance or reciprocal duties of assistance. None of the Dominions has any automatic military obligation towards Britain.[1] But while it is reasonably certain that Australia, New Zealand and Canada will be on the side of Britain in any war

[1] Except Canada, who has a duty to assist Britain in case of attack, not as a Dominion, but as a party to the North Atlantic Treaty.

of defence, this is far from certain in the case of the Asian Dominions. It is clear that they wish to concentrate their energies on internal development, and their international policies are generally neutralist. Even the older Dominions will for many purposes have to be considered as parts of new continental regions. Canada is militarily, economically and financially already predominantly a part of the American Continent.

Australia and New Zealand have realized for some time that they need new regional defence arrangements. The strategic interest of the United States in the defence of the Indian Ocean and the South-west Pacific area led in 1951 to the conclusion of a security treaty between the United States, Australia and New Zealand, which in substance and form, is closely modelled upon the North Atlantic Treaty. Its most important provision is that 'each party recognizes that an armed attack in the Pacific area on any of the parties would be dangerous to its own people and safety, and it declares that it would act to meet the common danger in accordance with its constitutional processes'. A further article defines an armed attack on any of the parties as including 'an armed attack on the metropolitan territory of any of the parties, or on the island territories under its jurisdiction in the Pacific area, or on its armed forces, public vessels, or aircraft in the Pacific'.

Australia and New Zealand have also been active supporters of a newer regional defence arrangement, the South-East Asia Treaty Organization (SEATO), established in September 1954. This Treaty — designed to protect South-east Asia against further Communist advances, and concluded in reaction to the Western defeat in Indo-China — has only two members which are neither members of the British Commonwealth nor Western Powers: the Philippines and Thailand. Two other Commonwealth members, Britain and Pakistan, have joined the Pact, whose main military backer and sponsor is, as in the case of Anzus, the United States. SEATO is designed to provide joint action of the parties in the case of aggression against certain designated territories in Asia (excluding Hong Kong), but SEATO shares the weakness of Anzus in being only consultative, and it has the added weakness of linking States with very disparate political strategic interests. Especially since the recent estrangement of Pakistan, the protective value of this organization must be regarded as very dubious.

Third, the political ties between the various parts of the

Commonwealth are very uneven. The links that have for many generations bound the great majority of Australians and New Zealanders, and of the English-speaking Canadians, to Britain — links symbolized by their whole-hearted participation on the side of Britain in two world wars — are still strong. But the younger generation of Australians and Canadians are more conscious of their own countries. Their sentimental attachment to Britain is weaker than that of their ancestors. They are also aware of the drastically altered strategic and political situation, which puts the relation to Britain in a very different perspective from that preceding the First or even the Second World War. The situation of Canada is a particularly complicated one. English-speaking Canadians, like Australians and New Zealanders, share with Britain the common heritage of history, race, culture and law. These are however countered by the natural attraction of Canada's giant continental neighbour, the United States. The people of Ontario, politically the most British-oriented of the Canadian provinces, are also those who in their habits and economic links are closest to the United States. The economic predominance of the United States in many of the basic industries of Canada, and the very large investment of American capital in Canada, has however produced a reaction against American influence, which in part expresses itself in a tendency to strengthen the traditional ties with Britain, and to welcome economic investment from Britain and other non-American countries. But the principal preoccupation of Canadians is the increasingly severe threat posed to the very existence of the nation by the militant nationalism of French-speaking Quebec. This province, with over a third of Canada's population, is divided from the English-speaking provinces by history, language, culture, religion and law. Ever since the annexation of Quebec by England, after the Battle of Abraham Heights in 1759, Quebec has striven with singular success to maintain the integrity of its institutions and heritage. However, in the period immediately following the last war, when a French-speaking Quebec Canadian, Louis Saint-Laurent, was Prime Minister of Canada, and Canada under Lester Pearson's guidance took a lead in the NATO alliance and other international associations, it seemed that the political force of Quebec nationalism was ebbing. But in recent years a new generation has pushed Quebec nationalism far beyond previous aspirations, to the point where a loose confederation of an essentially English-speaking, and essentially French-speaking Canada, or — on the part of a minority of extremists — even complete separation is seriously discussed. Quebec nationalism is reflected not only in the political, but also in the economic and financial field. There is strong pressure for a partial return of the federal taxing powers to the Provinces. Even if only a fraction of the actual demands of the more extreme Quebec nationalists is implemented, the strength of their influence on the Federal Government is apt to weaken Canada's national posture. This is accentuated by the recent tendency of Quebec nationalism to forge political, as distinct from merely cultural, links with a nationalist Gaullist France which is distancing herself more and more from the 'Anglo-Saxons'. The result is certainly a relative loosening of the strong ties developed in the earlier post-war period with both Britain and the United States.

Of the other older Dominions, the Republic of South Africa ceased to be a member of the Commonwealth in 1961. Quite apart from this formal severance of ties, the dominance of a Boer Government which is in many ways antagonistic to the British element, and even more the intransigent racialist policy of 'apartheid' which is repugnant to the great majority of the now predominantly non-white member-States of the Commonwealth, has alienated South Africa from the Commonwealth. Since the advent of a government in Southern Rhodesia — a colony with near-Dominion status — that is close to South Africa's white supremacy policy, tensions between Britain and the black African members of the Commonwealth on the one side, and Southern Rhodesia, on the other, have also risen to the point where Southern Rhodesia may break away from its British and Commonwealth association, even though its ruling class is of British stock and its economic links with Britain are strong.

For the newer non-white members of the Commonwealth — i.e. the ex-colonies of Asia, Africa and the West Indies — the principal reason for continued association is not political or military alignment with Britain. They are pledged to a policy of detachment from the Cold War and of aloofness from alliances. This is as true of India as of Nigeria, of Ceylon as of Tanganyika or Trinidad. The main value of the Commonwealth association for all these countries is the continuation of links that have developed, through centuries of — a formerly enforced and now voluntary — close association with British education, the common law, methods of administration, and ways of life which have so far survived political independence. Anybody who moves from one of the former British to one of the former French colonies of Africa is immediately struck by the extent to which both have been influenced by the ways of life and administration of their former masters. The ceremonies of opening Parliaments in Nigeria, and even more the passion for cricket, survive in countries that are no longer in any way subject to British control. The Commonwealth is essentially a club, whose members are represented by a board of trustees — the heads of Government or their deputies — who meet periodically for consultations but have no voting rules or any other definite procedure.

This loose association is cemented by certain more solid pillars: the link of a common basic currency, described as the Sterling Area (except for Canada); the continuance of a freedom of movement between most if not all the members of the Commonwealth, which is symbolized by a general British or 'Commonwealth' nationality; the continuing importance of mutual trade between Britain and the other Commonwealth members; the maintenance, on the part of Britain, of economic assistance for the many newer members of the Commonwealth — especially in Africa and the West Indies — which are as yet in a precarious financial and economic condition; the continuing, though rapidly diminishing, role of British civil servants in the administration of the newer States; finally, certain defence arrangements which, though not intended to be permanent, may prove to be more important to the governments of the newly independent States than they expected. In January 1964, the heads of Government of Tanganyika, Kenya and Uganda — all of which had achieved independence within the last few years — requested British military assistance for the suppression of local army mutinies.

Despite the continuing strength of these many formal and informal associations, the various parts of the Commonwealth — and especially its non-white members — are likely to go more and more their own and separate ways. To the extent that India may lean more heavily on Western military and economic aid to meet the threat from Communist China, such support will come from a coalition of Western Powers led by the United States, rather than from Britain as such. Economic aid to India or Nigeria comes from international institutions such as the World Bank, the United States or from public–private consortia, in all of which Britain plays an important but not a dominant part. British influence is apt to recede as the remainder of the British administrators leave and as a new generation of nationalist Africans grows up, whose association with British education and traditions is weaker than that of their parents.

The Political and Ideological Importance of the Commonwealth

In terms of constitutional machinery, of military and political links, of geographical or economic cohesion, the Commonwealth is now a very elusive association. It means little more than that a number of nations, separated by geography, race, history and civilization, wish to continue a special though informal association, which implies no concrete obligations of a political, military or economic character. But this very fact — and in particular, the fact that almost all the former colonies of Britain have chosen to maintain a special association with their former master, in conditions of freedom and equality — is an important factor in world politics. It is a practical vindication of the policy of evolutionary progress towards freedom. During the last world war, when Nehru was in prison and Mahatma Gandhi expressed his protests against British rule in repeated fasts, it did not seem likely that Indian nationalism and British policy could come together in an agreed solution, or that British businessmen would be welcome to India after independence. Yet a few years later independence was achieved by agreement and ever since official and unofficial relations between Britain and India — sustained by mutual knowledge acquired in centuries — have been friendly. Most of the African States invited British administrators and other advisers to remain, at least as long as there were not sufficient native administrators trained to take over. With the possible exception of Ghana, where the erratic and emotional leadership of President Nkrumah makes relations with other powers highly uncertain, Britain's political relations with all its former colonies are friendly, and in many cases cordial.

As an implementation of the principle of racial tolerance and of the possibilities of peaceful evolution from subjection to freedom, the Commonwealth has on the whole been a triumphant success. But it has failed to come up to hopes and aspirations in other respects. A few years ago it seemed that the newly independent members of the Commonwealth would follow the political pattern of British-style democracy, and adhere to the ideals of political freedom which many of their leaders had imbibed through their British education. Personal ambitions and the hard facts of life have largely frustrated this hope. The forms of Parliamentary democracy were introduced almost everywhere. But it is only in two — although very major — of the new members of the Commonwealth that Parliamentary democracy survives effectively, though not without difficulty. These two are India and Nigeria. In India, freedom of discussion and the predominance of Parliament are maintained, although it is doubtful how long Parliamentary democracy will continue after the death of Nehru, or if Congress ceased to be the predominant party able to control Parliament. In Nigeria the tensions between the three — now four — major regions, which to some extent correspond to the different parties and leaders, are serious. Elsewhere in Africa, democracy has disappeared, in substance and increasingly also in name. For reasons which will be analysed in a different chapter, one State after another — Pakistan, Ghana, Tanganyika and many others — have established some form of one-party State often accompanied by drastic restrictions on freedom of expression and judicial independence. The rapidity of the transition from political dependence and a low state of economic as well as administrative development, has made the working of democracy difficult. This inevitably affects the homogeneity of the Commonwealth and its influence as a moderating and civilizing factor in world affairs. But for all these weaknesses and strains, it is still an important and salutary, though intangible, force in world affairs.

Economic Prospects of the British Commonwealth and their Effect on International Politics

The looseness of constitutional and legal ties between the independent members of the Commonwealth is to some extent countered by a still close economic relationship cemented — except for Canada — by the sterling currency.

In her relations with the Dominions, Britain still retains to some extent the position which she occupied generally in the nineteenth century. She is a steady and large buyer of foodstuffs and certain raw materials from the Dominions, which she supplies in return with capital equipment and other manufactured goods. All the Dominions are making steady, and in some cases rapid, progress towards greater industrial autonomy. But some figures illustrate the degree of mutual dependence which still exists. For all the Dominions the United Kingdom is still by far the greatest single customer,[1] although the share of the United Kingdom in the total trade of the Commonwealth is slowly declining. In 1957, 45% of Britain's imports came from the Commonwealth (including Eire) while over 48% of British exports went to the Commonwealth as well as the greater part of Britain's foreign investments (estimated at about £200 million p.a.). In 1962, out of a greatly expanded export volume (£3,791·8 million), only a little over 35% (£1,343·0 million) went to the Commonwealth. Correspondingly, the proportion of British imports from the Commonwealth shrank to just over 24% of total imports.

The great expansion of Britain's trade in the last decade has therefore entirely occurred outside the Commonwealth. At the same time, the trade relations of the other Commonwealth countries have become increasingly diversified. Thus Canada, for whom the U.S. has long been the principal trading partner — in 1962, 59% of her exports, 69% of her imports — in 1962 only obtained 9% of her imports from the U.K., while exporting 14% of her total to the U.K. But for some other major Commonwealth members, the economic links with Britain remain very strong.

New Zealand is economically most closely bound to the U.K. — where in 1962 she still sent 49% of her exports and from where she obtained 42% of her imports. The corresponding figures for Australia were 19% and 31%, for India 23% and 25%, for Pakistan 14% and 20%, for Nigeria 41% and 33% and for the (now dissolved) Federation of Rhodesia and Nyasaland 42% and 33%.

That Canada's Commonwealth trade is well below that of the other major Dominions is due to Canada being a member of the dollar, not the sterling, area, as well as to participation in the growing economic links that rearmament, United States investments in Canada and the partial integration of their industrial production

[1] For some statistical details see below, p. 374.

and trade forge between the United States and Canada. Yet for all parts of the Commonwealth, not excluding Canada, the collapse of the British market would be an economic disaster. It would be a serious blow to wool production in Australia, to wheat and pig farming in Canada, to tea plantations in India, Pakistan and Ceylon, to dairy and sheep farming in New Zealand. Not only would all these countries be unable to find alternative markets; they could not satisfy most of their vital requirements for machinery and certain consumer goods. This applies particularly, but not exclusively, to members of the sterling area, and it is accentuated by the devaluation of sterling. The standard of living would drop catastrophically, and such countries as Australia and India would have to slow down greatly their ambitious efforts for industrial development. But Canada, too, although within the dollar area, has a vital interest in the maintenance of her trade relations with Britain. Although Canada can obtain many of her requirements from the neighbouring United States, she has usually been able to cover her chronic deficit with that country only by the conversion of her sterling surplus with Britain. Moreover, it is essential for the political independence of Canada that she should not be exclusively dependent on the American market.

Theoretically every member of the sterling area within the Commonwealth is free to leave the sterling group. But the facts just given show why they cannot do so without a drastic economic upheaval. Britain still acts as the financial centre for the Commonwealth in so far as its members customarily hold their sterling balances in London. This expresses the many financial and economic ties that still link the different parts of the Commonwealth. Moreover, the predominance of the Commonwealth for British investment — both public and private — finds institutional expression in the government-owned Commonwealth Development Corporation (formerly Colonial Development Corporation) (C.D.C.), and the privately owned Commonwealth Development Finance Company. The former had, by the end of 1963, total outstanding investments of £119,271,000 spread over 115 projects in all parts of the Commonwealth, mainly in basic utilities, primary production and processing, and housing. The latter, established more recently by a group of private banks and other enterprises for the encouragement of private Commonwealth development, has invested about £25 million in a variety of industrial enterprises, some of it by equity participations. The economic cohesion of the Commonwealth seemed to have reached its nadir when Britain applied for membership in the European Common Market, a membership which after a transitional period would have meant the end of Commonwealth Preference and a threat to the market that Britain has supplied for generations to the agricultural produce of New Zealand, Australia and other parts of the Commonwealth. The collapse of the negotiations between Britain and the European Economic Community has somewhat revived the economic as well as the sentimental interest in the Commonwealth ties. From time to time proposals for closer organizational economic links have been put forward. Among such proposals are those for an Export Council, a Development Council, a Commonwealth Bank, or a co-ordinated programme of financial and technical aid within the Commonwealth. It is true that in 1962, the sterling area — which means mainly, though not exclusively, the Commonwealth — still accounted for one-fifth to one-quarter of world trade, and that the Commonwealth as a whole does or can produce a major proportion of the vital raw materials and farm products, as well as an industrial potential which outside of the U.K. and Canada is only beginning to develop. It is easy to put together the Commonwealth production of such vital commodities as nickel, steel, cocoa, rubber, wool, rice or sugar and to arrive at dazzling estimates of their economic potential. The basic fallacy of such estimates is the assumption that the Commonwealth can be regarded as an economic unit, for purposes going beyond the gradual diminishing mutuality of trade and financial relationships. It is a political rather than an economic question and it is because of the political realities that it would seem absurd to regard not only such newer units of the Commonwealth as India, Ghana or Nigeria, but also older Dominions such as Australia and Canada, as parts of a potential economic unit which would plan and develop in unison. The image of the Commonwealth as an economic unit is in fact essentially one of the past when the undeveloped colonial members of the Empire supplied primary products to Britain and received manufactured goods in return. But now all these countries, including the older Dominions such as Australia, are determined to expand their own manufacturing industries and have no hesitation in using tariffs, import quotas and any other protective device to achieve national economic development. The protests that several members of the Commonwealth raised against Britain's proposed membership in the Common Market were the normal actions of countries that feared the loss of traditional markets, but neither Australia nor Canada, let alone the newer members of the Commonwealth, would consider for one moment abandoning economic policies which they regard to be in their national interest, out of consideration for Britain. As the former Economic Adviser to the British Treasury, Sir Robert Hall, has recently put it,[1] it seems to be frequently suggested that 'Britain alone has some special obligation not to enter groups unless they are favourably regarded by all the other members of the Commonwealth . . . but the economic links are not what they were and it is becoming harder to regard the Commonwealth as an action group and more necessary than it was to think in terms of other groups, some of which may be outside and others may be inside.' In other words, there are still many economic associations between *specific* members of the Commonwealth, e.g. in the development of beef cattle in Australia for British consumption, production of cotton in India and Pakistan or of tobacco in Southern Rhodesia, but this will have to be dealt with by specific arrangements such as bilateral trade agreements or investment plans. They do not extend to the Commonwealth as a whole.

An important contribution of the British Commonwealth to international developments is its outstanding part in post-war migration. On an average about half a million have annually migrated from Europe overseas, and by far the greatest proportion has gone to British Dominions, and in particular to Australia and Canada.[2] Both Dominions have in recent years taken immigrants at a rate approaching two hundred thousand a year. Migration to New Zealand and South Africa, too, has been considerable, though not approaching the rate of Australia and Canada. Not only has this immigration policy helped to solve human distress and overcrowding in Europe. What is perhaps even more important is the alteration in the racial composition of the Dominions, which is one consequence of their present immigration policy. Australia and New Zealand, for example, will for

[1] *The Listener*, February 13, 1964.

[2] On migration, see further below, pp. 327 *et seq*.

the first time have a considerable proportion of non-British Europeans — a fact of great cultural and sociological significance.

This immigration policy has been dictated by enlightened self-interest. The Dominions are in a phase of vigorous industrial development, and are anxious, for strategic reasons, to increase their (white) population. Even though far more will have to be done to redress the balance between the Old and the New World, the British Commonwealth has played, and is likely to play in the future, a notable part in helping towards the solution of this problem.

New Regional Associations and the Commonwealth

Its very elasticity makes it easier for the British Commonwealth than for more rigid associations to adapt itself to new patterns of international organization. For the purposes of membership of the United Nations and its specialized agencies, Britain and the Dominions act as independent States which often, but not invariably, act in concert. As the previous pages have shown, the Commonwealth has in the post-war period become increasingly diversified in composition, structure, policies and interests. Hence, the periodic proposals to create some kind of political and constitutional organization for the Commonwealth are not only unrealistic but would probably damage rather than improve such cohesion as exists. The main strength of the Commonwealth lies in its flexibility, in associations and methods of consultation that would most likely wither under the strain of institutionalization. To quote Sir Robert Hall again: '. . . the Commonwealth today is an association of sovereign States. It is unique among such associations because it contains States that differ very widely indeed on important issues. . . . This is not a bad thing but it is certain that if there were an attempt to form a coherent Commonwealth policy on some of these issues, the result would be to break up the Commonwealth.'

The interests and policies of the different members of the Commonwealth coincide in some fields, but diverge in others. For purposes of defence, Britain, Canada, Australia and New Zealand are closely aligned, and will probably continue to act in close concert. But geography and the threat of nuclear warfare have created close defence links between Canada and the United States. The two countries now have a common continental radar warning system and joint air defence arrangements. Even though Canada is now linked directly to Britain through the North Atlantic Treaty, the only formal defence link of Australia and New Zealand with Britain is indirect — through the new Security Treaty with the United States. Australia's strategic and geographical position was the main cause of her recent decision to re-equip her air force with American, not British, fighter planes.

Thus, it is intangible ties, rather than any specific community of military, political or even economic interests that makes the Commonwealth survive.[1]

[1] The strength as well as the elasticity of these ties was seldom more clearly demonstrated than at the annual Conference of Commonwealth Prime Ministers held at London in July 1964. It had been widely feared that the bitterness of the African members against Southern Rhodesia's new 'white supremacy' government, and impatience with Britain's cautious handling of Southern Rhodesia, would lead to bitter divisions, and perhaps ruptures. Instead, unanimous resolutions were passed and the newest member, Malawi's Prime Minister Dr. Banda, praised the Commonwealth. It was some of the African members that proposed the creation of a Commonwealth Secretariat, regarded with scepticism by most older members.

CHAPTER 8

THE EMERGENCE OF ASIA

AFTER centuries of unchallenged Western supremacy, it is not easy for the people of the West to adjust their thoughts and actions to a world situation in which the balance of world politics would be determined by Asia rather than by Europe or even North America. Yet the East has dominated the West before. Between the ninth and twelfth centuries the Arabs were not only physical masters of Southern Europe, but the centre of a civilization which had absorbed Greek, Jewish and Christian influences. Mongolian invasions, under Attila, Genghis Khan and Tamerlane, kept large parts of Europe subdued for long periods. Some centuries later the Ottoman Turks controlled considerable parts of Europe. In 1299 the Italian traveller Marco Polo told his astonished contemporaries of the vastly superior civilization of China.

The comparative study of history has shown that the supremacy of any one nation or civilization is a passing phenomenon, covering at best a span of a few centuries. Whatever cause the philosophers of history may single out as the dominant motive in the sudden rise and expansion of a nation such as the Greeks, the Romans or the modern British, it is certain that it does not lie in superiority of numbers. It is only in association with certain other factors that large numbers may become a decisive factor in international politics. The amazing rise and expansion of the nations of Western Europe is due to the combination of a new ideology with the development of modern technological science and concentration on the economic organization of society. The ideology of the Renaissance gave the individual a new consciousness of his own powers and freed him from the bonds of a static religious and feudal society. This individualism was reinforced by Protestantism, which, especially in its Calvinist version, made the acquisition of wealth a visible sign of divine grace and favour and gave an ethical justification to what Tawney has described as 'the acquisitive society'. These ideological developments also set free the thirst for knowledge and the conquest of Nature, which in turn provided the means for the technical mastery of the many new tasks now facing the Western nations: navigation of the oceans, improvement of transport, agriculture and trade, and finally the mechanization of production. No less important is a third factor: political organization on a vaster and more complex basis. Without the development of the modern national State, with its machinery of central government and administration of justice, its armed forces, its tax-gathering apparatus and the professional Civil Service, Western supremacy could not have been attained. With changing emphasis, these various developments have reacted upon each other. Without the new philosophy of the individual, there would have been no discoveries or scientific research; without the protective and organizing power of the modern State, neither Capitalism nor Socialism would have been possible. The modern Western State itself owes most of its power to the economic and technical improvements which the ideology of 'economic man', helped by science, has produced.

It is the absence of all these very factors that accounts for the political impotence of the vast masses of Asians: 750 million Chinese, 450 million Hindu Indians, 100 million Indonesians, hundreds of millions of Pakistani and Arab Moslems. In the past few centuries all these peoples have lived either under the cover of comparative obscurity and remoteness from the West, or they have been directly dominated by it.

The gap between the economic conditions of East and West has steadily widened. The vast majority of the Asians are peasants, and their ways of gaining their livelihood have not materially changed for many hundreds of years. Hand labour, the wooden plough, the ox and the water-buffalo are still the chief implements of agriculture. Mechanized farming and modern scientific methods of raising yields, by chemical fertilizers, or by improved seeds, have as yet hardly affected the vast majority of the peasant economies of the East. With the exception of Russia, there are only three industrial regions of any importance in Asia: Japan, Manchuria (part of China) and India, although Communist China is now rapidly developing other industrial areas. Of these three, Japan, the one Asian State which had quickly and completely absorbed Western methods of industrial production, military organization and centralized government, was the only one to become a major international Power previous to the Second World War. The relative international importance of these three industrial centres has for the time being decreased, as a result of the war. Japan, fighting against a desperate shortage of raw materials, is now making great strides to recover her position as a highly competitive exporter of industrial goods, with American help. Manchuria was stripped of most of its industrial equipment by the Russian armies which occupied it for a short period after the war. India's industrial production is almost fully absorbed by the needs of her rapidly increasing population.

The two factors mainly responsible for the rise in the standard of living of the Western nations — greater agricultural efficiency and industrial production — have not so far affected more than a very small proportion of the people of the East. A few years ago the average productivity of a Chinese farmworker was estimated as being less than one-tenth that of a United States farmworker. Various other factors have traditionally contributed to keeping the average Asian peasant not even in a state of primitive, though healthy, self-sufficiency, but in a condition of unceasing struggle for mere survival and subsistence: recurrent famines, due to drought, uncontrolled floods, or the disruptions of war and civil disorder; a still very widespread system of middlemen who collect excessive dues on behalf of absentee landlords; lack of proper health, education and other services.

Below a minimum level of economic conditions, teeming masses are an obstacle to effective political action. Wars and revolutions have been won by nations and classes which had begun to rise above the sheer daily struggle for survival. Modern war and political power demand efficient soldiers and skilled industrial workers; both presuppose a society in which a minimum standard of living is assured.

The vastness of the territories, the low standards of living, communications, education, account for the relative weakness of well-organized and efficient governments in Asia. The political rise of France and England was largely explained by their early development of a machinery of central government. But in Asia the range of effective government is still limited. Life and loyalty of the Asian peasant are still largely concentrated on family, village, caste or local leaders. The phenomenal rise of modern

Japan was made possible by the rapid conversion of the lower nobility (Samurai), the feudal chiefs (Daimyo) and the big merchants (Chonin) into pillars of the modern State, to which they supplied the military leaders, the new captains of industry and business, and the Civil Service. To this corresponded the conversion of the feudal serf into the modern industrial worker and soldier. The relationship of command and obedience was little affected, but its function was radically changed. None of the other independent Asian States has until recently achieved a similar transformation. Those countries which, like India, Pakistan and Indonesia, have been developed under European administration have in that way been provided with the foundations of modern States, but they have only recently begun to use them for their own political purposes. The dramatic rise in China's political, military and industrial power became possible only with the establishment of a highly centralized State organization.

Lastly, Oriental philosophies and religions, again with the significant exception of the Japanese Emperor-cult (Shinto), have not on the whole favoured the development of an ideology which demands closely knit political organization, dynamic evolution and conquest. This is a theme of infinite complexity, and the subject of many comparative studies by philosophers and historians. Without detracting from the many divergencies between the different religions and philosophies of the Orient, it may, however, be said that Hinduism, Buddhism and Chinese Confucianism are essentially contemplative rather than activist, that they see the individual as a receptive part of the universe rather than as a conqueror of nature, that they are concerned with the moral perfection of the individual, with his conduct and thought rather than with a yearning for individual fulfilment in action, or subordination to a greater entity. Modern Western philosophy, on the other hand, through such thinkers as Descartes, Hume, Kant, Hegel and others, has developed the ego as the thinking and willing centre of the universe. This has branched out into a philosophy of individual equality, of human rights and of democracy, as in the teaching of Locke, Paine, Bentham and the American Constitution. But it has also led to philosophies and political systems which see the fulfilment of the individual in his identification with a collective will. This trend of thought, inherent in the philosophy of Rousseau and Hegel, ultimately leads to the glorification of the collective, and the utter mental and physical subordination of the individual in modern Fascism and Communism. Even where such thinking does not lead to war and conquest, it urges the individual to try himself in a constant battle with the forces outside him, it makes him engage in discoveries, research or moral crusades. This is also the reason why Christianity has not acted as an effective brake on war and suppression. It is a religion of humility, but organized Christian religion has been turned, by the nations adopting it, into a missionary, crusading and conquering force. As Northrop has pointed out,[1] only three of the world's major religions have the crusading zeal — Christianity, Islam and the Japanese Shinto. All three have been used in the service of conquest and Imperialism. Christianity has served as a pretext for the mediæval crusades, for the Spanish Inquisition and for the virtual extinction of the peoples of South America, in the search for gold and Empire. The faith of Islam has inspired the Arab conquests of the Middle Ages and the Mogul Empire in India. The cult of the rising sun has given a unifying symbol to the recent Japanese venture in Imperialism.

Major Factors in the Revolution of Asia

Japan was the first Asian State to transform a primitive feudal society into an efficient modern industrial and military State through the whole-hearted adoption of Western techniques of civilization. Now, Western ideologies, Western forms of political organization and Western methods of economic, scientific and technical development are spreading all over Asia. The political leaders of Asia, men like Shastri, Mao Tse-tung, Ayub, Sukarno, talk and plan in terms of Western political philosophy and economic theory. They adopt or reject, praise or condemn, Nationalism, Capitalism, Socialism, Fascism, Democracy or Communism in terms adopted from the West. They speak of land reform, of the socialization of industries or of health services in a way perfectly intelligible to any Western politician. They aim at national sovereignty, at the scientific development of the nation's resources, in a way entirely borrowed from the technique of modern Western government. This is partly because the very ideology of national independence and sovereignty implies the adoption of suitable means in the political, economic, social and

[1] *The Meeting of East and West*, pp. 409–11.

cultural fields. But this Westernization of policy and thinking is underlined and emphasized by the intensity with which the awakening nations of Asia are drawn into the international struggle. And even if the balance of power should increasingly shift from the West to the East, the issues are stated in terms of Western political, economic and social philosophy.

This does not necessarily mean that Indian democracy will function exactly like Western democracy, or that Chinese Communism will slavishly imitate Soviet Communism. Differences of religion, social structure, historical tradition and racial characteristics may profoundly affect the evolution of the political revolution in the different countries of Asia.

The speeches of Nehru displayed a mixture of Gandhi's philosophy of non-violence and political victory through persuasion rather than force, with the attitudes of a Western-trained nationalist statesman. To some extent Nehru used such language and arguments in order to justify India's present policy of not committing herself in the struggle between East and West. The military and political actions of India since her emancipation have not been very different from those of any other State in a comparable position. India settled a long-drawn-out argument on the accession of the independent State of Hyderabad by military occupation. More recently, she occupied Portuguese Goa. She resisted China's attack on her northern frontiers by force. Indonesia's profession of faith in the principles of Panch Shila (peaceful co-existence) has not prevented her from using force in her disputes with Holland and Malaysia.

On the whole, the indications are that the common attributes that go to the organization of a modern State, to the transformation of a rural and primitive peasant society into an industrialized and urbanized society, to the control of the masses by modern media of communication, tend to reduce traditional national customs and distinctive characteristics, and to produce, for better or worse, a remarkable uniformity of thinking, living and slogans.

The Major Political Storm-Centres in Asia

Every one of the nations which, in the Far East or in the Southwest Pacific area, has achieved or is struggling to achieve political independence, presents certain special problems, caused by its particular religious, racial, economic or social conditions. But in a general survey of the international implications of the rise of Asian nationalism, it is perhaps sufficient to single out the major storm-centres of Asian nationalism, each of which has a particular impact upon world politics.

Japan

Japan, not so long ago the only Asian State which ranked as a major Power — with a permanent seat on the Council of the League of Nations, and a party to most important international treaties between the two wars — is again emerging as a major factor in world politics. Two main reasons combine to give Japan special international importance: in the first place, it is the one Asian Power which already has applied Western methods of government, of industrialization, of scientific cultivation of the soil, to a small, densely populated island group. Poorer than Germany in raw materials and other natural resources, Japan has a highly disciplined, industrious and intelligent population of 95 million. For many years the Japanese nation has been able to earn its living only by an intensive export trade. Owing to what by international standards were exceptionally low wages and long working hours, Japan before the war succeeded in flooding Asian and even many European markets with cheap exports. The attempt to substitute a policy of 'conquer or die' for that of 'export or die' led, after the Japanese defeat, only to an intensification of Japan's economic problem. The United States acquired sole responsibility and executive control over defeated Japan. The other Powers which had participated in the Far Eastern War, including Soviet Russia and Britain, were reduced to advisory functions in an Advisory Council which the imperious personality of General MacArthur soon reduced to utter impotence. The price which the United States paid for complete control was responsibility for Japan's economic recovery, as well as for her political and social future. For several years the American taxpayer paid immense Japanese subsidies on basic commodities which reduced the price of such vital raw materials as coal, pig iron and steel to less than half the American price.

Politically and socially the American authorities were guided by ideas similar to those applied in Germany. But, being in sole control of Japan, they could work with far greater effectiveness. The pattern was that of a moderately conservative parliamentary democracy. In Japan, as in Western Germany, the United States has sponsored a democratic constitution fashioned after the American Constitution. Under MacArthur's guidance, this was coupled with a conservative social policy. Free trade unions were restored and strengthened as compared with the pre-war position — but the right to strike and collective bargaining has been severely limited. At the same time, efforts to break up the industrial and banking concerns which, in Japan, held a position of economic and political power even greater than their counterparts in Germany, came to a far earlier stop than in Germany. The same forces which controlled Japan's economic power in the past have largely regained their influence. In both countries American policy has been strongly opposed to public ownership. It has also been anxious to restore efficiency in production, which is more easily attained by a few large concerns than by a large number of small units, especially in the heavy industries. The most important measure of social reform has been the redistribution of land among peasant farmers, which has converted some three million tenants into owners with apparently excellent social and economic effects, including mechanization without collectivization.

The Communist movement in Japan is not outlawed, but virtually all its leaders are under prosecution and prohibited from taking any active part in the political life of the country. In the elections held in November 1963, the Liberal-Democratic Party, despite its name a conservative party, increased its commanding lead, gaining an absolute majority, and it forms the Government under Prime Minister Sato. The Socialists, divided into left-wing and right-wing groups, are the second strongest party. The continued strength of the politically and socially conservative Liberal-Democratic Party reflects the spreading prosperity of post-war Japan, under a political and social order that, except for a brief period after the end of the last world war, has not basically altered the social and economic pattern of the country, but has brought substantial progress and benefits to the middle classes, the farmers and organized labour. Private enterprise dominates by far, especially in Japan's increasingly important shipbuilding, textile, steel, engineering and chemical industries. But a State monopoly controls the tobacco and salt industries.

The economic expansion and progress of Japan have been one

of the most remarkable phenomena of the post-war world. After having received decisive economic and technical help from the United States during its critical years of recovery, somewhat comparable to the Marshall Plan help that West Germany received in the critical period of reconstruction, Japan has had one of the fastest rates of industrial growth of any country in the world. Between 1960 and 1963 industrial production has risen by 43%, outstripping the also considerable rise in wages and prices. Exports — which are vital to a country that is densely populated and cannot be self-sufficient in food or raw materials, despite a most intensive and scientific cultivation of her sparse land — have risen from year to year (12% overall average in 1963, 17·3% at the end of 1963), Japan's shipbuilding industry has become the world's leader, and Japanese textile machines or photographic cameras are used all over the world. While the wage standards of Japanese labour have risen very considerably compared with the near-feudal conditions of pre-war days, the cost of Japanese production is still highly competitive, as compared with those of the principal Western industrial nations. The United States is far and away Japan's most important customer, buying currently about one-third of all her exports. In recent years Japan has made considerable efforts to widen her economic relations with the underdeveloped countries. A start was made with the Reparations Agreements concluded after the war with Burma, Indonesia and the Philippines, which were implemented by the export of Japanese machinery, engineers and technical advice. While development aid in the strict sense — i.e. grants and long-term loans to developing countries — is still of very modest proportions, amounting to some 280 million dollars in 1962 — less than one-fifteenth of the corresponding figures for the United States and one-third of those for the United Kingdom — Japanese trade with the developing countries, helped by Government guarantees, is expanding steadily, especially in Asia, where Japanese industrial equipment and technical skill are playing an increasing role. The growing importance of Japan as a major industrial Power of the non-Communist world is symbolized by her recent accession to the membership of the Organization for Economic Co-operation and Development (O.E.C.D.).

Like Great Britain and West Germany, Japan is chronically dependent on exports and foreign trade. She is far from self-sufficient in food and vital raw materials. Thus she cannot be isolationist in any sense of the word. After the initially highly successful and ultimately disastrous attempt to repair the lack of indigenous natural resources by military conquest — first, through the occupation of Manchuria and later through the military conquest of much of South-east Asia, the chief reservoir of rice — Japan appears to have abandoned recourse to militarism for the peaceful pursuit of economic expansion, accompanied by a not inconsiderable anti-militarist sentiment. In terms of political alignment, cultural and social contacts, and even in a far-reaching transformation of traditional ways of life, Japan has modelled herself upon the Western world.

Yet it is by no means certain how deep the attachment of the Japanese people to Western ideas, and in particular, to American politics and interests, really goes. Official Japanese policy is unquestionably one of close military, political and economic association with the West, and most of all with the United States. Yet, a few years ago, strong outbursts of pro-Communist and other anti-Western as well as 'neutralist' demonstrations greeted official American visitors. An economic depression accompanied by unemployment might well produce a reversal of Japanese policy.

The United States has a vital interest in Japanese economic and political stability. Faced with the utter inability of defending all or even a substantial proportion of the Far Eastern positions by Western military strength, American policy has to rely more and more on Japan. Like West Germany in Europe, the hated enemy of the last war has become the indispensable ally. The assumption is that Japan will remain strongly anti-Communist and, in the world-wide struggle, continue to ally herself with Western policy, even at the risk of war. In September 1951 the United States and Japan concluded a Treaty of Peace at San Francisco which recognizes Japan as a sovereign nation, with the right of self-defence. Japan agreed to maintain an American force in and about Japan, 'so as to deter armed attack upon Japan'. While the 1951 treaty still preserved certain American prerogatives on Japanese territory, a further treaty in 1960 restored full Japanese sovereignty and, by a somewhat ambiguous formula, seems to give Japan the power of decision over the use of nuclear weapons on Japanese territory.

American policy stands and falls with the correctness of the assumption that Japan will remain firmly anti-Communist. Under strong American pressure, the Japanese Government was induced to enter into negotiations for a peace treaty with the Nationalist Chinese Government. But even the strongly conservative and anti-Communist Japanese Government has been careful not to commit itself to any definite recognition of the Chiang Kai-shek Government as the legitimate Government of China. Few Japanese have any illusions about the prospects of Chiang Kai-shek's regime in China, short of a third world war. On the other hand, China is Japan's most important market, especially for the products of her textile and other light industries. On the whole, the representatives of Japan's heavy industries — dependent largely on American raw materials — favour American policy, while the representatives of her other industries are more inclined to compromise with China. The forces favouring stronger economic relations with Communist China may well be strengthened by France's recent diplomatic recognition of the Peking government.

It is also doubtful how far those who dream of another revival of Japanese power plan for continued association with the West. After the emergence of Soviet Russia and Communist China as major and militant Powers in the Far East, there is very little prospect of Japan's becoming again the dominant Power of Asia. But far from negligible military, political and economic considerations may tempt her to enter into a closer association with Communist China, whose Government is certainly not unaware of its favourable position towards Japan. There are many parallels between the Japanese and the German position. Whereas West Germany is tied to the West, by its strong participation in the North Atlantic Alliance and by its membership in the European Communities, there is no corresponding organic link between the West and Japan. The extraordinary industrial and general development of Japan can easily conceal the fact that it is a small island group, facing a continent dominated by two giant Communist States.

China

The emergence of China as a unified national Power under Communist leadership is the most important international event of recent years. For centuries, the country which, long before Marco Polo testified to its power and the high development of its civilization, had been a mighty and, by comparison to the Europe of the Middle Ages, a highly civilized State, had been in decline. Degenerate dynasties, corrupt administrations, recurrent famines, floods of immense proportions, and lack of communications turned the world's most populous country for a long time into a slumbering giant, the object rather than the subject of international politics. At a time when China was at the nadir of its political power and cohesion — during the latter part of the nineteenth and the beginning of the twentieth century — the leading Western Powers, and Great Britain in particular, were at the height of their power, prosperity and expansion. China's greatest ports and trading centres, such as Hong Kong, Shanghai and Canton, were economically Western dependencies, a status symbolized by the extra-territoriality enjoyed by the nationals of the major Western Powers in China. The Boxer Revolution of 1900 produced a joint Western military punitive expedition which emphasized the weakness and the humiliation of China.

The national and political rebirth of China dates from the proclamation of Sun Yat-sen's Three Principles of 1912 (the Sun Min Chu I): Nationalism, Democracy and the People's Livelihood. But it has taken more than another generation before the aspirations embodied in these principles began to be implemented in a new Chinese State. The Kuomintang, which was intended to implement Sun Yat-sen's principles, disintegrated under the increasingly inefficient and corrupt regime of Chiang Kai-shek. It was not the repeated Japanese invasions — beginning with the conquest of Manchuria in 1931 — that destroyed the Kuomintang; for national resistance against a hated invader has often proved to be the strongest cement of national unity and rebirth. The Nationalist regime succumbed of its own weakness, of its inability to weld the hundreds of millions of Chinese into an effective new nation. Otherwise, it could not have been defeated so thoroughly by what was originally a small and poorly equipped Communist guerrilla force under Mao Tse-tung. No amount of wishful thinking can disguise the fact that the Communists gradually conquered and drove the Chiang Kai-shek regime from the mainland, because they were infinitely better disciplined, and had a greater sense of purpose. Unlike the

Communist regimes of Eastern Europe, they were not pushed into power by the help of the Soviet Union. On the contrary, the Soviet Union in 1927 recognized the Kuomintang led by Chiang Kai-shek as the legitimate Government of China, and she did not withdraw this recognition until the Communists were in substantial control of the country. Stalin is known to have been sceptical of the prospects of Mao Tse-tung, in his attempt to obtain control of the whole of China. The Chinese Communist leaders had little cause for gratitude towards Stalin. They had furthermore some reason to fear Soviet ambitions in the Far East, a fear which could only be strengthened by the control of Manchuria and some of the Japanese islands which the Soviet Union obtained as a result of the Second World War.

During and immediately after the Second World War, the future political and economic orientation of Communist China was still open to some doubt. Most likely, its policy would have been anti-Western, in so far as, here as in so many other countries of Asia and Africa struggling for independence, the West had, for a long time, exercised strong economic control and legal privileges even though China had not been an actual colony or protectorate of any Western power. On the other hand, the Communists needed economic support, especially capital goods, to promote the industrial development of China. For the first few years after the last world war such help could be obtained only from the West, since Japan was not only the hated invader of the thirties and early forties, but also industrially paralysed, while Russia was absorbed in the reconstruction of her devastated land.

When the Communists, in 1949, had obtained effective control of mainland China, i.e. of the overwhelming proportion of Chinese territory and its people, the case for official recognition and the opening of reasonably normal relations therefore became very strong. A number of States, including Great Britain, India and the Scandinavian States, proceeded to grant diplomatic recognition to the new Government — an act which, in the overwhelming tradition of international law, does not signify political or ideological approval, but the acknowledgment of the fact that a new government is in effective control of the State.[1] A logical sequel of widespread recognition by other States would have been the substitution of the Communist Government for that of

[1] See below, pp. 357 *et seq.*

Chiang Kai-shek as the representative of the Chinese State in the United Nations. Such a development was, however, arrested by the policy of the United States, without whose support the recognition of the new Government, e.g. by Great Britain, could not lead beyond formal gestures, for at that time, more than at present, all the Western Powers were too deeply dependent on the political and economic support of the United States to pursue basically different policies. It is, of course, extremely difficult to say how the international policy of Communist China would have developed if the United States, in 1949 or shortly thereafter, had decided to open normal relations with Communist China. There is at least a possibility that Communist China would not have been pushed into as complete a military, political and economic alliance with Soviet Russia as, in fact, happened. In 1947, General Marshall, after the failure of his efforts to mediate in the Chinese Civil War on behalf of the President, was sufficiently disillusioned by the weakness and corruption of the Chiang Kai-shek Government to advise strict American neutrality, but American assistance for Chiang Kai-shek continued in the face of this advice. Vast supplies of arms were sent, only to find their way through defeat or corruption to the Communist forces, which were thus largely equipped by American arms. On the other hand, the American Government failed to obtain any influence on the direction of political, social and military affairs in Nationalist China. American policy failed to arrest the Nationalist decline, but it was substantial enough to stamp the United States, in the eyes of most Chinese, as the ally of Chiang Kai-shek and a foreign imperialist Power, intervening in the Civil War on the side of the defenders of absentee landlords and corrupt business.

The fruits of this policy were gathered by Soviet Russia. Having failed to support Mao Tse-tung in the years of struggle, she utilized the bitterness of the Chinese Communists against the United States to make up for lost time. Once convinced of the final defeat of Chiang Kai-shek, Soviet Russia gave strong support to the claims of the Communist Government for recognition by the United Nations, and helped it with industrial supplies, weapons and technical advisers. In the Soviet–Chinese Treaty, concluded in February 1950, Soviet Russia promised China credits of £300 million. Further credits were granted in an Agreement of 1959. The 1950 Treaty provided for a military alliance between China and the Soviet Union. On the other hand, China extracted from Soviet Russia the promise to surrender her rights in Manchuria (control over Port Arthur and the Trunk Railways) after the conclusion of a Peace Treaty with Japan, or 1952, whichever was the earlier. The Chinese Government is now in effective control of Manchuria.

The Korean war for some years cemented the new alliance and increased the hostility between Communist China and the United States, who lost many thousands of dead and wounded in the Korean war. Whether the Korean war was planned in Moscow or in Peking is a matter of guesswork, although Russia had initially a more direct influence on North Korean affairs. But Russia did not openly intervene in the war. On the other hand, Communist China, convinced of the lasting hostility of the Western Powers, and in particular of the United States, intervened with large 'volunteer' forces and equipment, much of it supplied by the U.S.S.R., on the side of the North Koreans after General MacArthur's forces had crossed the thirty-eighth parallel.

Since the Armistice that concluded the Korean war in 1952 and which, under the supervision of an Armistice Commission, keeps North Korean forces, with Chinese support, and South Korean as well as American troops on opposite sides of a border which divides Korea, there has been no direct military confrontation between Communist China and the United States. Twice in the intervening years conflicts seemed near, when China prepared to occupy the offshore islands of Matsu and Quemoy which formed part of the territory controlled by the Chaing Kai-shek government, and when the United States, despite grave doubts about the justifiability of keeping these small islands separate from the mainland at the cost of a possible world war, seemed prepared to defend them. While Communist China has reasserted time and again its claim not only to the offshore islands but to the larger island of Taiwan — the mainstay of the Nationalist Government, which the United States is pledged to defend — she has chosen other means to expand her influence. The pressures exercised by a country, whose population now stands at about 750 million, increasing at the rate of at least 15 million a year, and which in terms of size, population, military strength and economic potential, dwarfs any other State, or even combination of States, in Asia, have been partly political and partly military. Direct military action included the occupation of Tibet in 1959 through the brutal suppression of a revolt of that ancient and remote country, led by the adherents of the Dalai Lama. The control of Tibet — which is being extended at the present time by the construction of roads and the establishment of close political ties with the Kingdom of Nepal, a country that appears to be moving from the Indian to the Chinese orbit — greatly improved China's access to the Himalayan passes and into India. Three years later, after several years of fruitless negotiations with an Indian Government which only a few years earlier had co-sponsored — with Communist China — the five principles of peaceful co-existence, China invaded the northern Indian frontier at two places — in the north-west and the north-east. The Chinese forces decisively defeated the poorly equipped Indian forces, thus opening up an acute danger of penetration into Assam and Bengal in the east, and into Kashmir and the North Indian plains in the west. Having demonstrated their military superiority, the Chinese halted their attack, probably for a variety of reasons. One was the acute danger of direct confrontation with American and British forces, since both countries, in response to a call for aid from India, immediately proceeded to supply military advisers and equipment. Another was probably the doubtful advantage of any deep penetration into, or even occupation of India, a source of great potential hostility and immeasurable burdens of political and economic responsibility for China. But it is doubtful that China ever intended to make full-scale war against India. By securing certain strategic advantages, and even more by forcing India to divert a substantial part of her already greatly strained economic resources to military defence, China succeeded in substantially weakening the next largest country in Asia, and the only democratic State in that part of the world. While relations between China and India have calmed down in the last few years, no definite settlement of the disputed frontier question has been reached. Perhaps the most important indirect advantage gained by China through this operation was the opportunity for closer political relations with Pakistan. Disturbed by the rearmament of India with Western help, Pakistan, in 1962 and 1963, became increasingly critical of her Western ties and concluded a non-aggression pact with Communist China, which may have strategic as well as general political significance. A parallel move has been the recent strengthening of political ties with the Kingdom of Cambodia, which was neutralized by the Geneva Conference of 1954, after the withdrawal of French and Vietminh troops, under the shaky supervision of an International Commission.

For the rest, Communist China has in recent years preferred to extend her military and political influence indirectly through Chinese-trained Communist-led guerrilla forces, which control the northern part of Laos under the Communist Laotian Prince Souphannouvong, and in North Vietnam where the Communist forces of Ho Chi Minh are increasingly successful against the American-supported forces of South Vietnam.

These extensions of control and influence by Communist China give only a foretaste of the enormous potential power wielded by that country. In Burma, Indonesia, Malaysia and Thailand, there are important Chinese minorities, usually wielding economic power out of proportion to their numbers. Given the traditional strength of national and family loyalties of the Chinese, all of these constitute a potential Fifth Column. Burma — which would be almost defenceless against a Chinese attack — has concluded a non-aggression pact with Communist China, while Indonesia, despite strong pro-Communist leanings of the Sukarno Government and the existence of a powerful Communist party, would view a continuing expansion of Chinese control in that part of the world with great apprehension. Malaysia and Thailand have so far remained politically and militarily linked to the West, but live in constant apprehension of the Chinese danger.

Apart from the threat of a possible direct military confrontation with the United States, and the more recent tensions — to be described later — between Communist China and the Soviet Union, the principal factor in the relative caution of Communist China has undoubtedly been her economic weakness. Several years ago the regime of Mao Tse-tung, which had at first appeared to choose a relatively moderate social revolution by the redistribution of land to tenant farmers, the expropriation of absentee landlords, the abolition of middlemen and the development of co-operative industrial enterprises, changed to a far more radical policy. A sweeping programme of rapid industrialization was enforced by a degree of regimentation and control over the minds and bodies of the people, unusual even for a totalitarian state. Thousands of districts were organized into 'communes', which were pressed into a relentless drive for the rapid increase of agricultural and industrial production, under rigid collective discipline and control over their personal lives. The failure of this ruthless effort coincided with several successive harvest failures, caused by a combination of exceptional droughts and floods. The economic crisis was deepened by the growing tension between China and the U.S.S.R. which led to the virtual cancellation of Soviet economic and technical aid and the withdrawal of thousands of Soviet engineers and technicians. At the same time the continuing explosive growth of the Chinese population, encouraged only a few years ago by official hostility to birth control, created further economic problems, since the growth of the population outstripped available food and other economic resources. Although the agricultural situation has improved in the last few years, the combination of adverse factors — some man-made, some nature-made — has undoubtedly retarded China's very ambitious economic goals, and thus indirectly her immediate capacity for major foreign adventures. It would be dangerous to think that this setback is more than temporary. A country that has already an impressive reservoir of highly trained scientists, engineers and technicians, a rigidly disciplined population that, after fifteen years of Communist government, shows few signs of effective revolt, and supplies an almost limitless reservoir of manpower, is certain to grow in political and economic power from year to year. Behind this stands a militant ideology which rejects 'revisionism' and the possibility of more than temporary co-existence with Capitalism and which, alone of the major Powers, appears to believe that a nuclear war would end in the victory of the only country which could afford to lose even hundreds of millions of people without ceasing to exist as an organized entity. The detonation of a small but relatively advanced nuclear fission bomb, in October 1964, underlined China's potential power.

Relations between Communist China and the Soviet Union

In the last few years, the close ideological, military, political and economic alliance between Communist China and the Soviet Union has given way to open rivalry, tension and even hostility. Whether such tensions would have developed to anything like the same degree under a Stalinist regime in the Soviet Union, is an open question. The strong espousal of the doctrine of 'peaceful co-existence' between Communist and Capitalist States by Krushchev became an increasingly bitter source of conflict between Russia and China. While it is possible that the dismissal of Krushchev in October 1964 may lessen the tension or even herald a rapprochement, the causes of tension between the two Communist giants lie deeper. Ideology, while figuring prominently in the disputes between the dogma-oriented leaders of Communism, is only one factor in this tension.[1] The growing conflict is based on political and pragmatic rather than ideological considerations. The U.S.S.R. has, in recent years, become relatively developed and contented. After many years of deprivation of consumer goods for the sake of general economic progress and productivity, the people of the Soviet Union demand a better life for themselves. At the same time, an increasingly numerous, educated and more sophisticated intellectual élite has begun to break out of the mental isolation of the Stalinist period. It seeks scientific and cultural contacts with the West. These links and orientations underline the fact that the Russians, or at least the Soviet élite, feel themselves to be part of Western civilization, Europeans in the majority, and members of the white race. Though Communist ideology and the policy of the Soviet Union reject racialism, this has again become a factor in contemporary international politics, since almost all the national States are non-white, Africans or Asians. As the Soviet Union moves towards greater prosperity and increased contacts with the West, the contrast between her and the non-white nations — of whom China is the biggest — becomes more pronounced. The leaders of Communist China have not been averse — to the great discomfort of the Soviet leadership — to exploiting this advantage by an appeal to the underprivileged peoples of Asia, and more recently of Africa. This has accentuated an open competition between the Soviet Union and Communist China for the leadership of Communist movements throughout the world. Divisions of geography, civilization and race are having increasing importance in a movement that rejected all these divisions and appealed to the antagonism of classes, not of races or nations. The Soviet Union still has general leadership of the Communist parties of Europe and to a lesser extent of Latin America, although the Governments of the satellite Communist States of South-east Europe show increasing

[1] See, on the ideological dispute, above, pp. 71 *et seq.*

signs of independence. Chinese influence predominates in the Communist parties of Indonesia and most other Asian States, while even the Communist Party of India, despite the wave of national hostility against China after the invasion of a few years ago, is divided. The visit of Chou En-lai to a number of African States in 1964 was unquestionably designed to present to these mostly very underdeveloped countries an image of a China that was more genuinely concerned with their situation than a semi-bourgeois Soviet Union.

Lastly, there are national and territorial disputes between China and the U.S.S.R. which have nothing to do with Communist or any political ideology. Certain areas which stretch southwards from the western borders of Mongolia were ceded to the Soviet Union by China in several nineteenth-century treaties, when China was politically weak and decadent. The Peking regime now disavows these treaties as having been concluded under conditions of 'inequality' — an argument often used by Soviet international lawyers against treaties concluded with the Western world — although she does not yet threaten armed action. For some time to come the Soviet Union will have great technical military superiority over China. But the potentiality of Chinese pressure must form a major factor in Soviet military and political strategy. The Chinese threat compels the Soviet Union to avoid a possible war on two fronts. This simple strategic consideration may account for such efforts to lessen the tension between the U.S.S.R. and the West as have hitherto been made. From time to time both Soviet and Chinese leaders emphasize the basic solidarity of their alliance, in the face of possible threats from elsewhere. This may well be true. It would be highly dangerous for the West to count on Soviet–Chinese tensions as irrevocable, or even as more important than the many basic conflicts that still divide the Communist States from the Western world, in Europe and elsewhere. What is undeniable, however, is that the solidity of the alliance between the two giant Communist States can no longer be taken for granted, that the alignments within the Communist bloc have become at least as fluid and unpredictable as the shifts within the Western alliance. In these circumstances, present United States policy has been to assume that the hostility of Communist China is irredeemable, and to reduce as far as possible the more acute tensions and dangers of armed conflict between the West and the U.S.S.R. Having failed to recognize the Communist Government years ago when such a move would have been natural, American policy sees no way of changing its attitude now, despite the increasing absurdity of non-recognition of a government which rules the world's largest State and has been in undisputed control of all but a minute portion of China for 15 years. France, under de Gaulle, has chosen the alternative course of establishing diplomatic relations with Communist China, in the assumption that China will be less dangerous if not completely isolated. There is little doubt that France's policy is more realistic than that of the United States, in recognizing the fact of Communist China's power and permanency, and that the U.S. will find herself increasingly isolated in a policy that is mainly explained though not justified, by domestic reasons. Sooner or later, the United States will have to recognize the diplomatic as well as the political and military reality of Communist China. If, as appears to be the case, Communist China is preparing for a number of years of essentially political manœuvring, seeking to extend her influence in Asia and Africa, partly at the expense of the West, and partly at the expense of the Soviet Union, the availability of official diplomatic contacts will be even more necessary than at present. At a time when the United States leadership is far less generally accepted than even a few years ago, many other states will act independently of the United States; the pressure for seating of Communist China in the United Nations will increase, and the United States may eventually go down to another diplomatic defeat.

India

With a rapidly increasing population which, even after the political separation of Pakistan, now exceeds 450 million, and as one of the Asian States that has been longest and most strongly influenced by nationalist ideology and political ambition, India is China's most obvious rival for Asian leadership. Under Nehru's guidance India, since her full political emancipation in 1947, repeatedly asserted this claim, by organizing a Pan-Asian conference at New Delhi, by taking a leading part in the organization of the African–Asian Conference at Bandung in 1955 and by becoming Asia's major spokesman in the United Nations. Yet, from an international angle, India, as well as the other two

Dominions of the Indian Peninsula, Pakistan and Ceylon, presents problems and prospects very different from those of China or Japan. The latter two have developed their nationalism, in conscious adoption of Western ideologies and methods of government, and in an increasingly militant reaction to Western political and economic supremacy, which contact with the West and the education of their intellectuals in Western countries enabled them to feel more acutely. But neither country has been under direct Western rule. China has had to accept a measure of foreign domination, with the International Settlement at Shanghai, the British control of Hong Kong and the extra-territorial privileges enjoyed by the Western Powers, which were only recently abolished. The country as a whole, while helpless against the domination of foreign economic interests, never sank to colonial status. But India is the most important of a number of Asian countries that have developed under, and eventually reacted against, direct foreign domination. Such reaction is likely to be more violent than that of countries which merely want to shake off economic interests or spheres of interest. Once national consciousness is aroused, the presence of foreign soldiers, administrators and businessmen is a daily reminder of impotence, and of either real or imagined exploitation. The Netherlands in Indonesia, and France in Indo-China, have experienced the full danger of such a development. Indian nationalism and struggle for independence threatened for many years to become the greatest and most violent of the Asian uprisings against Western domination. The bold decision of the Attlee Government, in 1947, to grant full and unconditional independence to India, Ceylon and Burma, and to accept the new Moslem State of Pakistan, all this without any guarantees of a constitutional, military[1] or economic character, has entirely transformed the situation. Having been given their full freedom of action, the new States felt psychologically free to weigh soberly and independently the advantages of further close association with the West, and in particular with Britain and the Commonwealth. They could now freely acknowledge the benefit of British principles of political life, methods of administration and educational ideas. As a result, some of the dangers forecast by the opponents of full emancipation have not materialized.

[1] Except for the now terminated use of naval bases in Ceylon by the British Navy.

There has been no wholesale collapse of law and order, no war between India and Pakistan, despite grave tension over Kashmir and religious minorities in Bengal as well as over the use of the Indus and its tributaries, no economic anarchy; the new States were no longer able to place the responsibility for all their troubles on Britain — the responsibility was now squarely their own. They have decided to retain their membership of the British Commonwealth, their trade relations with Britain have developed — though this is partly due to the large sterling balances accumulated in London during the war — and British traditions in administration and military organization remain strong. Indian Congress decided a few years ago to retain English as the national language for another fifteen years. The general development of the international situation has tended to strengthen these ties, and thus incidentally to underline the differences between the Far East and South-east Asia. The constitutions of the new Dominions have been framed under the influence of British parliamentary democracy. The plans and programmes of the new States correspondingly represent a mixture of nationalization plans for some industries, land reform, the improvement of social services, economic development plans through a mixture of public and private enterprise, and other devices familiar to modern Western Governments.

Of the newly independent countries of South Asia, India is by far the most populous, industrially the most developed and ambitious, and politically the one most dedicated to achievement of her goals by democratic processes. At the same time, India faces problems of almost unbelievable magnitude, in seeking to improve the minimum standard of living, the health and the education of her vast population, which, according to the most recent surveys, increases by some 8 million every year (at a geometrical rate), and still lives overwhelmingly in a state of poverty and illiteracy. The attempt to achieve all these aims without recourse to dictatorial government or strong-man methods is one of the great human and social enterprises of our time. It deserves sympathy and support for its own sake, although unquestionably the fact that India's great Eastern neighbour, China, is pursuing a similar transformation by the ruthless methods of totalitarian government and Communist principles, is adding pungency to India's struggle.

Politically, India has, since independence, scrupulously adhered to parliamentary democratic methods and achieved amazing success in the degree of participation by her people, in the national and regional elections. The difficulties of this process have so far been mitigated by the predominance of one party, the Congress Party, and the pre-eminence of India's political leaders — Mahatma Gandhi and, from 1947 until his death in May 1964, Pandit Nehru. It is generally admitted that without the unique prestige of Nehru's leadership, Congress might easily have split into factions, without any acknowledged leader of national stature, and that political schisms, factions and struggles might have added to the tremendous social and economic problems of the country. So far Congress has prevailed on the State as well as on the Federal level, and only one State — Kerala — elected a Communist Government into power which, after violent disorders, was ousted by the Central Government in 1959. Overwhelmingly, Indian public opinion, Parliament and Government policy is hostile to Communism, although it has hitherto sought to distinguish between Communism as an internal Indian political movement, and foreign Communist Governments. Under the influence of the strongly pro-Communist and anti-Western former Defence Minister, Krishna Menon, the Nehru Government made strong efforts to establish friendly relations with both the Soviet Union and Communist China. With the latter, India co-sponsored the 'co-existence' principles of the Bandung Conference of 1955. Relations between the two States began to deteriorate when China laid claim to extensive frontier divisions, against India, asserting that the boundaries had been drawn by 'imperialists' (McMahon line). A period of prolonged tension was followed by a limited and victorious Chinese invasion of parts of India's north-western and north-eastern frontiers. This led to a wave of intense anti-Chinese nationalism in India, and despite a halt of military operations, the political relations between the two countries remain tense. By contrast, India's relations with the Soviet Union — which offered limited military assistance to aid India, through the supply of jet fighters — continue to be friendly. This is of course partly influenced by the deterioration of relations between the Soviet Union and Communist China.

The Communist attack also led India to a partial revision of her neutralist position. She turned to and promptly received military equipment and assistance from Britain and the United States. Moreover, these two Western countries were both prompter and less inhibited in their offers of help to India than the Soviet Union. Coupled with the overwhelming share of Western, especially United States' economic aid to India, India's dependence on Western aid and friendship is now great.

Nevertheless it is unlikely that India will abandon her policy of non-commitment to any military alliance. This policy is not only the expression of a deep apprehension about the split of the world into two giant antagonistic military coalitions, but also of the need for India to live in peace, and as far as possible, in collaboration with all the major Powers of the world. This is regarded by the great majority of the Indian leaders as essential, if the country is to solve its paramount problem of social and economic development. In order to win the desperate race against poverty, illiteracy, recurrent droughts and, above all, the as yet unchecked huge annual population increase, India needs financial aid, capital goods and technical assistance from all the industrially advanced countries of the world that are willing to give her such aid. Until recently, only the Western world had the industrial potential, the managerial experience and the technical knowledge available, and until the political emancipation in 1947, it was overwhelmingly British investment and British methods that accounted for India's gradual progress in industry, administration and education. Today, the Soviet Union and Japan are able to compete with the West in the supply of machinery, and of scientific and technical assistance. Moreover, the Soviet Union is able to determine the measure and direction of economic aid to be given, by political rather than commercial principles. The rate of interest for long-term loans, at present set at 2½ per cent, is part of the general planning and budgetary policy of the Soviet State, while engineers, teachers and advisers can be sent to work in foreign countries for limited periods of time, as a matter of political direction. For India, this competition has certain advantages. It is symbolized by the three recently completed competitive steel-mill projects. One of these is a steel mill equipped with Russian machinery, planned by Russian engineers and financed by a cheap loan from the Soviet Union. Another is directed and equipped by a consortium of German firms, also on the basis of long-term loans, while a third steel mill has been built by a group of British firms, helped by a low-interest loan from the British Treasury. While British investment and personnel still predominate among foreign activities in India — largely as a result of centuries-old links, and reinforced by a new era of friendship and respect that followed Britain's voluntary withdrawal from India in 1947 — today, United States, German, French and Japanese enterprises as well as the Soviet Union all participate in the gigantic task of India's industrial development. Yet India's problems are far from solved. India's economic system is one of mixed public and private economic enterprise, guided by general economic development plans. Gradually, India has built up a complex and intricate machinery of economic planning, in which the Ministry of Economics, the National Planning Commission and federal, State and private development corporations play important parts. India is now approaching the end of her third successive five-year plan. Unlike most of the new countries, India has the advantage of an extremely able, British-trained staff of senior civil servants, who carry the main burden of their country's administration. The general standards of integrity and government exceed those of most other underdeveloped countries. Moreover, the key position of India, as Asia's major democracy struggling for the maintenance of a progressive alternative to Communism against enormous handicaps, has gained increasing recognition in the Western world. India is far and away the biggest single recipient both of World Bank loans and of United States aid. Under the guidance of the World Bank, the principal Western countries, including the United States, Britain, West Germany and Japan, have formed an informal 'India Club', a consortium whose members meet periodically with each other as well as with representatives of the Indian Government, to discuss and meet as far as possible India's immense needs in foreign capital and industrial aid. For the first two years of the third five-year plan, the combined aid promised by six Western countries, as well as the World Bank and its affiliates, amounted to $2,225,000,000. Even this enormous contribution to India's foreign exchange needs left an estimated Indian payment deficit of over 1,500 million dollars, which has since considerably increased. With every succeeding year of discrepancy between India's minimum development needs and its available resources, the burden of interest payments on foreign aid increases, despite the generally low rates of interest charged by institutions such as the International Development Association or the U.S. Agency for International Development, or the Soviet Union. A growing burden of foreign obligations and the hitherto unchecked rate of population growth are barely balanced by increases in productivity, so that in terms of the individual, India seems to stand still rather than to move forward. The situation has been further aggravated by the need to divert manufacturing and financial resources for defence, after the Chinese attack of a few years ago.

The present difficulties may well conceal the enormous scientific, industrial and educational progress made by India in the last decade. Whether the increasing number of educated Indians — which includes an excessively high proportion of lawyers and arts graduates — will be a factor for progress or for growing discontent, will depend on the outcome of the desperate race between goals and achievement. Apart from the dangers of external aggression, the greatest single threat to India's stability is the continued growth of its population. Despite the energetic sponsorship of birth control by the Government, progress in a country where illiterate peasants and village communities still form the great majority of the population has hitherto been negligible. Success in the substantial slowing down of this ruinous growth — which constantly outstrips all efforts at economic and social improvement — is a minimum condition of India's stability. A balanced growth cannot be achieved overnight. Through the years of transition, India will need freedom from external aggression, and continued major help from the developed countries. The fulfilment of these conditions will make India's evolutionary growth and her survival as a democracy more likely, though not certain.

The death of Nehru — who had led India virtually for the entire first seventeen years of her independence — in May 1964, poses grave new problems for India's political future. Despite the quick, constitutional formation of a new government under a moderate follower of Nehru, Mr. Lal Bahadur Shastri, the disappearance of the one universally revered national leader of towering stature may revive many deep-seated conflicts, passions and fissures. Nehru's strong secularism, his hostility to religious taboos and caste divisions, his position as a symbol of Indian national unity contained, but did not eliminate, the religious, social, communal and linguistic divisions of India's many divergent groups. North and South remain divided in many ways; Hindi, the official national language, is spoken by barely one half of the people; the caste system, while legally abolished, continues to dominate social life. Violence between the Hindu majority and India's 40 million Moslems broke out in Bengal and elsewhere, even before Nehru's death. Fear of new religious massacre may have strongly contributed to Nehru's refusal to settle the Kashmir problem with Pakistan. His courageous, though belated, freeing of Sheikh Abdullah, the popular Kashmir leader, as a possible mediator between India and Pakistan aroused much opposition in India. But Nehru's successor appears determined to continue the attempt to find a Kashmir solution with Pakistan. Meanwhile the leaders of India's major States exercise increased influence in New Delhi, at the expense of central direction. Only an unexpectedly strong successor, a mature collective sense of national responsibility of India's political leaders, or perhaps another urgent threat from abroad, will hold together the still precarious national fabric of India. The effort must mainly come from within, although the West — and perhaps the U.S.S.R. too — can help greatly by sustained and unobtrusive help in India's economic development.

Pakistan

Pakistan achieved its independence as a sovereign State, together with India, in 1947. The foundation of the new State was the Moslem religion, which also deeply affects social habits and ways of living. With a rapidly increasing population of 95 million, Pakistan is, with Indonesia, the most populous and important of the Moslem States. The bitterly fought-for separation of a Moslem State from the formerly unified Indian Peninsula was, however, established at a heavy price. Pakistan consists of two halves separated not only by thousands of miles but also deeply divergent in economic interests and political outlook. The capital, and the political centre, of the new State was established in West Pakistan. But East Pakistan, with slightly more than half the total population, is far more densely settled and, by economics as well as by geography, much more closely linked with neighbouring India. It also has a very substantial Hindu minority. The immense political and administrative difficulties of holding together a State consisting of two such divergent parts, separated by thousands of miles from each other, are greatly increased by the lack of a Civil Service of adequate standards and integrity. After the partition, India retained the lion's share of the small, but crucially important, group of highly trained and capable senior civil servants who had gradually been prepared to take over responsibility under British guidance, in the Indian Civil Service (I.C.S.). Because of the generally lower educational background of the Moslem population, only a small minority of these administrative leaders were left in Pakistan. The attempts of Pakistan to devise a democratic constitution were greatly impeded, not only by the political tensions between East and West Pakistan and the lack of sufficient political and administrative leaders, but also by the split between those who wanted to turn the country into an essentially theocratically governed Moslem State and those who wanted to make of it a more modern and secular democracy. After years of debate and fruitless attempts to compromise, the effort to establish a parliamentary democracy foundered altogether. In October 1958, by a bloodless revolution, General Ayub took over the government of the country, seeking to reform both the standards of government and administration, and to effect, by non-revolutionary means, a redistribution of land and other resources. How far he will succeed in this goal, without clashing with a small but powerful group of big landowners, is as yet uncertain. If he achieves stability and an improvement of administrative standards, Pakistan is likely to attract more foreign private investment and public loans.

Economically, Pakistan is far less industrialized than India. It is still mainly dependent on the export of cotton and jute. The high prices and world-wide needs for these commodities put Pakistan into a favourable financial position until after the end of the Korean war, when a surplus was converted into a heavy deficit. Since then, Pakistan has painfully sought to re-establish an equilibrium between exports and imports and, at the same time, with considerable help from the Colombo Plan, proceeded towards the development of resources and industries. The share of the State is predominant. Two government-controlled corporations, the Pakistan Industrial Development Corporation and the Pakistan Industrial Finance Corporation, seek to promote industrial investment. Foreign industrial investment has recently been encouraged by guarantees given by the Government to foreign investors in regard to capital, profits and shareholding.

Internationally, too, the position of Pakistan differs in some vital respects from that of India. As the largest of the Moslem States, Pakistan is linked by ties of sympathy with the Arab States of the Middle East. Unlike India, Pakistan soon after having gained her independence, decided on close political and military association with the West. She concluded bilateral agreements with the United States, according the latter certain facilities for military bases. She joined both the SEATO and Central Treaty Organization, which were conceived as links in the chain of the Western, anti-Communist defence system, but have never gained real strength or cohesion. The disparity of the national interests of the members has prevented both political and military consolidation, as it has occurred — at least until the recent partial defection of France — in the North Atlantic Treaty Organization. Pakistan's links with the West have recently been further weakened by growing hostility to India and her consequent alienation from the major Western Powers, especially the United States and Britain, which have given India military assistance after the Chinese invasion of 1962. Pakistan's dispute with India over the control of Kashmir — which is overwhelmingly Moslem and whose population, as Pakistan claims with considerable justification, would in a free vote probably decide for affiliation with Pakistan — remains unsolved. Any strengthening of India's military power means for the Pakistanis primarily a more acute threat to Pakistan. Without openly defecting from her alliances, Pakistan has recently moved closer to Communist China. She has concluded a non-aggression pact with China and is seeking to strengthen commercial and political ties. At the same time her fear of a Soviet attack (via Afghanistan), which was a predominant factor in her earlier policies, has subsided in view of the less aggressive posture of the Soviet Union. In 1964 President Ayub took the initiative in moving towards a closer political and economic association with Iran and Turkey, two fellow Moslem States. Pakistan continues to receive important economic aid from the World Bank and the United

States. Another source of friction with India, the loss of the use of the Indus tributaries, was removed in 1960 when, under the guidance of the World Bank, the Indus water scheme made provision for the construction of an extensive system of canals to compensate Pakistan for the loss of irrigation vital to her cotton and jute plantations, with massive financial help from the United States, Britain and other Commonwealth States, and the World Bank itself. But too many other military, political and religious conflicts remained to bring a lasting rapprochement between the two neighbours. While leaders like Shastri and Ayub realize the folly of a war between their two countries, they are both subjected to strong nationalist pressures from their peoples.

Hong Kong and Malaysia

In some of the other storm-centres of Asia the problem of emancipation from Western colonial rule is as important for their future international position as it has been for the new Dominions of the Indian Peninsula. The position of the British colony of Hong Kong presents no problem of principle or ideology. There is little doubt that the new Chinese Government will seek the recovery of this part of China as soon as it feels it expedient to press this claim. For the present, an open international trading centre and port offers many advantages. Conversely, the preservation of Hong Kong as a British colony is for Britain purely a matter of strategy and economic interests.

The transformation of the economically and strategically important Malay Peninsula from colonial and protected status to independence, posed exceptional problems both for Britain and the political leaders of the independence movement. The principal problem was how to combine the states of Malaya proper — which had been British protectorates — with the Crown Colony of Singapore, one of the world's most important harbours and strategic posts. While in Malaya — which became a federation and an independent member of the Commonwealth in 1957 — the Malayans, predominantly of the Moslem religion, outnumber the Chinese at the rate of approximately 3 to 2, Singapore's 1·7 million people are almost entirely Chinese. The union of Singapore with the rest of Malaya thus produces a Chinese majority. Britain was also concerned to retain certain military rights in Singapore, which is Britain's only remaining base in the Far East.

In 1963 the problem was solved by the constitution of the State of Malaysia, which not only united Singapore and the Malayan Peninsula, but added the two smaller States of Sarawak and Sabah (North Borneo) which form the northern third of the huge island of Borneo. The rest of this island forms part of Indonesia.

By themselves, Malaya and Singapore constitute the economically most prosperous and developed unit of South-east Asia. The thriving commerce of Singapore is joined to the rich natural resources of the Malayan Peninsula, which include the world's largest rubber production accounting for average annual exports valued at nearly two thousand million dollars, large rice, tea and palm oil production, and important deposits of tin concentrates. In recent years the Federation of Malaya, under the moderate leadership of Tunku Abdul Rahman, has made important progress towards industrialization. By contrast, Sarawak and Sabah, with a combined population of about 1,200,000 people, are economically and politically very backward. In terms of geography, race, religion and development they are far away from the centre of Malaysia. The reason for the British wish to join the British-held northern part of Borneo with Malaya, was a desire to prevent a splintering of unviable independent states in that area, to protect important British economic interests (especially in oil) and to prevent their absorption by Indonesia. For the same reason, Indonesia has bitterly opposed the formation of Malaysia, with some support from the Philippines which laid claim to North Borneo as a continuation of their southern Philippine chain of islands. Indonesia's President Sukarno declared undying hostility to the new State, broke off diplomatic and economic relations with Malaysia and sent guerrillas into Borneo territory. Indonesia regards the joining of northern Borneo to Malaysia as a machination of British 'imperialism', all the more so as by virtue of defence arrangements with Malaysia, British and some Australian troops are poised to defend northern Borneo against invasion. An American mediation effort early in 1964, designed to bring Indonesia, Malaysia and the Philippines at least to an agreement to abstain from hostilities as a prelude to more amicable relations, appears to have failed, owing to Indonesian intransigence.

Indo-China

In the world-wide search of the Communist Powers for soft spots in the Western front, Indo-China offers one of the most promising targets. Communist China borders on Vietnam, and is able to direct support to the Vietnamese rebels and their Communist leader, Ho Chi Minh, in manpower, weapons and political organization.

Moreover, the State of Vietnam, and the kingdoms of Laos and Cambodia — formerly combined in French Indo-China — form an arc which partly envelops the neighbouring state of Thailand (Siam). Laos, as well as China, has a large contiguous frontier with Burma, in the very regions where revolt and unrest have plagued the Burmese Government since the country achieved its political independence in 1947. There is no doubt that the Power which politically controls Indo-China has Thailand at its mercy, can exercise great pressure on Burma, and ultimately isolate the Malayan Peninsula. President Eisenhower has compared the situation aptly with a row of dominoes, where the fall of one brings the whole lot down.

On the other hand, recent developments have shown that it is impossible for the West to hold on to Asian territory — colonial or otherwise — unless there is positive support in the country, and a stable, efficient and popular government, willing to collaborate with the West. In 1954 it became obvious that neither the tremendous French military effort in Indo-China, which cost the country the flower of its regular corps of officers and non-commissioned officers, nor vast American aid could achieve victory, or even a stalemate against the Communist and Nationalist elements led by Ho Chi Minh, and increasingly supported, with weapons, supplies and technicians, by Communist China. War weariness and pessimism about the developments gave Prime Minister Mendès-France almost unanimous support for an attempt to end the war. After heroic resistance, the fortress of Dien Bien Phu fell to the Communist forces, with many of the best French officers and troops. After this, it was only a question of obtaining the best possible conditions from a victorious and confident enemy. At the Geneva Conference in 1954 — in which Great Britain, apart from France and Communist China, played a very active role, but the United States was only a spectator — the country was partitioned. In the partition, the Ho Chi Minh Communist-controlled government obtained control over the northern ports of Hanoi and Haiphong. The part conceded to the Vietnamese Communists also contained the more important raw-material resources, and one of the major rice-producing areas. South Vietnam consists mainly of Cochin-China, the port of Saigon and parts of Annam.

A few years of uneasy co-existence between North and South Vietnam gave way to open warfare which continues with increasing bitterness. The North Vietnamese (Vietcong) operate through well-trained, highly disciplined and increasingly well-equipped guerrilla forces, with strong backing from Communist China which affords a vast and friendly hinterland. Like the Chinese Communists in the days of Chiang Kai-shek's control of mainland China, they avoid open battle and concentrate on surprise attacks, on villages and individual units of the South Vietnamese. The latter receive heavy military and economic assistance from the United States which, apart from paying for the bulk of the war effort, maintains some 17,000 combat and technical troops in support of the Vietnamese Army. For some years, until 1963, the United States strongly supported the regime of Ngo Dinh Diem, the head of a Roman Catholic family who seemed to promise a fight against corruption, social reform and an energetic war against the Communists. Late in 1963 the United States welcomed a military coup which deposed the regime and led to the execution of Diem and his brother, the police chief. But with a series of successive changes in the government and military command, the various Juntas has so far shown few signs of stability, and the situation continues to deteriorate, as the portion of South Vietnam solidly held by the Government forces shrinks and the guerrillas of North Vietnam increasingly seize the initiative.

For the United States the problem of Vietnam represents in its sharpest form the dilemma of her entire Asian policy: how to contain an enemy who in that part of the world has almost all the geographic and strategic advantages, as well as a greater sense of purpose and discipline, while the United States' allies have governments that are divided or irresolute, and have at most the lukewarm support of their people. The alternative of withdrawing from positions that will be a continuing drain on American manpower, finances and political patience in the face of a diminishing belief in ultimate success, is not yet seriously contemplated; the intention, reaffirmed by Secretary of Defence McNamara in February 1964, to withdraw the bulk of American troops from South Vietnam before the end of 1965, has been replaced by declaration of America's determination to support South Vietnam against growing attacks from the Vietcong in the realization that this may mean many years of American involvement.

Indonesia

After years of negotiations with the Netherlands, interrupted by recurrent conflicts, the new Republic of Indonesia, with a population of 100 million, attained full political independence in 1949. All legal and constitutional links with the Netherlands have been severed. Until 1962 the Netherlands retained control of their part of New Guinea, the other part being under an Australian trusteeship administration. But after several years of increasingly militant Indonesian pressure for the incorporation of 'Irian' into Indonesia, the Netherlands was induced, under strong pressure from the United States, to accept a settlement in 1962 under which, after a temporary period of supervision by the United Nations, Indonesia would take over the administration of former Dutch New Guinea and eventually organize a plebiscite under her own administration. This settlement was undoubtedly a thinly disguised victory for Indonesia, who achieved by threats what she could not have achieved by force, except with massive intervention from outside. However, it may well be that the settlement which freed the Netherlands from a political, financial and administrative burden is a blessing at a time when the status of a colonial Power becomes increasingly undesirable. Moreover, since the settlement, relations between Indonesia and the Netherlands, both officially and unofficially, have begun to improve despite the nationalization a few years ago of the vast Dutch-owned tobacco plantations and of other Dutch enterprises.

More recently Indonesia has shown herself strongly hostile to the newly formed State of Malaysia. Reference to this dispute, which also involves the Philippines, has already been made.[1]

Indonesia maintains large military forces, including a considerable Soviet-supplied navy. Indonesia's military posture, and the disproportionate amount of her resources devoted to military

[1] See above, p. 259.

expenditure, is both explained by and in turn aggravates her chronic economic difficulties.

Of all the Asian States which have attained political independence after a long period of colonial rule, Indonesia is one of the least stable. The country is basically in a relatively sound economic position. The majority of its people are smallholders, able, unlike the majority of smallholders in less-favoured countries, to feed themselves and live adequately by the cultivation of their soil. Indonesia is also an important exporter of certain vital raw materials, such as rubber, oil and tin. The fluctuation in prices and demand for these raw materials has, however, caused a series of economic upheavals in recent years. Moreover, the islands differ considerably in wealth and population. Much the most densely populated — Java — is also the poorest, and it is there that the Communist Party has had its greatest electoral successes. The oil wealth is mainly concentrated in Sumatra, and only a much more efficiently established central government could effect a major redistribution as between the different parts.

Indonesia consists of five major and hundreds of small islands, and a multitude of races, religions and languages. Although both Hinduism and Buddhism have adherents in Indonesia, the bulk of the population professes the Moslem religion. Modern Indonesia has been shaped and developed by over three centuries of Dutch administration. On the whole, the Dutch government of Indonesia was benevolent, efficient and beneficial to the development of the country. But it was essentially autocratic. Somewhat like the French, but unlike the British administrators, the Dutch in considerable numbers settled in what was formerly known as the Netherlands East Indies. They heavily invested in the country, developed it, frequently intermarried and produced a considerable Eurasian population. As a result, the Dutch, like the French *colons*, became far more intensively mixed up with the life of the country than the British in their colonies. One consequence of such a development, however, is the greater difficulty of transition to independence. Compared, for example, with India, Indonesia has few trained administrators, engineers or doctors. The strength of nationalist emotions is in no way matched by administrative experience. To this have been added deep internal divisions and conflicts between the constituent parts of the Indonesian Republic. A weak central government has repeatedly had to fight local and regional rebellions. Moreover, the position of the central government is inherently unstable. For several years unstable coalition governments which depended for their survival on the support of the Communist Party — itself outside the Government — pursued a 'neutralist' policy marked by suspicion of Western colonialism and hostility to Western industrial investment. In 1959 President Sukarno proclaimed the principle of 'guided democracy', a polite term for government not based on democratic methods. In subsequent regional elections the Communist Party scored major successes, especially in over-populated Java. A military, secessionalist revolt in some of the islands failed in its major purpose of changing the Government, but showed the lack of stability and central control in the Republic. In June 1959 a state of emergency was declared by the Chief of Staff of the Army, which, in response to the refusal by the Assembly to grant the President the requested dictatorial powers, prohibits political discussion and movements. Indonesia thus has joined the growing number of Asian States which have abandoned or at least suspended the attempt to govern by Western democratic methods and are reverting to autocratic government — mainly in the form of military rule. In its foreign policy Indonesia is, with the United Arab Republic, Iraq and Yugoslavia, one of the principal supporters of neutralism. But, unable or unwilling to tackle Indonesia's internal economic and social problems, President Sukarno has in recent years turned increasingly to expansionist policies, supported by a large, Soviet-equipped military establishment.

Burma and Thailand

Of the other major Asian States, Burma gained her independence at the same time as India, Pakistan and Ceylon, but, unlike these countries, chose to leave the British Commonwealth. Thailand on the other hand has, since the middle of the nineteenth century, been able to preserve an exceptional degree of independence. It has achieved this rather unusual position, first by skilfully balancing between the major Powers — Britain and France in the nineteenth and early twentieth centuries, Japan and the Western Allies during the last war — and, secondly, by a sound economic position helped by relatively stable conditions of government. Neither country can, however, remain outside the international conflict, which is accentuated by the advance of the Chinese Communists. At present Thailand enjoys relative tranquillity and prosperity under a semi-autocratic regime, which tends to control elections and the Press, but under a strong leader, Marshal Sarit, who died late in 1963, began the herculean task of cleansing the Government and Civil Service of deeply ingrained traditions of corruption — under which police chiefs were, for example, able to run profitable brothels. Thailand, almost alone among the Far Eastern countries, has a relatively prosperous peasantry and a fairly stable economy. The latter is largely based on the value of Thailand's rice exports. But Thailand's economic prosperity, and her rice surplus in particular, makes it a more tempting objective for Communist China. Her position would become almost untenable if Vietnam came under Communist control, or if on the other side Burma fell to the Communists.

In this precarious position, Thailand has — contrary to her traditional balancing policy — decided to cast in her lot with the West. Among the States of Far Eastern and South-east Asia, the Philippines, Thailand and Pakistan have been the lonely sponsors of military alliance with the West, and they have all joined the SEATO.

Together with Thailand and Ceylon, Burma is the most intensely Buddhist of all Asian countries, and a mixture of Buddhist contemplativeness and desire for Western progress dominates the policy of the country. This has produced an Eastern version of a Social-Democratic welfare State. Industrial development by State planning is the dominant aspect of Burma's internal policy. Internationally, Burma is a firm supporter of India's neutralist policy, although the Burmese Government has had years of hard struggle with Communist insurgent groups and is by no means unaware of the threat of Communist revolt or of the international aspects of Communist policies. Although Burma welcomed some foreign investments and assistance in its technical development, she will not tolerate any exclusive or predominant control by foreign capital and has recently become both more socialistic and nationalistic in her industrial policy. The gaining of independence was, as in the other former British colonies, accompanied by the introduction of parliamentary democracy. Until 1958, the governing People's Party — of moderate Socialist persuasion — had an overwhelming majority, but in

1958 it split into two rival factions — each led by prominent members of the Government. Although the military regime, in February 1960, permitted the holding of free elections which resulted in the return of the former Prime Minister, U-Nu, General Ne Win staged another military takeover in 1962, which led to more rigorous measures. Parliament was again suspended, U Nu put under house arrest and a strongly nationalistic economic policy was initiated, which is apt to discourage foreign investment. Burma has concluded a non-aggression treaty with Communist China, which has of course overwhelming power, as compared with Burma.

Australia, New Zealand and the South-west Pacific

In the vast ocean of Asian peoples, the two 'white' Western outposts, the British Dominions of Australia and New Zealand, are (in terms of population) small but important islands. Except for the Australian control of New Guinea and Papua, and some mandates over smaller islands, neither Dominion is a colonial Power. Both are isolated British and Western outposts. Their combined population is now over twelve million, amidst overwhelmingly larger numbers of Asians. Australia has, in the last decade, embarked on a vigorous policy of growth and industrial development, increasing her population by 20 per cent, and her gross national product by 90 per cent. By means of a vigorous immigration policy which is bringing hundreds of thousands of British and other European settlers yearly into the country, Australia hopes to double her population within a generation. But even this would not materially affect the proportion of whites to Asians. New Zealand has assimilated her native Maori population to the white majority and can therefore face the Asian States with a record of racial tolerance and equality. But it is the bigger and industrially more developed Commonwealth of Australia which has conducted a far more active international policy, and is at the same time faced with far greater problems. Since the constitution of the Commonwealth of Australia in 1900 the Dominion has pursued the so-called 'White Australia' policy. Immigration laws which in theory control immigration from any country are applied so as to strictly exclude the immigration of any people of coloured race. The motive behind this policy is fundamentally economic. The people of Australia enjoy a high standard of living, protected by an exceptionally strong and closely knit trade-union organization and an extensive system of social insurance. Any large-scale immigration of Asian labour would threaten to undermine this state of affairs. The Labour movement is therefore the strongest supporter of this policy. Australia's foreign policy has been greatly influenced by the desire to maintain friendly relations with the rising States of Asia. Australia has actively supported the Indonesian Republic against the Dutch, sent delegates to various Pan-Asian conferences and pleaded eloquently for racial equality and human rights at the United Nations Conferences. More important, perhaps, is Australia's practical contribution to the Colombo Plan.[1] But the systematic pursuit of this policy and its extension towards such countries as Malaysia or Thailand are greatly handicapped by the psychological effect of the White Australia policy. Certainly the opening up of Australia to Asian immigration would not even begin to solve the emigration problems of such countries as Japan, China or India. These countries must solve the problem of their economic and social development mainly by scientific, technical and social development, for which they will need foreign assistance. But newly emancipated nations are particularly sensitive to matters of national prestige. The refusal to admit or expel a particular coloured person on a ground of principle has an effect out of all proportion to numbers. For Asians it is a symbol of detestable white superiority. Unless, therefore, Australia applies her immigration policy more elastically, with more discretion and in such a manner as to make it conform to the new trend of her foreign policy, she will be handicapped in the attempt to enter into friendly relations with the new States of Asia.

Pan-Asianism

During the last war Japan attempted, not altogether unsuccessfully, to unite the various movements of resistance against European and Western domination in a positive movement of Pan-Asianism under Japanese leadership. India and China are certain to revive similar attempts under different formulas. What foundations are there for a Pan-Asiatic movement sufficiently united to become a political force and to take common action?

In the first place, it had undoubted importance as a slogan of defiance and resistance. The formula 'Asia for the Asians' helped

[1] See below, p. 275.

the Japanese to gain some support in Burma, India, Thailand, Indonesia and elsewhere. Nehru was able to focus some feeling of Asian solidarity in condemnation of Dutch military action in Indonesia. Chinese Communists are likely to mix the same appeal with nationalist and Socialist formulas in their attempts to stimulate revolution in the different parts of Asia where European interests are still important.

There is, however, a vast gap between the use of slogans of defiance, sometimes as convenient disguises for the Imperialism of a major Power, be it Japan, China or India, and its impact as a positive, supra-national ideology. Just as the Pan-European movement is faced with the deep political, national and racial divisions of Europe, as Pan-Islamism remains a vague formula, in view of the bitter dissensions and jealousies of the different Moslem leaders, the nations of Asia are deeply split by internal religious, racial or other tensions. In India the antagonism of Hindus and Moslems has led to the partition of a formerly unified State. In Malaysia, and other parts of South Asia, Malays, Chinese and Indians live in uneasy or hostile association, for economic as well as racial reasons. In Burma the Government is trying to suppress the rebellion of the Karens. The Chinese regard the Japanese as inferior in civilization, whereas the Japanese have occupied and exploited China when they were strong, and China disorganized. Koreans resent the Japanese as oppressors, and the Formosans feel similarly towards the Chinese. Indonesia, Malaysia, Thailand and Burma regard their Chinese minorities as both a political and economic problem.

It has been rightly pointed out by students of Asia that the divisions of religion, history, civilization and government in Asia go far deeper than those of the Western world. There has been nothing comparable to the unifying influence of the Greco-Roman civilizations as modified by Christian influences. Deepest of all, perhaps, are the religious differences, which in the nations of the East, far more than in the West, deeply affect the ways of life and thinking of the people. There can be no more contrasting religions than those of Islam, which predominates in the Middle East and in Pakistan, Indonesia and parts of Malaya, and Buddhism, which is predominant in Burma, Ceylon, Thailand and parts of Japan and China (though in two varieties). As history has shown, Islam makes for a disciplined, militant and sometimes aggressive community of behaviour, where Buddhism is essentially contemplative and non-aggressive. Hinduism, which predominates in India, is again a completely different system, both in its religious and social impact. In between there are important pockets of Christian denominations. Thus Premier Diem of South Vietnam was a Roman Catholic. Chiang Kai-shek is a Christian Methodist. If to these deep-seated divergences of religion and civilization are added the paucity of communications until the very recent past, and the diversity of political control to which the countries of Asia have been subjected in the past few centuries, it is not surprising that we find today a vast variety of political systems: moderately left-wing parliamentary democracy of the British pattern in India; a Buddhist–Socialist welfare State in Burma; a semi-fascist dictatorship in Thailand; benevolent autocracy under a military leader in Pakistan; a Communist regime in most of China; and various intermediate forms of government in the rest of Asia.

Ironically, it is not any community of Asian civilization or religion or history which is bringing the Asian nations together, but their common contact with Western civilization and the impact of Western industrialization and technology. It is where the veneer of Western ways of life has been superimposed upon the basic pattern of Asian civilizations, i.e. mainly in the capitals of the Asian States, that one finds common and familiar aspects, from Singapore to Peking. Nor is it surprising that the only possible common language at Pan-Asian conferences is English. And, as has been pointed out before, such community of outlook and interest as is inspired by contemporary Asian nationalism, anti-Western and anti-capitalist tendencies is itself of Western origin.

In Europe political compulsion or sheer force has overcome racial and political antagonisms in the countries which have come under Soviet domination. Without the same degree of compulsion, the non-Communist nations of Europe find it difficult enough to overcome their antagonisms, despite the political and economic pressures for unity. Similarly, the strongest prospect for a political and social unification of Asia lies in the advance of a political creed which, like Chinese Communism, would feel justified and be ruthless enough to overcome national, racial and religious differences for the sake of a common political and social order.

Democracy and Totalitarianism in Asia

The experience of the West shows that democracy — if it is to rest on solid foundations — needs a prolonged period of peace, of internal stability, and the building up of a political tradition based on education and a sense of civic responsibility. The democracies of Britain, France and the United States have been developed over centuries, and under the shelter of greater stability and safety than the twentieth century provides. The theoretically perfect democracy of the German Weimar Republic collapsed quickly under the onslaught of economic crises, nationalist agitation and international uncertainties. The Italian democracy proved little more resilient, while democracy has never firmly established itself in the economically backward and politically unstable countries of the Balkans. The Allied Military Occupation of Germany and Japan has produced a new batch of democratic constitutions, strongly influenced by the United States. How fertile these grafts will prove is still an open question. On the other hand, the democracies of Britain and some other European countries have proved resistant to severe political and economic pressure.

Most of the new States of Asia have gained their independence and shaped the pattern of their political life in conditions of great internal and international tension. Governments are formed which claim independence from foreign control and assume power over populations that are mostly underfed, illiterate and politically uneducated. Almost all the States face tremendous problems in the reorganization of Government administration — without the experience and training of the British, French or Dutch administrators who left or were thrown out with independence. Yet, all these States were eager at first to adopt the forms and patterns of the countries that formerly controlled them, and this influence was strengthened by the training of the intellectual leaders, many of whom received their higher education and political philosophy at the Universities of London or Oxford, Paris or Leyden — and, in recent years, increasingly at Columbia, Yale or Harvard. Consequently, parliamentary democracy was introduced everywhere, with its apparatus of Constituent Assembly and Parliament, general elections, Bills of Rights, independent law courts and other pillars of democratic constitutions. One by one, most of these democratic experiments have failed, under the pressure of economic emergencies, social unrest or open rebellion. In the last few years, Pakistan, Burma and Indonesia have all adopted more or less open forms of military dictatorship, with a corresponding abolition or curtailment of the parliamentary system and freedom of political discussion. The older State of Thailand observes the forms of democracy together with a strong-man government and many restrictions on political freedom. The new State of South Vietnam has indefinitely postponed general elections, and democracy in Ceylon is precarious since the assassination of Premier Bandaranaike. In its attempt to carry on, and to solve its problems without the sacrifice of political democracy and personal freedoms, India now stands almost alone in that part of the world. But even in India it is doubtful how long democracy will survive, once the Congress Party were to lose the pre-eminence which has so far placed it in charge of the government as a matter of course. Both its unity and its pre-eminence are now threatened with the death of Nehru, the chief unifying factor. Unless the West continues to help in the solution of India's overwhelming economic problems by a far more extensive and concerted programme of long-term loans and industrial investment, the prospects for democracy are doubtful in India, while they are definitely bleak for the rest of Asia. We have seen that even in the West the dangers of concentration of more power in fewer hands are steadily increasing, and this inevitably threatens democracy. In Asia there is hardly any tradition of democracy and liberalism to overcome. The main accent of contemporary revolutionary ideologies is on efficient control of the masses, made acceptable by the satisfaction of their minimum needs, on war potential and on technical development. The greater the pressure for political emancipation in Asia, the smaller would seem to be the chances of democracy.

This state of affairs favours both Fascism and Communism, which, as we have seen,[1] have many principles and methods of government in common. But Communism would seem, on balance, to have the greater prospects. The two great issues which dominate the Asian awakening are Nationalism and the revolt of the under-privileged against the exploiters. As long as the exploiters are foreigners, Europeans, Chinese or Indians, Nationalism and social revolution can reinforce each other. And it is

[1] See above, pp. 79 *et seq.*

largely with this in mind that recent Communist doctrine and propaganda have taken a strong Nationalistic flavour. But when it comes to far-reaching social change, Communism has the advantage over Fascism. It has a better doctrine and a better record on such issues as the breaking-down of inequalities of race or caste, the elimination of absentee landlords and middlemen, the redistribution of land to smallholders and tenant farmers, or the organization of industry on co-operative lines. Fascist Nationalism, while full of catch-phrases for the common man, has always fought shy of radical social change, whether in Germany, Italy, Japan, China or Spain. In all the Asian countries there are now small, determined groups of military, political and intellectual leaders, able and willing to seize power, and capable of expressing the grievances of the inarticulate masses. A century ago, in conditions of greater international tranquillity and a far stronger belief in liberal democracy, the political emancipation of Asia would have been more likely to proceed according to the democratic pattern. Today the formulas of democracy are widely used, but the reality behind it is mostly autocratic government.

Marxist and Leninist doctrine placed its faith in Communist revolutions organized by an intelligent and advanced *avant-garde* of industrial workers. In recent years, however, industrially and socially advanced countries have shown far more resistance to Communism than undeveloped and socially backward countries. In Europe a further advance of Communism is likely to be achieved only as a result of exceptional economic calamities, or by sheer force. But in Asia, Communist movements led by small groups of determined, capable and thoroughly indoctrinated leaders have achieved triumphant results in China and Indo-China, and they constitute a powerful force in Japan, Korea, Burma, the Philippines, India and Indonesia. This underlines the problem of a co-ordinated and realistic Western policy in Asia.

Asian Development and Foreign Assistance

Western policy towards the Asian nations outside the Communist sphere of control poses many complex problems. From the Philippines to Pakistan, a number of countries, almost all of which have gained their political independence since the last world war, are determined to shape their destinies as sovereign Powers, and with overwhelming emphasis on the economic and social improvement of their countries and their peoples. Legacies of anti-Western resentment on the one hand and the suspicion of Communist totalitarianism on the other combine to reinforce an attitude which is understandable enough in their situation: the avoidance of military and political commitments to either side in the Cold War. Yet the situation of these countries and their future development are vital not only to the relative position of the antagonists in the Cold War but also to the whole structure of international relations. In recent years the major Western Powers, to which Japan may be added in a political though not a geographical sense, have sought to oppose the greater military pressure and the political attractions offered by Asian Communism, not only by military counter-measures but also by various schemes of economic aid and technical assistance. Today they must compete even in this field with rapidly growing attempts by the Soviet Union, and now by Communist China, to counter Western aid with similar forms of assistance. Indeed, this aspect of the battle for Asia, the compelling need for either side in the Cold War to prevent the remaining independent countries from sliding into the other camp by assisting them in their emancipation and development, is one of the more constructive aspects of the political division that splits the world. Moreover, this group of countries is important and potentially powerful enough to compel both sides to proceed with moderation. Respect for national sensitivity — which is never stronger than in recently emancipated countries — compels the United States, as well as the Soviet Union, to offer its help without political strings attached. Even the suspicion, in India or Indonesia, that a shipment of wheat or of machinery may be coupled with some expectation of a promise of military bases, political support or propaganda facilities, may suffice to undo years of patient labour. On the other hand, the channelling of aid, from a Western country or an international organization, through the Government of the assisted country, may present grave problems. Even in some European countries, Marshall Aid was used by the assisted Government in such a way as to widen the gap between rich and poor, or to increase corruption. In Asia these dangers are infinitely more serious.

The assisted nations in Europe have behind them centuries of civilization and a highly developed technique of government, backed by a professional and generally efficient and honest Civil Service. With the partial exception of India, Pakistan, Burma and Ceylon, which have had a long period of training in British administration, the new States of Asia are without administrative experience and traditions of honest government. Nepotism and corruption are widespread. Foreign help and investment have often increased the gap between rich and poor in Asia and the Middle East, and have thus inflamed the hatred of the average Asian for the foreigner. European advisers, businessmen and technicians have had similar experiences in the Arab States of the Middle East and in most of the independent States of Asia. It would thus be only logical and prudent for Western Governments, as well as private economic interests, to couple economic or technical assistance with certain conditions ensuring their honest and efficient use. But such conditions encounter the particularly sensitive Nationalism of newly emancipated States, even if that Nationalism is often a pretext for unwillingness of the recipients to tolerate any reform in the government or the social conditions of their country. The extreme example of blind and emotional nationalism in this respect was the willingness of the Mossadegh Government in Iran to let the Abadan oil refineries go to ruin, and thousands of Iranians be unemployed, as well as to face the enormous loss of revenue to the Government, rather than accept anything less than complete and exclusive Iranian control. The calm acceptance of this challenge by the West, which proceeded to develop oil-refining facilities in other Middle East countries, hastened the downfall of the Mossadegh Government and the subsequent re-opening of the refineries by agreement between a new Iranian Government and a consortium of Western oil companies. The investment of foreign capital and skill cannot be a one-sided affair. There must be some give and take on both sides. It is understandable that the reaction against the long era of Western imperialism and colonialism has made the pendulum swing back too far. The first exuberance of sovereignty and national independence is fading, while the burdens and responsibilities of guiding one's own affairs become evident to the nations of Asia. Not only Iran has revised its position. Such countries as India, Pakistan, the Philippines and Thailand have worked out ways to utilize the still vastly superior resources, experience and skill of the more industrialized countries without prejudice to their sovereignty and independence. In countries such as these, the slogans of Western imperialism and capitalist exploitation are slowly fading. The countries in which they are kept alive, such as Indonesia, are apt to use the memories rather than the present reality of Western colonialism and exploitation as a diversion from their unwillingness to face their own problems. No amount of foreign assistance can replace the need for sober economic planning and a programme of austerity, as the leading Communist powers, the Soviet Union and China, adopted it for many years in their early stages of economic development. But foreign capital and technical assistance, now available from international institutions as well as from the major powers of the West and the East, could enable the struggling States of Asia to shorten the period of transition and avoid many unnecessary setbacks caused by lack of skill and experience. The Western powers, on the other hand, and particularly the United States, have had to learn that the transfer of methods and policies adapted to highly developed and mature countries is not necessarily suitable to the problems of developing countries. There is some hope — for example, in the methods of economic collaboration and development assistance that have been worked out as between India and Pakistan, the principal Western Powers and the World Bank — that insight and experience have improved mutual understanding and collaboration.

In recent years such agencies as the United Nations Technical Assistance Administration and Special Fund, the Food and Agriculture Organizations or the World Health Organization, all of them special United Nations agencies, the Colombo Plan administration and the United States Peace Corps have done much to bring scientific advice, technical knowledge and guidance to the nations of Asia, Africa and Latin America. But the material resources in capital and manpower, as well as the executive authority of these agencies, are insufficient to cope with the many problems. The United States operates a vast programme of bilateral assistance to most of the non-Communist nations of Asia. In those countries which have accepted a political alignment with SEATO or other American-sponsored organizations, much of the assistance is in the form of military aid. In the others it comes under the heading of technical co-operation, special programmes and development assistance.[1]

Under the so-called Colombo Plan the more highly developed countries of the British Commonwealth, joined by the United States, are giving assistance to a number of Asian countries which not only include members of the Commonwealth (India, Pakistan, Ceylon), but also Burma, Thailand, Indonesia, and the Philippines. Most of the funds contributed by the donor countries have so far gone into agricultural and power projects. Finally, increasing significance attaches to the schemes by which the free Asian countries themselves plan their development in association with foreign capital and enterprise. In underdeveloped countries with scarcity of capital resources, State planning always plays a greater part than in highly capitalized and industrialized countries. In the case of the most important of the Asian non-Communist countries, such as India, Burma, Pakistan and Indonesia, this is reinforced by a Socialist philosophy and the desire not to let private interests, national or foreign, dictate the development of the country. All these countries have five-year plans or similar programmes underpinned by State agencies, such as industrial development and industrial finance corporations, controlled by the Government, but possessing a greater or smaller degree of commercial flexibility. Increasingly, these countries have come to experiment in joint enterprise with foreign capital. This may be done by contracts with foreign firms or State enterprises as in the case of the Indian steel-mill projects, or by joint capital ventures as they have been set up between Indian (public or private) enterprises on the one hand and British, German or American manufacturers on the other hand — in the production of diesel trucks, pharmaceuticals, bicycles or other consumer products. But for many years to come the incentives for private investment by Western enterprise in Asia will be grossly insufficient for development needs. Both national and international public assistance will be of crucial importance for a long time.

Western Policy Problems

But economic development aid and technical assistance cannot solve certain more basic and agonizing policy problems that confront the West in its future Asian policy. In this, as in so many other respects, a phase of world politics dominated by the over-

[1] See further below, Ch. 12.

whelming importance of the Cold War division is coming to an end and giving way to a more fluid and many-sided situation. During that period, it was the basic Western — and in particular the principal American — objective to strengthen anti-Communist and weaken Communist forces everywhere in the world as much as possible. But even at the height of the Cold War this seemingly simple objective was tempered by the political and strategic realities. A shooting war in a way simplifies problems. It means the disruption of all normal political and economic relations and the defeat of the enemy by all possible means. But in a situation which is characterized by many twilight zones between peace and war, a workable compromise between peace and war strategy has to be found.

As in the previous phase of post-war policy, the West is still faced in Asia with three groups of nations: friends, neutrals and enemies. But not only have there been significant shifts within these groups, the methods of dealing with them may also need basic revision.

Among the nations that can be counted as political, or even military allies, a distinction must be made between those whose closeness to the West rests by and large on popular consent and strong links, and those which are in the Western camp as long as an unpopular government sustained by Western military and economic aid maintains itself in power. At this time only Japan and the Philippines can be clearly considered to be in the first group. In Japan, despite occasional outbursts of anti-Western sentiment, mainly on the part of left-wing intellectuals, and the more widespread opposition to Japanese involvement in a nuclear war, successive elections have shown a consistent pro-Western trend. Moreover, Japan has, even since the cessation of aid, exceptionally strong economic links with the United States and co-operated closely with such Western organizations as the O.E.C.D. By a significant twist of history, it is the principal ex-enemies in Asia and Europe that today prove the closest supporters of the United States and its general international policy. It is the continuing strength of economic links which is also the greatest single factor in the Philippines' orientation towards the United States. In 1963, 50% of Philippine exports went to the U.S., providing a comfortable surplus of $55 million in her favour. Imports from the U.S. constituted 44% of the Philippines' total trade. Under the leadership of President Macapagal, the Philippines — an ex-colony of the United States that gained its independence by consent — may prove a valuable political intermediary between the West and the Malayan peoples of South-east Asia.

On the other hand, Pakistan — formerly linked to the West by its membership in SEATO and the Central Treaty Organization, is now moving out of the Western camp. It is doubtful how far the above-mentioned treaties of alliance are at this time more than pieces of paper. They are not backed by any firm collective organization. Pakistan has recently moved towards friendly relations with Communist China, including a mutual non-aggression pact, which does not accord with the strongly anti-Chinese orientation of Western policy in Asia. Moreover, China has recently declared her support for the Pakistan position in the Kashmir dispute, a move directed not only against India but also against the U.S.S.R., which leans towards support for India.

Apart from Japan, Pakistan and the Philippines, there is a group of states that are at this time allies — not of the West as a whole — but of the United States, and are strongly supported militarily or economically by the latter. In the Far East they are Taiwan and South Korea; in the South-east Asian region they are Thailand and South Vietnam. In all these states, the United States is strongly committed to military assistance and thereby to the maintenance of the existing regime, though not of a particular government. She is firmly pledged to defend Taiwan and South Korea, where substantial U.S. forces still remain, side by side with the South Korean army. Britain is similarly pledged to assist Malaysia — now threatened by Indonesia. The United States is particularly deeply engaged in South Vietnam, through the military and economic support she gives to the war against North Vietnam. But there is increasing uneasiness, not only in other Western countries, but in the United States itself, about the long-term possibilities of maintaining such far-flung support for regimes that might not survive the withdrawal of American help. The question becomes more acute as the strength of Communist China increases and the balance of power shifts more and more in favour of the giant of the Asian continent. In recognition of this situation, de Gaulle's France, in January 1964, established diplomatic relations with Communist China, a policy justified by the realities of the situation and the tradition of international law, and controversial only because of its implied challenge to American policy. France also advocates the neutralization of a vast area, including at least Vietnam, Cambodia and Laos. It is unlikely that either General de Gaulle or any Western Government believes that a neutralization — which is already on the verge of collapse in Laos, despite an international agreement of 1962 — would bring lasting pacification to that area, or more than delay its ultimate control by Communist China. But there are many responsible Western statesmen and publicists who believe that the immense outpouring of American economic and military aid may not attain its long-term objective of creating strong and viable pro-Western governments while the effort is an increasing military and financial burden upon the West's leader. This sentiment is possibly beginning to be shared by the U.S. Government, which in February 1964 declared that it would withdraw most of the American troops from South Vietnam before the end of 1965, although subsequent Communist advances in Laos and Vietnam have induced commitments to increased economic and military assistance by the United States. Neutralization may be the most respectable way of retreating from an untenable situation.

On the other hand, the considerations that moved the United States to undertake all these supports in the first place still prevail as long as the maintenance of pro-Western regimes in Asia remains a paramount objective of Western policy. The effective loss of Vietnam, Cambodia and Laos would threaten the independence of Thailand, an important rice bowl — and ultimately of Malaysia, which Britain, as much as the United States, regards as a vital Western bastion.

A policy of mere military strategy or anti-Communism is not enough. No amount of economic or military support will indefinitely maintain a weak or a corrupt regime. It is unlikely that any Asian Government which does not satisfy a minimum of national and social aspirations has any prospect of survival. If it is generally true that one cannot sit on bayonets, this applies particularly to Western bayonets, which are much farther from the scene of Asian conflict than Communist bayonets. It might be seriously argued that the wisest, the most economic and, in a sense, the most courageous policy for the West would be to withdraw from all possessions or commitments in Asia. The great political success of the British withdrawal from India and Burma, and the disastrous consequences of the French failure to come to a timely arrangement with the nationalist forces in Vietnam, would seem to support such a policy. But it would be impossible at present to extend it to the whole of Asia. As long as the Cold War lasts and the Communist and non-Communist worlds remain opposed to each other, a complete Western withdrawal from Asia would fatally weaken its position in the rest of the world. But even if none of the Great Powers may be willing to risk an open and major clash, the likelihood of continuous regional conflicts in Asia is great. In Europe the fronts are now fairly clearly defined. Armed conflict in any part of Europe would almost certainly lead to general war, but in Asia both the military and ideological fronts are fluid and ill-defined. Soviet Russia and, in particular, China can support internal risings in many parts of Asia which are genuine and led by native leaders and national forces. On the other hand, the Western Powers are divided in their reaction to further Communist infiltration. Whereas American policy has often inclined towards open support of any anti-Communist faction, however unpopular or discredited, the other Western Powers recognize to a far greater degree the strength of Communism in such countries as China and Indo-China, as well as the increasing strain which the Asian conflicts put on Western resources. The United States' persistent refusal to recognize Communist China or let her be seated in the United Nations has done relatively little harm to China, but aggravated intra-Western divisions, demonstrated by France's recognition of the Communist Government in January 1964.

At a time when so many positions are in flux, it may be that unexpected support for the maintenance of some Western positions in that area will come from the Soviet Union. Already the U.S.S.R. has, over the last few years, acted with relative moderation in areas like Vietnam, or Laos. The reason for this is of course her increasing apprehension of the growing strength and hostility of Communist China. To the extent that such hostility should prevail and deepen, it would be logical for the U.S.S.R. to seek at least an accommodation with the pro-Western forces, rather than to work towards the complete control of the whole region by Communist China. This may be all the more so, as all the natural advantages of geography, race and ideology lie with China rather than with Russia in that part of the world.

It is possible that some of these dangerous situations will resolve themselves by internal rather than international decisions. It is conceivable that after the death of Chiang Kai-shek, the influence of the minority of mainland Chinese will further decline and that Taiwan will move towards a position of neutrality, or even a closer association with Communist China. If this should be the case, the United States could hardly oppose such a development by military force. Again it is not impossible, especially after a prolonged military impasse, that the two parts of Vietnam may come together on their own accord. Such developments would not mitigate the weakening of the Western global position, but they would facilitate a painful but probably inevitable change in the pattern of world politics: a change in which the growing strength of Communist China would lead to her supremacy in East Asia.

It would, however, require great optimism to believe that such an evolution could occur peacefully. At some point it is likely that a battle would occur — perhaps over the control of Malaysia or of Taiwan. It is extremely unlikely that such a battle would not develop into a world-wide conflagration which would make all further speculation on the political future of this or any other part of the world irrelevant.

Only if Communist China should come to share the awareness of the other two super-Powers, of the catastrophic and universal effects of another world war, is there a reasonable chance that an adjustment of strategic positions, including certain areas of neutralization, would constitute more than a brief transitory phase. But even if a third world war can be avoided, it is difficult to see how the West can avoid the gradual strengthening of the influence of Communist China, supported by many Chinese minorities in the key States of Asia.

It is finally clear that if such a development occurs, the genuinely neutral States, notably India, will not be able to resist effectively without continuing massive help from the West. Such help is likely to be forthcoming in the case of a direct military attack, as it occurred on a limited scale from China in 1962. It is hardly likely to be given to a neutralist India which would have to seek a way how to live with an immensely strengthened Communist China.

Beyond the immediate future, almost any speculation as to the long-term developments in Asia must be highly tentative. The odds are heavily weighted against the West and the nations friendly to it. The greatest — though still a slender — hope lies in the possibility that, with Japan as a strong bastion in the Far East, the nations of South-east Asia — and most of all the 450 million people of India — may, with Western help, acquire sufficient political, economic and social strength to resist Chinese power through their own resources, and not through precarious dependence on Western help. This alone makes the continuance and strengthening of long-term economic and technical aid a vital necessity, even though the political results of such help must remain in doubt.

CHAPTER 9

AFRICAN TURMOIL

BEFORE the last world war there were four independent States in Africa: Ethiopia, the Union of South Africa, Egypt and Liberia. Today there are thirty-six independent African States, the great majority of which have attained independence within the last five years. These sober figures alone indicate the explosive and dramatic transformation that Africa has undergone since the end of the last war, and particularly within the last decade. The continent which, between the middle of the nineteenth century and the beginning of the First World War, had almost entirely been divided up between four European colonial powers, France, Great Britain, Belgium and Portugal — although some of the colonies date further back — is now overwhelmingly composed of a large number of independent, 'sovereign' states. Of the remaining dependent territories, Northern Rhodesia and Southern Rhodesia, which until recently formed with Nyasaland the ill-fated Central African Federation, have now become separate States. The dependent territories remaining after that consist mainly of the two Portuguese colonies of Angola and Mozambique, which are likely to achieve independence either through revolution and war, or through continued pressure, from Africa and outside, on the only remaining major colonial power, Portugal. South-West Africa is a United Nations Trust Territory, although to all intents and purposes it has for many years been treated by the Republic of South Africa as part of its own territory and administration. There remain the three British protectorates of Bechuanaland, Basutoland and Swaziland, and certain scattered small enclaves and territories throughout the continent, insignificant in size and importance, as compared with independent Africa.

The Principal Groupings of African States

The history of Africa, and especially the colonial divisions, still influence the status, characteristics and orientation of the various States sufficiently to justify a rough grouping largely influenced by their history and former allegiance.

The first group, the four States that had political independence before the last world war, have no other link between themselves. By far the oldest of these is Ethiopia, a country that dates its independence back to A.D. 1040, a Christian State whose Hamite population is racially quite distinct, both from the Moslem Arabs and from the Africans who surround them. Egypt (called 'United Arab Republic' since its temporary union with Syria), one of the most ancient countries in the history of mankind, emerged to limited independence in 1922, after centuries of political and economic eclipse and domination by other powers (notably Turkey and Britain). It achieved full sovereignty only in 1936, after the withdrawal of British troops from the Suez Canal Zone. The Republic of South Africa which, between the end of the Boer War in 1901 and 1962, was a member of the British Commonwealth of Nations, is now under a strongly Nationalist Government formed by the Dutch (Boer) element, the most radical supporters in the world of a policy of white supremacy over non-white people. In any but a geographical sense, the rulers of South Africa have never considered themselves as Africans. A white minority of some three million people rules a native black population of 11 million and 2 million other non-whites as a subject race, which is denied voting and other civic rights, subjected to a severe regime of police supervision and denial of equal access to law. About 13·7% of the territory of the Republic of South Africa — mainly poor land — has been allocated to the native black population as 'Bantustan'. Finally, Liberia, founded in 1846 by American philanthropic societies as a haven of refuge for liberated slaves from America, preceded by more than a century the large number of independent African negro states that now cover most of Africa. Thus each of the older independent states in Africa has a completely different history, religion, racial composition and political orientation.

The second group consists of the four Arab–Moslem States of North Africa, which extend from the western border of the United Arab Republic to the Atlantic coast. One of these, the smallest in population, Libya, gained its independence in 1952, under United Nations auspices. The other three obtained their independence from French control between 1956 and 1962.

Morocco and Tunisia had been French protectorates since 1912 and 1881 respectively, and they gained their independence peacefully, by negotiation with France. The third, Algeria, had been constitutionally an Overseas Department of metropolitan France for more than a century, and achieved independence after one of the bitterest and bloodiest colonial wars of modern times, in 1961. The decision to terminate the civil war and to grant independence to the Algerian Arabs, despite the presence of about one million French *colons*, was made and carried out by General de Gaulle in the face of bitter resistance from strong elements of the French Army and the overwhelming majority of the French in Algeria. While Algeria forms in theory the Maghreb, with Morocco and Tunisia, its relations with either of these neighbours have not always been harmonious. To this group may be added the Sudan, a predominantly, though by no means purely, Arab–Moslem country which gained its political independence (from a British–Egyptian condominium) in 1956.

The third group consists of the thirteen States — all contiguous in West and Central Africa, except for the island republic of Malagasy — which achieved independence from France in 1960. The suddenness of this transition from a status of colonial, political and economic dependence and backwardness, to full independence — another dramatic decision made by General de Gaulle, after his assumption of power in France in 1958 — is all the more remarkable as France had traditionally differed from the principles of British colonial policy in seeking to integrate the French African colonies gradually, by extending the privilege of French citizenship to an increasing proportion of Africans, under the French flag. Troops from the African colonies had for many decades formed vitally important elements of the French Army, and served with distinction in both world wars. The transformation effected by de Gaulle implied the adoption of the British idea of a 'Commonwealth of Nations', i.e. the association of independent States in a community of equals. The former colonies, except Guinea, accepted the offer of such an association, and in return retained the vitally important aid that France had given for many years, in terms of administration, technical and educational assistance, and capital development. Overwhelmingly, the French-speaking West and Equatorial African States are dependent on the production of one or a few agricultural staple commodities, such as peanuts, cocoa, cotton or palm oil. They continue to be dependent on French economic aid, much of it in the form of price supports, i.e. the payment of a substantial margin between the prevailing world market prices and the prices paid by France for the staple products of these States. These subsidies will, however, come to an end as the result of the association of the French-speaking African States with the European Community, which, it is expected, will give them compensating advantages. In language, law, cultural orientation and economic dependence, the thirteen States — which form the *Union Africaine et Malgache* (UAM) — retain a strong link with France where the great majority of the present leaders of these States were educated and received their political apprenticeship. The younger leaders in these States are, however, beginning to pursue a more independent line.

The next group consists of the former British colonies of West and East Africa. The difference between these two areas is not only geographical. In the West, Ghana and Nigeria — and to a lesser extent Sierra Leone — are relatively prosperous, mainly through the successful marketing and export of important staple products, such as cocoa and palm oil. A perhaps more important difference between them and British East Africa results from British policies and methods of administration. The humid and until recently very unhealthy climate of West Africa did not entice British settlers. Britain governed these colonies — as she has done in Asia — through soldiers and civil servants, a superstructure of foreign controllers who stayed as a matter of duty and never made Africa their home. The counterpart of this lack of any permanent British settlement, coupled with the relative prosperity of a limited middle class of Africans, was the gradual training of many Ghanaians and Nigerians in law and administration, mainly in Britain. Moreover, British involvement in West Africa is several decades older than in East Africa. As a result, both these countries at the time of independence — which Ghana achieved in 1957, Nigeria in 1961 — disposed of a small nucleus of trained administrators and a professional class which enabled them to take over the government with a certain degree of preparedness. By contrast, the East African colonies found themselves in a state of economic backwardness and virtually without any nationals trained in law, administration, education or engineering.

In the case of Kenya, the attractiveness of the country induced British settlers since the beginning of the century to settle in the highlands. They came to feel entirely at home in a country that offered them rich returns for their labour, and a highly enjoyable though exclusive life. In the case of Uganda, also a land of great natural beauty and fertility, the traditional rivalries between the new nationalist parties and the hereditary governing groups of the four traditional kingdoms of Uganda, especially the powerful kingdom of Buganda, which contained the majority of the relatively wealthy and educated élite of Uganda, impeded political progress. It was only in a constitutional conference in 1962 that the major internal rivalries were overcome to the extent of providing a basis for independence. In the case of Tanganyika, whose climate and economic resources are less favoured, the almost complete absence of an educated African élite, is in part due to the fact that after having been for several decades a German colony, Tanganyika became after the First World War a British-administered League of Nations Mandate, and later a United Nations Trust Territory. Furthermore, it is only after the Second World War that the colonial Powers felt an obligation to compensate for inequalities of resources in their colonies by welfare and development grants. On the other hand, Britain had established a certain link between these three States, through a High Commission, now renamed 'Common Services Organization' which is a kind of prototype for the European Common Market, in so far as it administers a customs union and common services in transport and communications. Thus the groundwork was laid for a possible federation, which the three now independent States have so far failed to achieve.

The fourth group consists of the former Belgian possessions, now the Republic of the Congo, Rwanda and Burundi. The Congo, which was practically unknown until discovered by Stanley in the 1870s, had soon after been explored and exploited by Belgium under the leadership of King Leopold II, and been recognized as a Belgian possession in the Berlin Conference of 1884. Since then Belgium had administered this vast country of some 14,000,000 people by an entirely autocratic though benevolent government. The province of Katanga had been for decades a source of rich revenue through its ample resources in cobalt, diamonds, copper and tin. These were operated by the *Union*

Minière, a large and powerful company controlled mainly by Belgian and British financial interests.

Whereas in the British Empire the gradual attainment of self-government and eventual political independence had for many years become an accepted goal, with the consequence that, except for parts of East Africa, natives received some administrative and technical training, Belgium never began to envisage a corresponding development until it decided with abrupt suddenness in 1960 to fall in with the general trend, and granted the Congo complete political independence. The sudden and unprepared transition, made more chaotic by the all but complete absence of even a small nucleus of trained and educated Congolese, greatly contributed to the destructive civil war, provoked by the secession of its richest province, Katanga, under Tshombe, whose separatist tendencies were encouraged by the Belgian and British interests and by its neighbour, Southern Rhodesia. In January 1963 the unity of the Congo was precariously re-established through the intervention of a United Nations Force, mainly composed of Indian and African contingents, and the economic life and revenues of the country, which were mainly supplied by Katanga, were more or less restored. But the country continues to be plagued by civil strife and especially by tribal revolts, one of which at least is now under Communist leadership. The spread of these — apparently Chinese master-minded — Communist advances, threatens to engulf not only the Congo, but other parts of Central and East Africa, and to revive the dangers of foreign involvement which the late Dag Hammarskjöld sought to meet by U.N. intervention.[1]

The next group consists of the remaining dependent territories under British control. Of these, Southern Rhodesia is politically and socially close to its neighbour, the Republic of South Africa. Constitutionally, it is a self-governing British colony, but in fact has been treated, to all intents and purposes, as an independent part of the Commonwealth. Its small minority of

[1] Late in 1964, when Tshombe, now the Western-backed Prime Minister of the Congo, was fighting a left-wing rebel government in Stanleyville with the help of white mercenaries, an American–Belgian airlift of some 1,500 white rebel-held hostages threatened to make the Congo again the centre of international conflict. The airlift was bitterly opposed by the great majority of African States, vigorously supported by Communist China and the U.S.S.R.

some 225,000 Europeans rules over nearly four million Africans. The position was, until recently, similar in neighbouring prosperous Northern Rhodesia, a British protectorate which in 1962 had a gross national product of five hundred and fifty-five million dollars, more than half of which came from the mining of copper and other minerals. In 1953 Britain attempted a historic experiment in multiracial government by joining Northern and Southern Rhodesia, both dominated by small and prosperous white minorities, and the almost entirely African-populated and economically backward Nyasaland. The idea behind this federation was a partnership between whites and Africans, by a gradual increase of African voting rights and participation in government. From the beginning this attempt was resisted by both sides. The white minority objected to the aim of eventual political and possibly even economic equality and, in 1962, dismissed the relatively liberal incumbent Prime Minister, Sir Edgar Whitehead and his party, in favour of a more militant anti-African party led by Winston Field. In 1964 he was in turn displaced by a more radical champion of white supremacy, Ian Smith. The Africans on the other hand, stimulated by the rapid growth of many independent African States, such as neighbouring Tanganyika, resented the paternalism and the slowness of their proposed progress towards self-government and equality. The growth of tensions forced the British Government in 1963 to dissolve the Central African Federation. As a result, Nyasaland, now renamed Malawi, became independent in 1964 and will probably seek close association with its East African neighbours, in particular Tanzania. Southern Rhodesia shows every sign of moving more closely to the policies of its neighbour South Africa, the main bastion of white supremacy. Northern Rhodesia, which was under British protectorate, became in October 1964 the independent, African-controlled State of Zambia, led by the moderate Kenneth Kaunda. Independence was marred by a bitter dispute between the new government and the British South Africa Company, which claims full compensation for the loss of its rich mining licences originally acquired by Cecil Rhodes from a native chief, and guaranteed by a previous (British-controlled) government until 1986. One of the first acts of the new British Labour Government was to settle this dispute by a compromise. There remain the three British protectorates of Basutoland,

Bechuanaland and Swaziland, uncomfortably close to, and potentially threatened by, South Africa, which has repeatedly suggested to Britain that she should abandon her protectorate and have these territories made part of South Africa. This policy is of course totally unacceptable to Britain, as long as South Africa pursues a radical policy of apartheid, which would engulf the entirely African protectorates. If relations between South Africa and Britain should deteriorate further, the use of armed force and annexation of these territories by South Africa is not beyond the realm of possibility.

There remain the last Portuguese colonies of Angola and Mozambique, and a number of less important Spanish and French enclaves. Portugal has hitherto adamantly refused to follow the general trend of granting independence to colonies, and Angola has for several years been the scene of internal warfare between various groups of African nationalists and the Portuguese. All the independent African States have, with greater or lesser emphasis, vowed to fight for the independence of the Portuguese colonies. In the United Nations Portugal is essentially isolated, although most of the Western Powers do not follow the more radical resolutions pushed by the African members.

Political and International Orientations

The great diversity in the political and international orientations of the different groups of African States corresponds, to some extent, to the divergencies in their ethnic, racial and political history. Thus, South Africa and Southern Rhodesia, geographical neighbours, are close to each other in their general political and social orientation, and the apprehension felt by a politically and economically dominant white minority against the claims of the African majority. But the dominant group in South Africa are the Boer descendants of the Dutch, with the British in moderate opposition, while the rulers of Southern Rhodesia are of British stock. The latter (220,000 out of 3,900,000) are a much smaller proportion of the total population than the whites in South Africa. Moreover, their policies are restrained by association with the British Commonwealth, and a residuary policy control by Britain. On the whole, the political and economic status of the black population of Southern Rhodesia, while greatly inferior to that of the whites, is far superior to the apartheid status of their

South African brothers. The dissolution of the Central African Federation and the recent installation of African Governments in both Northern Rhodesia and Nyasaland may, however, bring Southern Rhodesia closer to South Africa and even lead to its dissociation from Britain and the Commonwealth.

At the other end of the continent a considerable measure of unity is provided by the ties of Arab race and the Moslem religion. These ties unite, up to a point, the United Arab Republic, Libya, Tunisia, Algeria, Morocco and Sudan, all of whom are members of the Arab League. But there are also many major differences: between the strongly nationalist and moderately Socialist 'middle-class revolution against Capitalism and Communism' of Nasser's Egypt — which also aspires to the leadership of the entire Arab world; the underpopulated and conservative monarchy of Libya — which is, however, in a process of economic change through the discovery of important oil deposits now under concession to many foreign companies; the moderately nationalistic and, under the leadership of Habib Bourguiba, essentially pro-Western political and economic orientation of Tunisia; the strongly Socialist and militant State of Algeria which emerged from eight years of bitter war with France, under the leadership of Ben Bella; and the kingdom of Morocco, where a king, as Chief of State, head of Government and the principal religious leader, seeks to hold together the many heterogeneous elements of the State and to transform it gradually from a backward agricultural country into a more diversified modern economy. There are also conflicting claims of Algeria and Morocco to the oil-bearing districts of the Sahara Region which are likely to be a major source of revenue for any country controlling them. The incidence of oil in the Middle East is the major source of wealth in an area where general poverty contrasts with the great wealth of some rulers and a small clan of landowners.

To the south of the Arab–Moslem group of States, certain States contain a mixture of Arab–Moor and black African populations, a mixture which almost invariably produces religious and social tensions, especially since the Arabs have for centuries exercised political and economic dominance over the black Africans, often as slave traders — and still tend to consider themselves as superior in civilization and status. There are also the religious differences between Islam and various forms of tribal religions as well as Christianity, although considerable numbers of black Africans have adopted the Moslem religion. Tensions between the Arab and the black African populations exist in most of these states, notably in the Sudan, where the dominant Moslem population rules, with much bloodshed, a primitive and generally underprivileged black population concentrated in the southern Sudan; in Mauritania, which belongs to the recently emancipated group of former French colonies; and in the island of Zanzibar, once a principal centre of slave traders, where the dominant Arab minority was recently displaced by a left-wing revolution, bringing the African majority party into power.

The French-speaking group of States which achieved independence from France in 1960 constitute what is on the whole the politically most cohesive group of States in Africa. Shortly after independence they formed an association (*Union Africaine et Malgache*), which is now being merged in the wider Organization of African Unity. Ties between these States rest on the community of language, law and institutions introduced by France, and the strong impact of French culture and education on the leaders of these new States. French civil servants and educators continue to occupy most of the key positions in the new administrations — though increasingly as advisers rather than executives — but most important is the extraordinary degree of economic dependence on French economic trade and aid. The French-speaking ex-colonies of France have associate membership in the European Economic Community, which ensures privileged trading conditions for their products. This status also qualifies them for development aid from the Community's European Development Fund.

While these States retain their strong pro-French political, social and economic orientation, some of them have taken a more independent line from the beginning, and a new generation of leaders is likely to pursue a more vigorous and independent African nationalism. Already there are tentative moves to break out of the exclusive French orientation through contacts with the neighbouring English-speaking States, and through membership in Pan-African movements and associations. A stronger emphasis on African nationalism usually goes together with left-wing tendencies. Guinea, which broke away from the French Commonwealth immediately after independence, has a strongly

Socialist Government led by President Touré, and Mali, which dissolved an association with neighbouring Senegal, also has a strong Socialist movement seeking to link Mali more closely to the Soviet bloc. In Gabon, the French restored, by military intervention, an elderly ruler deposed by a revolt of oppressive elements in January 1964, and thus probably caused national resentment. The political and international orientation of the former British colonies is far more diverse than that of the French group. Ghana, the first to achieve full independence in 1957, under the ambitious and erratic Nkrumah, has vacillated between extreme nationalist and Socialist policies and more moderate attitudes. In 1962 the Government concluded a series of agreements for the development of the Volta River with a variety of public and private international foreign participants. The Ghanaian Volta River Authority was established. The World Bank, the United States and Britain each provided major loans and credits for the purchase of machinery and materials, while an aluminium smelter will be operated as a joint venture by a consortium of aluminium companies. This consortium in turn has both private capital and major dollar loans from the United States Export–Import Bank and the AID. But despite this important involvement of Western, and particularly United States, funds, Ghana has recently veered again to a strongly anti-Western attitude, which makes the future of her relations with the West highly uncertain. Constitutionally, all pretence of democracy has been abandoned. Ghana is a totalitarian one-party State, in which independence of the judiciary and freedom of opinion as well as the vestiges of parliamentary democracy have been abolished.

By contrast the vastly bigger (between 40 and 50 million inhabitants) Federation of Nigeria has hitherto retained a parliamentary system and moderate policies, and, while avoiding any political entanglements or partisanship in the Cold War, maintains strong links with the West. Nigeria's ambitious development plans depend on a sustained aid programme from foreign sources. The principal of these is an informal group constituted by the World Bank and the major Western countries in which Britain and the United States take a leading part. The economic situation of Nigeria is one of the most favourable of the African continent. While 60% of its gross national product still comes from agriculture, and cocoa, palm oil, rubber and cotton are the principal export earners, important natural resources, such as iron, tin, hydroelectric power and, more recently, important oil deposits in Eastern Nigeria, help to spur industrial growth and to diversify the economy. Nigeria's economic development plans are designed not only to attract continued capital help from Western and international public sources, but also private investment, preferably in the form of joint ventures with Nigerian public and private enterprise. The maintenance of a parliamentary democracy and a generally independent system of administration of justice is helped by the federal structure of Nigeria and the need to maintain a balance between the principal regions — Nigeria's main political problem. Whereas Northern Nigeria is predominantly Moslem, in the Eastern and Western regions of Nigeria the Ibo and Yoruba tribes predominate. A moderate line pursued in international and economic policy under the leadership of Prime Minister Sir Abubakar Tafawa Balewa conceals to some extent the much more nationalist and anti-Western outlook of many of the younger political leaders of Nigeria. On the whole, however, Nigeria is not only the largest State, but one of the stablest factors in contemporary African politics.

The situation of the East African States — Tanganyika, Kenya, Uganda and Zanzibar — all of which have gained independence in recent years, is more precarious. These States were economically and administratively linked for several decades by a kind of common market which administers a common currency, a common customs tariff, railways and postal services and which it was hoped would provide a forerunner for closer economic and political integration. However, here as elsewhere in Africa, the strength of separate national ambitions, ironically clustering around national units which in large measure have been the artificial creation of Western colonization — in the nineteenth and early twentieth centuries — has tended to work against larger and organic units. Under the responsible and moderate leadership of Julius Nyerere, Tanganyika, a country of some nine million Africans with a very small European minority, was the first to achieve independence in December 1961. It was followed nearly a year later by Uganda, which, like Tanganyika, has no white settler problem, but has been plagued by the internal tensions between the traditional kingdoms and the rest of the country. Under the leadership of Prime Minister Obote, Uganda is however making slow progress towards nationhood, although it has continued to maintain strong reservations about federal union with Tanganyika and Kenya. The last of the three to achieve independence, in December 1963, was Kenya. The peaceful transition to independence was a remarkable achievement, after years of strife between the nationalist African leaders and the European settlers, and between the different African tribes that compose the population of Kenya. Unlike Tanganyika and Uganda, Kenya, a country endowed with great natural beauty, a healthy climate and fertile highlands, became attractive to white settlers, who even after the considerable exodus of recent years still number about 55,000. Unlike the British in West Africa and most other parts of the British Empire, these settlers were intent on staying permanently in a country that offered them beauty, privileges and wealth. Rising tensions with the growing nationalist movement culminated in the bloody Mau Mau revolt of 1952–54. A situation comparable to South Africa might have developed, except for the continuing control of Kenya by the British Government, which, after the Mau Mau revolt had subsided, accepted the principle of African majority rule and permitted the formation of African parties. After years of detention, Jomo Kenyatta became the leader of the majority party, the Kenya African National Union (KANU). As has often happened in the history of the British Empire and Commonwealth, the decision to entrust the leaders of strong nationalist movements (often after a period of prolonged imprisonment[1]) paid off in terms of a political reconciliation and even co-operation. The promise of national independence under African rule was accompanied by a land reform scheme, under which the white-settled highlands will be made available for African settlement. The financing of the compensation for this change was in part provided by a loan from the World Bank, in conjunction with British Government support.

As the problem of the relations with the white settlers neared solution, the internal tribal tensions achieved greater significance. KANU represents essentially the majority tribes (Kikuyu, Luo and Kamba), while most of the minority tribes have coalesced into another party (KADU) which stands for regional decentralization in contrast with KANU's centralizing tendencies. A compromise constitution agreed upon between the British and

[1] Other examples are Nehru in India, and Hastings Banda in Nyasaland.

the rival Kenya parties is unlikely to last. The Kenyatta government, whose party gained a sweeping electoral victory in May 1963, has since assumed most of the powers promised by the constitution to the region for the central government.

While leaders of all three States, but particularly those of Kenya and Tanganyika, have expressed strong desires for a speedy federation of the three East African States, with the likely inclusion of Zanzibar as a small fourth partner, progress has been dilatory. This is in part due to the suspicions entertained by the other partners of Kenya's relative economic predominance. In January 1964, a revolution in Zanzibar which displaced the ruling Arab minority and brought the African majority party under a generally left-wing leadership into power was followed by army mutinies in Tanganyika, Kenya and Uganda. The leaders of all three countries were compelled to invoke the assistance of the British armed forces, which suppressed the mutinies effortlessly and without bloodshed. Nevertheless, the invocation by the African national leaders of the help of the former colonial Power, however necessary and legally justified, is apt to undermine their authority, especially among the younger increasingly intransigent nationalist elements which will be even more inclined to combine their nationalism with anti-Western, and correspondingly pro-Communist, sentiments. In the tiny but strategically important Zanzibar the revolution of January 1964 led to increasing dominance of pro-Communist leaders, with the U.S.S.R., East Germany and China competing for influence through diplomatic, economic and military ties. The increasing lead of China in that race led, in April 1964, to a counter-move by Tanganyika, which, with the support of the more moderate Zanzibar leaders produced the United Republic of Tanganyika and Zanzibar[1], the strength of which is doubtful. It may be that present unrest may give an additional spur to the lagging efforts at achieving the East African Federation, a development that would not only be a logical continuation of the Common Market but would effectively counteract the many disintegrating tendencies in contemporary African nationalism and make the voice of East Africa one of the most important among the new African nations. Such a Federation might well attract the newly independent Nyasaland (Malawi) and Northern Rhodesia (Zambia). Because of its potential size and im-

[1] Renamed 'Tanzania' in October 1964.

portance, such a movement is however violently opposed by President Nkrumah, who sees in an East African Confederation a further challenge to his own predominance already threatened by Nigeria.

African Development Problems

The overwhelming majority of the African States face the problem of trying to bridge in a time very much shorter than that accorded to the older nations of Europe, and even to the newer nations of Asia and Latin America, the enormous gap between their present state of economic and social development, and the minimum aspirations of a modern State. The political and legal status of a sovereign State requires embassies in other countries and at the United Nations, and an apparatus of government modelled on that of more advanced States at home; the aspirations of economic development require a general improvement of the standard of living, a diversification of the economy and the establishment of links with many other parts of the world. Teachers, engineers, scientists, administrators, lawyers, doctors have to be trained. Moreover, the existence of a small élite of politicians, administrators and professionally trained men emphasizes the stark contrasts between them and the vast majority of villagers, farmers and workmen. The latter no longer accept their status passively as in former times, but they will seethe with discontent and easily turn to radical leaders, who can exploit not only the depressed conditions of the majority, but link them with the generally still prevailing ties between the present leaders of the African States and their former colonizers as well as other Western Powers. Thus, development in Africa, as in other underdeveloped countries, is not only a question of economic advancement and a rise in the standard of living. It also presents crucial problems of educational progress, and of social and political tensions. It is too late to argue whether the people of Africa might be happier if they had been left alone, in their ancient tribal customs and organization, in their primitive but self-sufficient agricultural economy, free from the ambitions of modern nation-States. The Africans did not ask to be disturbed in their ways of life by the West. It is the latter who brought with them not only the aspirations to a different way of life, but also the seeds of nationalism that now celebrates its belated triumph in contemporary Africa. The move towards nationhood, organized in modern States, is now irreversible. The problem that remains is how to bridge the enormous gap between reality and aspirations.

A state of economic and social underdevelopment is generally proportionate to the predominance of agriculture over commerce and industry. Only two States of Africa might be described as economically advanced, and they are characteristically not only the two most industrialized countries of Africa, but also the two that politically stand in the sharpest opposition to the rest of the Continent: South Africa and Southern Rhodesia. The Republic of South Africa, which leads the world in the production of gold, diamonds, asbestos and chrome ore, and has important reserves of other vital minerals, also has a highly advanced banking system and the highest degree of industrialization on the continent. Southern Rhodesia has in the last decade rapidly developed its secondary industry, and manufacturing now constitutes the largest component in its national product. Much of this progress was however due to the federation with Northern Rhodesia which has now been dissolved. All the other independent states of Africa are in varying stages of underdevelopment. Nigeria, while still largely dependent on the export-earning capacity of its staple agricultural products, is well on the way towards the development of secondary industries and economic diversification, and thanks to the relative political stability and confidence Nigeria enjoys in the Western world and the international financial agencies, Nigeria is making steady progress. The important aid given to it by the World Bank since 1958 in a series of loans, testifies to the confidence in its future. In the north of Africa, the much smaller and poorer country of Tunisia is also making rapid economic progress under the moderate leadership of Bourguiba, with concentration on agricultural reform and modernization. Guided by a realistic development plan Tunisia has attracted an unusual amount of foreign assistance from the World Bank, the United States and many other nations including the Soviet Union. Of the English-speaking countries, apart from Nigeria, Ghana is in a state of considerable economic development. Mention has already been made of the multinational Volta River Project which will give a great spur to the development of industry. The people of Ghana are relatively literate and developed, but the political whims of Nkrumah and the strong leanings towards a one-party Socialist State are likely to greatly curtail the flow of public and private Western investment while possibly leading to a correspondingly greater economic and technical support from Communist countries, notably the U.S.S.R. — which has already supplied the bulk of Ghana's commercial aviation fleet, technical assistance and the development of gold refining, State farms and a number of other economic activities. The East African States still depend on their staple agricultural commodities such as coffee, and with the partial exception of Kenya, are well behind their minimum aspirations in the state of industrial development. The French-speaking group of States is still overwhelmingly agricultural and correspondingly dependent on the continuation of French economic aid for technical and educational progress, and the still modest level of industrial development, although their association with the E.E.C. now makes them eligible for development aid from Community funds.

While World Bank and Western aid predominates in the majority of the African States, the Soviet bloc plays an important part in the development of some of them. The Soviet credit and technical direction of the huge Aswan Dam in Egypt is the most spectacular example of aid from the Communist bloc. But the U.S.S.R., Czechoslovakia, Yugoslavia also give aid to a number of projects, both in States that politically lean towards the Soviet bloc, such as Ghana or Guinea, and in States that deliberately emphasize a policy of neutralism and seek assistance from whatever quarter it may come, such as the United Arab Republic (Egypt), Somalia, the Sudan and Ethiopia. As mentioned in another context, the technically and scientifically highly developed though capital-poor State of Israel plays an important part in the technical and agricultural development of a large number of African States.[1]

The World Bank and more recently the United States have come to accept more and more the necessity of long-term economic development planning in virtually all the African States. Only economic development plans can provide for the kind of growth that will not encourage non-essentials at the expense of basic services and industries, that can correlate the growth of industry

[1] More recently Communist China has taken an active part in African affairs. Political and military missions in Zanzibar, Burundi, revolutionary Congo; interest-free loans to Kenya and Zanzibar; offers of trade agreements and technical assistance, mainly to African States; all these indicate that China regards Africa as one of its major strategic objectives.

and the modernization of agriculture with the training of skilled manpower on all levels. It acknowledges the inevitably predominant role of the State and of public enterprise in the earlier stage of economic development. It is sound economic development planning that has largely contributed to the favourable position enjoyed by such States as Nigeria and Tunisia in the flow of foreign funds towards their development.

Pan-African Movements

As the foregoing survey has shown, the new States of Africa show an amazing diversity in their history, their religious affiliations, their political orientation, their state of development and their general aspirations. Many divisions have been imported into the continent by the often extremely arbitrary boundaries of colonization in the nineteenth and early twentieth centuries. However arbitrary, these divisions have produced many lasting differences in the affiliations and habits of life of the African people. The differences in language, law, institutions and habits of life between the former French or Belgian and the English-speaking countries of Africa are obvious even to the casual visitor. Tribes have been artificially separated, for example in the national borders that now separate Ghana from Togo or Nigeria from the Cameroun Federation, or Somalia from Kenya and Ethiopia. The differences have often been accentuated by the rival ambitions of the present African leaders. President Nasser seeks to play a major part in the politics of Africa, as well as in the leadership of the Arab nations of the Middle and Near East. President Nkrumah, as the leader of the first of the newly independent African States, looks with jealousy upon the much bigger Nigeria, and on efforts to create an East African Federation. The Emperor of Ethiopia seeks to play a leading role in African politics, by virtue of the *ancienneté* of his country and its relative freedom from political alignments.

The differences of political orientation found expression in the formation of the three separate groupings of African States: the *Union Africaine et Malgache*, combining the former French colonies, in a generally pro-French orientation; the so-called Casablanca group, formed by the Arab States of North Africa with Ghana and Egypt; and the so-called Monrovia group, combining the moderately pro-Western group of States, such as Nigeria and Liberia. In May 1963 a Summit Conference of independent African States meeting in Addis Ababa, the capital of Ethiopia, formed an Organization of African Unity, whose charter expresses the 'common determination to promote understanding among our peoples and co-operation among our states in response to the aspirations of our people for brotherhood and solidarity, in a larger unity transcending ethnic and national differences'. To what extent this new organization will overcome the divergent purposes of the different States and groupings which, in theory, have emerged in the new organization, remains to be seen.

Another, possibly even more important, recent development is the establishment of an African Development Bank. Although in many ways modelled upon the Inter-American Development Bank, the African Development Bank differs from this regional model in confining membership and capital subscription to African States. Obviously, it cannot replace the vitally needed aid from non-African bilateral and multilateral sources; it is designed to assist 'the capital needs of the African states for the execution of the economic development programmes by concerted action in the public and private sectors'. Subscriptions will be allocated on the basis of each member's economic capacity, subject to a minimum subscription of one million U.S. dollars and a maximum subscription of thirty million U.S. dollars. Following the model of the World Bank Charter, each member will have an equal number of minimum votes, with additional votes in proportion to subscribed shares. While the top level of the management of the Bank will be entirely African, non-African experts will be used on other levels. If this Bank — which is due to start operations before the end of 1964 — succeeds in its objective of economic and financial co-operation between the many African States, it will prove an important element in the promotion of African unity.

Prospects and Problems

A continent which, in the span of a few years, has been transformed from a high preponderance of colonies administered by four European Powers, to one in which nearly forty independent States confront a few surviving dependent territories — almost all of which will achieve independence in the next few years — is bound to be beset with internal and international problems. The suddenness of the transition from colonial status to independence is aggravated by the great poverty and backwardness of the majority of these States, a backwardness expressed not only in terms of economic, but also of educational and social standards. With the partial exception of Nigeria and Ghana, where the British encouraged the training of a native class of administrators and professionally trained people, and perhaps for the two most developed of the French-speaking States, the Ivory Coast and Senegal, the new African States are desperately short of the trained élite needed to administer and develop a modern State. Yet owing to the rival political pressures of the Western States and the Soviet bloc, and the general sympathy for the aspirations to independence, all of them have been admitted to United Nations membership, virtually on the day of independence. This, and other factors, have increased the status-consciousness of many, and political ambitions well in advance of present realities. An excessive proportion of the desperately few trained administrators and diplomats must be used in relatively sterile diplomatic missions established at the United Nations or in a number of foreign countries. The desire for economic development is not always coupled with sober estimates of the kind of development best adapted to the growth and needs of the country. A steel mill or an oil refinery becomes a status symbol, sometimes unrelated to the capacities of the country. A disproportionate amount of the inadequate resources may be devoted to spectacular palaces, government buildings or television stations.

But a far greater threat than that presented by the infantile disorders of the early stages of independence comes from the excessive national divisions of Africa. This is perhaps the worst legacy left by the colonizing Powers of the nineteenth century, which grabbed the continent in rivalry with each other as opportunities presented themselves, and often without regard to the natural, ethnic, geographical or economic needs of the country in question. The administrative and political divisions introduced by the European Powers have on the whole been transformed into national divisions, in stark contrast to the realities of our time and the needs of Africa. All the French colonies have become independent States, even though many of them could not survive without continued French assistance, or the merger into a larger union. National rivalries and suspicions impede the formation of an East African Federation. Political and racial antagonisms have dissolved the economically highly advantageous federation of Southern Rhodesia, Northern Rhodesia and Nyasaland. As shown in the previous section, there are now some important moves towards greater unity and co-operation among the African States, but the divisive factors of national ambitions still prevail by far.[1]

As long as the fight for independence from European domination was the paramount objective, internal tribal and racial divisions did not become as obvious as they have since the attainment of independence. With the removal of the foreign rulers, tribal divisions have threatened the existence of more than one African State. In Kenya, sharp antagonism continues between the majority tribes represented in the ruling party of KANU and the minority tribes formerly represented by the now dissolved KADU. In the Republic of the Congo, and neighbouring Rwanda, tribal conflicts have raged almost continuously since independence. Somalia claims parts of Ethiopia and northern Kenya on racial grounds. The Federation of Nigeria is precariously balanced between the regions, each of which is dominated by a different tribe or race. In Uganda the people of the Kingdom of Buganda and of some other lesser kingdoms continue to be opposed to the rest of Uganda. Most of the French-speaking African States have no economic and little political stability. Often the symbols but not the reality of national unity have been achieved, with the granting of independence.

The excessively large number of different national States, coupled with their economic and political weaknesses, encourages not only social ferment but also the rival aspirations of foreign Powers. The great majority of the new African States profess a policy of neutralism, i.e. of non-alignment in a political and military sense. But there are many differences in the degree of their association with the rival major Powers of the world. Through their continued dependence on France and their associate membership in the European Economic Community, the French-speaking States are still strongly Western-oriented. The same applies to a lesser extent to the present leadership of the English-speaking States, except for the strongly leftist Ghana. But many of the younger political leaders have been or are being trained in

[1] The common unifying element is anti-colonialism, as shown by the almost unanimous protest by African States against the Belgian–American airlift of rebel-held hostages in the Congo (November 1964).

the Soviet Union or in Communist China. This is particularly true of the refugees from the still colonized territories, notably Portuguese Angola and Mozambique, and from the white-supremacy countries of southern Africa. A Communist-trained guerrilla leader is engaged in a prolonged civil war with the relatively moderate government of the Congo. This is apt to be repeated in other African States, in proportion to their weakness or the degree of dissatisfaction with the existing political and social conditions. The recent visit of the Communist Chinese Premier, Chou En-lai, to Africa, was undoubtedly a token of the strong interest taken by the more radical of the two Communist world Powers in the future of the African continent.

In conclusion, the future of Africa is clouded, most of all by the unresolved and increasingly bitter conflicts between the majority of independent African States and the white-led bastion of South Africa (with the possible addition of the South African Trust Territory of South-West Africa and of Southern Rhodesia); second, by the weakness and economic backwardness of the majority of the African States; third, by the radicalism of a dissatisfied political intelligentsia which, as elsewhere in the world, is more conscious of the known former colonizers of Western Europe than of the possible future tyranny of the Communist Powers.

Given all these immense difficulties, it is truly remarkable that the unexpectedly rapid transition from dependence to independence should have been accomplished with relatively little bloodshed and violence. The Belgian Congo, where transition from complete paternalism and dependence to independence was irresponsibly short, is the most notable exception. The new African States have some leaders of international stature, such as Tanganyika's Nyerere, Nigeria's Balewa or Guinea's Touré. In the United Nations, the majority of African States have acted responsibly and with a remarkable awareness of world problems. That this moderation should not extend to their attitudes towards the Republic of South Africa and Portugal is not altogether surprising. The greatest need in Africa is for greater political and economic co-operation, and for the merger of some of its less viable units into more viable States. The greatest help that the outside world can give is in assisting the growth of a responsible class of leaders, who will put the long-term needs of their nations and of the continent before status and prestige.

CHAPTER 10

LATIN AMERICA AND WORLD POLITICS

UNTIL recently, the twenty States of Central and South America, which are commonly described by the collective name of 'Latin America', stood outside the mainstream of world politics. Most of them had gained their political independence early in the nineteenth century, i.e. at a time when the state of communications made physical distance from the main theatres of international conflict still a major factor in the degree of international involvement. Moreover, the Latin American States, even those which, like Cuba or Panama, gained their independence around the beginning of the twentieth century, achieved political sovereignty at a time when evolutionary or revolutionary demands for economic development and social betterment were not yet an inevitable concomitant of political independence. In this they differed drastically from the circumstances under which the majority of Asian and African States have gained their independence in the post-war period.

Mostly, the new Latin American States continued to be governed, politically and economically, by a small dominating class of Spanish or Portuguese ancestry — closely linked culturally to the civilization and religion of Catholic Latin Europe, and generally separated by an enormous social and economic gulf from their own native peasant populations — largely of Indian stock. Economically, the ruling classes of Latin America, unlike their counterparts in Britain, the United States, Germany or other countries that became the leaders of industrial progress, displayed little dynamism in the direction of commercial or industrial enterprise, or general economic development. Their wealth was — as it still largely is — that of great landowners, raising livestock, and producing coffee, sugar or other staple commodities, with the labour of a large and underprivileged peasantry, effectively though not legally tied to the ranches and plantations. The natural suitability of many of the Latin American countries for the large-scale production of one or a few staple commodities favoured such an economic condition. But the more recent efforts at diversification, industrialization and economic development show that this is by no means inevitable and is rather a condition favoured by social and political factors, and the attitude of the leading classes in these countries. The latter were — as they still are to a considerable extent — supported by disproportionately large armed forces, predominantly engaged in internal political manœuvres or local wars, but not in international conflicts of any major scale.

The lack of economic dynamism and the overwhelming importance of staple commodity exports were extremely useful to Latin America's powerful neighbour, the United States, as it developed into the world's leading industrial Power. The United States became — as it still is — by far the most important single purchaser of Latin America's staple exports. On the other hand, Latin America became an important market for the United States' consumer goods and other industrial products, and generally a suitable region for foreign investments in the extraction or cultivation of primary products for export and in related facilities. During the nineteenth century the investments were European, but they were later supplanted by American investments. The basic utilities — communications, power and railways — were until recently predominantly owned and operated by industrial and capital interests from outside Latin America.[1]

Internationally, the Monroe Doctrine, proclaimed in 1823 by the United States — at a time when most of the Latin American States were gaining their independence from Spain or Portugal — has continued to be, until recently, the more or less accepted reality of the international position of Latin America. By the Monroe Doctrine, the United States unilaterally proclaimed its concern with the immunity of the American Hemisphere from foreign

[1] The degree of the continuing economic dependence of most Latin American countries on the export of one staple commodity is illustrated by the following brief survey: four States (Brazil, Colombia, Guatemala, El Salvador) depend to a major or even controlling extent on the export of coffee; one country (Cuba) lives on its exports of sugar, which is the second or third major export item for Brazil as well; Argentina depends still predominantly on its exports of livestock and wheat; Uruguay on that of wool and Honduras on that of bananas. Vital minerals dominate the economies of three other countries (copper for Chile, tin for Bolivia and oil for Venezuela).

interference and its claim to take action against any intervention. This position was consolidated by the result of the American Civil War, in which Great Britain had sympathized with the Confederates. It was generally accepted in Latin America.

At the beginning of the twentieth century, such specifically 'Latin American' doctrines of international law as the Calvo Clause and the Drago Doctrine indicated an incipient revolt of Latin America against the legal and military enforcement of foreign economic interests. They were harbingers of Latin American nationalism. The Calvo Clause, which insisted that aliens have no rights not accorded to nationals, and therefore should submit their claims to national jurisdictions only, and not invoke the protection of their own governments, is a defensive shield against the use of powerful foreign governments by foreign investors. The Drago Doctrine rejects the use of military force for the recovery of public debts, a reaction to the naval bombardment of Venezuela in 1902 by British and German forces, designed to teach a lesson to governments defaulting on their public debt.

The beginning of a major change in the attitude of the States of Latin America can be traced to the social and political revolution of Mexico, which began shortly before the First World War. This revolution was not only an internal one, against the Catholic Church and the economic and social predominance of the ruling landowners; it was also directed against the power of foreign economic interests, culminating in the expropriation of foreign, particularly American, landholdings and oil interests shortly before the Second World War. The pattern set by Mexico — a State which, having started its revolution relatively early, now entertains friendly economic and political relations with the United States and many other foreign countries — still characterizes the predominant direction of more recent Latin American activism: a combination of nationalist and to some extent Socialist philosophies, directed in many but by no means all countries against the national ruling classes, but in all cases against the predominance of foreign economic — i.e. mainly United States — interests although in many different shades of intensity.

The Change in the International Position of Latin America — Some Major Factors

The factors which account for the end of the long period of relative isolation of Latin America from international affairs can be briefly summed up as follows:

1. There is the important role that the 20 States of Latin America play in the United Nations. Although not actively involved in the Second World War, the entire group became founder-members of the United Nations, while the defeated Axis Powers and many other important States remained outside. Reinforced by the impotence of the Security Council, this gave the Latin American States a quite disproportionate weight in the United Nations until a few years ago. But at the same time this state of affairs involved the Latin American nations in world affairs to a far greater extent than under the European-dominated League of Nations.

2. The dramatic transformation in international communications — both peaceful and destructive — increasingly eliminated the physical protection of nineteenth-century remoteness. The world-wide ideological and power conflict between the Communist and the anti-Communist blocs, which at a time of military stalemate is increasingly directed to countries in a state of social and economic ferment, could therefore be extended to Latin America. This was most dramatically illustrated, in October 1962, by the direct confrontation of the United States and the Soviet Union when the latter installed missiles in Cuba, under the pro-Communist regime of Castro. The unprecedented attempt of the leading Communist Power to secure a strategic base, in a friendly country, at the very doorstep of its principal opponent, was made possible by the ideological harmony of the Castro regime and the Soviet Union, and it was reinforced by the United States policy of economic boycott which made Castro look to an alternative consumer and supplier, in a characteristic combination of political and economic strategy. But whatever the motivations, after the confrontation of October 1962, which led the world to the brink of another world war, the strategic and political isolation of Latin America is a thing of the past.

3. The nationalistic aspects of the Latin American revolt have, as an immediate objective, the removal of foreign privileges that remain from an era when the Western Powers had unchallenged

predominance and when they could even send punitive military expeditions for the maintenance of extra-territorial privileges or the enforcement of economic claims (such as the bombardment of Venezuela by British and German naval units in 1902 mentioned above, or the intervention of U.S. Marines in Nicaragua at various times up to 1933). The two remaining symbols of extra-territorial privileges — both in the hands of the United States — are the Guantánamo naval base in Cuba — not at present negotiable because of the political tension between the U.S. and Cuba — and the extra-territorial privileges of the United States in the Panama Canal Zone, which gave rise to violent riots in January 1964. Under a treaty of 1903, concluded when the United States supported Panama's secession from Colombia, the U.S. controls a strip of Panamanian territory on either side of the Panama Canal, in return for certain payments generally considered to be inadequate at the present time. The Panamanian demand for abrogation of these extra-territorial privileges is characteristic of similar demands all over the world. The treaty is attacked as having been concluded under 'unequal' conditions — a contention that is hardly challengeable in the conditions prevailing in 1903 between the United States and the newly formed State of Panama — and the maintenance of extra-territorial sovereignty as incompatible with contemporary conditions, as symbolized in the United Nations.

4. The claims for economic development and social change express themselves in a variety of one-sided measures taken by Latin American governments against the legal status of foreign interests. Given the economic preponderance of United States investments, these measures overwhelmingly affect American interests. The nationalization of land and later of oil enterprises (mainly American-owned) by Mexico in 1938 has been followed in recent years by the nationalization of American-owned sugar refineries in Cuba (1961), the nationalization of foreign-owned utilities in Brazil and Mexico during the last few years, and the cancellation or threat of cancellation of foreign oil concessions in Argentina and Peru in 1963. Such measures not only affect the economic relations between the expropriating country and the country of the expropriated interests or enterprises; they also involve a wider pattern of international economic relations, especially since an increasingly important part in economic

development is played by the financial aid of international financial institutions, such as the World Bank, and by lending agencies of the United States Government.

Economic Development Problems and Latin American Unrest

Conditions of economic and social unrest in Latin America, like anywhere else in the world, can no longer be regarded as purely internal phenomena. They inevitably involve foreign economic interests, foreign political reaction and, especially at a time when the main emphasis in the Cold War rivalry of the major blocs has turned from the military to the economic and social field, rival moves of the various contending powers. Nor is this any longer entirely a matter of contest between the United States and the Soviet Union. At a time when both the Western and the Communist blocs have lost much of their cohesion and solidity, a strongly nationalist and independent France — as shown by de Gaulle's visit to Latin America in 1964 — may utilize Latin American resentment against the United States for her own purposes, while Communist China may compete with the Soviet Union for influence among the more radical political movements of the Latin American countries. Hence the revolt of the great majority of the nations of Latin America against the essentially static and backward economic and social conditions that have prevailed for over a century has international as well as national implications.

All the nations of Latin America are still primarily agricultural and depend, both for the satisfaction of minimum national needs and the payment of needed imports, on the exports of certain staple commodities. There is, however, now a widespread desire to diversify the economies and to industrialize. This is spearheaded by some relatively advanced nations, such as Brazil and Mexico. These two countries lead Latin America not only in terms of their respective populations of 75 million and 40 million, but in terms of technical advancement, industrial diversification and foreign investment. But even in these relatively developed countries, industrial production can only supply a limited, though increasing, share of national consumption. The earnings of foreign exchange still depend on exports of agricultural products or minerals. And, like all other countries in a similar stage of development, the Latin American States continue to depend on a constant flow of external investment to achieve a satisfactory rate of development of their industrial and agricultural production, and the diversification of their economies. While this investment, like the entire nexus of economic relations, has been overwhelmingly American, some Latin American countries, such as Argentina, Brazil or Mexico, have in recent years had an increasing influx of non-American investment, mainly from the United Kingdom, Germany, Italy and Japan.

The need for foreign investment, both of capital and of technical know-how, is frustrated and at times paralysed by internal weaknesses shared by the great majority of the Latin American States. The negative factors are political, economic and social. Politically, the great majority of the Latin American nations suffer from chronic instability. Oversized armies, with an excessive proportion of high officers, are far more often engaged in political moves than in the defence of the country. They engineer revolts and control governments. The military junta is usually closely linked with the economic and social aristocracy of the country, and thus tends to be a defender of economic privileges, but sometimes, as in the case of the former Argentine dictator, Perón, it allies itself with the populace. It is too early to say, at this writing, whether the army-led revolt, which in 1964 deposed the left-wing government of Goulart and installed a semi-authoritarian regime under General Branco, will be essentially a defender of economic and social privileges, or use its power to promote reforms. There are indications that the younger generation of military leaders in several other Latin American countries is becoming more sympathetic to demands for social and economic change. While the number of complete dictatorships in Latin America has declined, as compared with some years ago, genuine democracies with any degree of stability are still in the minority. At the present time parliamentary democracy in varying degrees exists in Chile, Mexico, Colombia, Uruguay, Venezuela and Costa Rica. In the international relations of Latin America, however, it is the frequency of violent changes of regimes, rather than the degree of parliamentary democracy, that causes disturbance. Where there is stability under political dictatorships, they are also often accompanied by a high degree of oppression, tyranny and corruption. Of the deposed dictators of Latin American States, such as Perón of Argentina, Batista of Cuba, Trujillo of the Dominican Republic, or Pérez Jiménez of Venezuela, none failed to acquire an inordinate amount of personal wealth, enabling them to live in comfort and affluence even in exile.

Political instability is often accompanied by fiscal irresponsibility, leading to a high dose of inflation. At the present time, this is most evident in the largest of the Latin American States, Brazil, where inflation constantly outstrips and endangers the economic progress of a potentially very rich and promising country. There are however deeper organic causes for economic instability. As already mentioned, the countries of Latin America still overwhelmingly depend on the export of certain commodities. During the last decade, the prices of commodities such as coffee, sugar or tin have slumped while the prices of vitally needed industrial imports have risen. The loss suffered by the Latin American exports of these commodities in recent years, through the slump in world market prices for their commodities, outstrips the total of the vast economic aid given to these countries by external public lending agencies. The first recent year to show a substantial recovery in the prices of these commodities, such as coffee, was 1963, and the conclusion of an international coffee agreement may help to stabilize the price of this commodity on which the livelihood of several Latin American States depends. Thus both internal and external causes contribute to the economic instability of many of the Latin American countries.

The social problems can be broadly summed up in four major factors: first, general backwardness; second, inequality of the distribution of wealth; third, corruption in government; and fourth, a high rate of population growth.

Backwardness and inequality are closely linked. As the small top layer of affluent landowners, businessmen and politicians is separated from the vast majority of poor and underprivileged peasants and city dwellers, so the education of a highly sophisticated top level contrasts with the illiteracy of the great majority of the population.

Any planned economic development, which must largely rest on the integrity of administration and public enterprise, depends upon a standard of government which the majority of Latin American States have not attained. The Civil Services are generally underpaid and unstable, as successive governments follow each other, often in rapid succession as a result of military or other political coups. In other continents such as Africa or Asia, colonial domination has, at least in some States, such as India or Nigeria, had the positive by-product of laying the foundations for an efficient and honest Civil Service; the States of Latin America have not had any corresponding advantage. Government administrations have mostly been the tools of the military, political and economic rulers.

The annual rate of population increase in Latin America stands at 2·4%, as compared with Asia's 1·8% and Africa's 1·9%. It is estimated that the present population of approximately 225 million will have increased to at least 600 million by the year 2000. Nor is there any great hope that this disastrous rate of increase — which, as everywhere, is largest among the poorest sections of the population — will be mitigated by any widespread degree of birth control. More than any other region of the earth, Latin America is, officially and unofficially, under the spiritual control of the Catholic Church, which still adamantly opposes any form of birth control by the use of contraceptives.

International Participation in Latin American Development

The general concern with economic development, and the increasing realization in the United States that the economically undeveloped and socially restive Latin America will be a growing menace to American stability and thus indirectly to world peace, has led to more American and international involvement in the economic development of Latin America. The easiest and most natural way of assisting Latin America in the expansion and diversification of her economy would have been a continued flow of private investment. This would have been natural, since hundreds of American, and a lesser number of other foreign enterprises have for many years had branches, subsidiaries or joint ventures with local entrepreneurs in a vast variety of manufacturing industries and utilities. The combination of political instability, inflation and nationalist revolts leading to a series of nationalizations of foreign enterprises have however virtually stopped the inflow of new private capital, especially from the United States, in recent years and even produced a small net overall outflow (though not in manufacturing). This has shifted the emphasis from the private to the public sector, and from the commercial to the political aspects of economic development. The U.S. Government for a good many years participated in the economic development of Latin America mainly through the government-owned Export–Import Bank, which has not only financed export credits but also given a large number of loans for industrial and utilities investment in Latin America. In the post-war period the activities of the Export–Import Bank have been supplemented by other official aid agencies, now consolidated in the Agency for International Development. U.S. public funds in the amount of about $1 billion annually have been committed to Latin America during the last two years.

In view of the sensitivity that governs relations between the United States and Latin America, it became increasingly desirable to put the public sources of economic assistance to Latin America on a wider international basis. The World Bank and its recent affiliate, the International Development Association, have played a substantial part in the flow of loans to Latin America. While in both institutions the United States is the principal subscriber, they are in their structure and orientation international.

The growing need for financing institutions specifically devoted to Latin American needs led a few years ago to the establishment of the Inter-American Development Bank in which the United States, as the principal subscriber, and all the Latin American nations except Cuba participate. Under the presidency of a Latin American, Felipe Herrera, the Bank is playing an increasingly important part in the economic development of Latin America. From its first loan in February 1961 to September 30, 1963, the Bank authorized $775 million of loans and disbursed $158 million. Institutionally, the significance of the I.D.B. is that it is a joint enterprise between the United States — still far and away the most important investor, supplier and customer of Latin America — and the Latin American States.

These important institutional efforts were supplemented in 1961, under President Kennedy's Administration, by the initiation of a long-term plan for the economic development and social progress of Latin America, the *Alianza para el Progreso.* Its constitutive document, the Charter of Punta del Este, states that: 'it is the purpose of the Alliance for Progress to enlist the full energies of the peoples and governments of the American republics in a great co-operative effort to accelerate the economic and social development of the participating countries of Latin America, so that they may achieve maximum levels of well-being, with equal opportunities for all in democratic societies adapted to their own needs and desires.' Specifically, the goals stated in the Alliance are the development of co-ordinated national programmes of public investment and the encouragement of private investment, various schemes devoted to social progress and institutional reforms, including land reform, tax reform, education, public health and housing, and an extended scheme of external technical and financial assistance. The total external investment for these purposes over a ten-year period was put at 20 billion dollars. As previously indicated, the U.S. pledge of $1 billion of public funds per year has been met. Other sources of foreign financial assistance are private foreign investment and public capital from Europe, Canada and Japan. The novelty of this plan lies in the coupling of economic development and social reform, with the realization that progress in Latin America requires not only economic growth but also correction of the maldistribution of the social product among the different classes.

After the first few years of operation, the prospects of the Alliance remain somewhat in doubt. Some countries with relatively stable and enlightened governments had initiated important social and economic reforms, such as Colombia, Venezuela and El Salvador.[1] But many of the purposes of the Alliance were frustrated by the chronic phenomena of internal instability and upheavals, inflation and poor export earnings. It was mainly some of the smaller Latin American countries that made economic and social progress, while some of the largest, especially Argentina and Brazil, remained plagued by political unrest and economic inflation. In many countries the unabated population increase outpaced modest improvements in the national product and in export income. The rate of private investment from the United States declined sharply. The political spirit of this great co-operative enterprise between the United States and its Latin American neighbours was marred by the tension between the United States and Castro's Cuba, and by the revolt of Panama

[1] The election of Senator Eduardo Frei, a left-wing Christian Democrat, as President of Chile (September 1964) promises an energetic programme of economic and social change within the framework of the Alliance.

against the Panama Canal Treaty, for which there is widespread emotional support in Latin America.

The last few years have, however, also brought important, though still far from complete, efforts by groups of Latin American States to eliminate or reduce the economic barriers between them, and thus to create wider markets and a greater measure of unity. Two of these efforts might be briefly noted: the Latin American Free Trade Association and the Organization of Central American States (Guatemala, El Salvador, Honduras, Nicaragua and Costa Rica). The latter is rapidly moving towards a miniature Common Market, like that of the European Economic Community; and the former resembles the European Free Trade Association, as an effort to eliminate tariff barriers, import quotas and the like among nine Latin American countries, including the principal countries of the region (Argentina, Brazil, Chile, Colombia, Ecuador, Mexico, Paraguay, Peru and Uruguay).

United States and Latin America

The relations between the United States and Latin America remain the single most important factor in the relations of Latin America to the outer world, although they are now increasingly intermingled with wider international problems. The evolution of these relations has been admirably summarized by a distinguished Brazilian economist and diplomat who, after a period of service as Brazilian Ambassador to the United States, in 1964 became Minister of Planning in the Branco government.[1]

In the overall perspective, from 1823 to 1964, the attitude of the United States towards its Latin American neighbours has undergone dramatic changes. It has evolved from the unilateral patronage of the Monroe Doctrine and the unabashed interventionism of Theodore Roosevelt (in Cuba) and subsequent acts of armed intervention in Nicaragua, Mexico, Haiti, the Dominican Republic and Panama, to the Good Neighbour Policy of Franklin D. Roosevelt, and the sustained economic assistance programme since the Second World War, culminating in the Alliance for Progress. In the political field, this evolution

[1] Roberto de Oliviera Campos, 'Relations between the United States and Latin America', in *Latin America: Evolution or Explosion?*, Council on World Tensions Symposium, New York, 1963.

has been accompanied by a series of Pan-American organizations which started with the Pan American Union in 1890 — now called the Organization of American States (O.A.S.). This Organization, whose present Charter was formulated in 1948, is now an important international institution whose significance in international affairs has increased with the growing importance and potential international danger of inter-American conflicts. Its key articles[1] stipulate that any aggression against the territorial integrity or inviolability or against the sovereignty or political independence of an American State will be considered an act of aggression against the other American States, and its applicability extends to conflicts other than armed attacks, and other situations endangering the peace of America, whether as a result of intervention by a non-American State or of conflicts between American States. In implementation of this Charter, the O.A.S. has played an important role in recent conflicts, such as the dispatch of guerrilla forces and weapons by Castro's Cuba to Venezuelan Communists, in territorial disputes between Nicaragua and Honduras, in the quarantine imposed by the United States against Cuba in connection with the shipment and installation of Soviet missiles in Cuba, and most recently in the dispute between the United States and Panama on the revision of the Panama Canal Treaty. The function of the O.A.S. has been essentially a mediating one, and complete inter-American unity has seldom been achieved in view of the many divergent policies, and the reluctance of almost all the Latin American States to identify themselves completely with any military or economic sanctions initiated by the United States. But it does provide a permanent organ of consultation and collective action, less diffuse than the United Nations. Although the United States would ultimately have acted alone against Cuba and the Soviet Union, in the missile crisis of 1962, she did obtain the sanction of the O.A.S. for her quarantine.

In the economic field, the United States has moved from the unilateral domination of its investment in Latin America — accompanied in earlier decades by the all but complete control by certain American enterprises of some of the Central American republics — to a sustained and co-operative aid effort culminating in the Alliance for Progress. The general approach of recent U.S.

[1] For the text, see below, pp. 402 *et seq.*

governments is characterized by Roberto Campos as 'pluralistic', marked by the following features:

1. a more pragmatic attitude towards the basic neutralism of Latin American States in regard to international conflicts;
2. a deep concern with the promotion of economic and social development of the Latin American area;
3. the utilization of foreign assistance as leverage for social and fiscal reforms;
4. the reluctant acceptance — contrary to the predominant United States philosophy of private enterprise — of the vital part which has to be played in the development of Latin America by Government planning, public enterprise and mixed public–private economic systems. This implies the recognition of the insufficiency of private investment for adequate progress in Latin America.

This new attitude diminishes, but far from eliminates, the many remaining tensions and divergencies between United States policy and that of most of its Latin American neighbours. The predominant trend in the increasingly nationalistic climate of the majority of the Latin American States is for greater reliance on the direct role of the State — Government and Government-owned development corporations — as promoters of economic development. They are therefore impatient with the continuing reluctance of the official U.S. aid agencies and of the World Bank — though not of the Inter-American Development Bank — to assist State-owned enterprises. They are generally mistrustful of foreign private investments, especially from the United States, although more disposed to accept such investment through joint ventures with national, public or private capital. They are impatient to achieve rapid industrialization and to reduce their continuing independence on agricultural staple commodities, with the attendant danger of hasty industrialization schemes and insufficiently based development plans. Because of the continuing strength of the entrenched wealthy classes, many of these countries are far from vigorous in the initiation of the needed fiscal, economic and social reforms, which would achieve a better distribution of wealth, a speeding up of technical and general education, and a more efficient and less corrupt administration.

But some of them, such as Colombia or Venezuela, have made important progress in this direction.

The removal of the more acute political tensions between the United States and the Latin American group is inevitable for peaceful progress and amicable relations. Existing extra-territorial privileges, as in Panama, will certainly have to be given up before long. On the other hand, not only private investment, but also the continuing flow of public aid financed by the U.S. taxpayer, will be increasingly imperilled by confiscatory measures which do not provide for reasonable compensation. Already the U.S. Foreign Assistance Act of 1962 prohibits the continuance of aid to any country which enacts such measures without adequate compensation.

The sharp antagonism between a pro-Communist Cuba and the United States provides a continuing source of tension and irritation. Hitherto, few other American States have been noticeably influenced by Communist philosophy, but radical nationalist movements tend to couple anti-foreign sentiment with social radicalism and there is a widespread tendency to sympathize with Castro's Cuba, or with the Panamanian revolt, not so much for ideological reasons but because they represent the resistance of small countries against the powerful neighbour from the north. All this means the necessity of continuous consultation, in the O.A.S., the Inter-American Development Bank, other Alliance for Progress agencies, and the many other institutional and non-institutional links between the United States and Latin America. It also means patience, a great deal of give and take on both sides, and a 'pluralistic' approach by the United States to the manifold and diverse problems of Latin America.

The International Posture of Latin America

As compared with previous decades, the involvement of Latin America in world affairs is now irrevocable and will probably gain in importance. The Latin American group plays a vital role in the United Nations. It will play an increasingly important part in the different world-wide efforts to liberalize international trade and the conditions of economic development. Whatever the tensions and the disparities between the different Latin American States, they will fight unitedly for international commodity agreements, designed to stabilize the prices of their vital staple exports, and the removal of import restrictions by the more developed States on their exports. In the process they may well make further progress in the incipient economic unions and free trade areas, within Latin America.

In their general international posture, the Latin American States will continue to seek a diversification of their political and economic relations with States other than the United States. Most of them are not only developing trade and investment relations with the Western European Powers such as Britain, West Germany, France and Italy, but also with the Soviet Union and other Communist States. Latin America is overwhelmingly in favour of 'non-alignment', i.e. of a policy that will avoid political commitments on behalf of one of the opposing groups in the Cold War. Their military participation in any collective action outside the American hemisphere, whether under United Nations or in alignment with any particular group of powers, is likely to be non-existent or minimal (as illustrated by the refusal of Brazil to participate in the U.N. order force for Cyprus in 1964). They will continue to favour any disarmament or nuclear test-ban treaty, or any other international act designed to reduce the danger of war. In conformity with their own increasingly nationalist and anti-imperialist tendencies, they will often, though not invariably, side with the views and policies of the developing countries of Asia and Africa. But their predominant preoccupation will for many years continue to be their own development, and the transformation of their relations with the United States, which remains far and away the most important single Power in the perspective of Latin America.

PART III — CHALLENGES TO MANKIND

CHAPTER II

POPULATION PRESSURES AND INTERNATIONAL POLITICS

In recent years the optimism which made Malthus's *Essay on Population*, first published in 1798, appear to most people as an historical oddity, has once again given way to widespread pessimism on the race between the growth of the human population and the development of the means for its sustenance. Some of the causes for this scare operate all over the world, in particular the dangers of soil-erosion, over-cultivation, deforestation and other ways of depleting natural resources in modern industrialized society. But hitherto mankind has always been able to open up new resources or sources of energy when old ones threatened to be exhausted. There is a good chance that the diminishing water resources for cultivation and irrigation may, in due course, be replaced by economic methods of purifying sea-water. Oil is replacing coal to such an extent that at the present time coal stocks are piling up at the pitheads of the mines of Western Europe. As oil resources get depleted in some parts of the world (e.g. the United States), new oilfields are constantly being discovered, in the Middle East, Latin America, Canada, Africa or Asia. Natural gas deposits have greatly improved the fuel position of oil-poor countries like Italy or the Netherlands. Nuclear energy, already beginning to replace other sources of energy in some parts (e.g. in Britain), is potentially unlimited. If the world food shortage became more serious, far more energetic efforts would be made to utilize the resources of the sea and convert them into products suitable for human nutrition. At the present time, the immediate problem is not one of an absolute shortage of food, but of maldistribution, even though conservation of soil and other natural resources is still gravely insufficient. Whereas stocks of wheat, eggs, butter or coffee pile up in various parts of America, and particularly in the United States, hundreds of millions in other parts of the world do not get the minimum amount of calories necessary for a healthy survival. This maldistribution is, in part, the result of the difference in the methods and efficiency of production, as between the industrially developed and the underdeveloped countries. Thanks to the use of modern machinery and of scientific methods of cultivation, the rate of output per man of a United States farmer is many times that of the Indian peasant. For India, the main problem is still how to produce enough food for its rapidly swelling population. For the United States, it is how to prevent its diminishing farm population from producing too much food. The bitter irony of this situation could — and to some extent is — mitigated by international mechanisms that would equalize between surplus and deficiency areas. This was a vision that Lord Boyd-Orr and others had, at the end of the last world war, for the new Food and Agriculture Organization. Instead of a clearing-house and a pool for the equalization of surplus and deficiency areas, this organization has so far been merely an advisory and a research body. Instead, numerous unilateral, bilateral and multilateral schemes have sought to provide some measure of equalization between unsaleable surpluses in some, and desperate deficiencies in other, parts of the world. Foremost among them have been the numerous grant, loan, barter, sale and similar aid schemes executed by the United States, as the world's chief and wealthiest surplus area.

It is likely that, in the absence of another murderous conflict, international distribution schemes, on a regional or universal basis, will grow and improve. But towering over all the abovementioned problems is that of the explosive increase in the world population. Until the present century, a combination of wars, famines, floods and diseases provided a cruel but effective corrective to the natural increase of populations. Of these, only war has so far ceased to be eliminated or reduced in the affairs of mankind. But even the slaughter of the last two world wars, with all the misery they brought to millions of families, was a relatively minor factor in the development of the world population.[1] Until

[1] The death, during the last world war, of some twenty to thirty million Russians, military and civilian, has had the effect of temporarily slowing down the growth of the Russian population. The slaughter of some five to six million Jews in concentration camps and gas ovens by the Nazi Government of Germany has drastically reduced the number of Jews. Apart from this, the general effect of the war on world population has been relatively small.

recently, millions of Chinese or Indians regularly disappeared through the recurrent catastrophes of floods and famines. These causes of death are increasingly being brought under control by famine relief schemes — often inadequate to ensure a decent minimum standard, but sufficient to keep millions of people alive. This change will become more noticeable as the industrialization and communication systems of vast countries, such as China and India, increase and improve. But much the most potent single factor in the decimation of populations has been the prevalence of disease. We have no reliable statistics for past centuries, but a random comparison of the effects of the Black Death in the fourteenth century, the housing conditions of London or Paris two centuries ago, or the chronicles of infant mortality even among the princes of Europe (such as the death of all of Queen Anne's seventeen children) explains to a large extent why the world's population increased very slowly, if at all, until the advent of the Industrial Revolution. For a long time, however, the latter remained confined to a limited part of the Western world, while the rest — Asia, Latin America, Africa — went on in its own ways, suffering the consequences of disease, famine and other natural catastrophes. It is in these very areas that the change is most dramatic. According to recent United Nations estimates,[1] the world's population, containing 2,500 million people in 1950, will have grown to over 3,800 million in 1975, and to over 6,000 million in the year 2000. If these figures are correct — and in the recent past all projections of population growth have tended to be much too conservative[2] — the human race will add to itself annually over seventy-five million by 1975 and over 125 million by 2000. More alarming than this fact is the distribution of this projected population increase — which is based on well-tested scientific estimates that only a global nuclear war would drastically affect. The currently underdeveloped areas of the world are ex-

[1] Quoted from Kingsley Davis, *New York Times Magazine*, March 15, 1959.

[2] An estimate published in the *A.I.D. Digest* of Jan. 1962, for example, puts the expected population of Latin America for the year 2000 at 650 million, as against the usual estimate of 600 million. A relatively slight difference in the initial estimate has a multiplier effect, since it produces a growing diversity in the numerical base for reproduction. In 1962, according to the *U.N. Demographic Yearbook* for 1963, the world population increased by 62 million, at an annual rate of increase of 2·1% (2·4% in Africa, 2·8% in Latin America, 2·3% in Asia, 0·9% in Europe).

pected to grow twice as fast as the industrial countries. Most of the former can reduce their already lowered death rate much further, while they have so far shown little sign or ability of reducing their, in some cases fantastically high, birth rates. Generally, population growth will tend to be greatest where people are poorest. Even in the industrially developed and sophisticated countries of north-western Europe, the birth rate has picked up remarkably, as compared with pre-war depression standards. But it is insignificant compared with the rate of growth of (Communist) China, which at present increases by approximately fifteen million every year (the annual growth thus nearly equalling the total population of Canada). However, the fastest-growing region of the world is not China — nor any other part of the Communist world — but Latin America. Thus the net rate of increase in Mexico is nearly 3·5% a year, and the average for Latin America as a whole is almost 2·5% annually. By the year 2000 it is estimated that the present population of Latin America of about 225 million will have grown to over 600 million! The proportion of Europeans — 20·6% of the world total in 1900 — will have shrunk to 9·5% in 2000 (Council of Europe Report summarized in *Forward in Europe*, Feb. 1964). As the same report points out, the proportion of people aged 65 and over will have grown to 16%, as compared with 3% before he demographic revolution.

As we have seen, these explosive changes are essentially the result of the transition of a particular country or region from primitive and backward conditions to those of modern life, i.e. of communications, industrialization and the spread of modern medical and pharmaceutical remedies against disease. The open question is to what extent the increasing productivity resulting from industrialization will keep up with the increase in the number of people to be fed, clothed and otherwise maintained. The evidence so far is inconclusive and uneven. Political and economic policies influence the interpretation of the cold statistical facts. Perhaps the Communist regime of China, which puts everybody to work and is willing to sacrifice family life, individual freedom of choice, and all but the most elementary standards of comfort, to national production and power, may be able to increase its agricultural and industrial output at a faster rate than democratic India, which seeks to act by persuasion and maintains a mixed economy, of public and private enterprise. Again, in most of the States of Latin America, where small numbers of very wealthy landowners and businessmen face vast numbers of underpaid and underfed labourers and peasants, social tensions appear to rise as the gap between the few and the many increases. Politically speaking, the plight of the non-Communist countries, such as India or many of the Latin American States, places a moral and financial responsibility upon the industrialized nations of the West, and in particular the United States. Social unrest and discontent in all these countries are likely to favour Communism (especially when it is blended with nationalism). The evidence presented in recent years by the growth of production and technology in both the U.S.S.R. and China is impressive, whereas the price to be paid in terms of human freedom is not easily apparent to those who have not experienced Communist discipline themselves.

Not only the total growth of the world population, but far more the unevenness of its distribution, and the social pressure which it produces in some of the poorest regions of the world, will more and more increase the danger of social or international explosions. The temptation will be great to gain 'Lebensraum' by conquest, or at least by threats. But regardless of the political dangers, the world as a whole — and again, in particular, the underdeveloped regions — must restore the balance between life and death which, in previous centuries, was provided by natural causes. With the exception of a few countries — notably North-west Europe and, more recently, Japan, which in the last few years has legalized abortion and officially encouraged the use of contraceptives — the countries of the world with the most explosive growth rate of population have done little to counteract the drastic decline in the death rate with a reduction of the birth rate. In some cases this is a matter of deliberate policy. The U.S.S.R. and Communist China not only wish to restore the losses of the world war period, but also seem confident that their vast spaces and growing power of control over them will provide an adequate livelihood for any population increase likely to occur in the foreseeable future. Recently, however, China, alarmed by the combination of bad harvests and explosive population increases, has reverted to official advocacy of birth control. In most cases, notably in India and Latin America, lack of birth control is the result either of ignorance or of religious inhibition. Ignorance of birth-control methods prevails in primitive peasant communities, certainly as long as a simple device, such as a pill, is not generally and cheaply available. In Latin America the adamant opposition of the Catholic Church to any form of birth control — other than by the so-called 'rhythm' method — is a decisive influence. It is not possible to argue against the belief that the procreation of life is one of the purposes of God, with which deliberate interference must not be permitted. It is, however, legitimate to point out that the Christian and natural-law postulate of human dignity will become a caricature when, as is already occurring and more likely to occur in the future, millions of underfed, overcrowded and in every way degraded human individuals are committed to lead an existence somewhere between life and death. Mankind has — with the approval of the Catholic Church, as of almost everybody else — proceeded to control nature increasingly, through the taming of the elements, the progress of medicine, the control of catastrophes and even the production of energy out of the particles of the universe. Why mankind should stop at the control of numbers — no more and no less of a human device interfering with the course of nature than hundreds of forms of surgery or preventive medicine — it is difficult to see. For it is man's exploitation and mastery of nature that has brought about the danger of suffocating overpopulation.[1]

Migration and World Politics

Mass migration between continents is an idea bold in conception and appealing to the imagination. Its practical execution, however, is beset with theoretical and practical difficulties. Yet migration can at least make a modest contribution to the solution of the towering problem of overpopulation and maldistribution.

The migration problem presents a special challenge to the Western democracies. It is, in fact, one of the greatest, most urgent and most constructive tasks facing the North Atlantic Treaty Powers, as well as the nations of the British Commonwealth, and between them these two associations of nations provide today the main physical and moral reserve of the Western democracies. Only co-operation and joint action will lead to the solution of a problem which is political as well as economic and human.

[1] For signs of an impending change in official Catholic doctrine, see above, p. 90.

When, in 1933, Nazi policy forced large numbers of Jews and political opponents out of Germany, migration had come to a virtual standstill. The people who, as mathematicians, scientists, doctors, jurists, economists, philosophers and politicians, went to live and work in Britain and the Dominions, in the United States and, to a lesser extent, in Latin America, were only a tiny segment of the world's population, but they have exercised a deep influence on the thought, research and international outlook of all these countries. They have stimulated fundamental, as distinct from applied, research in the United States; broken into the isolationism of many parts of America; and produced an almost revolutionary change of outlook in such countries as Australia or New Zealand.

Migration since the War

The mass deportations of the last war, which left millions of people, from almost any European country, stranded in Germany, will perhaps prove even more significant. What Hitler wanted was to turn Slavs and other Europeans into a new slave class under their Germanic masters, while the vast spaces of eastern Europe were resettled with people of Germanic stock. What he achieved was that the German-speaking peasants from the borderland between Roumania and Hungary — settled there for over 700 years — are now refugees from Poland somewhere in Western Germany, and from there begin to emigrate to Canada or Australasia; that Estonian professors, Soviet lawyers, Czech craftsmen or German-Jewish scientists now find themselves in Canada, Australia or Brazil.

Between 1945 and 1952, four and a half million men and women emigrated from Europe overseas (United Nations figures prepared for the World Population Conference, Rome 1954). Of these, over one million were removed by the International Refugee Organization (I.R.O.), which has gone out of existence. It has been replaced by an Intergovernmental Committee (ICEM), which, by the end of 1956, had organized or assisted the emigration of another half million people from Europe. The achievement of the I.R.O. has been as magnificent as it has been unspectacular. It has selected, trained and counselled a particularly difficult and heterogeneous collection of people left uprooted, poor and embittered in Germany after the collapse. It has chartered ships, negotiated with a number of governments, and had the lion's share in solving at least one of the major problems of Central Europe. Its record is magnificent proof of what an international agency can do, if it is given a task and inspired with a sense of purpose.

The principal immigration countries together appear to take about half a million immigrants yearly, although the number fluctuates, depending upon the economic and employment conditions in the country of immigration. This is about one-fiftieth of one per cent of the present world population. Yet the psychological and political significance of this emigration, which is certain to go on for some years, is far greater than the numbers suggest. From the successive waves of nineteenth-century emigration it differs in two ways. Nineteenth-century emigration — overwhelmingly to America — was, on the whole, spontaneous. Its main motive power was poverty and, for some, a sense of adventure. The great majority of the emigrants were farmers and agricultural labourers, going to settle the empty and promising spaces of the American continent. Now, the main motive of emigration is force or fear. The vast majority of emigrants from Europe leave because they have been expelled from their homes and countries, either by Nazi Germany or by the Communist countries of Eastern Europe, or because they want to leave the fears and uncertainties of the Old World behind them. The social and economic background of the post-war migrant, too, differs greatly from that of the nineteenth century. Among the migrants there are still large numbers of East European, Italian or German peasants. But the countries which today absorb the great majority of the emigrants, that is in particular the United States, Australia, Canada, Latin America and Israel, are in a stage of vigorous transition from providers of foodstuffs and raw materials to highly industrialized nations. Their main demand is for skilled tradesmen of all kinds, for engineers and scientists; that is, for a more educated and urbanized type of immigrant.

The background of present-day emigration also accounts for the relatively large number of intellectual and professional people who go overseas. Their absorption — except for scientists — is in many ways more difficult than that of the farmer or skilled tradesman, but their influence on the intellectual, scientific and cultural life of the recipient nations is likely to be considerable.

In such countries as Australia and New Zealand, which hitherto have had a small and homogeneous population, the impact of the newcomers from European countries, many of them artists or academic scholars of high standing, is already noticeable.

Migration today is essentially a planned movement and linked with Government policy. The Governments of Canada and Australia and other countries lay down annual targets, set up immigration missions and decide what nationalities to admit and exclude, and generally regard immigration as part of their economic and defence policy. The annual emigration of several hundred thousand people from Britain and Europe to America and Australasia may not mean much in terms of world population, but it is an important factor in the internal and international position of these countries. The assimilation of hundreds of thousands of uprooted and embittered immigrants, a considerable proportion of whom are educated and articulate, presents both greater opportunities and greater dangers in the process of assimilation. A large proportion of the immigrants today carry with them a legacy of persecution, hatred and national tensions. No country which receives them can afford to leave them entirely to their own devices.

Barriers to Migration

What can migration contribute to the solution of the burning problems of our time? First, it can do little to the long-term problem of overpopulation of our globe. The countries where the increase of population threatens to outstrip their resources at an ever-increasing rate are mainly in Asia and South America. Outside the Western Hemisphere, it is in such countries as India or Bolivia that modern civilization has been effective enough to decimate disease or mortality through lack of hygiene, but not effective enough to lead to an increase or better distribution of food and land or to the adoption of new social habits such as birth control. The present migration movement leaves such countries out completely. None of the receiving countries will accept other than white immigrants, except on a token basis. Australia, in particular, is certain to adhere to its 'White Australia' policy from which no Government has departed since the establishment of the Commonwealth in 1900. It is fear that Australia's high living standards would be threatened by an influx of cheap Asian labour, rather than racial prejudice, which sustains this policy regardless of party difference. A few years ago Great Britain — alarmed by the social and economic tensions caused by the influx of West Indians — abandoned her tradition of freedom of immigration for all British subjects and imposed certain tests of proof of employment or financial independence, designed to reduce the flow of non-white immigrants. The United States' immigration quotas, while greatly favouring the original immigrant stock, notably British, German and Scandinavian, only allow a fraction of potential emigrants from southern Europe, and a small trickle from other countries. Even if Australia or Canada modified their policies, no more than a small fraction of the surplus populations of Asia or the West Indies could be absorbed. The influx of hundreds of thousands of Indians, Indonesians, Chinese or Japanese into Australasia or the American continent might have a disturbing effect on the social or economic structure of the receiving country, but it would hardly make any impact on the Asian population problem. The Colombo Plan, the field work of the Food and Agriculture Organization and other United Nations agencies, or the United States' Economic Development Loan Fund are attempts to provide an alternative to Asian migration, by creating a better balance between populations and resources.

The second great barrier to migration is the Iron Curtain. Apart from the legacy of displaced persons left in Germany after the war, and unwilling to return to their home countries, there has been virtually no movement of populations between the Communist and non-Communist countries. The only exception, the illegal movement of some 150,000 Germans annually across the 'green frontier' from Eastern to Western Germany, was virtually stopped by the Berlin wall erected by East Germany in 1961. The thousands of Czechs, Poles, Ukrainians, Hungarians and others who have, since the war, come to America and Australasia are all refugees.

Migration on any considerable scale today affects only a few countries both at the giving and the receiving end, but the political importance of the movement is far greater than numbers suggest. The population pressure in Italy is chronic, but its political significance has never been greater than today, when Italy's association with the Western democracies, in particular through NATO, is of outstanding political and strategic significance. Migration can never be a substitute for the solution of Italy's internal problems, but it can at least help to ease a situation which constantly threatens the political stability of Western Europe. The swelling of the population of Western Germany, on the other hand, is almost entirely the product of post-war developments. Nine million refugees flooded an already disrupted country, expelled from eastern Germany by the Poles and from the Sudetenland by the Czechs. They have been completely absorbed. Growing German prosperity, the removal of post-war barriers to German immigration in most countries and the shortage of workers caused by the decline of births during the war has eliminated a potentially dangerous situation.

Migration as a Problem of International Collaboration

As we have seen, migration is, in practice, confined to certain areas. The overpopulation problem of the teeming masses of Asia may be eased by inter-Asian migration, or by technical and economic assistance from the West, or by a combination of both. But emigration from Asia to the Western world, on any major scale, is not within the realm of practical politics. All the countries behind the Iron Curtain are also sealed off except for a trickle of refugees. In the Western world there are certain European countries in which the population pressure is becoming an economic and political problem. These countries are Eire, Austria, Italy, the Netherlands and Greece. The main areas of reception are the United States and the overseas Dominions of the British Commonwealth and, in particular, Australia and Canada. The United States has not so far liberalized its immigration policy to any considerable extent. In 1950 she permitted the immigration of 50,000 'Volksdeutsche', that is, people of German ethnic origin, but not necessarily of German nationality. In 1956 she gave special permission for the immigration of a few thousand Hungarian political refugees after the suppression, by the U.S.S.R. and its satellite Hungarian government, of the October revolt. The United States has also liberalized her immigration regulations by permitting the very small national quotas to be anticipated. Thus the Latvian quota of immigrants has already been filled for more than three centuries in advance. Latin America is of particular interest to emigrants from southern Europe, to whom it is racially and climatically more congenial. But the Latin American States altogether took only an average of 140,000 immigrants in recent years. The policies of most of these States are fickle, and their political stability uncertain. It would be difficult to count on them as a major factor in an international migration policy.

The immigration policy of Israel is even more difficult to fit into an international programme. Israel has been built up by immigration of Jews from all over the world. It is determined to keep its doors open, though its capacity for further large-scale immigration is decreasing, but its policy can only indirectly form part of an international migration programme.

Within the Common Market area of the European Communities, the free movement of persons, and in particular of labour, is a stated objective of the treaties. Because of problems which have been briefly outlined earlier in this book,[1] the full attainment of this objective will take some time. Meanwhile, a remarkable degree of intra-European migration has occurred in recent years, not as a result of formal treaties, but of the labour shortage of Europe's most prosperous industrial countries, notably West Germany and Switzerland. Hundreds of thousands of Greek, Italian and Spanish workers now work in the industrial plants of West Germany and Switzerland, where there is a shortage of labour, and they thus help to relieve the chronic population pressures, as well as the more depressed conditions of these countries. The higher standards of wages and other social services prevailing in Western Europe are beginning to have an effect in Italy, and more especially in Spain, where the conditions and organization of labour have been under rigid control by the Fascist regime of General Franco. A high proportion of this vast migrant labour force is, however, likely to return eventually to their homeland and will thus not produce permanent changes in the population pattern.

In the light of all these factors, a number of highly authoritative estimates have recently been made both of the needs and possibilities of intercontinental migration. They are a healthy corrective to the fantastic figures often circulated by publicists equipped with imagination rather than solid information. After many years of study, scientists, demographers, engineers and others have come to the conclusion that a target of twenty-five million people for Australia is a reasonable one, and this involves tremendous efforts in organization, housing, food production, education and other fields. It is easy to under-estimate the

[1] See above, p. 207.

amount of expense and organization involved in the absorption of 150,000–200,000 immigrants from dozens of countries in one year, in Australia or Canada. Short of Wellsian revolutions in the harnessing of atomic, solar or other forms of energy, or new ways of irrigation, the vast sand deserts of Australia and the ice deserts of Canada will remain uninhabitable. The targets set by responsible international organizations are fortunately more realistic. A few years ago, the International Labour Organization put forward proposals for the setting up of an International Migration Administration under the auspices of the I.L.O. A Migration Council, within the framework of the I.L.O., was to be entrusted with the task of moving 1,700,000 Europeans within five years. This Council, composed of both immigration and emigration countries, was to have gathered data, drawn up projects, organized centres of training and transportation, managed a loan and grant fund and provided facilities in the receiving countries. The funds were to be provided by the participating countries.

This Plan was rejected by three countries whose votes matter most — the United States, Australia and Canada.

None of them was prepared to entrust to an international agency the delicate and explosive problem of what numbers and types of immigrants they should admit.

Yet it would be deplorable if migration policy continued to remain a purely national business. Few statesmen, parliamentarians and publicists seem to have as yet grasped the outstanding practical importance of a co-ordinated migration policy. The main countries of emigration and immigration are either parties to the North Atlantic Treaty Organization or members of the British Commonwealth, that is, of the two international associations which today constitute the main collective defence of the Western world. Britain and Canada belong to both, and the United States, through its defence treaty with Australia and New Zealand, has now created direct links with these Pacific members of the Commonwealth. At present, immigration policy is a purely national affair. Co-ordination of immigration policies within the British Commonwealth is certainly urgent. But it is an even more important task for the Atlantic group of nations. These problems cannot be solved by a stroke of the pen. They are part of the immense task of creating a sense of unity in Europe which will make vital and obvious common interests overcome history and national prejudices. The European Economic Community of six States is at least aiming at freedom of migration within its borders. It should not be beyond the ingenuity and resourcefulness of the West to set up a Migration Committee in which those nations of the British Commonwealth principally interested in immigration would co-operate with the NATO Powers themselves on the political as well as the economic co-ordination of migration policies. Within this framework we have the basic community of interests which is lacking in the wider and less homogeneous forum of the I.L.O. In 1959, British initiative was responsible for the organization of 'World Refugee Year', in which the nations of the West hoped to raise enough funds to make some contribution to the resettlement of the twenty million unsettled refugees — among them one million Arab exiles in Palestine, and 800,000 Chinese in Hong Kong. Five years later, both groups are still where they were. In some cases national hatreds frustrate any reasonable solution of population problems — as they do notably in the case of the Palestine refugees. In many more cases, racial antagonisms still prevent migration on a world-wide scale. In others, such hatreds prevent peaceful co-existence. In Cyprus, clashes between the Greek majority and the Turkish minority during 1964 brought the economic life of the island to a standstill and threatened to provide a major international war. On the one hand, the fusion of the two groups in a Cypriot nation has proved impossible. On the other, the transfer of 100,000 Turkish Cypriots to Turkey, while perhaps feasible, would mean an unacceptable political defeat for Britain and Turkey as guarantors of their status.

An imaginative, realistic and far-sighted migration policy is no panacea for the ills of our world. But it is a most vital, challenging and constructive task, and in the long run the world can solve it only in unison.

CHAPTER 12

ECONOMIC AID AND INTERNATIONAL DEVELOPMENT

THE importance, for the structure and orientation of international relations, of the emergence of many new States in the continents of Africa and Asia is of far more than quantitative significance; it is not confined to strategic factors, or to a shift in the balance of power inside and outside the United Nations. The great majority of the new nations have reached political independence, after a short and sometimes non-existent transition from a static, backward and rural economy, to the expectations entertained by almost any modern State, of economic diversification, industrial development and a general rise in the standard of living. These expectations have spread from the newly independent nations to those which, notably in Latin America, have enjoyed political independence for more than a century, but retained dominantly rural, staple commodity economies and a generally low level of industrial development. Countries like Colombia, Peru, Libya, Ghana, Tanganyika, Burma, India or the Philippines can be divided from each other in terms of history, civilization, geography, race, religion and political alignments. But they are now united in their expectations of economic development and the claim that it is the responsibility of the wealthier and more developed part of the world to assist them in these aspirations. Nor are the major industrial nations of the world in any position to deny these aspirations. A general sense of obligation to assist in the economic and social development of the economically backward countries has moral, political and economic aspects. The sense of moral obligation extends from a still faint and very uneven, but increasing, feeling for the kinship of men, the universality of human aspirations and stirrings of conscience about stark contrasts between affluence in some countries and misery in others. The knowledge of the immense disparity in the economic conditions of the different nations and peoples of the world has been very greatly increased by modern communications, the immeasurably increased opportunities of travel, the impact of television and other visual media, and the daily contacts of representatives of nations — rich and poor — in the United Nations and many other international organizations and conferences. But there is a great gap between knowledge of conditions and the practical desire to remedy them. It would be easy to exaggerate the sense of moral obligation felt, for example, by the average American, German or Englishman, towards the average Bolivian, Somalian or Indian. There are after all glaring inequalities left within most States. Even in the United States, the most advanced model of the 'affluent society', at least one-fifth of the population still has an income officially considered as below a decent minimum standard of family living ($3,000), and in the big cities millions of people live in slums and sanitary conditions that may not be superior to the living conditions of the poorest peasants in South Asia. Yet the war on 'poverty' proclaimed by President Johnson in 1964 is bitterly opposed by many Americans as an improper encroachment on local autonomy and private enterprise. If such inequalities persist, in an age of overwhelming *national* loyalties, and at a time when the philosophy of the welfare State and the 'century of the common man' are generally accepted in the political philosophies and programmes of all the major parties, the appeal of the Tanganyikan villager or the unemployed of Calcutta to the conscience of other nations is infinitely weaker. Yet there are important segments of public opinion, in Parliaments, universities, churches and social organizations in the United States, Great Britain or Germany, which feel and articulate the sense of responsibility of the rich nations towards the poor, and of the unity of mankind.[1] It would be as easy to underestimate the strength of these basic humanitarian motives as it would be to overrate them.

[1] Humanitarian scruples also contribute to the failure of economic boycotts as instruments of international policy. The average American may detest the Castro regime in Cuba or the Verwoerd regime in South Africa. But it is unfortunately impossible to starve objectionable governments, it is the people who suffer generally. Economic boycotts, such as the United States boycott of Castro's Cuba, have been conspicuous failures, because other countries have, at least to some extent, filled the gaps left by the policy of the boycotting nation. But if such a policy were successful to the point where the average person in the boycotted country were dying of hunger or disease, there would be an instinctive revulsion against the consequences of boycott.

There is, secondly, a powerful economic argument in favour of economic development aid flowing from the wealthier to the poorer countries. In a sense such a flow is but a continuation of the process which has gone on at least since the beginning of the Industrial Revolution, by which industrial, scientific and technical progress spread from Britain to Germany, the United States and many other countries, generally contributing to a vast and continuing increase in standards of living and international trade, even though the immediate consequence of industrialization in a particular country is a loss of exports, at least of particular goods, for the country which until then supplied the goods and services. The great majority of economists are agreed that a rise in the economic levels of the many underdeveloped countries of Africa, Asia and Latin America will, in the long run, lead to an increase in their standard of living, demands for a greater diversity of goods and services, and a general rise in international trade. It is also agreed that while the improvement of agricultural methods and productivity is essential for countries that still struggle for the attainment of minimum standards in the quantity and quality of food for the average person, a major improvement in the standard of living has always arisen from industrialization — although not from indiscriminate industrialization, spurred by prestige and status considerations rather than sound economic planning. The steady increase in the volume of trade between the industrially developed countries of the North American continent and Western Europe is a phenomenon that could be a product of economic development in many other parts of the world.

But probably the most important immediate cause of the emergence of foreign and international development aid as a major policy factor in the post-war world has been political and strategic. Assistance in economic development has come to be seen as a major factor in leading the underdeveloped countries — a vast majority of the present States — towards peaceful evolution rather than social unrest and violent revolution. In the immediate post-war period, it was hoped that international development assistance would become a universal international concern and responsibility, corresponding to the function of the United Nations as a universal organization safeguarding peace and promoting political and economic collaboration among the nations of the world. It was in this expectation that the International Bank for Reconstruction and Development was established, together with the International Monetary Fund, in December 1945. But while the great majority of the States — over a hundred at the time of writing — are now members of the Bank, the Communist bloc does not participate at all. It has during the last decade developed its own policies and system of development aid. Of the total capital subscriptions to the Bank, over 31% are held by the United States, nearly 13% by the United Kingdom and over 5% each by France and West Germany. And although the great majority of the underdeveloped nations are members of the Bank, their subscriptions are small or minimal, and their membership reflects mainly their interest in the receipt of aid. The same position is repeated in the younger affiliate institutions of the World Bank, the International Development Association (I.D.A.) and the International Finance Corporation (I.F.C.). In the management and policies of the Bank and its sister institutions, the United States has played a dominant role. While the United Nations itself reflects the political conflicts and power coalitions of the world, as long as the Communist bloc — with the exception of Communist China — actively participates, the international financial institutions reflect essentially the policies of the major industrial nations of the Western, non-Communist, world. The only limited exceptions are the United Nations' technical assistance programmes and its Special Fund, a relatively modest fund now spending some eighty million dollars a year for pilot projects designed to spur scientific, agricultural, and technical development, to which the Soviet Union contributes a small amount.

Despite this reflection of the political schisms of the world in the membership of the international financial organizations, the World Bank and its affiliate institutions constitute the main pillars of international development aid. In 1962 their combined outlays amounted to nearly 1½ billion dollars, overwhelmingly in the form of loans. The great majority of the loans made by the World Bank and the I.D.A. were to governments for basic development purposes, although the World Bank may make loans to private firms with Government guarantees and, as a matter of (U.S.-inspired) policy, prefers the encouragement of private enterprise to that of State-owned industry. But as under its Charter the Bank must have a Government guarantee for any loan made to a private enterprise, and also because the needs of the developing countries have been predominantly for 'infrastructure' projects, i.e. for basic utilities such as power generation, irrigation, road transport or harbours, the accent has been heavily on public development projects. The I.F.C. was specifically established to encourage private enterprise in the developing countries; but it is only since the abolition, a few years ago, of the prohibition to take equity participations in such enterprises that it has begun to play a somewhat more important part in international economic development. Of far greater importance are two essentially regional international development organizations, the Inter-American Development Bank (I.D.B.) and the European Development Fund of the E.E.C., each of which in 1962 disbursed about 150 million dollars in aid. As the name indicates, the I.D.B. has the purpose of encouraging economic development in the American Hemisphere, and in that institution, too, the United States is the most important single contributor. The E.E.C. Development Fund seeks to promote development in the associated overseas members of the Community, i.e. overwhelmingly the former French African colonies. An African Development Bank — established by the African States — is in process of formation.

The role of the international financial development institutions in general international economic development is important, and many of the developing countries would like to see them take over a great deal of the aid that is now being given on a bilateral basis, since this would greatly lessen their sense of political dependence on a particular donor country. Meanwhile, however, the proportion of bilateral aid, i.e. of economic assistance granted by one particular country to some other country, vastly exceeds that given by international institutions. According to the 1963 review published by the Organization for Economic Co-operation and Development (O.E.C.D.), of the total official development aid given by members of the O.E.C.D. in 1962 (grants, loans and contributions to multilateral agencies) of nearly 6 billion dollars, less than 700 million dollars consisted of contributions to the international finance institutions. The members of the O.E.C.D. include all the major aid-giving countries outside the Soviet bloc, both in terms of bilateral aid and of contributions to the international development institutions. The fact that the overwhelming proportion of development aid still is on a country to country basis underlines its political nature. Reference has already been made[1] to the development aid policies and institutions of the United States. Outside the United States, Great Britain and France have for many years been major aid-givers, mainly to their former colonies. France in particular gives almost all its economic assistance to the French-speaking countries of Africa, which continue to be economically dependent on their former colonizer. The United States — and among more recent important aid-giving countries, West Germany — do not concentrate their aid on specific areas or groups of countries to anything like the same extent. This does not, however, diminish the political orientation of their aid. That U.S. economic aid is on a world-wide basis reflects the world-wide political and strategic responsibilities and interests of the United States. Europe, which in the years of the Marshall Plan received the lion's share, has almost disappeared as an aid recipient, except for certain military expenditures of the United States classed as military assistance (they are of major dimensions in Spain). Instead the Near East and Asia have emerged as the regions receiving the largest share of U.S. aid, with India receiving about one-third of the total, followed by Pakistan, Turkey and Egypt. Despite the very strong economic, political and geographical interest of the United States in the American continent, Latin America follows a good distance behind, with aid receipts and authorizations in 1962 amounting to about $500 million dollars. It is followed by the Far East and Africa. Because the political responsibilities of the United States are more universal than those of any other country, its economic aid also comes much nearer than that of any other State to a universal aid policy. The large share of India for example, reflects the strong interest of the United States in the maintenance of a desperately under-privileged and populous democratic State, which in that part of the world competes with a centrally planned and Communist-led China. The important assistance given to Pakistan stems from the now increasingly shaky military association of that country with the Western Alliances and the need to counterbalance the aid given by the United States to a neutralist India, by support to a military ally. With regard to Latin America, United States aid is now far more institutionalized and systematized than in any other part of the world, since the establishment

[1] See above, pp. 108 *et seq.*

of the Inter-American Development Bank, largely with United States capital, but jointly run by the United States and the Latin American members of that institution. The Alliance for Progress is a long-term plan for the economic and social development of Latin America, supported by direct contributions from the United States, by actual and projected investment from private investors, by loans from international agencies such as the World Bank and its affiliates and the Inter-American Bank. In Africa the United States still takes a back seat behind the former colonial Powers, Britain and France, and the aid of international institutions. But the United States can certainly not disclaim interest in the future of that desperately under-privileged continent which, within a few years, has emerged from a predominantly colonial status to a bewildering variety of politically independent States struggling to achieve political stability and economic viability.

To some extent Western aid policies are co-ordinated. For several years the principal Western countries and Japan have, under the guidance of the World Bank, established informal aid consortia for India and Pakistan which discuss with the representatives of the Indian and Pakistani governments the respective needs of these two countries for foreign assistance in the light of their successive development plans. Looser consultative groups have been formed for Colombia, Nigeria, Sudan and Tunisia. To a limited extent the twelve Western countries (including the United States, Canada, Britain, France, Germany, Italy and Japan) which are members of the O.E.C.D. co-operate in their assistance policies through the Development Assistance Committee of the O.E.C.D. But the basic development aid policies as well as the amounts contributed from public national budgets to these purposes remain determined by national policy. The United States Congress retains its tight control over the annual appropriations for economic assistance, and it emphasizes the national policy interests of the United States. French aid is largely directed by the desire for strong continuing association with its former colonies in Africa. German aid is directed by the desire to strengthen existing or developing export possibilities in Latin America, the Near East, Africa or India. And in so far as the world-wide character of the United States aid can be regarded as diluting any specific political orientation, this is largely countered by the fact that, since 1960, most of the aid given in the form of loans is 'tied aid', i.e. it is linked to purchases for goods or services in the United States. This is designed both to protect the U.S. balance of payments and to give support to U.S. industries, in competition with that of other countries.

The political orientation and necessity of development aid is strengthened by the substantial increase and systematization of capital and technical aid flowing from the Communist bloc. The emergence of the U.S.S.R. as one of the world's major industrial and technological Powers has made it possible for that country to support her political aims and aspirations in the developing countries, and especially in the countries that have recently emerged from colonial rule by Britain, France, the Netherlands and Belgium, by economic and technical assistance. An important part, especially in the supplies of capital goods and technical services, is played by some of the other members of the Communist group with industrial and technical experience, notably Czechoslovakia, East Germany, Poland and Roumania. In the case of the Soviet bloc, it is extremely difficult to disentangle aid proper, i.e. grants or technical aid given and not paid for, from trade. The speeches and statistics published by the Communist countries emphasize on the one hand the predominant importance played by trade as the most honest means of helping the developing countries while at the same time stressing the altruistic character of the assistance given by the Soviet bloc, in contrast to the Capitalist world. It seems that the bulk of the increase in the economic relations between the Communist countries (other than China) and the developing countries[1] is accounted for by trade, mainly in the form of barter or exchange agreements for certain commodities, a form of trade commending itself to centrally controlled socialistic economies. The main form of genuine assistance consists in the cheap interest rate of loans ($2\frac{1}{2}\%$) which are used for the purchase of equipment and technical services in the donor country.

According to the latest information from Soviet sources,[2] the Soviet bloc (C.M.E.A.[3] countries) is now furnishing economic

[1] In the case of the Soviet Union, the total amount of trade with the developing countries increased from 258·2 million roubles in 1955 to 912·9 million roubles in 1960.

[2] *International Affairs*, February, 1964, p. 71.

[3] The bloc countries use this abbreviation for 'Council for Mutual Economic Assistance' rather than the Western abbreviation Comecon.

and technical assistance in the construction of 1,100 industrial enterprises and other projects in 40 developing States, including 166 projects in India, 50 in Indonesia, and 178 in the United Arab Republic. By the end of 1962, specialists of C.M.E.A. countries had trained about 53,000 workers, engaged at construction sites in the newly free countries. In 1962 C.M.E.A. countries sent 7,000 specialists to young States to provide various services. Over 10,000 people from Asian, African and Latin American countries are studying in educational establishments of C.M.E.A. States.

Much of this is financed by credits given for periods from five to fifteen years at an annual interest rate of 2½%. More than half of it is used for the development of key industries. The loans are usually repaid by 'traditional export goods' (i.e. mainly raw materials and staple commodities). Most of the Soviet-bloc 'aid' is thus trade financed by credits in which the 'aid-giver' receives commodities in exchange.

But much of the aid given in the form of development loans by Western countries is also linked with trade in so far as most of it is tied to purchases in the loan-giving country (as is most of the economic assistance given by the U.S., France and Britain). It is different in technique but not in substance. Only grants, loans or sales on non-commercial terms can be described as genuine 'aid'. It is in the terms of credit — such as the AID or I.D.A. loans given for forty or fifty years at very low rates of interest or in the sales of surplus commodities — that the 'aid' character of Western economic assistance is most pronounced.

Except for the small participation of the U.S.S.R. in the U.N. technical assistance programmes and Special Fund, there is no co-operation between the Western world and the Communist world in the aid to the developing countries. Deliberately, or tacitly, the two groups compete. A good illustration is the construction of several major steel mills in India. A few years ago three major steel mills were simultaneously in process of construction: one financed by a Soviet loan and built with Soviet materials and directed by Soviet engineers, the second directed by a British, and the third by a German consortium. All the aid-giving countries, Communist and Capitalist alike, have an interest in forging links with the recipient countries, as regards the source of equipment, commercial relations, the type of technical training, and the establishment of financial ties. Both the Western world — including the World Bank — and the Soviet bloc have concentrated on 'project' aid, i.e. on loans given for specific projects deemed worthy of support. This has the advantage of identification of the donor country with a specific steel plant or refinery or fertilizer factory. It also gives better possibilities to appraise the value of a specific undertaking. From the point of view of the recipient country, it has the disadvantage of neglecting the economic and social bases of development, and of encouraging extravagant industrial projects which absorb an excessive proportion of the country's insufficient resources. In recent years there have been, at least in the Western world, certain indications of changes in policy. The Inter-American Development Bank has a special social development fund administered in trust for the United States, which is designed to assist important social projects in the fields of housing, education and agrarian reform. In several cases, the United States Agency for International Development has given loans designed for general budgetary aid, and quite recently the President of the World Bank has indicated an intention of widening the loan policies of the Bank in the direction of general development projects. The recognition of such a change — hitherto still insignificant in practical terms — indicates a better understanding of the ubiquitous character of development aid, and in particular of the desperate poverty of the great majority of the developing countries in the educational and technical bases of development. There is an increasing, though still inadequate, recognition of the fact that the most carefully worked-out aid for specific industrial or agricultural or commercial development may be wasted unless the recipient country has an adequate minimum of trained administrators, teachers, scientists and technicians. On the other hand, general budgetary aid may lead to the squandering of resources, unless there is an adequate development plan and some control over its execution.

It may be asked whether the enormous, and politically, extremely sensitive, expenditure in development aid during the last fifteen years has paid, or is likely to pay political dividends in terms of alliance, friendship or even more generally, peaceful development. An unconditional affirmative answer can only be given in the case of the aid given to Western Europe after the war. But then the assisted countries were all countries of high development, temporarily thrown back by the exhaustion of the world war. In the case of the rest of the world, the answer is an open one. What can be said clearly is that the expectation of a direct *quid pro quo*, i.e. the reward for economic aid given, in terms of military or political alliance, is futile. The governments of the aid-giving countries — though by no means all the legislators or other sectors of public opinion — have come to accept this. Thus the coupling of aid with political conditions would probably have driven India, like any other newly independent and therefore extremely sensitive country, to wilder nationalism and anti-Western sentiment. Instead, the policy pursued by the Western Powers individually and collectively, of giving aid to India without political conditions, facilitated the cautious pro-Western turn taken by India in response to the Chinese attack on her borders a few years ago. It cannot even be forecast with certainty that economic aid will ensure the peaceful evolution of the assisted country. This is partly due to the fact that aid given in the past, or reasonably likely to be given in the future, will always fall far short of the minimum needs of any one country. Short of a much more effective and universal international organization of economic aid, and a far greater redistribution of wealth between the wealthy and the poor countries than is politically feasible at this time, the gap between needs and fulfilment will always remain wide. Without co-ordination between donors and recipients, there is also the danger that aid may be neutralized by inadequate administration or planning. It is easier to justify the continuance of aid in negative terms: if the United States, or Britain, or France, or Germany, should cease to give aid even within the present dimensions, the likelihood of economic and political penetration of any given country in Asia or Africa by the Communist bloc would be far greater than it is at present. It may, however, occur owing to quite different circumstances, and despite economic aid. This is the frustrating aspect of the whole problem, which troubles the governments of the Western countries year after year, when they present their economic aid budgets to their respective Parliaments. Moreover, it is always easier to point to the visible frustrations than to the invisible satisfactions. The impact that U.S. and other Western aid may have had on the basically friendly orientation of countries like Nigeria or India or Colombia cannot be measured. But a nationalization measure in Brazil, Ceylon or Indonesia attracts immediate publicity.

One argument often made by the critics of governmental aid to developing countries is patently fallacious: the argument that economic development should be left to private enterprise and investment. The figures of post-war development, and of the relative shares of public aid and private investment in the developing worlds, are clear. According to the most recent statistics of the O.E.C.D., in 1962 the total official aid, in form of grants, loans and contributions to multilateral agencies, of nearly six billion dollars, compared with less than two and one-half billion dollars representing the flow of private capital, and including export credits as well as direct investment. Moreover, the greatest single proportion of private investment in developing countries consists in the production and refinement of crude oil, overwhelmingly in the Near East. Private capital and enterprise in the Western countries are far more attracted by the investment opportunities in the developed world, i.e. in such countries as Canada, Western Europe and selected Latin American countries, such as Mexico, than in the more risky and uncertain investment in developing countries. Even the availability of Government guarantees against major investment risks (expropriation, inconvertibility, war) in the United States, Germany and Japan has not reversed the trend.

The U.N. Conference on Trade and Development, held in Geneva from March to June 1964, underlined the continuing gap between the minimum aspirations of the developing countries and the maximum offers of the developed ones. The former, constituting an almost solid bloc of 77 States, demanded far-reaching price stabilization for commodities, trade concessions, minimum pledges of continuing assistance — a figure of 1% of the gross national product was, in principle, conceded by the developing countries — and, above all, a permanent Council, in which the developing countries would have a clear majority, and which would have the power to pass binding resolutions. Most of these demands were rejected by the developed countries, which could hardly commit themselves to having their aid contributions and trade policies determined by an international body dominated by the aid-receiving States. But a permanent Board for trade and development was established and further conferences will be held.

The political significance of this conference lies in the fact that the developing countries, constituting a strong majority of the world's independent States, have formed a common front — although an implementation of their proposals would reveal many conflicts of interest between them — and that possibly the conflicts and adjustments between the economically developed and the economically underdeveloped nations will replace the Cold War as the major political issue of the next decade.

Thus, economic development aid remains a major and unsolved problem of international politics. It is a problem that neither Communist nor anti-Communist countries can evade; it is a necessity that is unpopular in every one of the aid-giving countries, and one which certainly does not pay short-term dividends, and quite possibly no long-term dividends either. It is a problem sharpened and made more difficult by the economic, social and political competition of the Communist and anti-Communist political and economic systems. It is likely to stay with us for the indefinite future, since the gap between minimum aspirations and fulfilled needs remains as wide as ever. It is linked with problems such as the population explosion, the size of military expenditures and many other factors that aggravate an already enormous burden. Economic development aid is more likely than any other item to be the victim of nationalist passions, resentments and economy drives. Yet its overwhelming importance in the long-term perspective is undeniable: a world in which a majority of the States remain in a state of — no longer passively accepted — poverty and stagnation while a minority of nations accumulate the bulk of the resources and wealth of the earth, cannot remain a peaceful or contented world. It is bound to result in explosions, which will deeply affect both the peace and the political balance of the world.

CHAPTER 13

PROSPECTS FOR WAR AND PEACE

THE last few years have brought profound changes in the texture of international relations. The dangers to the peace and survival of mankind are no less than they were; but they differ in many ways from the kind of threat that hung over mankind during the period of 'bipolar' division and confrontation of the two dominant Powers.

The major changes that have occurred can be summarized as follows:

1. The two most powerful States, the United States and the Soviet Union, still possess between them an overwhelming power of destruction, but they no longer dominate the direction of world politics. Even if they were in alliance, they would no longer exercise the control over the fate of mankind, which was in their hands until a few years ago. Divided as they are by conflicting purposes, policies and ideologies, their combined influence is very much weaker. In the uneasy balance of terror between the two giants, both reluctant to risk a direct clash but poised against each other in their military, political and economic policies all over the world, the individual and collective influence of other Powers has greatly increased.

2. Despite her economic setbacks and her continuing backwardness in industrial development and advanced technology, Communist China is emerging more and more clearly as the third world Power, with policies independent from those both of the United States and the Soviet Union. China's influence is bound to increase further, as she closes the gap in industrial and technological development. In some respects, Chinese and Russian policies may still be drawn together against the common enemy — for example, in the case of an extension of the conflict in Vietnam. If a major war is avoided, the development of three major spheres of imperial influence in the world may become more and more marked. More or less in line with George Orwell's

vision of the empires of Oceania, Eurasia and Eastasia, the United States would be the predominant Power in the Atlantic area, the Soviet Union in Eastern and Central Europe and certain adjoining parts of Asia, and China in most of the Asian continent.

3. The predominance of both the United States and the Soviet Union in their respective alliances has been greatly weakened by the increasing independence of their allies. Within the Communist bloc there is not only the conflict between the U.S.S.R. and China over the major principles and strategies of Communism, as well as national rivalries; there have been signs of growing independence on the part of the European members of the Soviet-Communist bloc, notably of Poland, Hungary and Roumania. In part this independence manifests itself in an attitude of neutrality towards the rivalries between the Soviet Union and China; but more significant is perhaps the tendency of all these countries to widen their international contacts, and especially those with the non-Communist world.

Within the Western Alliance, the defection of France from American leadership is now all but complete. It manifests itself in the virtual cessation of her active participation in the NATO Alliance, in the independence of her policies, in Europe, towards Communist China, in South-east Asia and elsewhere. The basic principles of French policy under de Gaulle, i.e. a Continental Europe — not federated but closely linked under French leadership — and a policy of neutrality in the parts of Asia in which the United States is deeply engaged in fighting against Communist forces backed by China, are entirely at cross-purposes with American policy. Even the demise of the NATO Alliance is a possibility, unless another acute military threat from the U.S.S.R. should draw the allies together once again. Apart from France, America's most important allies show a growing independence in their economic policies, and this has important political implications. Britain and the members of the European Community pursue their own economic objectives, even to the point of acute conflict with the United States over such matters as trade with Communist powers or Community tariffs against the outer world.

4. The rapid increase in the number of newly independent and politically unaligned States greatly increases the fluidity as well as the explosiveness of the international situation. Now that the struggle for independence from colonial domination is

almost over, the singlemindedness of the fight for independence gives way to a multitude of regional and internal conflicts, many of which bear the seeds of wider international strife. A significant and dangerous aspect of this development is the lack of restraint in the actions of some of the newer States. It is the major States — with the possible and ominous exception of Communist China — which are today restrained by the awesome burden and responsibility of power. The conflicts which at this time rage in areas such as Cyprus, Malaysia, Palestine or Vietnam each have in them the danger of 'escalation'. These conflicts, although essentially local, national or regional in character, are such that, unless a lasting solution is found, they will almost inevitably lead to wider international wars. On the other hand, real solutions, as distinct from temporary cease-fires or armistices, are not in sight. Thus, in Cyprus, elementary common sense would dictate a supreme attempt on the part of the 525,000 people of the island, to live together in peace and turn Cyprus into a small but viable State. But the racial and national feud between the Greek majority and the Turkish minority is so intense and bitter that no compromise between the will of the majority to abolish the internationally guaranteed privileges of the Turkish minority and the fear of the Turks for their survival can be found. While the United Nations may be able to delay war and violence, international police action cannot be a substitute for an organic solution. A failure to find such a solution may involve Britain, Greece, Turkey and possibly other States in hostilities. In Malaysia, Britain has too vital an interest in the maintenance of a State which includes the vital strategic base and harbour of Singapore, to let the vastly more populous and powerful Indonesia invade Malaysian territory with impunity. Any major intervention would be very likely to produce Chinese counter-reactions. The confrontation of the United States and the U.S.S.R. in Cuba, in October 1962, showed that any major political or military intervention of a foreign Power on the American continent, regardless of the validity and viability of the Monroe Doctrine, would involve acute conflict with the United States. In the Near East, there is not the glimmer of a solution to the bitter strife between the Arab States and Israel. Only disunity among the Arab States and the military strength of Israel have delayed a renewal of the war of 1948. The Arab States are more and more committed to hostile action at some time, and tension has been increased by the impending diversion of Jordan waters drawn from Israel territory, for the irrigation of the Negev. It is difficult to see how an involvement of this area in acute war would fail to develop into a wider conflagration. The U.S.S.R. has moved increasingly towards unconditional support of Arab nationalism and hostility to Israel, whereas the Western Powers, most clearly perhaps France, would stand on Israel's side, with the United States torn between the enormous interests of American companies in Arab-owned oil and strong sympathies for Israel. A great deal would depend on who is the actual aggressor.

5. Although the danger of war now arises increasingly from the possible 'escalation' of local or regional conflicts, there remain certain areas of continuing conflict — suspended at best by an uneasy truce — where the major Powers confront each other directly.

In the first place, the partition of Germany and Berlin remains a continuing source of friction. The partition of Germany into two States — a political though not yet a legal reality — is not likely to lead to war in the foreseeable future. By contrast the partition of Berlin can erupt into acute conflict at any time that the Soviet Union chooses to intensify the pressure. The long-term objective of the Soviet bloc is the absorption of Berlin, which is an enclave in Communist territory, while the West is not now in a position to withdraw, or even to concede an internationalization of West Berlin.

In the second place, the hostile forces of South Korea and the United States on the one side, and of North Korea and Communist China on the other side, confront each other on the 38th parallel, in a situation of uneasy armistice that in no way differs from 1952 when hostilities ended.

Thirdly — and perhaps most seriously — the United States and Communist China, with possible support from the Soviet Union, will confront each other directly in Vietnam with unforeseeable consequences, if the war should continue to go against South Vietnam and the United States should decide to extend rather than to reduce its commitment, by attacks upon North Vietnam. These areas of direct big-Power conflict are a reminder of the grim fact that only an uneasy balance of terror, and the awareness of the present leaders of the incalculable consequences of direct hostilities between the big Powers, stands between the present situation of uneasy peace and the possible destruction of civilized life on earth.

6. In all these immensely dangerous situations, the United Nations can and does exercise an important restraining, but not a controlling, function. That the United Nations — weak though it is — plays an indispensable role, is evident from the part it has had in many serious conflicts of recent date. On some occasions — in the Suez Canal hostilities of 1956, the civil war of the Congo and, most recently, in Cyprus — it has played an active role as an 'order' force. But its functions are severely limited not only by growing financial difficulties, but also by severe division of the Powers concerning the objectives and purposes of United Nations action. This, in turn, reflects basic political divisions. There is no prospect of an extension of *ad hoc* forces of the United Nations, let alone, in the foreseeable future, of a permanent international police force, which would intervene in areas and situations presenting acute threats to peace. The best that can be hoped for is the continuance of the role of the United Nations as an organized forum of discussion, where parties stalled in direct negotiations can meet without loss of face and seek, either with or without the formal intervention of the United Nations organs, to arrive at a settlement. In short, the United Nations is today a more indispensable link than ever in the complex and many-sided processes of the peaceful settlement of international disputes. Without it, the danger of impasse situations, of conflicts of prestige and interest in which the participants might see no other way out but war, would be vastly greater. But the United Nations has not attained, nor can it hope to attain in the foreseeable future, the status of a general international police authority. And, quite apart from the continued absence of one of the world's three major Powers from its ranks, it is threatened with disintegration, if France and the U.S.S.R. persist in their refusal to pay their shares of the United Nations expeditionary forces and the United States should press its move for denial of voting rights for defaulters under Article 19 of the Charter. The success of such a move would probably lead to the withdrawal of France and the U.S.S.R., its failure to the withdrawal of the United States.

7. While world conflict threatens no longer predominantly from the hostility of the two leading Powers, but from a multi-

tude of major or minor storm-centres and from the growing strength of Communist China, mankind's posture at this time is not purely one of conflict. For a number of years there have been massive and concerted efforts, on the part of the more developed and prosperous countries, to assist the developing countries by sustained economic development aid. This flows from international institutions, from the Western Powers and from the Communist bloc. Much of this aid has a competitive character and is closely linked with Cold War strategy. Nevertheless, it is one of the most positive by-products of the Cold War. There are also halting, and hitherto quite inadequate, efforts at international co-operation in matters of common concern to mankind. Though gravely deficient in the necessary minimum of executive powers, the special U.N. agencies in the fields of health, food, agriculture, atomic energy, labour and transport have begun to set the pattern for organized co-operative efforts of the majority of nations in the development of human resources. There is limited co-operation between the United States and U.S.S.R. in the exploration of outer space, weather observation and other scientific matters. But not only are these efforts inadequate, they are also unbalanced. While both national and international efforts have been largely successful in improving communications, sanitary and agricultural standards in many parts of the world, they are more than outpaced by an explosive population increase in which any co-ordinated international action is almost totally lacking.

Although the desperate inadequacy, and the danger to peace, of a vastly increased number of nominally sovereign national States is becoming daily more apparent, conflicts deriving from racial, social, religious, economic and ideological tensions still dominate the life of the nations. So numerous are these conflicts, so intense are the rifts and antagonisms that it requires great optimism to hope that none of them will within the next decade or so develop into a major conflagration, beyond the point of return. The fear of the consequences of a major war has not subdued the ancient instincts of hatred and strife. But it has helped to restrain them, to impose brakes where formerly there were none. The result is a twilight atmosphere of unresolved partitions, border conflicts, racial antagonisms, a state — in many parts of the world — of neither peace nor war.

8. The precariousness of mankind's future is aggravated by the

fact that irrevocable decisions on life and death of civilization depend to a greater extent than ever on relatively few individuals. Time and again since the end of the last war, and most dramatically during the height of the Cuba crisis in 1962, the survival of civilization depended on the lonely decisions of a few leaders. The power over the fateful decisions on peace or war is no longer greatly influenced by the differences between totalitarian and democratic forms of government. The decision whether to send bombers or missiles in anticipation of, or in reply to an imminent attack, must be made by one man, perhaps in consultation with a few military and political leaders. Once it is made, it is irrevocable and the nation must follow for better or worse. For this reason the impact of personality on international events is greater than ever, and it is not confined to the leaders of the major Powers. The recklessness of a Sukarno or the scheming of a Makarios may involve the fate of hundreds of millions.

9. The loneliness of the power and responsibility of the few men whose decisions can involve the fate of mankind, contrasts with the passivity and helplessness of the thousands of millions of individuals whom they govern. Such is the organization of modern life, such is the speed of modern communications and weapons that they can less than ever participate in the decisions that affect them. While their main concern is to live out their lives in peace, work and a modest minimum standard of living for themselves and their families, they may be hurled into disaster by the recklessness of a few men. Individuals, or groups of them, may be effective in local or limited action. This is shown by the great increase of spontaneous group action in the fight for desegregation in the United States. The masses may indirectly influence the political leaders by articulating their desire for peace, or at the other extreme, by outbursts of nationalist emotions, or racial hatreds (as shown by recent events in Panama or Cyprus, or in the periodic religious conflicts on the borders between India and Pakistan). But they can have little direct influence on the vital decisions over war and peace, which have to be made within hours, or perhaps minutes. It is this sense of impotence that serves to increase the tendencies inherent in the mass communications aspect of contemporary society which is largely directed to personal escapism and to the modern version of *panem et circenses*, the preoccupation with the latest boxing

or football match, the latest crime story or a Hollywood divorce.

Thus mankind uneasily stumbles along a rather narrow path, somewhere between unprecedented affluence and unimaginable disaster, between an almost boundless widening of the frontiers of knowledge and a possible relapse into primitive barbarism. More than ever the future of the nation depends on the moral and intellectual wisdom of a small élite of leaders.

APPENDICES

APPENDIX I

RECOGNITION, UNITED NATIONS MEMBERSHIP AND INTERNATIONAL DIPLOMACY

1. The International Status of China

THE Communist Government of China — which has control of all China (with an estimated population of 750 million people) except the island of Formosa (Taiwan) and a few small offshore islands — is firmly established as the effective government of that country; it also has, in the last few years, emerged as one of the major international Powers of the world. Yet it is the Government of Chiang Kai-shek — which in effect controls only the island of Taiwan (10 million inhabitants) — that at the time of writing represents China in the United Nations and is still recognized as the Government of China by a large number of States, in particular by the United States.

The main reason for this anomalous and dangerous situation is the intensity of the Cold War, and the bitterness of the antagonism between the Communist and non-Communist worlds. As the recognition of new governments is one of the most discussed problems of international law, and as no State wishes to put itself into a position of open defiance of international law, the legal position should be briefly summarized.

There are two major aspects to this problem: the recognition of the Communist Government of China by the other States, individually; and the admission of the Communist Government of China as the legitimate representative of one of the member-States (and a permanent member of the Security Council) of the United Nations.

It is generally recognized that the normal, and by far the most important, test for the recognition of a new government of an already existing State is 'effectiveness', i.e. the ability of the new government to control the territory and population of the State which it claims to represent, and its consequent ability to fulfil the international obligations of that State. By that test there could be no doubt that the effective government of China today — with the exception of the island of Taiwan — is the Communist Government of China. However, State practice, in particular that of the United States and Great Britain, has in the past on many occasions withheld or delayed the recognition of new governments for political reasons. The predominant reason for such delay has been hostility to the political character of the new regime.

The best-known modern example has been the delay in the recognition of the Soviet Union by the U.S. Government for thirteen years after the former had gained effective control of the country. It is, however, equally significant that, when a new government has maintained itself effectively in power for a prolonged period, recognition has always followed sooner or later. The justification for the delay or withholding of recognition of foreign governments has sometimes been rationalized, e.g. by Professor Lauterpacht in his book on *Recognition in International Law* (1947), as being dependent on the democratic character of the new regime. By that test, the willing consent of the governed is supposed to be an implied condition of the claim of the government to international recognition. The difficulty of that test is twofold. First, it is somewhat in conflict with the present basis of international law, namely, the irrelevance of internal political and social forms of government to international status. This, in turn, is a corollary of the present state of international society. Second, no State has been consistent in the theory that free consent of the governed is a precondition of international recognition of the new government. The United States, for example, and other Western democracies did not delay the recognition of the openly undemocratic government of Franco in Spain after it had seized effective control. The United States has long abandoned a short-lived attempt made under President Wilson's first administration to withhold recognition from revolutionary governments in Latin America that it considers undemocratic, and makes effective control the test. This, and not political approval, has been the reason for maintaining diplomatic relations with such military dictatorships as the former Perón regime of Argentina or the surviving one of Stroessner in Paraguay. On the other hand, State practice has permitted wide divergencies in the speed and manner in which existing governments recognize a revolutionary government of a foreign State. Great Britain, France, India, Burma, the Scandinavian countries and other States have certainly the presumption of correctness by international law on their side in having recognized the Communist Government of China as the legitimate government of China after it had established and maintained effective control for some time. The Communist Government claims that the island of Formosa (Taiwan) forms part of the Republic of China, that it is entitled to seize it by force as a matter of purely internal civil war with the Chiang Kai-shek forces, and that United States intervention on the side of Chiang Kai-shek is an unwarranted interference in the domestic affairs of a foreign State. The status of Formosa is, however, less clear than that claim makes out. Having been conquered and ruled by Japan from 1896 to 1945, the island of Formosa had ceased to be part of China for a very considerable period. The three major Allies at the Teheran Conference in 1943 recorded their agreement that Formosa should be returned to China after the war, but the form of this return was not settled. Nor was this declaration in the nature of an internationally binding treaty. After the end of the war, the civil war in China and the increasing antagonism between, in particular, the United States and the Communist forces in China, delayed any formal consolidation. It may, therefore, be claimed with some justification, though certainly not with unquestionable authority, that the international status of Formosa (Taiwan) is unsettled, and that in such a situation the United States is entitled to take such protective measures against conquest by force as it deems to be in its national interest.

No such justification, however, would legitimate armed intervention against an attempt by the Communist Government of China to seize the offshore islands of Matsu and Quemoy. They are unquestionably part of the mainland, and any direct assistance given to the Chiang Kai-shek forces stationed there against a Communist attempt to oust them would be intervention in a civil war.

The representation of the Communist Government of China within the United Nations poses somewhat different problems. Art. 4 of the U.N. Charter provides as follows:

> '1. Membership in the United Nations is open to all other peace-loving States which accept the obligations contained in the present Charter and, in the judgment of the Organization, are able and willing to carry out these obligations.
>
> '2. The admission of any such State to membership in the United Nations will be effected by a decision of the General Assembly upon the recommendation of the Security Council.'

The United States, and a number of other States usually accepting the lead of United States policy, have based their strong opposition to any admission of the Communist Chinese Government on the adjective 'peace-loving'. However, even if there were general international agreement on certain aggressive actions of the Communist Government, e.g. in North Korea, the interpretation of 'peace-loving' is open to many doubts. On the theory propounded by the United States, the Soviet Union itself, which is one of the permanent members of the Security Council, might be disqualified from membership for her actions against Finland in 1939, and Hungary in 1956. Britain and France, in occupying the Suez Canal, committed aggressive acts, as did India in occupying Goa, and Indonesia in attacking Malaysia. The practice of the United Nations has in many ways come to diverge from the Charter. In recent years, every newly formed State has been automatically admitted to U.N. membership, despite serious doubts about the 'ability' of some of them to carry out their obligations, in accordance with Art. 4. In the present state of world politics, the United Nations cannot fulfil its essential security function but is still the pre-eminent and indispensable forum where the nations of the world can meet, make contacts, exchange opinions and, on occasions, take joint action. This shift — and common sense — lends support to the view that membership of the United Nations should not be made dependent on moral tests but on the effective participation of a country in the affairs of the nations. Admission to membership should only be refused to States which have clearly defied the Charter. In any case, Art. 6 provides for the expulsion of any member of the United Nations 'which has persistently violated the principles contained in the present Charter'.

Technically, however, the recognition of the Communist Government of China in the United Nations is not a matter of membership. China has been one of the founder-members. It is a matter of credentials, of seating a particular government in the General Assembly and the Security Council, and in the affiliated organizations. This is, therefore, a matter on which the General Assembly and the Security Council may act separately, undesirable though this is.

Clearly, political considerations have prevailed over legal tests. But arguments of political strategy and expediency are far more vulnerable to the impact of changed conditions than legal tests. After fifteen years of continued control over all but a minute part of China — an island — and in view of the growing military, political and economic power of a State of 750 million people, continued non-recognition of Communist China by a decreasing number of States becomes increasingly ineffective. It greatly complicates the inevitable need of certain direct contacts which States of the importance of the United States and Communist China must maintain with each other, short of a full-scale shooting war. A state of political tension in many ways increases the need for such diplomatic contacts — as is shown by the installation of a 'hot line' between Moscow and Washington in 1963. Such contacts are in fact maintained, through periodical meetings of the United States and Chinese Ambassadors to Poland, through joint participation in certain international conferences, such as the Conference of 1962 concerning the neutralization of Laos. The necessity, because of non-recognition, to confine these contacts to subordinate and occasional diplomatic levels, greatly diminishes their efficacy. Since the reality of political power sooner or later determines legal relations, the legal isolation of Communist China is bound to be a wasting asset. This was dramatically illustrated when, in January 1964, France under de Gaulle's leadership extended full recognition to Communist China. This had of course been preceded for many years by diplomatic recognition on the part of Britain, Canada, several Scandinavian States and others. What can be foreseen with certainty is that, as the years go by, more and more States, especially those of Asia and Africa, will wish to normalize their relations with Communist China, leaving the United States in increasing isolation. This is likely to manifest itself both outside and inside the United Nations, in the latter institution through a vote that might admit Communist China to a seat in the General Assembly, even though the United States could block corresponding seating in the Security Council through the veto. The strongest argument in favour of full diplomatic participation by Communist China in international organizations and diplomatic relations is the futility of any international disarmament or arms control agreement without her participation. The urgency of full Chinese representation is underlined by the detonation of China's first atomic bomb in October 1964. The value of any test ban or other agreement is drastically reduced as long as Communist China remains outside the nexus of international legal relationships.

2. The International Status of Germany

As in the case of China, the international status of Germany — i.e. the recognition of East and West Germany, respectively, by the various Powers — has been a matter of political rather than legal considerations. The refusal on the part of the Western Powers and the majority of other States to recognize the State of East Germany (Deutsche Demokratische Republik) and the blocking, by mutual veto, of the admission of either of the two Germanies to the United Nations, is clearly a matter of politics, and more specifically, part of the 'Cold War' strategy. The Western Powers, under strong pressure from West Germany (Bundesrepublik Deutschland), have hitherto refused to grant recognition to East Germany, partly as a protest against the character and composition of a satellite Communist government controlled from Moscow, and partly as a protest against the continued partition of Germany. The Soviet Union, on the other hand, is pressing, and would probably make concessions in other fields, for the international recognition of East Germany, so as to consolidate the *status quo* in Central and Eastern Europe.

Legally, the international status of Germany differs from that of China, in that the former State of Germany no longer exists — except in the theory of eventual reunification. Both the West and East German Republics are new States. They developed out of the breakdown of the joint Allied military government of the whole of Germany, through the Allied Control Council in Berlin. Both the Soviet Union and the Western Powers accuse each other of having prevented the reunification of Germany in accordance with the Yalta and Potsdam

Agreements. The fact remains that both groups of occupying Powers proceeded to develop their occupation zones into new States, acting as entirely separate units and behaving like other States with an effective machinery of government, a territory and a population. The main difference is that the West German Government can claim to be based on a genuinely democratic constitution, whereas the East German Government would not expose itself to free elections. That West Germany has about three times the population of East Germany is not, of course, a relevant factor. Legally, the refusal to recognize East Germany could be based only on the above-mentioned political motivation: that it is not democratic and representative. This recalls the abortive theory of President Wilson with regard to the non-recognition of revolutionary regimes in Latin America, but is in contradiction with the recognition of many Communist and other totalitarian governments by the Western world. As in the case of Communist China, with every year that passes, the reality of a Communist-governed State of East Germany is likely to become more firmly established, and the continued refusal of recognition is likely to become more and more an empty gesture — since war is not contemplated as a means of reunifying Germany. Since public opinion in West Germany emphatically and almost unanimously rejects even a discussion of recognition of the East German regime, the present stalemate is, however, likely to continue indefinitely. The Soviet Union recognized the West German State and Government some years ago, but diplomatic relations between West Germany and the Communist satellite States have not yet been established.

Non-recognition has not meant absence of contacts. There are consular and economic relations between the two German States, which conclude trade as well as other agreements. There are strong arguments in favour of the theory that a gradual extension of these contacts — even though it may stop short of full diplomatic recognition — might have a stronger impact on the political situation in East Germany than the present policy. A by-product of the present West German official policy towards East Germany is the so-called 'Hallstein doctrine' under which West Germany refuses to establish or maintain diplomatic relations with any State that grants diplomatic recognition to East Germany. A few years ago this led to the breaking off by West Germany of diplomatic relations with Yugoslavia, an action whose political as well as economic wisdom is open to grave doubt.

The status of Germany is further complicated by the extraordinary position of Berlin, which is also partitioned into two entirely separate political and administrative units. The status of West Berlin — an enclave in Communist territory which has something like associate membership of the West German Federation, is guaranteed by the presence of Allied troops based on post-war agreements, predicated on the assumption of a united Germany controlled by a Four-Power Allied government pending the re-establishment of a democratic all-German government. The Soviet Union has repeatedly proposed internationalization of West Berlin only, under U.N. supervision, a proposal that is unacceptable to the West. If internationalization could be extended to the entire city — which would mean removal of the physical partition — and a reunified Berlin were guaranteed free access to both West and East Germany, the objections of the Western Powers would have less force, since Berlin as a whole, or divided, is not likely to become again the capital of Germany in the foreseeable future. There is, however, little prospect of such an agreement, which would mean for East Germany the abandonment of its capital, and for West Germany an indirect recognition of the partition of Germany.

A by-product of this policy is the inability of West Germany to join the United Nations, since the U.S.S.R. will veto admission in the Security Council unless East Germany is also admitted. While admission to the United Nations is not identical with recognition by individual member-States, the latter would probably have to go with the former. Given the near-universal character of the United Nations, and the extremely mixed political composition of its members, more would probably be gained by having both Germanies in the United Nations than to have both of them outside.

APPENDIX II

VITAL STATISTICS[1]

1. *Production Figures*

A. *Coal Production*

(1,000 metric tons, 1961)

	Coal.	Lignite.[2]
Belgium . .	21,539	—
Czechoslovakia .	26,382	65,302
France . .	52,358	2,906
India . . .	56,065	64
Japan . . .	54,484	1,309
Poland . .	106,606	10,338
United Kingdom[3] .	193,521	—
United States .	378,664	2,738
U.S.S.R. . .	377,019	153,516
West Germany and Saar . .	143,615[4]	97,267[5]

[1] *Source: United Nations Statistical Yearbook 1962*, except where otherwise indicated.

[2] Lignite and brown coal are inferior fuels generally about one-third the heating value of coal. Many countries, such as the United States of America, the United Kingdom, France, Japan, India and Belgium, produce virtually none.

[3] Great Britain only. Excluding coal produced at quarries, but including open-cast coal.

[4] Low-grade coal has been included at its hard-coal equivalent.

[5] Excluding *pechkohle*, the production of which varied from 1 to 2 million metric tons annually.

B. *World Steel*[1] *Production*, 1961

(1,000 metric tons, crude)

Australia[2]	3,939
Austria	3,101
Belgium	7,001
Canada	5,866
China	15,000[3]
Eastern Europe[4]	26,900
France	17,572
India	4,071
Italy	9,124
Japan	28,268
Luxembourg	4,113
Mexico[2]	1,728
Netherlands	1,971
South Africa	2,475
Spain	2,111
Sweden	3,530
U.S.S.R.	70,700
United Kingdom	22,440
United States	88,917
West Germany (incl. Saar)	33,458
Yugoslavia	1,532

[1] Steel ingots and steel for castings.
[2] Ingots only.
[3] *Source:* U.S. Bureau of Mines.
[4] Czechoslovakia, East Germany (ingots only), Hungary, Poland, Roumania.

C. *World Petroleum Reserves*,[1] 1963

(estimated in billions of barrels)

Middle East	207,368,000
United States and Canada	39,947,000
U.S.S.R. and other Communist States	29,500,000
(of which U.S.S.R.)	28,000,000
Total Western Hemisphere	64,252,000
Africa	16,375,500
Asia-Pacific	11,621,200
Europe	1,925,600

[1] *Source: Oil and Gas Journal*, December 30, 1963.

D. *World Petroleum Production*, 1963[1]

(thousands of barrels per day)

Algeria	502
Argentina	262
Canada	717
Indonesia	452
Iran	1,470
Iraq	1,120
Kuwait	1,930
Libya	470
Mexico	320
Saudi Arabia	1,618
U.S.S.R.	4,200
United States	7,537
Venezuela	3,246

[1] *Source: Oil and Gas Journal*, December 30, 1963.

E. *Natural Gas Production*

(millions of cubic metres, 1961[1])

Canada	18,293
Italy	6,863
Mexico	10,210[2]
Roumania	11,141[2]
U.S.S.R.	58,981
United States	380,391

[1] Provisional.
[2] Including gas repressured and wasted.

F. *Electric Power Production*[1]

(million kWh., 1962)

United States	946,933	West Germany	129,629
U.S.S.R.	347,000	France	83,100
United Kingdom	151,846	Italy	63,965
Canada	117,003	Sweden	39,499
Japan	136,758		

[1] *Source: The World Almanac*, 1964.

G. *Copper Production*

(1,000 metric tons, 1961)

United States . .	1,341	ex-Belgian Congo . .	295
Chile	502	West Germany . .	185
Canada . . .	364	Mexico	48
Northern Rhodesia. .	569	Japan	74

H. *Wool Production*

(1,000 metric tons, 1961–62[1])

Argentina . .	187
Australia . .	771
New Zealand .	266
South Africa .	151[2]
U.S.S.R. . .	345
United States .	144

[1] Provisional.
[2] Including Basutoland and South-west Africa.

I. *Lead Production*

(1,000 metric tons, 1961)

	Lead ore[1]	Smelter production
United States . .	238	745
Australia . . .	274	214
Mexico . . .	181	176
Canada . . .	209	156
Belgium . . .	—	100
West Germany .	50	141
France . . .	19	89

[1] Lead content.

J. *Rubber Production*

(1,000 metric tons, 1961)

Natural:	
Malaya[1]	749
Indonesia	682
Thailand[2]	185
Ceylon	98
North Borneo, Sarawak	72
Cambodia and Vietnam	119
Liberia[2]	43
Synthetic:	
United States	1,427
Canada	167

[1] Including Colony of Singapore.
[2] Net exports.

K. *Production of Motor Vehicles*[1]

(1961)

United States[2]	6,676,700
United Kingdom	1,464,200
U.S.S.R.	682,400
Canada	390,900
France	1,201,700
West Germany[3]	2,147,000
Japan[4]	1,038,502
Italy	759,400

[1] Excluding off-the-road vehicles, such as industrial and farm tractors and other construction machinery, as well as three-wheeled commercial vehicles.
[2] Factory sales. [3] Including the Saar.
[4] Including three-wheeled motor vehicles.

L. *Cement Production*

(1,000 metric tons, 1961)

United States	56,718
United Kingdom	14,376
U.S.S.R.	50,900
West Germany	27,144
France	15,685
Belgium[1]	4,754
Canada	5,483
Japan	24,632
Poland	7,364

[1] Excluding natural cement.

M. *Major Producers of Cereals*
(1,000 metric tons, 1961[1])

Wheat.

Country.	Amount.
U.S.S.R.	66,257
United States	33,603
China	31,294[2]
Canada	7,713
Argentina	5,100
Australia	6,703
India	10,992
Italy	8,292
Pakistan	3,847
France	9,574
Turkey	7,135
Spain	3,438

Rice.

Country.	Amount.
China	85,000[3]
India	51,223
Pakistan	16,118
Japan	15,524
Burma	6,589
Thailand	7,845
Indonesia	12,810[3]
South Korea	3,706
Philippines	3,909
Brazil	5,313[3]
United States	2,433

Rye.

Country.	Amount.
U.S.S.R.	16,324[3]
Germany (East)	1,504
(West) and Saar	2,512
Poland	8,356
Czechoslovakia	994
United States	692
Argentina	510
Canada	166

Maize (corn).

Country.	Amount.
United States	92,061
China	21,440[4]
Argentina	5,220
Roumania	5,740
U.S.S.R.	24,062
Yugoslavia	4,550

[1] Provisional. [2] 1959. [3] 1960. [4] 1957.

Note: In the more advanced countries, with a highly commercialized and mechanized agriculture, a large proportion of grain is fed to animals. In the Soviet Union the major part of grain produced is for direct human consumption, whereas in the United States grain forms a smaller proportion of human diet, and between 72% and 81% by weight is normally used for animal fodder.

2. *Selected Population Figures* (*The Economist Diary*), 1962

North America

Canada	18,600,000
Mexico	37,233,000
United States	186,591,000

South America

Argentina	21,079,000[1]
Brazil	75,271,000
Chile	8,001,000
Colombia	14,769,000
Peru	10,365,000[1]
Venezuela	7,872,000

[1] Mid-1961.

Communist Europe

Albania	1,660,000[1]
Bulgaria	7,943,000[1]
Czechoslovakia	13,856,000
East Germany	17,125,000[2]
Hungary	10,060,000
Poland	30,324,000
Roumania	18,567,000[1]
U.S.S.R.	221,465,000
Yugoslavia	18,841,000

Western Europe

Austria	7,081,000[1]
France	47,025,000
West Germany	56,946,000[3]
Greece	8,451,000
Italy	49,821,000
Spain	31,300,000[4]
Turkey	29,418,000
United Kingdom	53,301,000

[1] Mid-1961.
[2] Including East Berlin.
[3] Including West Berlin.
[4] Includes the Balearic and Canary Islands.

The Middle East

Iran	21,227,000
Iraq	7,263,000[1]
Israel	2,292,000
Jordan	1,690,000[2, 3]
Lebanon	1,646,000[4, 5]
Saudi Arabia	6,036,000[6]
Syria	4,555,000[7, 8]
United Arab Republic	26,593,000[1]

[1] Mid-1961.
[2] End 1961.
[3] Including 630,725 registered Palestinian refugees.
[4] Mid-1960.
[5] Excluding 136,561 registered Palestinian refugees.
[6] January 1, 1956.
[7] End 1960.
[8] Excluding 129,086 registered Palestinian refugees.

The Far East (mid-1961)

Burma	21,257,000
Cambodia	5,749,000[1]
Ceylon	10,167,000
China	686,400,000[2]
India	442,257,000
Indonesia	95,655,000
Japan	94,930,000[4]
Korea, North	8,430,000[3]
Korea, South	25,375,000
Laos	1,850,000
Malaya	8,824,000
Pakistan	96,558,000[4]
Philippines	28,727,000
Taiwan	10,971,000
Thailand	27,181,000
Vietnam, North	16,690,000[3]
Vietnam, South	14,494,000

[1] Mid-1962. [2] Mid-1960.
[3] Estimate. [4] 1962.

French-Speaking Africa

36,463,000

English-Speaking East Africa

(Kenya, Tanganyika, Uganda, Zanzibar)
23,846,000

Rhodesia–Nyasaland

9,380,000

Africa (mid-1961)

Algeria	10,784,000[1]
Congo (Leopoldville)	14,464,000
Ethiopia	21,000,000[2]
Morocco	11,925,000
Nigeria	36,473,000[3]
South Africa	16,236,000
Sudan	12,109,000
Tunisia	4,254,000

[1] Mid-1960. [2] Mid-1962.
[3] 1962. Recent Nigerian estimates give figures around 50 million.

3. *Recent Developments in Trade Between Eastern (Communist) and Western (non-Communist) European Countries*[1]

The General Level of Trade

Unit and year.	*Imports into Western Europe.*	*Exports from Western Europe.*
Current value (millions of dollars, imports c.i.f., exports f.o.b.)		
1950	801	643
1952	995	739
1959	2,062	1,709
1960	2,380	2,118
1961	2,510	2,302

Sources and methods: Calculated from the national trade statistics of Western European countries and O.E.E.C. statistics. For details of methods used, see 'Notes to statistics' in the *Economic Bulletin for Europe*, Vol. 12, No. 2.

[1] *Source: Economic Bulletin for Europe*, Volume 14, No. 1, September 1962.

The Share of Eastern Europe (including the Soviet Union) in the Total Trade of Western European Countries

Percentages

Country or area	Imports c.i.f.		Exports f.o.b.	
	1960	1961	1960	1961
(A)				
Belgium–Luxembourg	1·9	2·0	2·5	2·4
France	2·5	2·5	3·2	3·2
West Germany[1]	3·7	3·8	3·8	3·8
Italy	5·6	5·9	4·7	5·1
Netherlands	2·2	2·1	1·6	1·8
(A) Total E.E.C.	3·2	3·3	3·3	3·4

Sources: O.E.C.D. *Statistical Bulletins — Foreign Trade*, Series A.

[1] Including trade with East Germany.

The Share of Eastern Europe (including the Soviet Union) in the Total Trade of Western European Countries—contd.

Percentages

Country or area	Imports c.i.f.		Exports f.o.b.	
	1960	1961	1960	1961
(B)				
Austria	11·2	10·4	13·7	14·6
Denmark	4·3	4·2	3·8	3·1
Norway	3·1	3·0	4·4	4·0
Portugal	1·4	1·2	2·2	1·4
Sweden	4·2	4·4	4·3	4·2
Switzerland	2·2	2·3	3·3	3·2
United Kingdom[1]	3·0	3·5	2·1	2·9
(B) Total EFTA	3·7	3·9	3·5	3·8
(C)				
Finland	20·2	18·9	18·8	17·5
Greece	7·9	7·1	22·1	23·4
Iceland	22·8	23·0	23·1	14·1
Ireland	1·1	1·7	0·1	0·1
Spain	1·6	1·2	2·5	2·1
Turkey	9·1	7·7	12·2	8·6
Yugoslavia	25·6	18·6	32·2	30·2
(C) Total	12·5	10·0	14·8	13·4
TOTAL Western Europe	4·1	4·1	4·1	4·2

Sources: O.E.C.D. *Statistical Bulletins—Foreign Trade*, Series A; and national statistics for Finland.

[1] Special exports.

Share of Western World in Trade of Countries Joined in Council for Mutual Economic Assistance (C.M.E.A.)[1]

Between 1955 and 1962, the total foreign trade of C.M.E.A. countries rose from 14,100 million to 28,600 million roubles, with reciprocal trade between members increasing from 8,600 million to 18,500 million roubles.

Trade between C.M.E.A. members and the industrially developed capitalistic countries increased from 2,700 million roubles in 1955 to 5,500 million roubles in 1962. Trade between C.M.E.A. members and the newly developing States of Asia, Africa and Latin America exceeded 2,400 million roubles in 1962 and was nearly three times greater than in 1955.

[1] *Source: International Affairs*, published in Moscow, February 1964.

Notes

'A major problem preventing a faster expansion of east–west European trade continued to be — even more than in 1960 — the inability of the eastern European countries to earn enough western foreign exchange to cover both their growing imports of western European goods (mainly capital goods) and the deficits incurred with certain primary-producing countries requiring payment in western currencies. The continuation throughout 1961 of the trend already observed in 1960 for western Europe's exports to eastern Europe to grow faster than its imports from that region demonstrates that no solution to this problem has yet been found. Thus the long-standing western European trade deficit vis-à-vis eastern Europe — which had amounted to more than 17 per cent of imports in 1959 — shrank to little more than 8 per cent last year, and was less than 5 per cent if British re-exports are included. Indeed, if both western European imports and exports were calculated on a comparable f.o.b. basis the deficit might be seen to have disappeared, or to have been converted into a small export surplus. . . .

'When east–west European trade is broken down by broad commodity groups, the most striking changes between 1960 and 1961 are, first, the much higher share of foodstuffs in western European imports, reflecting enlarged imports of cereals and sugar in particular, and, second, the tendency for machinery to account for a steadily increasing share of western European exports.'[1]

From the summary of a report by a Committee of the Consultative Assembly of the Council of Europe, *Forward in Europe*, October 1963:

> 'There is no doubt that a commercial demand exists on both sides for increased trade. But behind this lies an essentially political problem. What are the advantages and disadvantages of trading with Communist countries?
>
> 'In the West, the price of any commercial product is usually a fair reflection of manufacturers' costs, together with a profit margin which cannot be too great if the producer is to remain in business. In Eastern Europe however, goods can be produced and sold at whatever price the state judges best, since there is no normal commercial competition. Thus, goods can be marketed at prices lower than their actual production costs if this fits in with the state's trading policy. The loss on any one item can always be made up in another way, either by direct or indirect taxation or by artificially increased prices for other goods.
>
> 'The contrast between these systems shows that it is impossible, for the present, to imagine a free trade area embracing both Western and Eastern Europe. Even the granting of quotas must be carefully examined to ensure that goods are not dumped in the West at an artificially low price level.

[1] Excerpts from *Economic Bulletin for Europe*, Volume 14, No. 1, September 1962, pp. 59, 61.

'Those members of the Committee who oppose the expansion of East–West trade hold that it remedies weaknesses and inefficiencies of production and supply in the Communist bloc. Such trade merely strengthens the economic and political basis of Communist regimes while in no way improving the living conditions of the ordinary people. Others who favour the expansion of East–West trade argue, on the contrary, that their opponents exaggerate the disadvantages. Western European states should be careful not to become too dependent on the Soviet bloc for any particular commodity. There should be a tightly controlled system of joint Western decisions on trade in strategic goods. It might also be wise to increase trade with the Communist countries to upset the renewed political centralisation under Moscow's control that is likely to accompany COMECON's new policy of achieving self-sufficiency within the Communist bloc. In addition the growth of East–West trade could promote contacts between the peoples of Eastern and Western Europe and might also extend Western political influence. Finally the whole Committee is agreed that the bilateral barter arrangements with Eastern European countries should be replaced by the adoption of a common Western European policy on East–West trade.'

4. *Trade between United Kingdom and Major Commonwealth Countries, 1962*

	£ million.
United Kingdom Exports to:	
Commonwealth countries and Irish Republic . . .	1,343·0
Other countries	2,448·8
United Kingdom Imports from:	
Commonwealth countries and Irish Republic . . .	1,697·2
Other countries	2,794·8

United Kingdom Trade with	Exports to (£ million).	Imports from (£ million).
Australia	231	185
Canada	194	349
Ceylon	25	42
India	118	136
New Zealand	148	103
Pakistan	44	29
Rhodesia and Nyasaland	42	96
Nigeria	65	73
Malaya and Singapore	87	45

Source: Economist Diary, 1964.

5. *World Trade*, 1962

(billions of United States dollars)

	Exports.	Imports.
World (Total)[1]	124·000	132·000
Sterling Area	26·300	29·700
(Of which United Kingdom)	11·058	12·576
North America (total)	27·875	24·338
(Of which United States)	21·644	17·971
(Of which Canada)	6·231	6·367
Latin America (total)	10·200[2]	10·200[2]
Western Europe	47·382	53·834
Asia	12·700	16·000
Middle East (including North-east Africa)	5·900	4·700
Africa	5·700	6·700
Oceania. (Australia and New Zealand)	3·300	3·600

Source: Economist Diary, 1964.

[1] Excludes China (mainland), U.S.S.R. and countries of Eastern Europe.
[2] Excludes Cuba.

6. *Economic Assistance to Less-Developed Countries*

A. *Flow of Assistance from Twelve Countries Joined in Development Assistan* (*O.E.C.D.*), 1962 (*Disbursements*)

(U.S

	BELGIUM	CANADA	DENMARK
A. *Total official and private, net* (B + C)	n.a.	n.a.	12·4
B. *Total official, net*	96·9	50·3	8·5
Total official bilateral, net	68·6	37·4	0·7
I. Grants	65·6	22·2	0·8
of which: Reparations and indemnification payments	—	—	—
II. Loans repayable in recipients' currencies, net[4, 5]	—	—	—
III. Transfer of resources through sales for recipients' currencies (net of resources realized by donor country by use of these currencies)	—	—	—
IV. Loans for more than 5 years, net[5]	3·0	15·2	—0·1
1. Loans for more than 5 years, gross	4·0	20·4	—
a) Loans for 20 years or more	—	—	—
b) Loans for more than 10, up to 20 years	—	5·5	—
c) Loans for more than 5, up to 10 years	4·0	14·8	—
2. Amortization received	1·0	5·2	0·1
V. Contribution to multilateral agencies, net	28·3	12·8[6]	7·8
a) Grants and capital subscription payments	28·3	12·8	7·9
b) Purchases of bonds, loans and participations	—	—	—0·1
C. *Flow of Private Capital, net*	n.a.	n.a.	3·9
I. Direct investment and other new lending	n.a.	n.a.	2·6
1. Direct investment (including reinvested earnings)	n.a.	n.a.	2·6
of which: reinvested earnings	n.a.	n.a.	n.a.
2. Other private capital and portfolio investment	n.a.	n.a.	—
II. Guaranteed private export credits for more than 5 years	23·3	—	1·3
III. Portfolio investment in multilateral agencies, net	—1·9	8·6	—

[1] Preliminary data based on official estimates.

[2] Totals include Secretariat estimate of French guaranteed private export credit

[3] Totals include Secretariat estimate of Belgian, Canadian and Portuguese privat investment.

[4] Net of amortization representing resource transfer in other than recipient currencies.

[5] Excludes assistance extended in recipients' currencies.

[6] Does not include $7 million maintenance of United States dollar value pay ments on I.D.A. and I.B.R.D. subscriptions.

ouncil (D.A.C.) *of the Organization for Economic Co-operation and Development*

illions)

FRANCE[1]	GERMANY (WEST)	ITALY	JAPAN	NETHERLANDS	NORWAY	PORTUGAL	UNITED KINGDOM	UNITED STATES	TOTAL D.A.C. COUNTRIES
(1,380·5)	681·4	278·0	281·9	(140·5)	3·1	n.a.	(836·7)	(4,520)	(8,400)[2,3]
995·9	426·9	66·4	165·1	85·7	1·5	37·3	416·7	3,606	5,957
879·2	324·6	34·9	158·0	42·0	1·3	37·2	377·2	3,328	5,289
771·7	107·7	34·5	74·6	37·8	1·3	3·1	214·7	1,339	2,673
—	70·0	20·2	66·8	—	—	—	—	—	157
—	—	—	—	—	—	—	—	435	435
—	1·5	—	—	—	—	—	—	869	871
107·5	215·4	0·4	83·4	4·3	−0·1	34·1	162·5	684	1,310
146·2	244·8	14·9	115·1	5·2	—	34·2	187·3	926	1,698
38·7	29·3	—	—	5·2	—	31·3	152·9	329	586
78·3	179·9	—	18·9	—	—	1·6	2·5	457	744
29·2	35·6	14·9	96·2	—	—	1·3	31·9	140	368
38·7	29·4	14·5	31·7	0·9	0·1	0·2	24·8	242	389
116·7	102·3	31·5	7·1	43·7	0·2	0·1	39·5	278	668
115·7	105·3	19·0	8·6	43·7	6·0	0·1	39·5	278	665
1·0	−3·0	12·5	−1·5	—	−5·8	—	—	—	3
(384·6)	254·5	211·6	116·8	(54·8)	1·6	n.a.	(420·0)	(914)	(2,443)[2,3]
284·6	150·5	169·5	82·4	(27·5)	1·6	n.a.	(399·1)	(719)	(1,932)
n.a.s.	92·6	143·3	68·4	−12·2	0·8[7]	n.a.	(399·1)	(517)	(1,289)
n.a.s.	44·0	n.a.s.	n.a.	n.a.	n.a.	n.a.	n.a.s.	(336)	n.a.s.
n.a.s.	57·9	26·2	14·0	39·7	0·8	17·4	n.a.	202	(358)
n.a.	104·4	24·2	33·7	16·0	—	—	13·7	35	(297)[2]
11·0	−0·4	17·9	0·7	11·3	—	—	7·2	160	214

Preliminary figure, based on incomplete information.

Minor discrepancies in totals are due to rounding.

Signs used: ( ) preliminary figure

n.a. not available

n.a.s. included in total, but not available separately.

— nil or negligible

rce: Organization for Economic Co-operation and Development 1963.

view of *Development Assistance Efforts and Policies.*

B. *Economic Assistance from Communist Countries*[1] (*Comecon, C.M.E.A.*)

According to official Soviet sources, the total trade between C.M.E.A. countries and developing States in Asia, Africa and Latin America trebled between 1955 and 1962, exceeding 2,400 million roubles in 1962. C.M.E.A. gave economic and technical aid in the construction of 1,100 industrial projects and enterprises in forty undeveloped countries. The country distribution of these projects was as follows:

United Arab Republic	178
India	166
Indonesia	50
Syria	48
Mali	17
Brazil	10
Argentina	9
Morocco	6

Note: Soviet and C.M.E.A. (Comecon) statistics, as far as available, are much less detailed than O.E.C.D. statistics and capable of different interpretations. In particular, it would appear from the figures and the many accompanying articles and speeches that the U.S.S.R. and other Communist countries regard trade with developing countries as the principal form of economic aid. Generally this means that the C.M.E.A. countries will sell industrial plants and technical assistance in exchange for certain staple commodities and other products, usually by way of bilateral agreements between the governments concerned. The 'aid' element consists of credits which, according to Soviet statistics, are generally given at an interest rate of 2½%, for periods ranging from five to fifteen years. In addition, the U.S.S.R. and other C.M.E.A. countries appear to have made occasional gifts such as hospital equipment to developing countries. The U.S.S.R. also contributes a modest amount to the technical assistance programme of the United Nations.

[1] *Source: International Affairs*, Moscow, February 1964.

APPENDIX III

SELECTED DOCUMENTS

I. International Organizations and Treaties (political and military)
1. Charter of the United Nations (Articles 1–54)
2. North Atlantic Treaty
3. Warsaw Pact
4. South-East Asia Collective Defence Treaty
5. Charter of the Organization of American States
6. Inter-American Treaty of Reciprocal Assistance
7. Charter of the Organization of African Unity

II. Economic Organizations and Treaties
1. European Community Treaties
2. Council for Mutual Economic Assistance
3. General Agreement on Tariffs and Trade

III. Functional International Agencies
1. Constitution of the Food and Agriculture Organization
2. Articles of Agreement of the International Bank for Reconstruction and Development.

I. INTERNATIONAL ORGANIZATIONS AND TREATIES (POLITICAL AND MILITARY)

1. CHARTER OF THE UNITED NATIONS (Excerpts)

Chapter I

Purposes and Principles

Article 1

The Purposes of the United Nations are:

1. To maintain international peace and security, and to that end: to take effective collective measures for the prevention and removal of threats to the peace, and for the suppression of acts of aggression or other breaches of the peace, and to bring about by peaceful means, and in conformity with the principles of justice and international law,

justment or settlement of international disputes or situations which might lead to a breach of the peace;

2. To develop friendly relations among nations based on respect for the principle of equal rights and self-determination of peoples, and to take other appropriate measures to strengthen universal peace;

3. To achieve international co-operation in solving international problems of an economic, social, cultural, or humanitarian character, and in promoting and encouraging respect for human rights and for fundamental freedoms for all without distinction as to race, sex, language or religion; and

4. To be a centre for harmonizing the actions of nations in the attainment of these common ends.

Article 2

The Organization and its Members, in pursuit of the Purposes stated in Article 1, shall act in accordance with the following Principles:

1. The Organization is based on the principle of the sovereign equality of all its Members.

2. All Members, in order to ensure to all of them the rights and benefits resulting from membership, shall fulfil in good faith the obligations assumed by them in accordance with the present Charter.

3. All Members shall settle their international disputes by peaceful means in such a manner that international peace and security, and justice, are not endangered.

4. All Members shall refrain in their international relations from the threat or use of force against the territorial integrity or political independence of any state, or in any other manner inconsistent with the Purposes of the United Nations.

5. All Members shall give the United Nations every assistance in any action it takes in accordance with the present Charter, and shall refrain from giving assistance to any state against which the United Nations is taking preventive or enforcement action.

6. The Organization shall ensure that states which are not Members of the United Nations act in accordance with these Principles so far as may be necessary for the maintenance of international peace and security.

7. Nothing contained in the present Charter shall authorize the United Nations to intervene in matters which are essentially within the domestic jurisdiction of any state or shall require the Members to submit such matters to settlement under the present Charter; but this principle shall not prejudice the application of enforcement measures under Chapter VII.

Chapter II

Membership

Article 3

The original Members of the United Nations shall be the states which, having participated in the United Nations Conference on International Organization at San Francisco, or having previously signed the Declaration by United Nations of 1 January 1942, sign the present Charter and ratify it in accordance with Article 110.

Article 4

1. Membership in the United Nations is open to all other peace-loving states which accept the obligations in the present Charter and, in the judgment of the Organization, are able and willing to carry out these obligations.

2. The admission of any such state to membership in the United Nations will be effected by a decision of the General Assembly upon the recommendation of the Security Council.

Article 5

A Member of the United Nations against which preventive or enforcement action has been taken by the Security Council may be suspended from the exercise of the rights and privileges of membership by the General Assembly upon the recommendation of the Security Council. The exercise of these rights and privileges may be restored by the Security Council.

Article 6

A Member of the United Nations which has persistently violated the Principles contained in the present Charter may be expelled from the Organization by the General Assembly upon the recommendation of the Security Council.

Chapter III

Organs

Article 7

1. There are established as the principal organs of the United Nations: a General Assembly, a Security Council, an Economic and

Social Council, a Trusteeship Council, an International Court of Justice and a Secretariat.

2. Such subsidiary organs as may be found necessary may be established in accordance with the present Charter.

Article 8

The United Nations shall place no restrictions on the eligibility of men and women to participate in any capacity and under conditions of equality in its principal and subsidiary organs.

Chapter IV

The General Assembly

Composition

Article 9

1. The General Assembly shall consist of all the Members of the United Nations.

2. Each Member shall have not more than five representatives in the General Assembly.

Functions and Powers

Article 10

The General Assembly may discuss any questions on any matters within the scope of the present Charter or relating to the powers and functions of any organs provided for in the present Charter, and, except as provided in Article 12, may make recommendations to the Members of the United Nations or to the Security Council or to both on any such questions or matters.

Article 11

1. The General Assembly may consider the general principles of co-operation in the maintenance of international peace and security, including the principles governing disarmament and the regulation of armaments, and may make recommendations with regard to such principles to the Members or to the Security Council or to both.

2. The General Assembly may discuss any questions relating to the maintenance of international peace and security brought before it by any Member of the United Nations, or by the Security Council, or by a state which is not a Member of the United Nations in accordance with Article 35, paragraph 2, and, except as provided in Article 12,

may make recommendations with regard to any such questions to the state or states concerned or to the Security Council or to both. Any such question on which action is necessary shall be referred to the Security Council by the General Assembly either before or after discussion.

Article 12

1. While the Security Council is exercising in respect of any dispute or situation the functions assigned to it in the present Charter, the General Assembly shall not make any recommendations with regard to that dispute or situation unless the Security Council so requests.

2. The Secretary-General, with the consent of the Security Council, shall notify the General Assembly at each session of any matters relative to the maintenance of international peace and security which are being dealt with by the Security Council and shall similarly notify the General Assembly, or the Members of the United Nations if the General Assembly is not in session, immediately the Security Council ceases to deal with such matters.

Article 13

1. The General Assembly shall initiate studies and make recommendations for the purpose of:

(*a*) promoting international co-operation in the political field and encouraging the progressive development of international law and its codification;

(*b*) promoting international co-operation in the economic, social, cultural, educational, and health fields, and assisting in the realization of human rights and fundamental freedoms for all without distinction as to race, sex, language or religion.

2. The further responsibilities, functions and powers of the General Assembly with respect to matters mentioned in paragraph 1 (*b*) above are set forth in Chapters IX and X.

Article 14

Subject to the provisions of Article 12, the General Assembly may recommend measures for the peaceful adjustment of any situation, regardless of origin, which seems likely to impair the general welfare or friendly relations among nations, including situations resulting from a violation of the provisions of the present Charter setting forth the Purposes and Principles of the United Nations.

Article 15

1. The General Assembly shall receive and consider annual and special reports from the Security Council; these reports shall include

an account of the measures that the Security Council has decided upon or taken to maintain international peace and security.

2. The General Assembly shall receive and consider reports from the other organs of the United Nations.

Article 18

1. Each member of the General Assembly shall have one vote.

2. Decisions of the General Assembly on important questions shall be made by a two-thirds majority of the members present and voting. These questions shall include: recommendations with respect to the maintenance of international peace and security, the election of the non-permanent members of the Security Council, the election of the members of the Economic and Social Council, the election of members of the Trusteeship Council in accordance with paragraph 1 (*c*) of Article 86, the admission of new Members to the United Nations, the suspension of the rights and privileges of membership, the expulsion of Members, questions relating to the operation of the trusteeship system, and budgetary questions.

3. Decisions on other questions, including the determination of additional categories of questions to be decided by a two-thirds majority, shall be made by a majority of the members present and voting.

Article 23

1. The Security Council shall consist of eleven Members of the United Nations. The Republic of China, France, the Union of Soviet Socialist Republics, the United Kingdom of Great Britain and Northern Ireland, and the United States of America shall be permanent members of the Security Council. The General Assembly shall elect six other Members of the United Nations to be non-permanent members of the Security Council, due regard being specially paid, in the first instance to the contribution of Members of the United Nations to the maintenance of international peace and security and to the other purposes of the Organization, and also to equitable geographical distribution.

2. The non-permanent members of the Security Council shall be elected for a term of two years. In the first election of the non-permanent members, however, three shall be chosen for a term of one year. A retiring member shall not be eligible for immediate re-election.

3. Each member of the Security Council shall have one representative.

Article 24

1. In order to ensure prompt and effective action by the United Nations, its Members confer on the Security Council primary responsibility for the maintenance of international peace and security, and

agree that in carrying out its duties under this responsibility the Security Council acts on their behalf.

2. In discharging these duties the Security Council shall act in accordance with the Purposes and Principles of the United Nations. The specific powers granted to the Security Council for the discharge of these duties are laid down in Chapters VI, VII, VIII and XII.

3. The Security Council shall submit annual and, when necessary, special reports to the General Assembly for its consideration.

Article 25

The members of the United Nations agree to accept and carry out the decisions of the Security Council in accordance with the present Charter.

Article 26

In order to promote the establishment and maintenance of international peace and security with the least diversion for armaments of the world's human and economic resources, the Security Council shall be responsible for formulating, with the assistance of the Military Staff Committee referred to in Article 47, plans to be submitted to the Members of the United Nations for the establishment of a system for the regulation of armaments.

Article 27

1. Each member of the Security Council shall have one vote.

2. Decisions of the Security Council on procedural matters shall be made by an affirmative vote of seven members.

3. Decisions of the Security Council on all other matters shall be made by an affirmative vote of seven members, including the concurring votes of the permanent members; provided that, in decisions under Chapter VI, and under paragraph 3 of Article 52, a party to a dispute shall abstain from voting.

Article 33

1. The parties to any dispute, the continuance of which is likely to endanger the maintenance of international peace and security, shall, first of all, seek a solution by negotiation, enquiry, mediation, conciliation, arbitration, judicial settlement, resort to regional agencies or arrangements, or other peaceful means of their own choice.

2. The Security Council shall, when it deems necessary, call upon the parties to settle their dispute by such means.

Article 34

The Security Council may investigate any dispute, or any situation which might lead to international friction or give rise to a dispute, in order to determine whether the continuance of the dispute or situation is likely to endanger the maintenance of international peace and security.

Article 35

1. Any Member of the United Nations may bring any dispute, or any situation of the nature referred to in Article 34, to the attention of the Security Council or of the General Assembly.

2. A state which is not a Member of the United Nations may bring to the attention of the Security Council or of the General Assembly any dispute to which it is a party if it accepts in advance, for the purposes of the dispute, the obligations of pacific settlement provided in the present Charter.

3. The proceedings of the General Assembly in respect of matters brought to its attention under this Article will be subject to the provisions of Articles 11 and 12.

Article 36

1. The Security Council may, at any stage of a dispute of the nature referred to in Article 33 or of a situation of like nature, recommend appropriate procedures or methods of adjustment.

2. The Security Council should take into consideration any procedures for the settlement of the dispute which have already been adopted by the parties.

3. In making recommendations under this Article the Security Council should also take into consideration that legal disputes should as a general rule be referred by the parties to the International Court of Justice in accordance with the provisions of the Statute of the Court.

Article 37

1. Should the parties to a dispute of the nature referred to in Article 33 fail to settle it by the means indicated in that Article, they shall refer it to the Security Council.

2. If the Security Council deems that the continuance of the dispute is in fact likely to endanger the maintenance of international peace and security, it shall decide whether to take action under Article 36 or to recommend such terms of settlement as it may consider appropriate.

Article 38

Without prejudice to the provisions of Articles 33 to 37, the Security Council may, if all the parties to any dispute so request, make recommendations to the parties with a view to a pacific settlement of the dispute.

Article 39

The Security Council shall determine the existence of any threat to the peace, breach of the peace, or act of aggression and shall make recommendations, or decide what measures shall be taken in accordance with Articles 41 and 42, to maintain or restore international peace and security.

Article 40

In order to prevent an aggravation of the situation, the Security Council may, before making the recommendations or deciding upon the measures provided for in Article 39, call upon the parties concerned to comply with such provisional measures as it deems necessary or desirable. Such provisional measures shall be without prejudice to the rights, claims, or position of the parties concerned. The Security Council shall duly take account of failure to comply with such provisional measures.

Article 41

The Security Council may decide what measures not involving the use of armed force are to be employed to give effect to its decisions, and it may call upon the Members of the United Nations to apply such measures. These may include complete or partial interruption of economic relations and of rail, sea, air, postal, telegraphic, radio, and other means of communication, and the severance of diplomatic relations.

Article 42

Should the Security Council consider that measures provided for in Article 41 would be inadequate or have proved to be inadequate, it may take such action by air, sea or land forces as may be necessary to maintain or restore international peace and security. Such action may include demonstrations, blockade and other operations by air, sea or land forces of Members of the United Nations.

Article 43

1. All Members of the United Nations, in order to contribute to the maintenance of international peace and security, undertake to make available to the Security Council, on its call and in accordance with a

special agreement or agreements, armed forces, assistance and facilities, including rights of passage, necessary for the purpose of maintaining international peace and security.

2. Such agreement or agreements shall govern the numbers and types of forces, their degree of readiness and general location, and the nature of the facilities and assistance to be provided.

3. The agreement or agreements shall be negotiated as soon as possible on the initiative of the Security Council. They shall be concluded between the Security Council and Members or between the Security Council and groups of Members and shall be subject to ratification by the signatory states in accordance with their respective constitutional processes.

Article 44

When the Security Council has decided to use force it shall, before calling upon a Member not represented on it to provide armed forces in fulfilment of the obligations assumed under Article 43, invite that Member, if the Member so desires, to participate in the decisions of the Security Council concerning the employment of contingents of that Member's armed forces.

Article 45

In order to enable the United Nations to take urgent military measures, Members shall hold immediately available national air-force contingents for combined international enforcement action. The strength and degree of readiness of these contingents and plans for their combined action shall be determined, within the limits laid down in the special agreement or agreements referred to in Article 43, by the Security Council with the assistance of the Military Staff Committee.

Article 46

Plans for the application of armed force shall be made by the Security Council with the assistance of the Military Staff Committee.

Article 47

1. There shall be established a Military Staff Committee to advise and assist the Security Council on all questions relating to the Security Council's military requirements for the maintenance of international peace and security, the employment and command of forces placed at its disposal, the regulation of armaments and possible disarmament.

2. The Military Staff Committee shall consist of the Chiefs of Staff of the permanent members of the Security Council or their repre-

sentatives. Any Member of the United Nations not permanently represented on the Committee shall be invited by the Committee to be associated with it when the efficient discharge of the Committee's responsibilities requires the participation of that Member in its work.

3. The Military Staff Committee shall be responsible under the Security Council for the strategic direction of any armed forces placed at the disposal of the Security Council. Questions relating to the command of such forces shall be worked out subsequently.

4. The Military Staff Committee, with the authorization of the Security Council and after consultation with appropriate regional agencies, may establish regional sub-committees.

Article 48

1. The action required to carry out the decisions of the Security Council for the maintenance of international peace and security shall be taken by all the Members of the United Nations or by some of them, as the Security Council may determine.

2. Such decisions shall be carried out by the Members of the United Nations directly and through their action in the appropriate international agencies of which they are members.

Article 49

The Members of the United Nations shall join in affording mutual assistance in carrying out the measures decided upon by the Security Council.

Article 50

If preventive or enforcement measures against any state are taken by the Security Council, any other state, whether a Member of the United Nations or not, which finds itself confronted with special economic problems arising from the carrying out of those measures shall have the right to consult the Security Council with regard to a solution of those problems.

Article 51

Nothing in the present Charter shall impair the inherent right of individual or collective self-defence if an armed attack occurs against a Member of the United Nations, until the Security Council has taken the measures necessary to maintain international peace and security. Measures taken by Members in the exercise of this right of self-defence shall be immediately reported to the Security Council and shall not in any way affect the authority and responsibility of the Security Council under the present Charter to take at any time such action as it deems necessary in order to maintain or restore international peace and security.

Article 52

1. Nothing in the present Charter precludes the existence of regional arrangements or agencies for dealing with such matters relating to the maintenance of international peace and security as are appropriate for regional action, provided that such arrangements or agencies and their activities are consistent with the Purposes and Principles of the United Nations.

2. The Members of the United Nations entering into such arrangements or constituting such agencies shall make every effort to achieve pacific settlement of local disputes through such regional arrangements or by such regional agencies before referring them to the Security Council.

3. The Security Council shall encourage the development of pacific settlement of local disputes through such regional arrangements or by such regional agencies either on the initiative of the states concerned or by reference from the Security Council.

4. This Article in no way impairs the application of Articles 34 and 35.

Article 53

1. The Security Council shall, where appropriate, utilize such regional arrangements or agencies for enforcement action under its authority. But no enforcement action shall be taken under regional arrangements or by regional agencies without the authorization of the Security Council, with the exception of measures against any enemy state, as defined in paragraph 2 of this Article, provided for pursuant to Article 107 or in regional arrangements directed against renewal of aggressive policy on the part of any such state, until such time as the Organization may, on request of the Governments concerned, be charged with the responsibility for preventing further aggression by such a state.

2. The term enemy state as used in paragraph 1 of this Article applies to any state which during the Second World War has been an enemy of any signatory of the present Charter.

Article 54

The Security Council shall at all times be kept fully informed of activities undertaken or in contemplation under regional arrangements or by regional agencies for the maintenance of international peace and security.

2. NORTH ATLANTIC TREATY

March 18, 1949[1]

The Parties to this Treaty reaffirm their faith in the purposes and principles of the Charter of the United Nations and their desire to live in peace with all peoples and all Governments.

They are determined to safeguard the freedom, common heritage and civilization of their peoples founded on the principles of democracy, individual liberty and the rule of law. They seek to promote stability and well-being in the North Atlantic area. They are resolved to unite their efforts for collective defence for the preservation of peace and security. They therefore agree to this North Atlantic Treaty.

Article 1

The parties undertake, as set forth in the Charter of the United Nations, to settle any international disputes in which they may be involved by peaceful means in such a manner that international peace and security and justice are not endangered and to refrain in their international relations from the threat or use of force in any manner inconsistent with the purposes of the United Nations.

Article 2

The Parties will contribute toward the further development of peaceful and friendly international relations by strengthening their free institutions, by bringing about a better understanding of the principles upon which these institutions are founded and by promoting conditions of stability and well-being. They will seek to eliminate conflict in their international economic policies and will encourage economic collaboration between any or all of them.

Article 3

In order more effectively to achieve the objectives of this Treaty the Parties separately and jointly by means of continuous and effective self-help and mutual aid will maintain and develop their individual and collective capacity to resist armed attack.

[1] Signatories: Belgium, Canada, Denmark, France, Iceland, Italy, Luxembourg, Netherlands, Norway, Portugal, United Kingdom, United States. Greece and Turkey joined by a Protocol signed on October 22, 1951, which modifies Article 6 so as to include the territory of Turkey and the Mediterranean Sea. West Germany joined in 1955.

Article 4

The Parties will consult together whenever in the opinion of any of them the territorial integrity, political independence or security of any of the Parties is threatened.

Article 5

The Parties agree that an armed attack against one or more of them in Europe or North America shall be considered an attack against them all and consequently they agree that if such an armed attack occurs each of them in exercise of the right of individual or collective self-defence recognized by Article 51 of the Charter of the United Nations will assist the Party or Parties so attacked by taking forthwith individually and in concert with the other Parties such action as it deems necessary including the use of armed force to restore and maintain the security of the North Atlantic area.

Any such armed attack and all measures taken as a result thereof shall be immediately reported to the Security Council. Such measures shall be terminated when the Security Council has taken the measures necessary to restore and maintain international peace and security.

Article 6

For the purpose of Article 5 an armed attack on one or more of the Parties is deemed to include an armed attack on the territory of any of the Parties in Europe or North America, on the Algerian departments of France, on the occupation forces of any Party in Europe, on the islands under the jurisdiction of any Party in the North Atlantic Area north of the Tropic of Cancer, or on the vessels or aircraft in this area of any of the Parties.

Article 7

This treaty does not affect and shall not be interpreted as affecting in any way the rights and obligations under the Charter of the Parties which are members of the United Nations or the primary responsibility of the Security Council for the maintenance of international peace and security.

Article 8

Each Party declares that none of the international engagements now in force between it and any other of the Parties or any third State is in conflict with the provisions of this Treaty and undertakes not to enter into any international engagement in conflict with this Treaty.

Article 9

The Parties hereby establish a Council on which each of them shall be represented to consider matters concerning the implementation of this Treaty. The Council shall be so organized as to be able to meet promptly at any time. The Council shall set up such subsidiary bodies as may be necessary; in particular it shall establish immediately a Defence Committee which shall recommend measures for the implementation of Articles 3 and 5.

Article 10

The Parties may by unanimous agreement invite any other European State in a position to further the principles of this Treaty and to contribute to the security of the North Atlantic area to accede to this Treaty. Any State so invited may become a Party to the Treaty by depositing its instrument of accession with the Government of the United States of America. The Government of the United States of America will inform each of the Parties of the deposit of each such instrument of accession.

Article 11

This Treaty shall be ratified and its provisions carried out by the Parties in accordance with their respective constitutional processes.

The instruments of ratification shall be deposited as soon as possible with the Government of the United States of America, which will notify all the other signatories of each deposit. The Treaty shall enter into force between the States which have ratified it as soon as the ratifications of the majority of the signatories including the ratifications of Belgium, Canada, France, Luxembourg, the Netherlands, the United Kingdom and the United States have been deposited, and shall come into effect with respect to other States on the date of the deposit of their ratifications.

Article 12

After the Treaty has been in force for ten years or at any time thereafter, the Parties shall, if any of them so request, consult together for the purpose of reviewing the Treaty, having regard for the factors then affecting peace and security in the North Atlantic area, including the development of universal as well as regional arrangements under the Charter of the United Nations for the maintenance of international peace and security.

Article 13

After the Treaty has been in force for twenty years any Party may cease to be a Party one year after its notice of denunciation has been given to the Government of the United States of America which will inform the Governments of the other Parties of the deposit of each notice of denunciation.

Article 14

This Treaty, of which the English and French texts are equally authentic, shall be deposited in the archives of the Government of the United States of America. Duly certified copies thereof will be transmitted by that Government to the Governments of each of the other signatories.

3. WARSAW PACT AND UNIFIED COMMAND ACCORD (May 14, 1955)

The Communiqué

In accordance with the pact of friendship, co-operation and mutual assistance between the People's Republic of Albania, the People's Republic of Bulgaria, the Hungarian People's Republic, the German Democratic Republic, the Polish People's Republic, the Rumanian People's Republic, the Union of Soviet Socialist Republics and the Czechoslovak Republic, the signatory States have decided to set up a unified command of Armed Forces.

This decision provides that general questions relating to the strengthening of the defence capacity and the organization of united Armed Forces of the participating countries are to be examined by the political and consultative communities, which will take appropriate decisions.

The Commander-in-Chief of the united Armed Forces contributed by the participating States is appointed in the person of Marshal of the Soviet Union Konev.

The deputies to the Commander-in-Chief of the united Armed Forces are appointed in the persons of the ministers of defence and military leaders of the participating States, who are to command the Armed Forces of each participating country contributing to the strength of the unified Armed Forces.

The question of the participation of the German Democratic Republic in measures regarding the Armed Forces of the unified command is to be examined later.

The Commander-in-Chief of the united Armed Forces is to set up a headquarters of the unified command of the participating countries, which is to include the permanent representatives of the general staffs of the participating countries.

The headquarters is to be located in Moscow.

The location of the united Armed Forces on the territories of the participating States is to be decided in accordance with the needs of mutual defence by agreement between these States.

The Treaty

The contracting parties

Confirm once again their striving for the creation of a system of collective security in Europe based on the participation of all European States, irrespective of their social or state structure, which would make it possible to unite their efforts in the interest of ensuring peace in Europe.

Taking into consideration at the same time the situation which has arisen in Europe as the result of the ratification of the Paris agreements envisaging the formation of a new military alignment in the form of the West European Union with the participation of Western Germany, which is being remilitarized, and her inclusion in the North Atlantic bloc, which increases the danger of a new war and creates a threat to the national security of peace-loving States;

Being convinced of the fact that in these circumstances peace-loving States in Europe must take measures necessary to safeguard their security and in the interests of preserving peace in Europe;

Guided by the aims and principles of the United Nations Charter, in the interests of the further strengthening and developing of friendship, collaboration and mutual assistance in accordance with the principles of respecting the independence and sovereignty of the States and non-interference in their internal affairs;

Have decided to conclude the present treaty of friendship, collaboration and mutual assistance, and have appointed as their representatives: [Names follow]

Who, representing their countries, agreed to the following:

Article 1

The high contracting parties undertake, in accordance with the United Nations Charter, to abstain in their international relations from threats of violence or its use and to settle international disputes by peaceful means, so as not to put each other or international peace in danger.

Article 2

The contracting parties declare their readiness to co-operate in all international actions with the purpose of ensuring international peace and security.

With that, the contracting parties will strive to reach agreement with States desiring to co-operate in that cause and take measures to reduce armaments and the ban of atomic, hydrogen and other kinds of weapons of mass destruction.

Article 3

The contracting parties will consult mutually on all important international problems affecting their common interests, taking as their guide the interests of strengthening international peace and security.

They will immediately consult each time in the event of a threat of armed attack against one or several States, signatories to the pact, in the interest of insuring their mutual defence and of maintaining peace and security.

Article 4

In case of armed aggression in Europe against one or several states party to the pact by a State or group of States, each state member of the pact, in order to put into practice the right to individual or collective self-defence, in accordance with Article 51 of the United Nations Charter, will afford to the State or States which are the objects of such an aggression immediate assistance, individually and in agreement with other States, party to the pact, with all means which appear necessary, including the use of armed force.

The parties to the pact will immediately take joint measures necessary to establish and preserve international peace and security.

Measures taken on the basis of this article will assist security in accordance with the United Nations Charter.

These measures will be stopped as soon as the Security Council takes measures necessary for establishing and preserving international peace and security.

Article 5

The contracting powers agree to set up a joint command of their Armed Forces to be allotted by agreement between the powers, at the disposal of this command and used on the basis of jointly established principles.

They will also take other agreed measures necessary to strengthen their defences in order to protect the peaceful toil of their peoples, guarantee the integrity of their frontiers and territories and ensure their defence against possible aggression.

Article 6

With the object of carrying out consultations provided by the present treaty between the States participating in the treaty and for the examination of questions arising in connection with the fulfilment of this treaty, a political consultative committee is being set up in which each State participating in the treaty will be represented by a member of its Government or another specially appointed representative.

The committee may set up any auxiliary organs it considers necessary.

Article 7

The contracting parties undertake not to enter into any coalitions or unions and not to enter into any agreements whose aims are contrary to the terms of this treaty.

The contracting parties declare that their obligations under existing international agreements are not contrary to the terms of the present treaty.

Article 8

The contracting parties declare that they will act in a spirit of friendship and co-operation in order further to develop the economic and cultural ties between them, and will be guided by principles of mutual respect and will not interfere in the internal affairs of each other.

Article 9

The present treaty is open to other States, irrespective of their social or Government regime, who declare their readiness to abide by the terms of this treaty in order to safeguard peace and security of the peoples.

The joining of this treaty by such countries will come into force in agreement with the States party to the treaty, after it has been handed over to the Government of Poland for safekeeping.

Article 10

The present treaty is subject to ratification, and the ratification instruments will be handed to Poland for safekeeping. It will come into force on the day the instruments are handed over to the Polish Government.

The Government of the Polish People's Republic will inform the other State signatories of the treaty when each ratification instrument is handed over.

Article 11

The present treaty will remain in force for twenty years. Those States which do not give notice of abrogation one year before the treaty expires will remain bound by it for a further ten years.

In the event of a system of collective security being set up in Europe and a pact to this effect being signed — to which each party to this treaty will direct its efforts — the present treaty will lapse from the day such a collective security treaty comes into force.

Drawn up in Warsaw May 14, 1955, in one copy each in Russian, Polish, Czech and German, each text being equally valid.

Attested copies of this treaty will be sent to the Governments of each party to the treaty by the Government of the Polish People's Republic.

In witness whereof the plenipotentiary representatives affixed their signatures and seal.

4. SOUTH-EAST ASIA COLLECTIVE DEFENCE TREATY

Eight Western and Asian governments on September 8, 1954, signed in Manila a South-East Asia security pact. The signatories were the United States, Britain, France, Australia, New Zealand, Thailand, Pakistan and the Philippines. India and other Asian neutralist countries refused to participate in the Manila conference.

The parties to this treaty,

Recognizing the sovereign equality of all the parties,

Reiterating their faith in the purposes and principles set forth in the Charter of the United Nations and their desire to live in peace with all peoples and all governments,

Reaffirming that, in accordance with the Charter of the United Nations, they uphold the principle of equal rights and self-determination of peoples, and declaring that they will earnestly strive by every peaceful means to promote self-government and to secure the independence of all countries whose peoples desire it and are able to undertake its responsibilities,

Intending to declare publicly and formally their sense of unity, so that any potential aggressor will appreciate that the parties stand together in the area, and

Desiring further to co-ordinate their efforts for collective defence for the preservation of peace and security,

Therefore agree as follows:

Article 1

The parties undertake, as set forth in the Charter of the United Nations, to settle any international disputes in which they may be involved by peaceful means in such a manner that international peace and security and justice are not endangered, and to refrain in their international relations from the threat or use of force in any manner inconsistent with the purposes of the United Nations.

Article 2

In order more effectively to achieve the objectives of this treaty, the parties separately and jointly, by means of continuous and effective self-help and mutual aid, will maintain and develop their individual and collective capacity to resist armed attack and to prevent and counter subversive activities directed from without against their territorial integrity and political stability.

Article 3

The parties undertake to strengthen their free institutions and to co-operate with one another in the further development of economic measures, including technical assistance, designed both to promote economic progress and social well-being and to further the individual and collective efforts of governments toward these ends.

Article 4

1. Each party recognizes that aggression by means of armed attack in the treaty area against any of the parties or against any State or territory which the parties by unanimous agreement may hereafter designate, would endanger its own peace and safety, and agrees that it will in that event act to meet the common danger in accordance with its constitutional processes. Measures taken under this paragraph shall be immediately reported to the Security Council of the United Nations.

2. If, in the opinion of any of the parties, the inviolability or the integrity of the territory or the sovereignty or political independence of any party in the treaty area or of any other State or territory to which the provisions of Paragraph 1 of this Article from time to time apply is threatened in any way other than by armed attack or is affected or threatened by any fact or situation which might endanger the peace of the area, the parties shall consult immediately in order to agree on the measures which should be taken for the common defence.

3. It is understood that no action on the territory of any State designated by unanimous agreement under Paragraph 1 of this Article or on any territory so designated shall be taken except at the invitation or with the consent of the government concerned.

Article 5

The parties hereby establish a Council, on which each of them shall be represented, to consider matters concerning the implementation of this Treaty. The Council shall provide for consultation with regard to military and any other planning as the situation obtaining in the Treaty area may from time to time require. The Council shall be so organized as to be able to meet at any time.

Article 6

This Treaty does not affect and shall not be interpreted as affecting in any way the rights and obligations of any of the parties under the Charter of the United Nations or the responsibility of the United Nations for the maintenance of international peace and security. Each party declares that none of the international engagements now in force between it and any other of the parties or any third party is in conflict with the provisions of this Treaty, and undertakes not to enter into any international engagement in conflict with this Treaty.

Article 7

Any other State in a position to further the objectives of this Treaty and to contribute to the security of the area may, by unanimous agreement of the parties, be invited to accede to this Treaty. Any State so invited may become a party to the Treaty by depositing its instrument of accession with the Government of the Republic of the Philippines. The Government of the Republic of the Philippines shall inform each of the parties of the deposit of each such instrument of accession.

Article 8

As used in this Treaty, the 'treaty area' is the general area of South-East Asia, including also the entire territories of the Asian parties, and the general area of the South-West Pacific not including the Pacific area north of 21 degrees 30 minutes North Latitude. The parties may, by unanimous agreement, amend this Article to include within the treaty area the territory of any State acceding to this Treaty in accordance with Article 7 or otherwise to change the treaty area.

Article 9

1. This Treaty shall be deposited in the archives of the Government of the Republic of the Philippines. Duly certified copies thereof shall be transmitted by that Government to the other signatories.

2. The Treaty shall be ratified and its provisions carried out by the parties in accordance with their respective constitutional processes. The instruments of ratification shall be deposited as soon as possible with the Government of the Republic of the Philippines, which shall notify all of the other signatories of such deposit.

3. The Treaty shall enter into force between the States which have ratified it as soon as the instruments of ratification of a majority of the signatories shall have been deposited, and shall come into effect with respect to each other State on the date of the deposit of its instrument of ratification.

Article 10

This Treaty shall remain in force indefinitely, but any party may cease to be a party one year after its notice of denunciation has been given to the Government of the Republic of the Philippines, which shall inform the governments of the other parties of the deposit of each notice of denunciation.

Article 11

The English text of this treaty is binding on the parties, but when the parties have agreed to the French text thereof and have so notified the Government of the Republic of the Philippines, the French text shall be equally authentic and binding on the parties.

Understanding of the United States of America

The delegation of the United States of America in signing the present treaty does so with the understanding that its recognition of the effect of aggression and armed attack and its agreement with reference thereto in Article 4, paragraph 1, apply only to communist aggression but affirms that in the event of other aggression or armed attack it will consult under the provisions of Article 4, paragraph 2.

In witness whereof, the undersigned plenipotentiaries have signed this treaty.

Done at Manila, this eighth day of September, 1954.

Protocol

Designation of States and territory as to which provisions of Article 4 and Article 3 are to be applicable:

The parties to the South-East Asia collective defence treaty unanimously designate for the purposes of Article 4 of the treaty the States of Cambodia and Laos and the Free Territory under the jurisdiction of the State of Viet-Nam.

The parties further agree that the above-mentioned states and territory shall be eligible in respect of the economic measures contemplated by Article 3.

This protocol shall come into force simultaneously with the coming into force of the treaty.

In witness whereof, the undersigned plenipotentiaries have signed this protocol to the South-East Asia Collective Defence Treaty.

Done at Manila, this eighth day of September, 1954.

5. CHARTER OF THE ORGANIZATION OF AMERICAN STATES (1948)

(Excerpts)

PART ONE

Chapter I

Nature and Purposes

Article 1

The American States establish by this Charter the international organization that they have developed to achieve an order of peace and justice, to promote their solidarity, to strengthen their collaboration, and to defend their sovereignty, their territorial integrity, and their independence. Within the United Nations, the Organization of American States is a regional agency.

Article 2

All American States that ratify the present Charter are Members of the Organization.

Article 3

Any new political entity that arises from the union of several Member States and that, as such, ratifies the present Charter, shall become a Member of the Organization. The entry of the new political entity into the Organization shall result in the loss of membership of each one of the States which constitute it.

Article 4

The Organization of American States, in order to put into practice the principles on which it is founded and to fulfil its regional obligations under the Charter of the United Nations, proclaims the following essential purposes:

(*a*) To strengthen the peace and security of the continent;
(*b*) to prevent possible causes of difficulties and to ensure the pacific settlement of disputes that may arise among the Member States;
(*c*) to provide for common action on the part of those States in the event of aggression;
(*d*) to seek the solution of political, juridical and economic problems that may arise among them; and
(*e*) to promote, by co-operative action, their economic, social and cultural development.

Chapter II

Principles

Article 5

(*a*) International law is the standard of conduct of States in their reciprocal relations;
(*b*) international order consists essentially of respect for the personality, sovereignty and independence of States, and the faithful fulfilment of obligations derived from treaties and other sources of international law;
(*c*) good faith shall govern the relations between States;
(*d*) the solidarity of the American States and the high aims which are sought through it require the political organization of those States on the basis of the effective exercise of representative democracy;
(*e*) the American States condemn war of aggression: Victory does not give rights;
(*f*) an act of aggression against one American State is an act of aggression against all the other American States;
(*g*) controversies of an international character arising between two or more American States shall be settled by peaceful procedures;
(*h*) social justice and social security are bases of lasting peace;
(*i*) economic co-operation is essential to the common welfare and prosperity of the peoples of the continent;
(*j*) the American States proclaim the fundamental rights of the individual without distinction as to race, nationality, creed or sex;
(*k*) the spiritual unity of the continent is based on respect for the cultural values of the American countries and requires their close co-operation for the high purposes of civilization;
(*l*) the education of peoples should be directed towards justice, freedom and peace.

Chapter III

Fundamental Rights and Duties of States

Article 6

States are juridically equal, enjoy equal rights and equal capacity to exercise these rights, and have equal duties. The rights of each State depend not upon its power to ensure the exercise thereof, but upon the mere fact of its existence as a person under international law.

Article 7

Every American State has the duty to respect the rights enjoyed by every other State in accordance with international law.

Article 8

The fundamental rights of States may not be impaired in any manner whatsoever.

Article 9

The political existence of the State is independent of recognition by other States. Even before being recognized, the State has the right to defend its integrity and independence, to provide for its preservation and prosperity, and consequently to organize itself as it sees fit, to legislate concerning its interests, to administer its services, and to determine the jurisdiction and competence of its courts. The exercise of these rights is limited only by the exercise of the rights of other States in accordance with international law.

Article 10

Recognition implies that the State granting it accepts the personality of the new State, with all the rights and duties that international law prescribes for the two States.

Article 11

The right of each State to protect itself and to live its own life does not authorize it to commit unjust acts against another State.

Article 12

The jurisdiction of States within the limits of their national territory is exercised equally over all the inhabitants, whether nationals or aliens.

Article 13

Each State has the right to develop its cultural, political and economic life freely and naturally. In this free development, the State shall respect the rights of the individual and the principles of universal morality.

Article 14

Respect for and the faithful observance of treaties constitute standards for the development of peaceful relations among States. International treaties and agreements should be public.

Article 15

No State or group of States has the right to intervene, directly or indirectly, for any reason whatever in the internal or external affairs of any other State. The foregoing principle prohibits not only armed force but also any other form of interference or attempted threat against the personality of the State or against its political, economic and cultural elements.

Article 16

No State may use or encourage the use of coercive measures of an economic or political character in order to force the sovereign will of another State and obtain from it advantages of any kind.

Article 17

The territory of a State is inviolable; it may not be the object, even temporarily, of military occupation or of other measures of force taken by another State, directly or indirectly, on any grounds whatever. No territorial acquisitions or special advantages obtained either by force or by other means of coercion shall be recognized.

Article 18

The American States bind themselves in their international relations not to have recourse to the use of force, except in the case of self-defence in accordance with existing treaties or in fulfilment thereof.

Article 19

Measures adopted for the maintenance of peace and security in accordance with existing treaties do not constitute a violation of the principles set forth in Articles 15 and 17.

Chapter IV

Pacific Settlement of Disputes

Article 20

All international disputes that may arise between American States shall be submitted to the peaceful procedures set forth in this Charter, before being referred to the Security Council of the United Nations.

Article 21

The following are peaceful procedures: direct negotiation, good offices, mediation, investigation and conciliation, judicial settlement, arbitration and those which the parties to the dispute may especially agree upon at any time.

Article 22

In the event that a dispute arises between two or more American States which, in the opinion of one of them, cannot be settled through the usual diplomatic channels, the Parties shall agree on some other peaceful procedure that will enable them to reach a solution.

Article 23

A special treaty will establish adequate procedures for the pacific settlement of disputes and will determine the appropriate means for their application, so that no dispute between American States shall fail of definitive settlement within a reasonable period.

Chapter V

Collective Security

Article 24

Every act of aggression by a State against the territorial integrity or the inviolability of the territory or against the sovereignty or political independence of an American State shall be considered an act of aggression against the other American States.

Article 25

If the inviolability or the integrity of the territory or the sovereignty or political independence of any American State should be affected by an armed attack or by an act of aggression that is not an armed attack, or by an extracontinental conflict, or by a conflict between two or more American States, or by any other fact or situation that might endanger the peace of America, the American States, in furtherance of the principles of continental solidarity or collective self-defence, shall apply the measures and procedures established in the special treaties on the subject.

PART TWO

Chapter IX

The Organs

Article 32

The Organization of American States accomplishes its purposes by means of: (*a*) The Inter-American Conference; (*b*) The Meeting of Consultation of Ministers of Foreign Affairs; (*c*) The Council; (*d*) The Pan American Union; (*e*) The Specialized Conferences; and (*f*) The Specialized Organizations.

Chapter X

The Inter-American Conference

Article 33

The Inter-American Conference is the supreme organ of the Organization of American States. It decides the general action and policy of the Organization and determines the structure and functions of its Organs, and has the authority to consider any matter relating to friendly relations among the American States. These functions shall be carried out in accordance with the provisions of this Charter and of other inter-American treaties.

Article 34

All Member States have the right to be represented at the Inter-American Conference. Each State has the right to one vote.

Article 35

The Conference shall convene every five years at the time fixed by the Council of the Organization, after consultation with the Government of the country where the Conference is to be held.

Article 36

In special circumstances and with the approval of two-thirds of the American Governments, a special Inter-American Conference may be held or the date of the next regular Conference may be changed.

Article 37

Each Inter-American Conference shall designate the place of meeting of the next Conference. If for any unforeseen reason the Conference cannot be held at the place designated, the Council of the Organization shall designate a new place.

Article 38

The programme and regulations of the Inter-American Conference shall be prepared by the Council of the Organization and submitted to the Member States for consideration.

Chapter XI

The Meeting of Consultation of Ministers of Foreign Affairs

Article 39

The Meeting of Consultation of Ministers of Foreign Affairs shall be held in order to consider problems of an urgent nature and of common interest to the American States, and to serve as the Organ of Consultation.

Article 40

Any Member State may request that a Meeting of Consultation be called. The request shall be addressed to the Council of the Organization, which shall decide by an absolute majority whether a meeting should be held.

Article 41

The programme and regulations of the Meeting of Consultation shall be prepared by the Council of the Organization and submitted to the Member States for consideration.

Article 42

If, for exceptional reasons, a Minister of Foreign Affairs is unable to attend the meeting, he shall be represented by a special delegate.

Article 43

In case of an armed attack within the territory of an American State or within the region of security delimited by treaties in force, a Meeting of Consultation shall be held without delay. Such Meeting shall be called immediately by the Chairman of the Council of the Organization, who shall at the same time call a meeting of the Council itself.

Article 44

An Advisory Defence Committee shall be established to advise the Organ of Consultation on problems of military co-operation that may arise in connection with the application of existing special treaties on collective security.

Article 45

The Advisory Defence Committee shall be composed of the highest military authorities of the American States participating in the Meeting of Consultation. Under exceptional circumstances the Governments may appoint substitutes. Each State shall be entitled to one vote.

Article 46

The Advisory Defence Committee shall be convoked under the same conditions as the Organ of Consultation, when the latter deals with matters relating to defence against aggression.

Article 47

The Committee shall also meet when the Conference or the Meeting of Consultation or the Governments, by a two-thirds majority of the Member States, assign to it technical studies or reports on specific subjects.

Chapter XII

The Council

Article 48

The Council of the Organization of American States is composed of one Representative of each Member State of the Organization especially appointed by the respective Government, with the rank of Ambassador. The appointment may be given to the diplomatic representative accredited to the Government of the country in which the Council has its seat. During the absence of the titular Representative, the Government may appoint an interim Representative.

Article 49

The Council shall elect a Chairman and a Vice-Chairman, who shall serve for one year and shall not be eligible for election to either of those positions for the term immediately following.

Article 50

The Council takes cognizance, within the limits of the present Charter and of inter-American treaties and agreements, of any matter referred to it by the Inter-American Conference or the Meeting of Consultation of Ministers of Foreign Affairs.

Article 51

The Council shall be responsible for the proper discharge by the Pan American Union of the duties assigned to it.

Article 52

The Council shall serve provisionally as the Organ of Consultation when the circumstances contemplated in Article 43 of this Charter arise.

Article 53

It is also the duty of the Council:

(*a*) to draft and submit to the Governments and to the Inter-American Conference proposals for the creation of new Specialized Organizations or for the combination, adaptation or elimination of existing ones, including matters relating to the financing and support thereof;

(*b*) to draft recommendations to the Governments, the Inter-American Conference, the Specialized Conferences or the Specialized Organizations, for the co-ordination of the activities and programmes of such organizations, after consultation with them;

(*c*) to conclude agreements with the Inter-American Specialized Organizations to determine the relations that shall exist between the respective agency and the Organization;

(*d*) to conclude agreements or special arrangements for co-operation with other American organizations of recognized international standing;

(*e*) to promote and facilitate collaboration between the Organization of American States and the United Nations, as well as between Inter-American Specialized Organizations and similar international agencies;

(*f*) to adopt resolutions that will enable the Secretary-General to perform the duties envisaged in Article 84;

(*g*) to perform the other duties assigned to it by the present Charter.

Article 54

The Council shall establish the bases for fixing the quota that each Government is to contribute to the maintenance of the Pan American Union, taking into account the ability to pay of the respective countries and their determination to contribute in an equitable manner. The budget, after approval by the Council, shall be transmitted to the Governments at least six months before the first day of the fiscal year, with a statement of the annual quota of each country. Decisions on budgetary matters require the approval of two-thirds of the members of the Council.

Article 55

The Council shall formulate its own regulations.

Article 56

The Council shall function at the seat of the Pan American Union.

Article 57

The following are organs of the Council of the Organization of American States: (*a*) The Inter-American Economic and Social Council; (*b*) The Inter-American Council of Jurists; and (*c*) The Inter-American Cultural Council.

Article 58

The organs referred to in the preceding article shall have technical autonomy within the limits of this Charter; but their decisions shall not encroach upon the sphere of action of the Council of the Organization.

Article 59

The organs of the Council of the Organization are composed of Representatives of all the Member States of the Organization.

Article 60

The organs of the Council of the Organization shall, as far as possible, render to the Governments such technical services as the latter may request; and they shall advise the Council of the Organization on matters within their jurisdiction.

Article 61

The organs of the Council of the Organization shall, in agreement with the Council, establish co-operative relations with the corresponding organs of the United Nations and with the national or international agencies that function within their respective spheres of action.

Article 62

The Council of the Organization, with the advice of the appropriate bodies and after consultation with the Governments, shall formulate the statutes of its organs in accordance with and in the execution of the provisions of this Charter. The organs shall formulate their own regulations.

Chapter XIII

The Pan American Union

Article 78

The Pan American Union is the central and permanent organ of the Organization of American States and the General Secretariat of the Organization. It shall perform the duties assigned to it in this Charter and such other duties as may be assigned to it in other inter-American treaties and agreements.

Article 79

There shall be a Secretary-General of the Organization, who shall be elected by the Council for a ten-year term and who may not be re-elected or be succeeded by a person of the same nationality. In the event of a vacancy in the office of Secretary-General, the Council shall, within the next ninety days, elect a successor to fill the office for the remainder of the term, who may be re-elected if the vacancy occurs during the second half of the term.

Article 80

The Secretary-General shall direct the Pan American Union and be the legal representative thereof.

Article 81

The Secretary-General shall participate with voice, but without vote, in the deliberations of the Inter-American Conference, the Meeting of Consultation of Ministers of Foreign Affairs, the Specialized Conferences and the Council and its organs.

Article 82

The Pan American Union, through its technical and information offices, shall, under the direction of the Council, promote economic, social, juridical and cultural relations among all the Member States of the Organization.

Article 83

The Pan American Union shall also perform the following functions: . . .

(*c*) Place, to the extent of its ability, at the disposal of the Government of the country where a conference is to be held, the technical aid and personnel which such Government may request;
(*d*) serve as custodian of the documents and archives of the Inter-American Conference, of the Meeting of Consultation of Ministers of Foreign Affairs, and, insofar as possible, of the Specialized Conferences;
(*e*) serve as depositary of the instruments of ratification of inter-American agreements;
(*f*) perform the functions entrusted to it by the Inter-American Conference, and the Meeting of Consultation of Ministers of Foreign Affairs;
(*g*) submit to the Council an annual report on the activities of the Organization;
(*h*) submit to the Inter-American Conference a report on the work accomplished by the Organs of the Organization since the previous Conference.

Article 84

It is the duty of the Secretary-General:

(*a*) To establish, with the approval of the Council, such technical and administrative offices of the Pan American Union as are necessary to accomplish its purposes;
(*b*) to determine the number of department heads, officers and employees of the Pan American Union; to appoint them, regulate their powers and duties, and fix their compensation, in accordance with general standards established by the Council.

Article 85

There shall be an Assistant Secretary-General, elected by the Council for a term of ten years and eligible for re-election. In the event of a vacancy in the office of Assistant Secretary-General, the Council shall, within the next ninety days, elect a successor to fill such office for the remainder of the term.

Article 86

[omitted]

Article 87

The Council, by a two-thirds vote of its members, may remove the Secretary-General or the Assistant Secretary-General whenever the proper function of the Organization so demands.

Article 88

[omitted]

Article 89

In the performance of their duties the personnel shall not seek or receive instructions from any government or from any other authority outside the Pan American Union. They shall refrain from any action that might reflect upon their position as international officials responsible only to the Union.

Article 90

Every Member of the Organization of American States pledges itself to respect the exclusively international character of the responsibilities of the Secretary-General and the personnel, and not to seek to influence them in the discharge of their duties.

Article 91

In selecting its personnel the Pan American Union shall give first consideration to efficiency, competence and integrity; but at the same time importance shall be given to the necessity of recruiting personnel on as broad a geographical basis as possible.

Article 92

The seat of the Pan American Union is the city of Washington.

6. INTER-AMERICAN TREATY OF RECIPROCAL ASSISTANCE (1947)

(Excerpts)

Article 3

1. The High Contracting Parties agree that an armed attack by any State against an American State shall be considered as an attack against all the American States and, consequently, each one of the said Contracting Parties undertakes to assist in meeting the attack in the exercise of the inherent right of individual or collective self-defence recognized by Article 51 of the Charter of the United Nations.

2. On the request of the State or States directly attacked and until the decision of the Organ of Consultation of the Inter-American System, each one of the Contracting Parties may determine the immediate measures which it may individually take in fulfilment of the obligation contained in the preceding paragraph and in accordance with the principle of continental solidarity. The Organ of Consultation shall meet without delay for the purpose of examining those measures and agreeing upon the measures of a collective character that should be taken.

3. The provisions of this Article shall be applied in case of any armed attack which takes place within the region described in Article 4 or within the territory of an American State. When the attack takes place outside of the said areas, the provisions of Article 6 shall be applied.

4. Measures of self-defence provided for under this Article may be taken until the Security Council of the United Nations has taken the measures necessary to maintain international peace and security.

Article 5

The High Contracting Parties shall immediately send to the Security Council of the United Nations, in conformity with Articles 51 and 54 of the Charter of the United Nations, complete information concerning the activities undertaken or in contemplation in the exercise of the right of self-defence or for the purpose of maintaining inter-American peace and security.

Article 6

If the inviolability or the integrity of the territory or the sovereignty or political independence of any American State should be affected by an aggression which is not an armed attack or by an extracontinental or intracontinental conflict, or by any other fact or situation that might endanger the peace of America, the Organ of Consultation shall meet immediately in order to agree on the measures which must be taken in case of aggression to assist the victim of the aggression or, in any case, the measures which should be taken for the common defence and for the maintenance of the peace and security of the continent.

Article 7

In the case of a conflict between two or more American States, without prejudice to the right of self-defence in conformity with Article 51 of the Charter of the United Nations, the High Contracting Parties, meeting in consultation, shall call upon the contending States to suspend hostilities and restore matters to the *status quo ante bellum*, and shall take in addition all other necessary measures to re-establish or maintain inter-American peace and security and for the solution of the conflict by peaceful means. The rejection of the pacifying action will be considered in the determination of the aggressor and in the application of the measures which the consultative meeting may agree upon.

Article 8

For the purposes of this Treaty, the measures on which the Organ of Consultation may agree will comprise one or more of the following: recall of chiefs of diplomatic missions; breaking of diplomatic relations; breaking of consular relations; partial or complete interruption of economic relations or of rail, sea, air, postal, telegraphic, telephonic and radiotelephonic or radiotelegraphic communications; and use of armed force.

Article 9

In addition to other acts which the Organ of Consultation may characterize as aggression, the following shall be considered as such:

(*a*) Unprovoked armed attack by a State against the territory, the people, or the land, sea, or air forces of another State.
(*b*) Invasion, by the armed forces of a State, of the territory of an American State, through the trespassing of boundaries demarcated in accordance with a treaty, judicial decision or arbitral award, or, in the absence of frontiers thus demarcated, invasion affecting a region which is under the effective jurisdiction of another State.

7. CHARTER OF THE ORGANIZATION OF AFRICAN UNITY

We, the Heads of African States and Governments assembled in the city of Addis Ababa, Ethiopia;

CONVINCED that it is the inalienable right of all people to control their own destiny;

CONSCIOUS of the fact that freedom, equality, justice, and dignity are essential objectives for the achievement of the legitimate aspirations of the African peoples;

CONSCIOUS of our responsibility to harness the natural and human resources of our continent for the total advancement of our peoples in spheres of human endeavour;

INSPIRED by a common determination to strengthen understanding and co-operation among our states in response to the aspirations of our peoples for brotherhood and solidarity, in a large unity transcending ethnic and national differences;

CONVINCED that, in order to translate this determination into a dynamic force in the cause of human progress, conditions for peace and security must be established and maintained;

DETERMINED to safeguard and consolidate the hard-won independence as well as the sovereignty and territorial integrity of our states, and to fight against neo-colonialism in all its forms;

DEDICATED to the general progress of Africa;

PERSUADED that the Charter of the United Nations and the Universal Declaration of Human Rights, to the principles of which we reaffirm our adherence, provide a solid foundation for peaceful and positive co-operation among states;

DESIROUS that all African states should henceforth unite so that the welfare and well-being of their peoples can be assured;

RESOLVED to reinforce the links between our states by establishing and strengthening common institutions;

HAVE agreed to the present Charter.

Establishment

Article I

(1) The High Contracting Parties to by the present Charter establish an organization to be known as the 'Organization of African Unity'.

(2) The organization shall include the continental African states, Madagascar, and all the islands surrounding Africa.

Purposes

Article II

(1) The organization shall have the following purposes: (a) to promote the unity and solidarity of the African states; (b) to co-ordinate and intensify their co-operation and efforts to achieve a better life for the peoples of Africa; (c) to defend their sovereignty, their territorial integrity, and independence; (d) to eradicate all forms of colonialism from Africa; and (e) to promote international co-operation, having due regard to the Charter of the United Nations and the Universal Declaration of Human Rights.

(2) To these ends, the member states shall co-ordinate and harmonize their general policies, especially in the following fields: (a) political and diplomatic co-operation; (b) economic co-operation, including transport and communications; (c) educational and cultural co-operation; (d) health, sanitation and nutritional co-operation; (e) scientific and technical co-operation; and (f) co-operation for defence and security.

Principles

Article III

The member states, in pursuit of the purposes stated in Article II, solemnly affirm and declare their adherence to the following principles:

(1) the sovereign equality of all member states;
(2) non-interference in the internal affairs of states;
(3) respect for the sovereignty and territorial integrity of each member state and for its inalienable right to independent existence;
(4) peaceful settlement of disputes by negotiation, mediation, conciliation or arbitration;
(5) unreserved condemnation, in all its forms, of political assassination as well as of subversive activities on the part of neighbouring states or any other states;
(6) absolute dedication to the total emancipation of the African territories which are still dependent;
(7) affirmation of a policy of non-alignment with regard to all blocs.

Membership

Article IV

Each independent sovereign African state shall be entitled to become a member of the organization.

Rights and Duties of Member States

Article V

All member states shall enjoy equal rights and have equal duties.

Article VI

The member states pledge themselves to observe scrupulously the principles enumerated in Article III of the present Charter.

Institutions

Article VII

The organization shall accomplish its purposes through the following principal institutions:

(1) the Assembly of Heads of State and Government;
(2) the Council of Ministers;
(3) the General Secretariat;
(4) the Commission of Mediation, Conciliation and Arbitration.

The Assembly of Heads of State and Government

Article VIII

The Assembly of Heads of State and Government shall be the supreme organ of the organization. It shall, subject to the provisions of this Charter, discuss matters of common concern to Africa with a view to co-ordinating and harmonizing the general policy of the organization. It may in addition review the structure, functions and acts of all the organs and any specialized agencies which may be created in accordance with the present Charter.

Article IX

The Assembly shall be composed of the Heads of State, Government or their duly accredited representatives and it shall meet at least *once a year*. At the request of any member state, and approval by the majority of the member states, the Assembly shall meet in extraordinary session.

Article X

(1) Each member state shall have one vote.

(2) All resolutions shall be determined by a two-thirds majority of the members of the organization.

(3) Questions of procedure shall require a simple majority. Whether or not a question is one of procedure shall be determined by a simple majority of all member states of the organization.

(4) Two-thirds of the total membership of the organization shall form a quorum at any meeting of the Assembly.

Article XI

The Assembly shall have the power to determine its own rules of procedure.

The Council of Ministers

Article XII

The Council of Ministers shall consist of Foreign Ministers or such other Ministers as are designated by the Governments of member states.

The Council of Ministers shall meet at least twice a year. When requested by any member state and approved by two-thirds of all member states, it shall meet in extraordinary session.

Article XIII

The Council of Ministers shall be responsible to the Assembly of Heads of State and Government. It shall be entrusted with the responsibility of preparing conferences of the Assembly.

It shall take cognizance of any matter referred to it by the Assembly. It shall be entrusted with the implementation of the decisions of the Assembly of Heads of State and Government. It shall co-ordinate inter-African co-operation in accordance with the instructions of the Assembly and in conformity with Article II (2) of the present Charter.

Article XIV

(1) Each member state shall have one vote.

(2) All resolutions shall be determined by a simple majority of the Council of Ministers.

(3) Two-thirds of the total membership of the Council shall form a quorum for any meeting of the Council.

Article XV

The Council shall have the power to determine its own rule of procedure.

General Secretariat

Article XVI

There shall be an Administrative Secretary-General of the organization, who shall be appointed by the Assembly of Heads of State and Government, on the recommendation of the Council of Ministers. The

Administrative Secretary-General shall direct the affairs of the Secretariat.

Article XVII

There shall be one or more Assistant Secretaries-General of the organization, who shall be appointed by the Assembly of Heads of State and Government.

Article XVIII

The functions and conditions of service of the Secretary-General, of the Assistant Secretaries-General and other employees of the Secretariat shall be governed by the provisions of this Charter and the regulations approved by the Assembly of Heads of State and Government.

(1) In the performance of their duties the Administrative Secretary-General and the staff shall not seek or receive instructions from any government or from any other authority external to the organization. They shall refrain from any action which might reflect on their position as international officials responsible only to the organization.

(2) Each member of the organization undertakes to respect the exclusive character of the responsibilities of the Administrative Secretary-General and the staff and not to seek to influence them in the discharge of their responsibilities.

Commission of Mediation, Conciliation and Arbitration

Article XIX

Member states pledge to settle all disputes among themselves by peaceful means and, to this end, decide to establish a Commission of Mediation, Conciliation and Arbitration, the composition of which and the condition of service shall be defined by a separate protocol to be approved by the Assembly of Heads of State and Government.

Specialized Commissions

Article XX

The Assembly shall establish such Specialized Commissions as it may deem necessary, including the following:

(1) Economic and Social Commission;
(2) Educational and Cultural Commission;
(3) Health, Sanitation and Nutrition Commission;
(4) Defence Commission;
(5) Scientific, Technical, and Research Commission.

Article XXI

Each Specialized Commission referred to in Article XX shall be composed of the Ministers concerned or other Ministers or Plenipotentiaries designated by the Governments of the member states.

Article XXII

The functions of the Specialized Commissions shall be carried out in accordance with the provisions of the present Charter and of the regulations approved by the Council of Ministers.

The Budget

Article XXIII

The budget of the organization prepared by the Administrative Secretary-General shall be approved by the Council of Ministers. The budget shall be provided by contributions from member states in accordance with the scale of assessment of the United Nations; provided, however, that no member state shall be assessed an amount exceeding twenty per cent of the yearly regular budget of the organization. The member states agree to pay their respective contributions regularly.

Signature and Ratification of Charter

Article XXIV

This Charter shall be open for signature to all independent sovereign African states and shall be ratified by the signatory states in accordance with their respective constitutional processes.

The original instrument, done, if possible, in African languages, in English and French, all texts being equally authentic, shall be deposited with the Government of Ethiopia, which shall transmit certified copies thereof to all independent sovereign African states.

Instruments of ratification shall be deposited with the Government of Ethiopia, which shall notify all signatories of each such deposit.

Entry into Force

Article XXV

This Charter shall enter into force immediately upon receipt by the Government of Ethiopia of the instruments of ratification from two-thirds of the signatory states.

Registration of the Charter

Article XXVI

This Charter shall, after due ratification, be registered with the Secretariat of the United Nations through the Government of Ethiopia in conformity with Article 102 of the Charter of the United Nations.

Interpretation of the Charter

Article XXVII

(1) Any question which may arise concerning the interpretation of this Charter shall be decided by a vote of two-thirds of the Assembly of Heads of State and Government of the organizations.

Adhesion and Accession

Article XXVIII

(1) Any independent sovereign African State may at any time notify the Administrative Secretary-General of its intention to adhere or accede to this Charter.

(2) The Administrative Secretary-General shall, on receipt of such notification, communicate a copy of it to all the member states. Admission shall be decided by a simple majority of member states. The decision of each member state shall be transmitted to the Administrative Secretary-General, who shall, upon receipt of the required number of votes, communicate the decision to the state concerned.

Miscellaneous

Article XXIX

The working languages of the organization and all its institutions shall be, if possible, African languages, English, and French.

Article XXX

The Administrative Secretary-General may accept on behalf of the organization, gifts, bequests, and other donations made to the organization, provided that this is approved by the Council of Ministers.

Article XXXI

The Council of Ministers shall decide on the privileges and immunities to be accorded to the personnel of the Secretariat in the respective territories of the member states.

Cessation of Membership

Article XXXII

Any state which desires to renounce its membership shall forward a written notification to the Administrative Secretary-General. At the end of one year from the date of such notification, if not withdrawn, the Charter shall cease to apply with respect to the renouncing state, which shall thereby cease to belong to the organization.

Amendment to the Charter

Article XXXIII

This Charter may be amended or revised if any member state makes a written request to the Administrative Secretary-General to that effect, provided, however, that the proposed amendment is not submitted to the Assembly for consideration until all the member states have been duly notified of it and a period of one year has elapsed. Such an amendment shall not be effective unless approved by at least two-thirds of all the member states.

In faith, whereof, We, the Heads of African State and Government, have signed this Charter.

Done in the City of Addis Ababa, Ethiopia, this 25th day of May, 1963.

1. Algeria: Premier Ahmed Ben Bella
2. Burundi: King Mwambutsa
3. Cameroun: President Ahmadou Ahidjo
4. Central African Republic: President David Dacko
5. Chad: President François Tombalbaye
6. Congo-Brazzaville: President Fulbert Youlou
7. Congo-Leopoldville: President Joseph Kasavubu
8. Dahomey: President Hubert Maga
9. Ethiopia: Emperor Haile Selassie I
10. Gabon: President Léon M'Ba
11. Ghana: President Kwame Nkrumah
12. Guinea: President Sékou Touré
13. Ivory Coast: President Félix Houphouët-Boigny
14. Liberia: President William V. S. Tubman
15. Libya: King Idris I
16. Malagasy Republic: President Philibert Tsiranana
17. Mali: President Modibo Keita
18. Mauritania: President Mokhtar Ould Daddah
19. Niger: President Hamani Diori

20. Nigeria: Prime Minister Alhaji Sir Abubakar Tafawa Balewa
21. Rwanda: Foreign Minister Callixte Habamenshi for President Grégoire Kayibanda
22. Senegal: President Léopold Sédar Senghor
23. Sierra Leone: Prime Minister Sir Milton Margai
24. Somali Republic: President Aden Abdullah Osman
25. Sudan: President Ibrahim Abboud
26. Tanganyika: President Julius Nyerere
27. Tunisia: President Habib Bourguiba
28. Uganda: Prime Minister Milton Obote
29. United Arab Republic: President Gamal Abdul Nasser
30. Upper Volta: President Maurice Yaméogo

Not Present:

1. Morocco: King Hassan II
2. Togo: President Nicolas Grunitzky

II. ECONOMIC ORGANIZATIONS AND TREATIES

1. EUROPEAN COMMUNITY TREATIES[1]

(*a*) Treaty Constituting the European Coal and Steel Community

Article 1

By the present Treaty the HIGH CONTRACTING PARTIES institute among themselves a EUROPEAN COAL AND STEEL COMMUNITY, based on a common market, common objectives and common institutions.

[1] The excerpts given below from the three community treaties now in operation are chosen so as to give the basic organization and principles of each of them. It should be borne in mind that the three treaties are interrelated and that the Assembly and the Court of Justice — concerning both of which the most important provisions are reprinted under the Coal and Steel Community Treaty — are now joint institutions for all three communities. In addition, most of the provisions dealing with the High Authority of the Coal and Steel Community have been reprinted, since its executive powers differ in substantial respects from those of the commissions of the other two communities. The merger of the executive authorities of the three Communities in a single Commission is likely to take place in 1965. For an analysis of the European communities see above, pp. 199 *et seq.*

Article 2

The mission of the European Coal and Steel Community is to contribute to economic expansion, the development of employment and the improvement of the standard of living in the participating countries through the institution, in harmony with the general economy of the member States, of a common market as defined in Article 4.

The Community must progressively establish conditions which will in themselves assure the most rational distribution of production at the highest possible level of productivity, while safeguarding the continuity of employment and avoiding the creation of fundamental and persistent disturbances in the economies of the member States.

Article 3

Within the framework of their respective powers and responsibilities and in the common interest, the institutions of the Community shall:

(*a*) see that the common market is regularly supplied, taking account of the needs of third countries;
(*b*) assure to all consumers in comparable positions within the common market equal access to the sources of production;
(*c*) seek the establishment of the lowest prices which are possible without requiring any corresponding rise either in the prices charged by the same enterprises in other transactions or in the price-level as a whole in another period, while at the same time permitting necessary amortization and providing normal possibilities of remuneration for capital invested;
(*d*) see that conditions are maintained which will encourage enterprises to expand and improve their ability to produce and to promote a policy of rational development of natural resources, avoiding inconsiderate exhaustion of such resources;
(*e*) promote the improvement of the living and working conditions of the labour force in each of the industries under its jurisdiction so as to make possible the equalization of such conditions in an upward direction;
(*f*) further the development of international trade and see that equitable limits are observed in prices charged on external markets;
(*g*) promote the regular expansion and the modernization of production as well as the improvement of its quality, under conditions which preclude any protection against competing industries except where justified by illegitimate action on the part of such industries or in their favour.

Article 4

The following are recognized to be incompatible with the common market for coal and steel, and are, therefore, abolished and prohibited within the Community in the manner set forth in the present Treaty:

(*a*) import and export duties, or charges with an equivalent effect, and quantitative restrictions on the movement of coal and steel;
(*b*) measures or practices discriminating among producers, among buyers or among consumers, specifically as concerns prices, delivery terms and transportation rates, as well as measures or practices which hamper the buyer in the free choice of his supplier;
(*c*) subsidies or state assistance, or special charges imposed by the state, in any form whatsoever;
(*d*) restrictive practices tending towards the division of markets or the exploitation of the consumer.

Article 5

The Community shall accomplish its mission, under the conditions provided for in the present Treaty, with limited direct intervention.

To this end, the Community will:

. . . assist the action of the interested parties by collecting information, organizing consultations and defining general objectives;

. . . place financial means at the disposal of enterprises for their investments and participate in the expenses of readaptation;

. . . assure the establishment, the maintenance and the observance of normal conditions of competition and take direct action with respect to production and the operation of the market only when circumstances make it absolutely necessary;

. . . publish the justifications for its action and take the necessary measures to ensure observance of the rules set forth in the present Treaty.

The institutions of the Community shall carry out these activities with as little administrative machinery as possible and in close cooperation with the interested parties.

Article 6

The Community shall have juridical personality.

In its international relationships, the Community shall enjoy the juridical capacity necessary to the exercise of its functions and the attainment of its ends.

In each of the member States, the Community shall enjoy the most extensive juridical capacity which is recognized for legal persons of the nationality of the country in question. Specifically, it may acquire and transfer real and personal property, and may sue and be sued in its own name.

The Community shall be represented by its institutions, each one of them acting within the framework of its own powers and responsibilities.

Article 7

The institutions of the Community shall be as follows:

. . . a HIGH AUTHORITY, assisted by a Consultative Committee;
. . . a COMMON ASSEMBLY, hereafter referred to as 'Assembly';
. . . a SPECIAL COUNCIL, composed of MINISTERS, hereafter referred to as 'the Council';
. . . a COURT OF JUSTICE, hereafter referred to as 'the Court'.

CHAPTER I. — THE HIGH AUTHORITY

Article 8

The High Authority shall be responsible for assuring the fulfilment of the purposes stated in the present Treaty under the terms thereof.

Article 9

The High Authority shall be composed of nine members designated for six years and chosen for their general competence.

A member shall be eligible for reappointment. The number of members of the High Authority may be reduced by unanimous decision of the Council.

Only nationals of the member States may be members of the High Authority.

The High Authority may not include more than two members of the same nationality.

The members of the High Authority shall exercise their functions in complete independence, in the general interest of the Community. In the fulfilment of their duties, they shall neither solicit nor accept instructions from any government or from any organization. They will abstain from all conduct incompatible with the supranational character of their functions.

Each member State agrees to respect this supranational character and to make no effort to influence the members of the High Authority in the execution of their duties.

The members of the High Authority may not exercise any business or professional activities, paid or unpaid, nor acquire or hold, directly or indirectly, any interest in any business related to coal and steel during their term of office or for a period of three years thereafter.

Article 13

The High Authority shall act by vote of a majority of its membership.

Its quorum shall be fixed by its rules of procedure. However, this quorum must be greater than one-half of its membership.

Article 14

In the execution of its responsibilities under the present Treaty and in accordance with the provisions thereof, the High Authority shall issue decisions, recommendations and opinions.

Decisions shall be binding in all their details.

Recommendations shall be binding with respect to the objectives which they specify but shall leave to those to whom they are directed the choice of appropriate means for attaining these objectives.

Opinions shall not be binding.

When the High Authority is empowered to issue a decision, it may limit itself to making a recommendation.

Article 15

The decisions, recommendations and opinions of the High Authority shall state the reasons therefor, and shall take note of the opinions which the High Authority is required to obtain.

When such decisions and recommendations are individual in character, they shall be binding on the interested party upon their notification to him.

In other cases, they shall take effect automatically upon publication.

The High Authority shall determine the manner in which the provisions of the present article are to be carried out.

(*b*) European Economic Community

PART ONE

PRINCIPLES

Article 1

By the present Treaty, the High Contracting Parties establish among themselves a European Economic Community.

Article 2

The Community's mission shall be, by establishing a common market and gradually removing differences between the economic policies of Member States, to promote throughout the Community the harmonious development of economic activities, continuous and balanced expansion, increased stability, a more rapid improvement in the standard of living and closer relations between its Member States.

Article 3

With the objects set out in the preceding Article the Community's action shall include, on the conditions and at the rates provided for in the present Treaty:

(*a*) the removal of customs duties, as between Member States, and of quantitative restrictions on the importation and exportation of goods as well as of all other measures with equivalent effect,
(*b*) the establishment of a common customs tariff and a common commercial policy towards States outside the Community,
(*c*) the abolition, as between Member States, of obstacles to the free movement of persons, services and capital,
(*d*) the inauguration of a common agricultural policy,
(*e*) the inauguration of a common transport policy,
(*f*) the establishment of a system ensuring that competition shall not be hampered in the common market,
(*g*) the adoption of procedures to enable the economic policies of Member States to be co-ordinated and to remedy disequilibria in their balances of payments,
(*h*) the removal of differences in national laws so far as is necessary for the operation of the common market,
(*i*) the creation of a European Social Fund in order to enhance possibilities of employment for workers and contribute to the raising of their standard of living,
(*j*) the establishment of a European Investment Bank to facilitate economic expansion of the Community by creating fresh resources,
(*k*) the association of overseas countries and territories with the Community with a view to increasing trade and to pursuing in common efforts towards economic and social development.

Article 4

1. Responsibility for carrying out the tasks entrusted to the Community shall be vested in

— an Assembly
— a Council
— a Commission
— a Court of Justice.

Each of these institutions shall act within the limits of the powers conferred upon it by the present Treaty.

2. The Council and the Commission shall be assisted by an Economic and Social Committee exercising advisory functions.

Article 5

Member States shall take all appropriate general or special measures to ensure the fulfilment of the obligations resulting from the present Treaty or from the decisions of the institutions of the Community, and shall facilitate the accomplishment of its mission.

They shall refrain from all measures likely to jeopardise achievement of the aims of the present Treaty.

Article 6

1. Member States, acting in close collaboration with the institutions of the Community, shall co-ordinate their respective economic policies so far as is necessary to achieve the aims of the present Treaty.

2. The institutions of the Community shall be careful not to endanger the internal and external financial stability of Member States.

Article 7

Within the field of application of the present Treaty and without prejudice to the special provisions included therein, all discrimination on the grounds of nationality shall be prohibited.

On the proposal of the Commission and after consulting the Assembly, the Council may, by the prescribed majority, lay down regulations prohibiting such discrimination.

Article 8

1. The common market shall be gradually established over a transitional period of 12 years.

The transitional period shall be divided into three stages of four years each, which may be altered on the conditions set out hereunder.

2. To each stage there shall be assigned a co-ordinated group of activities which must be undertaken and pursued concurrently.

3. Passage from the first to the second stage shall be conditional upon establishment of the fact that the main aims specifically laid down in the present Treaty for the first stage have been effectively achieved, and that, subject to the exceptions and procedures provided for in this Treaty, commitments have been met.

This fact shall be established at the end of the fourth year by the Council voting unanimously on a report by the Commission. However, a Member State may not prevent a unanimous decision by availing itself of its failure to fulfil its own obligations. In the absence of a unanimous decision the first stage shall automatically be extended for one year.

At the end of the fifth year, the Council shall establish the aforesaid fact under the same conditions. In the absence of a unanimous decision, the first stage shall be automatically extended for a further year.

At the end of the sixth year, the Council shall establish the aforesaid fact by a prescribed majority vote on a report by the Commission.

4. Within one month as from this last vote, each Member State which voted with the minority or, if the requisite majority was not obtained, any Member State shall be entitled to ask the Council to appoint an Arbitration Board whose decision shall bind all Member States and the institutions of the Community. The Arbitration Board shall consist of three members appointed by a unanimous vote of the Council taken on a proposal by the Commission.

If the Council has not appointed the members of the Arbitration Board within one month of being asked to do so, they shall be appointed by the Court of Justice within a further period of one month.

The Arbitration Board shall appoint its own President.

It shall give its award within six months of the date of the vote by the Council referred to in the last sub-paragraph of paragraph 3.

5. The second and third stages may not be extended or curtailed except by unanimous decision of the Council taken on a proposal by the Commission.

6. The provisions of the foregoing paragraphs shall not have as their result any extension of the transitional period beyond a total duration of fifteen years from the date of the entry into force of the present Treaty.

7. Subject to the exceptions or derogations provided for in the present Treaty, the expiration of the transitional period shall mark the final date for the entry into force of the whole body of regulations provided for, and for the completion of all the operations entailed by the establishment of the common market.

PART FIVE

ORGANS OF THE COMMUNITY

Chapter I

Provisions Governing Institutions

Section 1 ORGANS

Sub-section: The Assembly [1]

Article 137

The Assembly shall be composed of representatives of the peoples of the States forming the Community and shall enjoy the powers of decision and supervision conferred upon it by the present Treaty.

Article 138

1. The Assembly shall be composed of delegates whom the parliaments shall be called upon to appoint from among their own members in accordance with the procedure laid down by each Member State.

2. The number of these delegates shall be fixed as follows:

Belgium	14
France	36
Germany	36
Italy	36
Luxembourg	6
Netherlands	14

3. The Assembly shall draw up proposals for election by direct universal suffrage according to an identical procedure in all Member States.

The Council shall, by a unanimous vote, determine the provisions which it shall recommend for adoption by Member States in accordance with their respective constitutional rules.

Article 139

The Assembly shall hold annual sessions. It shall meet as of right on the third Tuesday in October.

At the request of a majority of its members, or at the request of the Council or of the Commission, the Assembly may meet in extraordinary session.

[1] The Assembly is now common to the Economic Community, the Coal and Steel Community and the Atomic Energy Authority.

Article 141

Except where otherwise provided in the present Treaty, the Assembly shall take its decisions by an absolute majority of the votes cast.

Article 143

The Assembly shall discuss in public meeting the Annual General Report which shall be submitted to it by the Commission.

Article 144

If a motion of censure concerning the operations of the Commission is tabled in the Assembly, the latter may decide thereon, by an open vote, only after not less than three days have elapsed from the tabling of the motion.

If the motion of censure is adopted by a two-thirds majority of the votes cast, representing a majority of the members of the Assembly, the members of the Commission shall resign their office in a body. They shall continue to deal with current business until they shall have been replaced in accordance with the provisions of Article 158.

Sub-section II: The Council

Article 145

With a view to ensuring achievement of the objectives laid down in the present Treaty, and under the conditions provided for therein, the Council shall

— be responsible for co-ordinating the general economic policies of Member States;
— exercise powers of decision.

Article 146

The Council shall be composed of representatives of Member States, each Government appointing to it one of its Members.

Each of the members of the Council shall act as Chairman for a period of six months in rotation, following the alphabetical order of the Member States.

Article 147

Meetings of the Council shall be called by the Chairman, on his own initiative, or at the request of one of its members or of the Commission.

Article 148

1. Except where otherwise provided in the present Treaty, decisions of the Council shall be taken by a majority of its members.

2. In the case of Council decisions requiring a prescribed majority the votes of its members shall be weighted as follows:

Belgium	2
France	4
Germany	4
Italy	4
Luxembourg	1
Netherlands	2

Decisions receiving at least the following number of votes shall be regarded as adopted:

— in the case of decisions which the present Treaty requires to be taken on a proposal by the Commission: twelve votes;
— in other cases: twelve votes representing a favourable vote by at least four members.

3. Abstentions by members either present in person or represented shall not prevent the adoption of Council decisions requiring unanimity.

Article 149

When the present Treaty requires that a Council decision be taken on a proposal by the Commission, the Council may amend such proposal only by a unanimous vote.

So long as the Council has not taken its decision, the Commission may amend its original proposal, in particular, in cases where the Assembly has been consulted on the proposal in question.

Sub-section III: The Commission

Article 155

With a view to ensuring the operation and development of the common market, the Commission shall

— supervise the application of the provisions of the present Treaty and of measures adopted by the organs of the Community in virtue thereof;
— formulate recommendations or opinions in regard to matters covered by the present Treaty, in cases where this is explicitly provided therein or where the Commission considers it necessary;

— enjoy independent powers of decision and take part in the preparation of decisions by the Council and Assembly, under the conditions laid down in the present Treaty;
— exercise the powers conferred on it by the Council with a view to the execution of the rules laid down by the latter.

Article 156

The Commission shall each year, at least one month before the opening of the Assembly Session, issue a General Report on the work of the Community.

Article 157

1. The Commission shall be composed of nine members, selected for their general competence and of unquestioned integrity.

The number of members of the Commission may be altered by a unanimous vote of the Council.

Members of the Commission must be nationals of Member States.

The Commission may not include more than two members who are nationals of the same State.

2. The members of the Commission shall carry out their functions in complete independence, in the general interest of the Community.

In the discharge of their duties they shall neither ask for nor accept instructions from any Government or other body and shall refrain from all action incompatible with the character of their functions. Each Member State shall undertake to respect this character and not to seek to influence the members of the Commission in the performance of their task.

During their term of office the members of the Commission may not engage in any other professional activity, whether paid or unpaid. When entering upon their duties, they shall give a solemn undertaking that, both during and after their term of office, they will respect the obligations resulting therefrom and in particular the duty of exercising honesty and discretion as regards the acceptance, after their term of office, of certain functions or advantages. Should these obligations not be respected, the Court of Justice, on the application of the Council or of the Commission, may, according to circumstances, decree that the member in question either be removed from office under the provisions of Article 160, or forfeit his right to a pension or other advantages in lieu thereof.

Article 158

The members of the Commission shall be appointed by agreement between the Governments of Member States.

They shall be appointed for a term of four years and shall be re-eligible.

Article 163

Decisions of the Commission shall be taken by a majority of the members provided for in Article 157.

Sub-section IV: The Court of Justice

Article 164

The Court of Justice shall ensure observance of the rules of law in the interpretation and application of the present Treaty.

Article 165

The Court of Justice shall be composed of seven judges.

The Court of Justice shall sit in plenary session. Nevertheless, it may set up within itself divisions, each composed of three or five judges, either for the purpose of conducting certain enquiries or for the purpose of judging certain types of cases, under conditions to be laid down in special regulations.

The Court of Justice shall, however, always sit in plenary session to hear cases submitted to it by a Member State or by one of the organs of the Community, or to deal with interlocutory questions submitted to it under Article 177.

Should the Court of Justice so request, the Council may, by a unanimous vote, increase the number of judges and make the consequent amendments to the second and third sub-paragraphs of the present Article and to the second sub-paragraph of Article 167.

Article 166

The Court of Justice shall have the assistance of two advocates-general.

The duty of the advocate-general shall be to present publicly, with complete impartiality and independence, reasoned conclusions on cases submitted to the Court of Justice, with a view to assisting the latter in the discharge of its mission as laid down in Article 164.

Should the Court of Justice so request, the Council may, by a unanimous vote, increase the number of advocates-general and make the consequent amendments to the third sub-paragraph of Article 167.

Article 167

The judges and the advocates-general shall be chosen from among persons of unquestioned impartiality who fulfil the conditions required in their respective countries for the holding of the highest legal offices or who are legal experts of wide repute. They shall be appointed for a term of six years by agreement between the Governments of Member States.

Article 170

Any Member State that considers that another Member State has failed to comply with any of its obligations under the present Treaty may bring the matter before the Court of Justice.

Before a Member State initiates, against another Member State, proceedings relating to an alleged violation of the obligations incumbent upon such other Member State in virtue of the present Treaty, it must bring the matter before the Commission.

After the States concerned have been given the opportunity to present observations and replies thereto, both orally and in writing, the Commission shall issue a reasoned pronouncement.

Article 173

The Court of Justice shall review the legality of decisions of the Council and Commission, but not of recommendations or opinions. To this end, it shall be competent to give judgment on appeals, lodged by a Member State, the Council or the Commission, on grounds of incompetence, procedural errors, infringement of the present Treaty or of any rule of law relating to its application, or abuse of powers.

Individuals or corporations may, under the same conditions, submit an appeal against decisions of which they are the object and against decisions which, although in the form of regulations or decisions addressed to another individual or corporation, are nevertheless of direct personal concern to themselves.

The appeals provided for in the present Article shall be lodged within two months dating, according to circumstances, either from the promulgation of the decision in question, or from its notification to the appellant or, failing that, from the day on which the latter had knowledge thereof.

Article 174

If the appeal is allowed, the Court of Justice shall declare the decision in question to be null and void.

Nevertheless, in the case of regulations, the Court of Justice shall, if it considers it necessary, state which of the effects of the regulations annulled shall be deemed to remain in force.

Article 175

Should the Council or the Commission fail to take a decision in cases where such decision is provided for under the present Treaty, the Member States and other organs of the community may bring the matter before the Court of Justice with a view to establishing that such violation of the Treaty has taken place.

Such an appeal shall be heard only if the organ in question has previously been invited to take action. If the aforesaid organ has not made its attitude known within two months of such invitation, an appeal may be lodged within a further period of two months.

In the case of a decision, but not in that of a recommendation or opinion, any individual or corporation may bring before the Court of Justice, under the conditions laid down in the preceding sub-paragraphs, a complaint against any of the organs of the Community for having failed to notify the said individual or corporation.

Article 176

The organ responsible for a decision declared null and void, and any organ whose failure to act has been declared contrary to the provisions of the present Treaty, shall be bound to take the necessary measures to comply with the judgment of the Court of Justice.

Article 179

The Court of Justice shall be competent to give judgment in any dispute between the Community and its agents, within the limits and under the conditions laid down in the rules or regulations applicable to the latter.

Article 180

The Court of Justice shall be competent, within the limits laid down hereunder, to hear cases concerning:

(*a*) the fulfilment by Member States of the obligations arising under the Statutes of the European Investment Bank. The Board of Directors of the Bank shall, in this matter, exercise the powers conferred upon the Commission by Article 169;

(*b*) decisions taken by the Board of Governors of the Bank. Any Member State, the Commission and the Board of Directors of the Bank may lodge an appeal against such decisions under the conditions laid down in Article 173;

(*c*) decisions taken by the Board of Directors of the Bank. In the case of these decisions, appeals may be lodged, under the conditions laid down in Article 173, only by a Member State or by the Commission, and only on the grounds of non-observance of the procedure laid down in paragraph 2 and paragraphs 5 to 7 inclusive of Article 21 of the Statutes of the Investment Bank.

Article 181

The Court of Justice shall be competent to give judgment in virtue of any arbitration clause contained in a contract concluded, under public or private law, by or on behalf of the Community.

Article 182

The Court of Justice shall be competent to give judgment in all disputes between Member States connected with the objects of the present Treaty, if such disputes are submitted to it under the terms of a special agreement.

Article 192

Decisions of the Council or of the Commission which impose a pecuniary obligation upon persons other than the States shall have executory force.

Forced execution shall be governed by the rules of civil procedure in effect in the State in whose territory it takes place. The writ of execution shall be appended, without other formality than the verification of the authenticity of the document, by the national authority which the Government of each of the Member States shall designate for this purpose and notify to the Commission and the Court of Justice.

After completion of these formalities at the request of the party concerned, the latter may proceed with the forced execution by direct application to the organ which is competent under the national law.

Forced execution can be suspended only in virtue of a decision of the Court of Justice. Nevertheless, verification of the regularity of the measures of execution shall be within the competence of the national judicial authorities.

Chapter II

Financial Dispositions

Article 199

Estimates must be drawn up for each financial year for all receipts and expenditures of the Community, including those relating to the European Social Fund, and must be shown in the budget.

The receipts and expenditures of the budget must balance.

Article 200

1. The budget receipts, apart from revenue from other sources, shall comprise the financial contributions of Member States, fixed on the following proportionate scale:

Belgium	7·9
France	28
Germany	28
Italy	28
Luxembourg	0·2
Netherlands	7·9

2. Nevertheless, the financial contributions of Member States which are intended to meet the expenses of the European Social Fund shall be fixed on the following proportionate scale:

Belgium	8·8
France	32
Germany	32
Italy	20
Luxembourg	0·2
Netherlands	7

3. The proportionate scales may be changed by the Council, voting unanimously.

Article 201

The Commission shall study the conditions under which the financial contributions of Member States as laid down in Article 200 might be replaced by other appropriate resources, more particularly by revenue accruing from the common customs tariff when this shall have been finally established.

The Commission shall submit proposals in this connection to the Council.

The Council, voting unanimously, may, after consulting the Assembly on these proposals, draw up provisions which it would recommend Member States to adopt in accordance with their respective constitutional rules.

Article 218

The Community shall enjoy, in the territories of the Member States, the privileges and immunities necessary for the fulfilment of its mission, under conditions specified in a separate Protocol.

Article 219

Member States undertake not to submit a dispute concerning the interpretation or application of the present Treaty to any method of settlement other than those provided for in the Treaty.

Article 220

Member States shall, so far as necessary, engage in negotiations with each other with a view to ensuring for their nationals

— the protection of persons and the enjoyment and protection of rights under the conditions granted by each State to its own nationals,
— the abolition of double taxation within the Community,

— mutual recognition of companies within the meaning of Article 58, paragraph 2, the retention of their legal personality in cases where the registered office is transferred from one country to another, and the possibility for companies subject to the laws of different Member States to form mergers,

— the simplification of the formalities governing the reciprocal recognition and execution of judicial decisions and arbitral awards.

Article 221

Within three years of the entry into force of the present Treaty, Member States shall accord to nationals of other Member States the same facilities as regards financial participation in the capital of companies within the meaning of Article 58 as they accord to their own nationals, without prejudice to application of the other provisions of the present Treaty.

Article 222

The present Treaty shall be entirely without prejudice to the system of ownership in Member States.

Article 223

1. The provisions of the present Treaty shall not be incompatible with the following rules:

(*a*) no State shall be obliged to supply information the disclosure of which it considers contrary to the vital interests of its security,

(*b*) each Member State may take the measures which it considers necessary to protect the vital interests of its security, and which are connected with the manufacture or sale of arms, munitions and war material; these measures must not interfere with conditions of competition in the common market in respect of products not intended for specifically military purposes.

Article 224

Member States shall consult one another for the purpose of taking in common the necessary measures to prevent the operation of the common market from being affected by measures which a Member State may be led to take in case of serious internal disturbances affecting public order, in case of war or serious international tension constituting a threat of war, or in order to fulfil undertakings into which it has entered for the purpose of maintaining peace and international security.

Article 237

Any European State may ask to join the Community. It shall address its request to the Council which, after taking the opinion of the Commission, shall decide by a unanimous vote.

The conditions of admission and the adaptations to the present Treaty entailed thereby shall be the subject of an agreement between the Member States and the applicant State. The said agreement shall be submitted for ratification by all the contracting States, in conformity with their respective constitutional rules.

(*c*) European Atomic Energy Community

Article 1

By the present Treaty, the High Contracting Parties establish among themselves a EUROPEAN ATOMIC ENERGY COMMUNITY (EURATOM).

It shall be the aim of the Community to contribute to the raising of the standard of living in Member States and to the development of commercial exchanges with other countries by the creation of conditions necessary for the speedy establishment and growth of nuclear industries.

Article 2

For the attainment of its aims the Community shall, in accordance with the provisions set out in this Treaty:

(*a*) develop research and ensure the dissemination of technical knowledge,

(*b*) establish, and ensure the application of, uniform safety standards to protect the health of workers and of the general public,

(*c*) facilitate investment and ensure, particularly by encouraging business enterprise, the construction of the basic facilities required for the development of nuclear energy within the Community,

(*d*) ensure a regular and equitable supply of ores and nuclear fuels to all users in the Community,

(*e*) guarantee, by appropriate measures of control, that nuclear materials are not diverted for purposes other than those for which they are intended,

(*f*) exercise the property rights conferred upon it in respect of special fissionable materials,

(*g*) ensure extensive markets and access to the best technical means by the creation of a common market for specialized materials and equipment, by the free movement of capital for nuclear investment, and by freedom of employment for specialists within the Community,

(*h*) establish with other countries and with international organizations any contacts likely to promote progress in the peaceful uses of nuclear energy.

Article 3

1. The achievement of the tasks entrusted to the Community shall be ensured by:

— an ASSEMBLY,
— a COUNCIL,
— a COMMISSION,
— a COURT OF JUSTICE.

Each of these institutions shall act within the limits of the powers conferred upon it by this Treaty.

2. The Council and the Commission shall be assisted by an Economic and Social Committee acting in a consultative capacity.

2. COUNCIL FOR MUTUAL ECONOMIC ASSISTANCE

Article 1: Aims and Principles

1. The Council for Mutual Economic Assistance shall have as its aim contributing, through the union and co-ordination of the forces of the member countries of the Council, to the planned development of the national economy and an acceleration of the economic and technical progress of these countries; raising the level of industrialization of the under-developed countries; an uninterrupted growth in labour productivity; and a steady rise in the well-being of the peoples of the member countries.

2. The Council for Mutual Economic Assistance shall be based on the principle of the sovereign equality of all the member countries of the Council.

The economic and scientific-technical co-operation of the member countries shall be accomplished in accordance with the principles of complete equality of rights, respect for sovereignty and national interests, mutual benefit and comradely mutual aid.

Article 2: Membership

1. The charter members of the Council for Mutual Economic Assistance shall be the countries signing and ratifying this Charter.

2. Admission to the Council shall be open to such other countries of Europe as share the aims and principles of the Council and agree to accept the obligations contained in this Charter.

The admission of new members to the Council shall be effected by decision of a Session of the Council upon the receipt of official requests from the relevant countries for such admission.

Article 3: Functions and Powers

1. In accordance with the aims and principles enumerated in Article 1 of this Charter, the Council for Mutual Economic Assistance: (*a*) shall organize:

[*i*] the many-sided economic and scientific-technical co-operation of the member countries of the Council with an aim to a more economical utilization of their natural resources and an acceleration of the growth of the productive forces;

[*ii*] the preparation of recommendations regarding the most important questions of economic relations resulting from the respective plans for the development of the national economy of the member countries of the Council, with a view to co-ordinating these plans;

[*iii*] the study of those economic problems encompassing the interests of the member countries of the Council;

(*b*) shall assist the member countries of the Council in working out and accomplishing joint measures in the following areas:

[*i*] the development of the industry and agriculture of the member countries of the Council on the basis of successive realization of the international socialist division of labour, specialization and co-operation in production;

[*ii*] the development of transport with the aim, first and foremost, of ensuring an increase in the export-import and transit freight of the member countries of the Council;

[*iii*] a more effective utilization of the capital investments allotted by the member countries of the Council for the construction of projects to be accomplished on the basis of joint participation;

[*iv*] the development of commodity turnover and trade between the member countries of the Council themselves and with other countries;

[*v*] the exchange of scientific-technical achievements and advanced production experience;

(*c*) shall undertake such other activities as are necessary for the achievement of the aims of the Council.

2. In the person of its organs acting within the limits of their competence, the Council for Mutual Economic Assistance shall be empowered to make recommendations and decisions in accordance with this Charter.

Article 4: Recommendations and Decisions

1. Recommendations shall be made on questions of economic and scientific-technical collaboration. The recommendations shall be communicated to the member countries of the Council for their consideration.

Realization by the member countries of the Council of the recommendations adopted by them shall be carried out according to the decisions of the Governments, or the competent organs, of the said countries in accordance with the relevant legislation.

2. Decisions shall be made on organizational and procedural questions. These decisions shall come into force, if not otherwise stipulated in the decisions themselves, on the day of the signing of the protocol of the session of the corresponding organ of the Council.

3. All recommendations and decisions of the Council shall be made only with the concurrence of those member countries of the Council concerned, each country having the right to express itself regarding its interests on each question considered in the Council.

Recommendations and decisions shall not extend to those countries expressing disinterest in the given question. However, any of these countries may subsequently concur in the recommendations and decisions made by other member countries of the Council.

Article 5: Organs

1. For execution of the functions and plenary powers specified in Article 3 of this Charter, the Council for Mutual Economic Assistance shall have the following basic organs: the Session of the Council, the Consultative Body of Representatives of the member countries of the Council, the Permanent Commissions, the Secretariat.

2. Such other organs as may be found necessary shall be established in conformity with this Charter.

Article 6: The Session of the Council

1. The Session of the Council shall represent the highest organ of the Council for Mutual Economic Assistance. It shall have full power to consider all questions falling within the competence of the Council, and to make recommendations and decisions in accordance with this Charter.

2. The Session of the Council shall consist of the delegations from all the member countries of the Council. The composition of the delegation of each country shall be determined by the government of the respective country.

3. Under the chairmanship of the head of the delegation of the country in which such Session is conducted, regular Sessions of the Council shall be convoked two times in successive capitals of the member countries of the Council.

4. An extraordinary Session of the Council shall be convoked upon the request of, or with the concurrence of, not less than one-third of the member countries of the Council.

5. The Session of the Council:

(*a*) shall examine:

[*i*] proposals on questions of economic and scientific-technical co-operation submitted by the member countries, and also by the Consultative Body of Representatives of the member countries of the Council, the Permanent Commissions and the Secretariat of the Council;

[*ii*] the report of the Secretariat of the Council on the activities of the Council;

(*b*) shall determine the basic direction of the activities of the other organs of the Council, and the basic questions of the agenda for the next Session of the Council;

(*c*) shall carry out such other functions as prove necessary for achieving the aims of the Council.

6. The Session of the Council shall be empowered to establish such organs as it considers necessary for carrying out the functions entrusted to the Council.

7. The Session of the Council shall establish its own rules of procedure.

Article 7: The Consultative Body of Representatives of Member Countries of the Council

1. The Consultative Body of Representatives of the member countries of the Council for Mutual Economic Assistance shall consist of representatives of all the member countries of the Council: specifically, one from each country.

At the seat of the Secretariat of the Council, the representative of each member country of the Council shall have a deputy, the necessary staff of advisers, and other co-workers. Upon authorization of the representative, such deputy shall perform the functions of the representative in the Consultative Body.

2. The Consultative Body shall conduct its sessions as necessary.

3. Within the limits of its competence, the Consultative Body shall have the right to make recommendations and decisions in conformity with this Charter. The Consultative Body shall also introduce proposals for consideration by the Session of the Council.

4. The Consultative Body:

(*a*) shall consider the proposals of the member countries of the Council, the Permanent Commissions and the Secretariat as regards ensuring the execution of the recommendations and decisions of the Session of the Council, as well as other questions of economic and scientific co-operation requiring decisions in the period between Sessions of the Council;

(*b*) shall consider ahead of time, when necessary, proposals of the member countries of the Council, the Permanent Commissions, and the Secretariat of the Council regarding questions for the agenda of the next Session of the Council;

(*c*) shall co-ordinate the work of the Permanent Commissions of the Council; shall examine their reports concerning the performance of the work and further activities;

(*d*) shall approve:

[*i*] the staffs and budget of the Secretariat of the Council, as well as the accounts of the Secretariat of the Council concerning the execution of the budget;

[*ii*] the status of the Permanent Commissions and Secretariat of the Council;

(*e*) shall create control organs for the verification of the financial activities of the Secretariat of the Council;

(*f*) shall perform such other functions as arise from the present Charter, as well as from the recommendations and decisions of the Session of the Council.

5. The Consultative Body shall create when necessary auxiliary organs for the preliminary working up of questions.

6. The Consultative Body shall establish its own rules of procedure.

Article 8*: The Permanent Commissions*

1. The Permanent Commissions of the Council for Mutual Economic Assistance shall be formed by the Session of the Council with an aim to contributing to the further development of the economic relations between the member countries of the Council, and to organizing many-sided economic and scientific-technical co-operation in the various sectors of the national economy of the said countries.

The status of the Permanent Commissions shall be approved by the

Consultative Body of Representatives of the member countries of the Council.

2. Each member country of the Council shall name its representatives to the Permanent Commissions.

3. The Permanent Commissions shall have the right to make recommendations and decisions, within the limits of their competence, in accordance with the present Charter. The Commissions may also introduce proposals for the consideration of the Session of the Council and the Consultative Body of Representatives of the member countries of the Council.

4. The Permanent Commissions shall elaborate measures and prepare proposals for the realization of the economic-technical cooperation indicated in paragraph 1 of this article. They shall also carry out such other functions as arise from this Charter, the recommendations and decisions of the Session of the Council, and the Consultative Body of Representatives of the member countries of the Council.

The Permanent Commissions shall present to the Consultative Body of Representatives of the member countries of the Council annual reports on the progress of their work and further activities.

5. The sessions of the Permanent Commissions shall be conducted, as a rule, at the place of their permanent abode, which shall be determined by the Session of the Council.

6. The Permanent Commissions shall form auxiliary organs when necessary. The composition and competence of these organs, as well as their place of meeting, shall be determined by the parent Commission.

7. Each Permanent Commission shall have a secretariat headed by the secretary of the Commission. The staff of the secretariat of such Commission shall become a constituent part of the Secretariat of the Council, and shall be maintained at the expense of its budget.

8. The Permanent Commissions shall establish their own rules of prodecure.

Article 9: The Secretariat

1. The Secretariat of the Council for Mutual Economic Assistance shall consist of the Secretary of the Council, his deputies and such personnel as may be required for carrying out the functions entrusted to the Secretariat.

The Secretary and his deputies shall be named by the Session of the Council, and shall direct the work of the Secretariat of the Council. The personnel of the Secretariat shall be recruited from among the citizens of the member countries of the Council, in accordance with the Regulations applicable to the Secretariat of the Council.

The Secretary shall be the head official of the Council. He shall represent the Council before the officials and organizations of the member countries of the Council and other countries, as well as before international organizations. The Secretary of the Council shall, where necessary, empower his deputies, as well as other employees of the Secretariat, to appear in his behalf.

The Secretary and his deputies shall be permitted to take part in all sessions of the organs of the Council.

2. The Secretariat of the Council:

(*a*) shall present a report on the activities of the Council to the regular Session of the Council;

(*b*) shall assist in the preparation and conduct of the Session of the Council, the Consultative Body of Representatives of the member countries of the Council, the sessions of the Permanent Commissions of the Council and the Consultative bodies formed by the decisions of these organs of the Council;

(*c*) shall prepare, under the authority of the Session of the Council or the Consultative Body of Representatives of the member countries of the Council, economic surveys and analyses according to the materials of the member countries of the Council, and shall also publish materials on questions of the economic and scientific-technical co-operation of these countries;

(*d*) [shall] prepare:

[*i*] proposals on questions of the work of the Council for the consideration of the corresponding organs of the Council;

[*ii*] informational and reference materials on questions of the economic and scientific-technical co-operation of the member countries of the Council;

(*e*) shall organize, jointly with the Permanent Commissions of the Council, the preparation of projects in relation to questions of economic and scientific-technical co-operation on the basis of the recommendations and decisions of the Session of the Council and the Consultative Body of Representatives of the member countries of the Council;

(*f*) shall undertake other activities arising from this Charter, the recommendations and decisions made by the Council, and the regulations applicable to the Secretariat of the Council.

3. The Secretary of the Council, his deputies and the personnel of the Secretariat shall act in the capacity of international officials in the performance of their official duties.

4. The seat of the Secretariat of the Council shall be Moscow.

Article 10: Participation of Other Countries in the Work of the Council

The Council of Mutual Economic Assistance shall be permitted to invite countries which are not members of the Council to take part in the work of the organs of the Council.

The conditions under which representatives of these countries may participate in the work of the organs of the Council shall be determined by the Council, in agreement with the respective countries concerned.

Article 11: Relations with International Organizations

The Council of Mutual Economic Assistance shall be permitted to establish and maintain relations with the economic organizations of the United Nations and with other international organizations.

The character and form of these relations shall be determined by the Council, in agreement with the respective international organizations concerned.

Article 12: Questions of Finance

1. The member countries of the Council of Mutual Economic Assistance shall bear the expenses incurred in the maintenance of the Secretariat and the execution of its activities. Each member country's share of these expenses shall be established by the Session of the Council; other financial questions shall be resolved by the Consultative Body of Representatives of the member countries of the Council.

2. The Secretariat of the Council shall present to the Consultative Body of Representatives of the member countries of the Council a report on the execution of the budget for each calendar year.

3. The expenses incurred by the participants in the Session of the Council, the Consultative Body of Representatives of the member countries of the Council, the Permanent Commissions of the Council, and the consultations conducted within the framework of the Council, shall be borne by the countries represented at these meetings and consultations.

4. The expenses incurred in connection with the meetings and consultations mentioned in paragraph 3 of this article shall be borne by the country in which the meetings and consultations are conducted.

Article 13: Various Enactments

1. The Council of Mutual Economic Assistance shall enjoy within the territory of each member country of the Council such capacities as are necessary for carrying out its functions and achieving its aims.

2. The Council, as well as the representatives of the member countries of the Council and the officials of the Council, shall enjoy, within the territory of each of these countries, such privileges and immunities as are necessary for carrying out the functions and achieving the aims foreseen by this Charter.

3. The capacities, privileges and immunities mentioned in this Article shall be specified in a special Convention.

4. The regulations of this Charter shall not affect such rights and obligations of the member countries of the Council as arise from membership in other international organizations, or from the conclusion of international treaties.

3. THE GENERAL AGREEMENT ON TARIFFS AND TRADE (1947–55)[1]

PART I

Objectives

Article 1

1. The contracting parties recognize that their relations in the field of trade and economic endeavour should be conducted with a view to raising standards of living, ensuring full employment and a large and steadily growing volume of real income and effective demand, developing the full use of the resources of the world and expanding the production and exchange of goods, and promoting the progressive development of the economies of all the contracting parties.

2. The contracting parties desire to contribute to these objectives through this Agreement by entering into reciprocal and mutually advantageous arrangements directed to the substantial reduction of tariffs and other barriers to trade and to the elimination of discriminatory treatment in international commerce.

General Most-Favoured-Nation Treatment

Article 2

1. With respect to customs duties and charges of any kind imposed on or in connection with importation or exportation or imposed on the international transfer of payments for imports or exports, and with

[1] The excerpts printed below are designed to convey an impression of the general objectives and structure of the GATT. The many qualifications and exemptions of this very complex document are omitted.

respect to the method of levying such duties and charges, and with respect to all rules and formalities in connection with importation and exportation, and with respect to the application of internal taxes to exported goods, and with respect to all matters referred to in paragraphs 2 and 4 of Article 4, any advantage, favour, privilege or immunity granted by any contracting party to any product originating in or destined for any other country shall be accorded immediately and unconditionally to the like product originating in or destined for the territories of all other contracting parties.

2. The provisions of paragraph 1 of this Article shall not require the elimination of any preferences in respect of import duties or charges which do not exceed the levels provided for in paragraph 4 of this Article and which fall within the following descriptions: [not reproduced].

PART II

National Treatment and Internal Taxation and Regulation

Article 4

1. The contracting parties recognize that internal taxes and other internal charges, and laws, regulations and requirements affecting the internal sale, offering for sale, purchase, transportation, distribution or use of products, and internal quantitative regulations requiring the mixture, processing or use of products in specified amounts or proportions, should not be applied to imported or domestic products so as to afford protection to domestic production.

2. The products of the territory of any contracting party imported into the territory of any other contracting party shall not be subject, directly or indirectly, to internal taxes or other internal charges of any kind in excess of those applied, directly or indirectly, to like domestic products. Moreover, no contracting party shall otherwise apply internal taxes or other internal charges to imported or domestic products in a manner contrary to the principles set forth in paragraph 1.

3. With respect to any existing internal tax which is inconsistent with the provisions of paragraph 2, but which is specifically authorized under a trade agreement, in force on 10 April 1947, in which the import duty on the taxed product is bound against increase, the contracting party imposing the tax shall be free to postpone the application of the provisions of paragraph 2 to such tax until such time as it can obtain release from the obligations of such trade agreement in order to permit the increase of such duty to the extent necessary to compensate for the elimination of the protective element of the tax.

4. The products of the territory of any contracting party imported into the territory of any other contracting party shall be accorded treatment no less favourable than that accorded to like products of national origin in respect of all laws, regulations and requirements affecting their internal sale, offering for sale, purchase, transportation, distribution or use. The provisions of this paragraph shall not prevent the application of differential internal transportation charges which are based exclusively on the economic operation of the means of transport and not on the nationality of the product.

Anti-dumping and Countervailing Duties

Article 6

1. The contracting parties recognize that dumping, by which products of one country are introduced into the commerce of another country at less than the normal value of the products, is to be condemned if it causes or threatens material injury to an established industry in the territory of a contracting party or materially retards the establishment of a domestic industry. For the purposes of this Article, a product is to be considered as being introduced into the commerce of an importing country at less than its normal value, if the price of the product exported from one country to another

(*a*) is less than the comparable price, in the ordinary course of trade, for the like product when destined for consumption in the exporting country, or,

(*b*) in the absence of such domestic price, is less than either

(i) the highest comparable price for the like product for export to any third country in the ordinary course of trade, or

(ii) the cost of production of the product in the country of origin plus a reasonable addition for selling cost and profit.

Due allowance shall be made in each case for differences in conditions and terms of sale, for differences in taxation, and for other differences affecting price comparability.

General Elimination of Quantitative Restrictions

Article 11

1. No prohibitions or restrictions other than duties, taxes or other charges, whether made effective through quotas, import or export licenses or other measures, shall be instituted or maintained by any contracting party on the importation of any product of the territory of any other contracting party or on the exportation or sale for export of any product destined for the territory of any other contracting party.

Restrictions to Safeguard the Balance of Payments

Article 12

1. Notwithstanding the provisions of paragraph 1 of Article 11, any contracting party, in order to safeguard its external financial position and its balance of payments, may restrict the quantity or value of merchandise permitted to be imported, subject to the provisions of the following paragraphs of this Article.

Non-discriminatory Administration of Quantitative Restrictions

Article 13

1. No prohibition or restriction shall be applied by any contracting party on the importation of any product of the territory of any other contracting party or on the exportation of any product destined for the territory of any other contracting party, unless the importation of the like product of all third countries or the exportation of the like product to all third countries is similarly prohibited or restricted.

Subsidies

Section A — Subsidies in General

Article 16

1. If any contracting party grants or maintains any subsidy, including any form of income or price support, which operates directly or indirectly to increase exports of any product from, or to reduce imports of any product into, its territory, it shall notify the Organization in writing of the extent and nature of the subsidization, of the estimated effect of the subsidization on the quantity of the affected product or products imported into or exported from its territory and of the circumstances making the subsidization necessary. In any case in which it is determined that serious prejudice to the interests of any other contracting party is caused or threatened by any such subsidization, the contracting party granting the subsidy shall, upon request, discuss with the other contracting party or parties concerned, or with the Organization, the possibility of limiting the subsidization.

State-trading Enterprises

Article 17

1. (*a*) Each contracting party undertakes that if it establishes or maintains a State enterprise, wherever located, or grants to any enterprise, formally or in effect, exclusive or special privileges, such

enterprise shall, in its purchases or sales involving either imports or exports, act in a manner consistent with the general principles of non-discriminatory treatment prescribed in this Agreement for governmental measures affecting imports or exports by private traders.

(*b*) The provisions of sub-paragraph (*a*) of this paragraph shall be understood to require that such enterprises shall, having due regard to the other provisions of this Agreement, make any such purchases or sales solely in accordance with commercial considerations, including price, quality, availability, marketability, transportation and other conditions of purchase or sale, and shall afford the enterprises of the other contracting parties adequate opportunity, in accordance with customary business practice, to compete for participation in such purchases or sales.

(*c*) No contracting party shall prevent any enterprise (whether or not an enterprise described in sub-paragraph (*a*) of this paragraph) under its jurisdiction from acting in accordance with the principles of sub-paragraphs (*a*) and (*b*) of this paragraph.

Governmental Assistance to Economic Development

Article 18

1. The contracting parties recognize that the attainment of the objectives of this Agreement will be facilitated by the progressive development of their economies, particularly of those contracting parties the economies of which can only support low standards of living and are in the early stages of development.

2. The contracting parties recognize further that it may be necessary for those contracting parties, in order to implement programmes and policies of economic development designed to raise the general standard of living of their people, to take protective or other measures affecting imports, and that such measures are justified in so far as they facilitate the attainment of the objectives of this Agreement. They agree, therefore, that those contracting parties should enjoy additional facilities to enable them (*a*) to maintain sufficient flexibility in their tariff structure to be able to grant the tariff protection required for the establishment of a particular industry and (*b*) to apply quantitative restrictions for balance of payments purposes in a manner which takes full account of the continued high level of demand for imports likely to be generated by their programmes of economic development.

Tariff Negotiations

Article 29

1. The contracting parties recognize that customs duties often constitute serious obstacles to trade; thus negotiations on a reciprocal and

mutually advantageous basis, directed to the substantial reduction of the general level of tariffs and other charges on imports and exports and in particular to the reduction of such high tariffs as discourage the importation even of minimum quantities, and conducted with due regard to the objectives of this Agreement and the varying needs of individual contracting parties, are of great importance to the expansion of international trade. The Organization may therefore sponsor such negotiations from time to time.

2. (*a*) Negotiations under this Article may be carried out on a selective product-by-product basis or by the application of such multilateral procedure as may be accepted by the contracting parties concerned. Such negotiations may be directed towards the reduction of duties, the binding of duties at then existing levels or undertakings that individual duties or the average duties on specified categories of products shall not exceed specified levels. The binding against increase of low duties or of duty-free treatment shall, in principle, be recognized as a concession equivalent in value to the reduction of high duties.

III. FUNCTIONAL INTERNATIONAL AGENCIES

1. CONSTITUTION OF THE FOOD AND AGRICULTURE ORGANIZATION OF THE UNITED NATIONS[1] (Excerpts)

(1945–57)

Functions of the Organization

Article 1

1. The Organization shall collect, analyse, interpret and disseminate information relating to nutrition, food, and agriculture. In this Constitution, the term 'agriculture' and its derivatives include fisheries, marine products, forestry and primary forestry products.[2]

2. The Organization shall promote and, where appropriate, shall recommend national and international action with respect to;

(*a*) scientific, technological, social, and economic research relating to nutrition, food, and agriculture;

(*b*) the improvement of education and administration relating to nutrition, food, and agriculture, and the spread of public knowledge of nutritional and agricultural science and practice;

[1] Published by the Food and Agriculture Organization.

[2] The second sentence of this paragraph is the whole of the original Article 16, Fish and Forest Products.

(*c*) the conservation of natural resources and the adoption of improved methods of agricultural production;
(*d*) the improvement of the processing, marketing, and distribution of food and agricultural products;
(*e*) the adoption of policies for the provision of adequate agricultural credit, national and international;
(*f*) the adoption of international polices with respect to agricultural commodity arrangements.

3. It shall also be the function of the Organization:

(*a*) to furnish such technical assistance as governments may request;
(*b*) to organize, in co-operation with the governments concerned, such missions as may be needed to assist them to fulfil the obligations arising from their acceptance of the recommendations of the United Nations Conference on Food and Agriculture and of this Constitution; and
(*c*) generally to take all necessary and appropriate action to implement the purposes of the Organizations as set forth in the Preamble.

The Conference

Article 3

1. There shall be a Conference of the Organization in which each Member Nation and Associate Member shall be represented by one delegate. Associate Members shall have the right to participate in the deliberations of the Conference but shall not hold office nor have the right to vote.

4. Each Member Nation shall have only one vote. A Member Nation which is in arrears in the payment of its financial contributions to the Organization shall have no vote in the Conference if the amount of its arrears equals or exceeds the amount of the contributions due from it for the two preceding financial years. The Conference may, nevertheless, permit such a Member Nation to vote if it is satisfied that the failure to pay is due to conditions beyond the control of the Member Nation.

Functions of the Conference

Article 4

1. The Conference shall determine the policy and approve the budget of the Organization and shall exercise the other powers conferred upon it by this Constitution.

2. The Conference shall adopt Rules of Procedure and Financial Regulations for the Organization.

3. The Conference may, by a two-thirds majority of the votes cast, make recommendations to Member Nations and Associate Members concerning questions relating to food and agriculture, for consideration by them with a view to implementation by national action.

4. The Conference may make recommendations to any international organization regarding any matter pertaining to the purposes of the Organization.

5. The Conference may review any decision taken by the Council or by any commission or committee of the Conference or Council, or by any subsidiary body of such commissions or committees.

Council of the Organization

Article 5

1. A Council of the Organization consisting of 24 Member Nations shall be elected by the Conference. Each Member Nation on the Council shall have one representative and shall have only one vote. Each Member of the Council may appoint an alternate, associates and advisers to its representative. The Council may determine the conditions for the participation of alternates, associates and advisers in its proceedings, but any such participation shall be without the right to vote, except in the case of an alternate, associate or adviser participating in the place of a representative. No representative may represent more than one Member of the Council. The tenure and other conditions of office of the Members of the Council shall be subject to rules made by the Conference.

2. The Conference shall, in addition, appoint an independent Chairman of the Council.

3. The Council shall have such powers as the Conference may delegate to it, but the Conference shall not delegate the powers set forth in paragraphs 2 and 3 of Article 2, Article 4, paragraph 1 of Article 7, Article 12, paragraph 4 of Article 13, paragraphs 1 and 6 of Article 14, and Article 20 of this Constitution.

4. The Council shall appoint its officers other than the Chairman and subject to any decisions of the Conference shall adopt its own rules of procedure.

5. Except as otherwise expressly provided in this Constitution or by rules made by the Conference or Council, all decisions of the Council shall be taken by a majority of the votes cast.

6. To assist the Council in performing its functions, the Council shall appoint a Programme Committee, a Finance Committee, a Committee on Commodity Problems and a Committee on Constitutional

and Legal Matters. These committees shall report to the Council and their composition and terms of reference shall be governed by rules adopted by the Conference.

The Director-General

Article 7

1. There shall be a Director-General of the Organization who shall be appointed by the Conference by such procedure and on such terms as it may determine.

2. Subject to the general supervision of the Conference and the Council, the Director-General shall have full power and authority to direct the work of the Organization.

3. The Director-General or a representative designated by him shall participate, without the right to vote, in all meetings of the Conference and of the Council and shall formulate for consideration by the Conference and the Council proposals for appropriate action in regard to matters coming before them.

Staff

Article 8

1. The staff of the Organization shall be appointed by the Director-General in accordance with such procedure as may be determined by rules made by the Conference.

2. The staff of the Organization shall be responsible to the Director-General. Their responsibilities shall be exclusively international in character and they shall not seek or receive instructions in regard to the discharge thereof from any authority external to the Organization. The Member Nations and Associate Members undertake fully to respect the international character of the responsibilities of the staff and not to seek to influence any of their nationals in the discharge of such responsibilities.

3. In appointing the staff the Director-General shall, subject to the paramount importance of securing the highest standards of efficiency and of technical competence, pay due regard to the importance of selecting personnel recruited on as wide a geographical basis as possible.

4. Each Member Nation and Associate Member undertakes, insofar as it may be possible under its constitutional procedure, to accord to the Director-General and senior staff diplomatic privileges and immunities and to accord to other members of the staff all facilities and immunities accorded to non-diplomatic personnel attached to diplomatic missions, or alternatively to accord to such other members of the staff the

immunities and facilities which may hereafter be accorded to equivalent members of the staffs of other public international organizations.

Conventions and Agreements

Article 14

1. The Conference may, by a two-thirds majority of the votes cast and in conformity with rules adopted by the Conference, approve and submit to Member Nations conventions and agreements concerning questions relating to food and agriculture.

2. The Council, under rules to be adopted by the Conference, may, by a vote concurred in by at least two-thirds of the membership of the Council, approve and submit to Member Nations:

(*a*) agreements concerning questions relating to food and agriculture which are of particular interest to Member Nations of geographical areas specified in such agreements and are designed to apply only to such areas;

(*b*) supplementary conventions or agreements designed to implement any convention or agreement which has come into force under paragraphs 1 or 2 (*a*).

Legal Status

Article 16

1. The Organization shall have the capacity of a legal person to perform any legal act appropriate to its purpose which is not beyond the powers granted to it by this Constitution.

2. Each Member Nation and Associate Member undertakes, insofar as it may be possible under its constitutional procedure, to accord to the Organization all the immunities and facilities which it accords to diplomatic missions, including inviolability of premises and archives, immunity from suit and exemptions from taxation.

3. The Conference shall make provision for the determination by an administrative tribunal of disputes relating to the conditions and terms of appointment of members of the staff.

Budget and Contributions

Article 18

1. The Director-General shall submit to each regular session of the Conference the budget of the Organization for approval.

2. Each Member Nation and Associate Member undertakes to contribute annually to the Organization its share of the budget, as apportioned by the Conference. When determining the contributions to be

paid by Member Nations and Associate Members, the Conference shall take into account the difference in status between Member Nations and Associate Members.

2. ARTICLES OF AGREEMENT OF THE INTERNATIONAL BANK FOR RECONSTRUCTION AND DEVELOPMENT (Excerpts)

The Governments on whose behalf the present Agreement is signed agree as follows:

Introductory Article

The International Bank for Reconstruction and Development is established and shall operate in accordance with the following provisions:

Article I

Purposes

The purposes of the Bank are:

(i) To assist in the reconstruction and development of territories of members by facilitating the investment of capital for productive purposes, including the restoration of economies destroyed or disrupted by war, the reconversion of productive facilities to peace-time needs and the encouragement of the development of productive facilities and resources in less developed countries.

(ii) To promote private foreign investment by means of guarantees or participations in loans and other investments made by private investors; and when private capital is not available on reasonable terms, to supplement private investment by providing, on suitable conditions, finance for productive purposes out of its own capital, funds raised by it and its other resources.

(iii) To promote the long-range balanced growth of international trade and the maintenance of equilibrium in balances of payments by encouraging international investment for the development of the productive resources of members, thereby assisting in raising productivity, the standard of living and conditions of labour in their territories.

(iv) To arrange the loans made or guaranteed by it in relation to international loans through other channels so that the more useful and urgent projects, large and small alike, will be dealt with first.

(v) To conduct its operations with due regard to the effect of international investment on business conditions in the territories of members and, in the immediate post-war years, to assist in bringing about a smooth transition from a war-time to a peace-time economy.

The Bank shall be guided in all its decisions by the purposes set forth above.

Article II

Membership in and Capital of the Bank

Section 1. *Membership*

(*a*) The original members of the Bank shall be those members of the International Monetary Fund which accept membership in the Bank before the date specified in Article XI, Section 2(*e*).

(*b*) Membership shall be open to other members of the Fund, at such times and in accordance with such terms as may be prescribed by the Bank.

Section 2. *Authorized capital*

(*a*) The authorized capital stock of the Bank shall be $10,000,000,000, in terms of United States dollars of the weight and fineness in effect on July 1, 1944. The capital stock shall be divided into 100,000 shares having a par value of $100,000 each, which shall be available for subscription only by members.

(*b*) The capital stock may be increased when the Bank deems it advisable by a three-fourths majority of the total voting power.

Section 3. *Subscription of shares*

(*a*) Each member shall subscribe shares of the capital stock of the Bank. The minimum number of shares to be subscribed by the original members shall be those set forth in Schedule A. The minimum number of shares to be subscribed by other members shall be determined by the Bank, which shall reserve a sufficient portion of its capital stock for subscription by such members.

(*b*) The Bank shall prescribe rules laying down the conditions under which members may subscribe shares of the authorized capital stock of the Bank in addition to their minimum subscriptions.

(*c*) If the authorized capital stock of the Bank is increased, each member shall have a reasonable opportunity to subscribe, under such conditions as the Bank shall decide, a proportion of the increase of stock equivalent to the proportion which its stock theretofore subscribed bears to the total capital stock of the Bank, but no member shall be obligated to subscribe any part of the increased capital.

Article IV

Operations

Section 1. *Methods of making or facilitating loans*

(*a*) The Bank may make or facilitate loans which satisfy the general conditions of Article III in any of the following ways:

(i) By making or participating in direct loans out of its own funds corresponding to its unimpaired paid-up capital and surplus and, subject to Section 6 of this Article, to its reserves.

(ii) By making or participating in direct loans out of funds raised in the market of a member, or otherwise borrowed by the Bank.

(iii) By guaranteeing in whole or in part loans made by private investors through the usual investment channels.

(*b*) The Bank may borrow funds under (*a*) (ii) above or guarantee loans under (*a*) (iii) above only with the approval of the member in whose markets the funds are raised and the member in whose currency the loan is denominated, and only if those members agree that the proceeds may be exchanged for the currency of any other member without restriction.

Article V

Organization and Management

Section 1. *Structure of the Bank*

The Bank shall have a Board of Governors, Executive Directors, a President and such other officers and staff to perform such duties as the Bank may determine.

Section 2. *Board of Governors*

(*a*) All the powers of the Bank shall be vested in the Board of Governors consisting of one governor and one alternate appointed by each member in such manner as it may determine. Each governor and each alternate shall serve for five years, subject to the pleasure of the member appointing him, and may be reappointed. No alternate may vote except in the absence of his principal. The Board shall select one of the governors as Chairman.

(*b*) The Board of Governors may delegate to the Executive Directors authority to exercise any powers of the Board, except the power to:

(i) Admit new members and determine the conditions of their admission;
(ii) Increase or decrease the capital stock;
(iii) Suspend a member;
(iv) Decide appeals from interpretations of this Agreement given by the Executive Directors;
(v) Make arrangements to co-operate with other international organizations (other than informal arrangements of a temporary and administrative character);
(vi) Decide to suspend permanently the operations of the Bank and to distribute its assets;
(vii) Determine the distribution of the net income of the Bank.

(*c*) The Board of Governors shall hold an annual meeting and such other meetings as may be provided for by the Board or called by the Executive Directors. Meetings of the Board shall be called by the Directors whenever requested by five members or by members having one-quarter of the total voting power.

(*d*) A quorum for any meeting of the Board of Governors shall be a majority of the Governors, exercising not less than two-thirds of the total voting power.

(*e*) The Board of Governors may by regulation establish a procedure whereby the Executive Directors, when they deem such action to be in the best interests of the Bank, may obtain a vote of the Governors on a specific question without calling a meeting of the Board.

(*f*) The Board of Governors, and the Executive Directors to the extent authorized, may adopt such rules and regulations as may be necessary or appropriate to conduct the business of the Bank.

(*g*) Governors and alternates shall serve as such without compensation from the Bank, but the Bank shall pay them reasonable expenses incurred in attending meetings.

(*h*) The Board of Governors shall determine the remuneration to be paid to the Executive Directors and the salary and terms of the contract of service of the President.

Section 3. *Voting*

(*a*) Each member shall have two hundred fifty votes plus one additional vote for each share of stock held.

(*b*) Except as otherwise specifically provided, all matters before the Bank shall be decided by a majority of the votes cast.

Section 4. *Executive Directors*

(*a*) The Executive Directors shall be responsible for the conduct of the general operations of the Bank, and for this purpose, shall exercise all the powers delegated to them by the Board of Governors.

(*b*) There shall be twelve Executive Directors, who need not be Governors, and of whom:

(i) five shall be appointed, one by each of the five members having the largest number of shares;
(ii) seven shall be elected according to Schedule B by all the Governors other than those appointed by the five members referred to in (i) above.

Section 5. *President and staff*

(*a*) The Executive Directors shall select a President who shall not be a governor or an executive director or an alternate for either. The President shall be Chairman of the Executive Directors, but shall have no vote except a deciding vote in case of an equal division. He may participate in meetings of the Board of Governors, but shall not vote at such meetings. The President shall cease to hold office when the Executive Directors so decide.

(*b*) The President shall be chief of the operating staff of the Bank and shall conduct, under the direction of the Executive Directors, the ordinary business of the Bank. Subject to the general control of the Executive Directors, he shall be responsible for the organization, appointment and dismissal of the officers and staff.

(*c*) The President, officers and staff of the Bank, in the discharge of their offices, owe their duty entirely to the Bank and to no other authority. Each member of the Bank shall respect the international character of this duty and shall refrain from all attempts to influence any of them in the discharge of their duties.

(*d*) In appointing the officers and staff the President shall, subject to the paramount importance of securing the highest standards of efficiency and of technical competence, pay due regard to the importance of recruiting personnel on as wide a geographical basis as possible.

Article VII

Status, Immunities and Privileges

Section 1. *Purposes of Article*

To enable the Bank to fulfil the functions with which it is entrusted, the status, immunities and privileges set forth in this Article shall be accorded to the Bank in the territories of each member.

Section 2. *Status of the Bank*

The Bank shall possess full juridical personality, and, in particular, the capacity:

(i) to contract;
(ii) to acquire and dispose of immovable and movable property;
(iii) to institute legal proceedings.

Section 3. *Position of the Bank with regard to judicial process*

Actions may be brought against the Bank only in a court of competent jurisdiction in the territories of a member in which the Bank has an office, has appointed an agent for the purpose of accepting service or notice of process, or has issued or guaranteed securities. No actions shall, however, be brought by members or persons acting for or deriving claims from members. The property and assets of the Bank shall, wheresoever located and by whomsoever held, be immune from all forms of seizure, attachment or execution before the delivery of final judgment against the Bank.

Section 4. *Immunity of assets from seizure*

Property and assets of the Bank, wherever located and by whomsoever held, shall be immune from search, requisition, confiscation, expropriation or any other form of seizure by executive or legislative action.

Section 5. *Immunity of archives*

The archives of the Bank shall be inviolable.

Section 6. *Freedom of assets from restrictions*

To the extent necessary to carry out the operations provided for in this Agreement and subject to the provisions of this Agreement, all property and assets of the Bank shall be free from restrictions, regulations, controls and moratoria of any nature.

Section 7. *Privilege for communications*

The official communications of the Bank shall be accorded by each member the same treatment that it accords to the official communications of other members.

Section 8. *Immunities and privileges of officers and employees*

All governors, executive directors, alternates, officers and employees of the Bank

(i) shall be immune from legal process with respect to acts performed by them in their official capacity except when the Bank waives this immunity;
(ii) not being local nationals, shall be accorded the same immunities from immigration restrictions, alien registration requirements and national service obligations and the same facilities as regards exchange restrictions as are accorded by members to the representatives, officials, and employees of comparable rank of other members;
(iii) shall be granted the same treatment in respect of travelling facilities as is accorded by members to representatives, officials and employees of comparable rank of other members.

Section 9. *Immunities from taxation*

(*a*) The Bank, its assets, property, income and its operations and transactions authorized by this Agreement, shall be immune from all taxation and from all customs duties. The Bank shall also be immune from liability for the collection or payment of any tax or duty.

(*b*) No tax shall be levied on or in respect of salaries and emoluments paid by the Bank to executive directors, alternates, officials or employees of the Bank who are not local citizens, local subjects or other local nationals.

(*c*) No taxation of any kind shall be levied on any obligation or security issued by the Bank (including any dividend or interest thereon) by whomsoever held—

(i) which discriminates against such obligation or security solely because it is issued by the Bank; or
(ii) if the sole jurisdictional basis for such taxation is the place or currency in which it is issued, made payable or paid, or the location of any office or place of business maintained by the Bank.

(*d*) No taxation of any kind shall be levied on any obligation or security guaranteed by the Bank (including any dividend or interest thereon) by whomsoever held—

(i) which discriminates against such obligation or security solely because it is guaranteed by the Bank; or

(ii) if the sole jurisdictional basis for such taxation is the location of any office or place of business maintained by the Bank.

Section 10. *Application of Article*

Each member shall take such action as is necessary in its own territories for the purpose of making effective in terms of its own law the principles set forth in this Article and shall inform the Bank of the detailed action which it has taken.

1. Germany and Austria

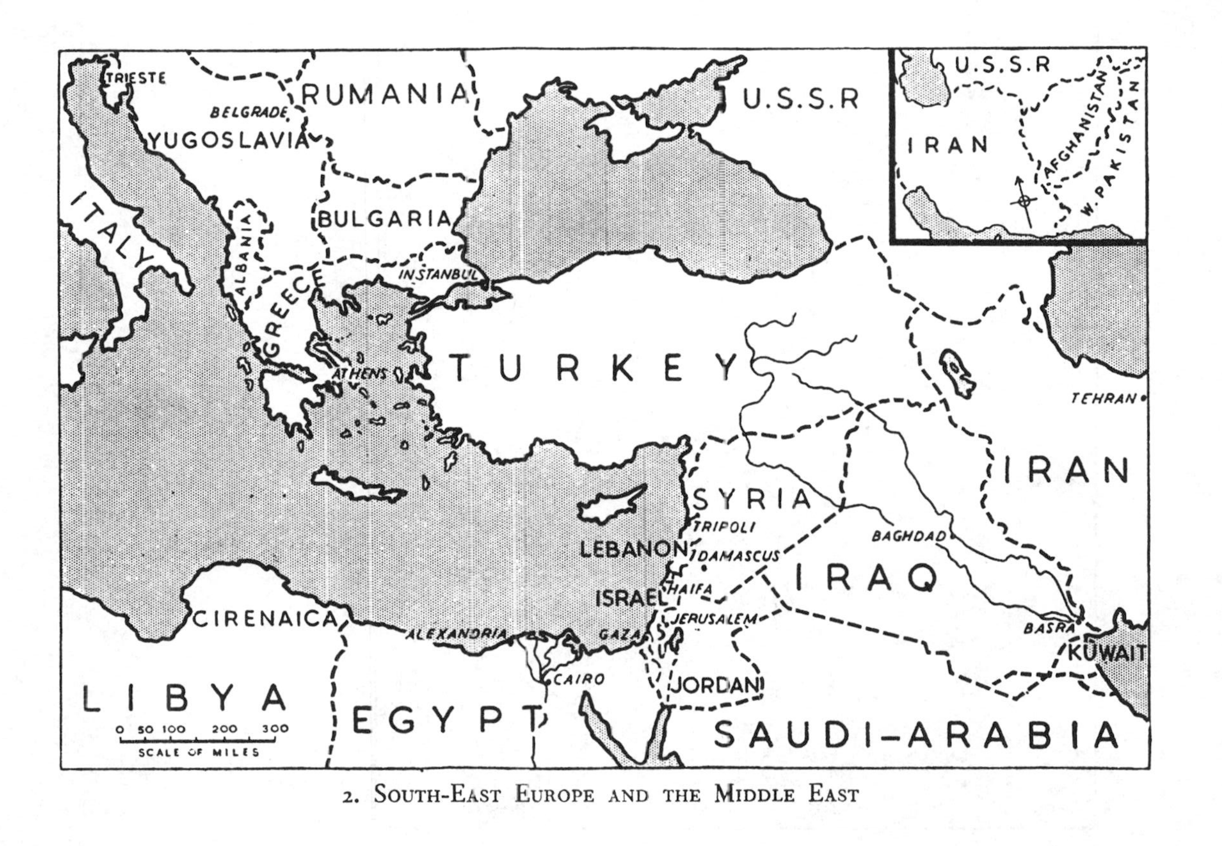

2. South-East Europe and the Middle East

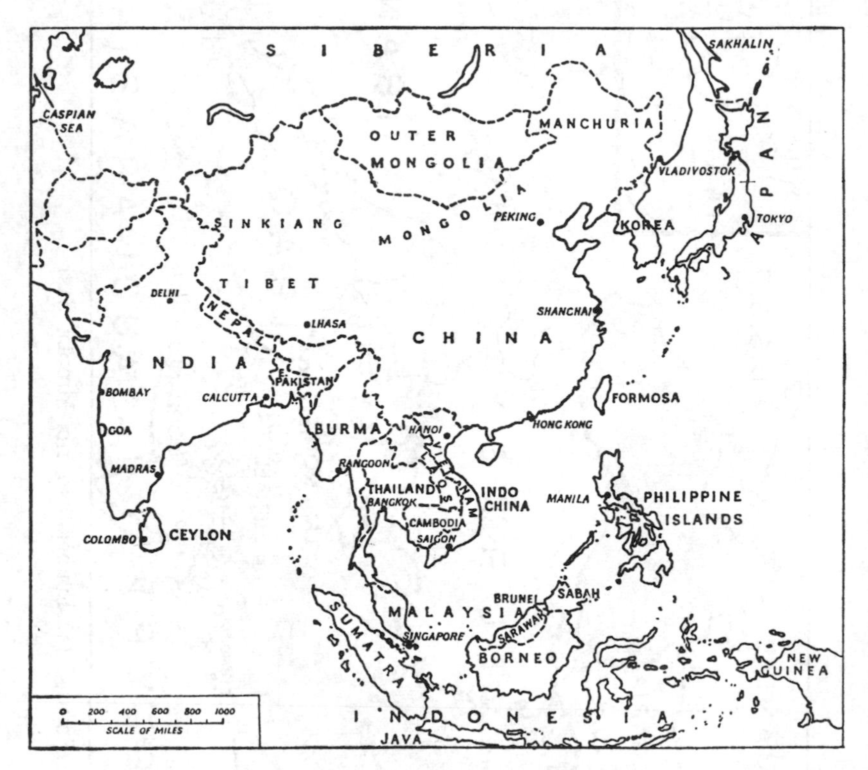

3. South-East Asia and the Far East

TUNISIA
0 1000
Miles
MOROCCO
ALGERIA
LIBYA
EGYPT
SP. SAHARA
MAURITANIA
MALI
NIGER
SENEGAL
CHAD
SUDAN
FR. SOMALILAND
VOLTA
GUINEA
GHANA
NIGERIA
SIERRA LEONE
IVORY COAST
LIBERIA
CAMEROON
CENTRAL AFRICA
ETHIOPIA
SOMALI REP.
SP. GUINEA
KENYA
UGANDA
GABON
CONGO REP.
CONGO
TANGANYIKA
CABINDA
ZANZIBAR
ANGOLA
NYASALAND
NORTHERN RHODESIA
MOZAMBIQUE
MADAGASCAR
SOUTHERN RHODESIA
SOUTH WEST AFRICA
BECHUANALD.
REP. OF SOUTH AFRICA
SWAZILAND
BASUTOLAND
1 GAMBIA
2 PORTUGUESE GUINEA
3 TOGO
4 DAHOMEY
5 RUANDA
6 BURUNDI

4. Africa

5. SOUTH AMERICA

SELECTED BIBLIOGRAPHY

CHAPTER 1

CARR, E. H. *Conditions of Peace* (London, Macmillan, 1942).
CHAMBERS, F. P. *This Age of Conflict* (New York, Harcourt, Brace, 1950).
CLAUDE, J. L., Jr. *Power and International Relations* (New York, Random House, 1962).
FOX, W. T. R. (ed.). *Theoretical Aspects of International Relations* (South Bend, Ind., University of Notre-Dame Press, 1959).
FROMM, E. *Fear of Freedom* (London, Kegan Paul, 1942).
GOODRICH, L. M. *The United Nations* (New York, Thomas Y. Crowell, 1959).
HOFFMANN, S. (ed.). *Contemporary Theory in International Relations* (New York, Prentice-Hall, 1960).
KAPLAN, M. A. *System and Process in International Politics* (New York, Wiley, 1957).
MARSHALL, C. B. *The Limits of Foreign Policy* (New York, Holt, 1954).
MORGENTHAU, H. J. *Politics Among Nations; the Struggle for Power and Peace*, 3rd ed. (New York, Knopf, 1960).
NIEBUHR, R. *Christian Realism and Political Problems* (New York, Scribner's, 1953).
RUSSELL, B. *Power*, 5th ed. (London, Allen & Unwin, 7th imp., 1958).
SCHUMAN, F. L. *International Politics: The Western State System and the World Community*, 6th ed. (New York, McGraw-Hill, 1958).
SCHWARZENBERGER, G. *Power Politics*, 3rd ed. (London, Stevens, 1951).
SPROUT, H., and SPROUT, M. *Foundations of International Politics* (Princeton, N.J., Van Nostrand, 1962).
STOESSINGER, J. *The Might of Nations: World Politics in Our Time* (New York, Random House, 1961).
TEMPLE, W. *Christianity and World Order* (Harmondsworth, Penguin, 1943).
TOYNBEE, A. *A Study of History* (abridged ed. by Somervell, D.C.) (Oxford, Oxford University Press, 1947).

CHAPTER 2

CARR, E. H. *Nationalism and After* (New York, St. Martin's Press, 1945).
COBBAN, A. B. *National Self-Determination* (Oxford, Oxford University Press, 1945).
EARLE, E. M. (ed.). *Nationalism and Internationalism* (New York, Columbia University Press, 1950).

FRIEDMANN, W. *The Crisis of the National State* (London, Macmillan, 1943).
KOHN, H. *The Idea of Nationalism*, 2nd ed. (New York, Macmillan, 1945).
AL RAZZAZ, M. *The Evolution of the Meaning of Nationalism* (New York, Doubleday, 1963).
Royal Institute of International Affairs, *Nationalism* (Oxford, Oxford University Press, 1939).
WRIGHT, W. (ed.). *The World Community* (Chicago, University of Chicago Press, 1948).

CHAPTER 3

ALMOND, G. A. *The American People and Foreign Policy* (New York, Harcourt Brace, 1950).
ARENDT, H. *The Origins of Totalitarianism* (New York, Harcourt, Brace, 1951).
BELOFF, M. *Foreign Policy and the Democratic Process* (Baltimore, Johns Hopkins Press, 1955).
CALVOCORESSI, P. *World Order and New States* (New York, Praeger, 1962).
CARR, E. H. *Studies in Revolution* (London, Macmillan, 1950).
——*A History of Soviet Russia, 1923–24*, 4 vols. (London, Macmillan, 1950–54).
COLE, I. *European Political Systems* (New York, Knopf, 1953).
CORBETT, P. E. *Law in Diplomacy* (Princeton, N.J., Princeton University Press, 1959).
FOX, W. T. R. *The Super Powers* (Baltimore, Johns Hopkins Press, 1944).
FRIEDRICH, C. J., and BRZEZINSKI, Z. K. *Totalitarian Dictatorship and Autocracy* (Cambridge, Mass., Harvard University Press, 1956).
GALBRAITH, J. K. *American Capitalism* (Cambridge, Mass., Houghton Mifflin, 1952).
GUNTHER, J. *Inside Russia Today* (New York, Harper, 1957).
HAYEK, E. A. *The Road to Serfdom* (London, Routledge, 1944).
KULSKI, W. W. *The Soviet Regime* (New York, Syracuse University Press, 1954).
NEUMANN, F. *Behemoth* (London, Gollancz, 1942).
ORWELL, G. *1984* (London, Secker & Warburg, 1949).
RUSH, M. *The Rise of Kruschchev* (Washington, D.C., Public Affairs Press, 1958).
RUSSELL, B. *Authority and the Individual* (London, Allen & Unwin, 1949).
SCHLESINGER, A. M. *Vital Center: The Politics of Freedom* (New York, Houghton, 1949).
SNYDER, R. C. *Decision-making as an Approach to the Study of International Politics* (Princeton, N.J., Princeton University Press, 1954).
WALTZ, K. N. *Man, the State, and War; A Theoretical Analysis* (New York, Columbia University Press, 1959).
WARD, B. *Five Ideas that Changed the World* (New York, Norton, 1959).
WOLFERS, A., and MARTIN, L. *The Anglo-American Tradition in Foreign Affairs* (New Haven, Yale University Press, 1956).
WOOTTON, Barbara. *Freedom Under Planning* (London, Allen & Unwin, 1946).

CHAPTER 4

ARON, R. *The Century of Total War* (New York, Doubleday, 1954).
BELOFF, M. *The Great Powers; Essays in Twentieth-Century Politics* (London, Macmillan, 1959).
BLACKETT, P. M. S. *Studies of War: Nuclear and Conventional* (New York, Hill & Wang, 1962).
BRZEZINSKI, Z. K. *The Soviet Bloc: Unity and Conflict* (Cambridge, Mass., Harvard University Press, 1960).
BULE, H. *The Control of the Arms Race* (New York, Praeger, 1961).
FEIS, H. *Between War and Peace: The Potsdam Conference* (Princeton, N.J., Princeton University Press, 1960).
FULBRIGHT, J. W. *Prospects for the West* (Cambridge, Mass., Harvard University Press, 1963).
GALLOIS, P. *The Balance of Terror* (Cambridge, Mass., Houghton Mifflin, 1961).
GARTHOFF, R. L. *Soviet Strategy in the Nuclear Age*, rev. ed. (New York, Praeger, 1962).
GROSS, E. A. *The United Nations: Structure for Peace* (New York, Harper, 1962).
HALPERN, M. H. *Limited War in the Nuclear Age* (New York, Wiley, 1963).
KAHN, H. *On Thermonuclear War* (Princeton, N.J., Princeton University Press, 1960).
—— *Thinking About the Unthinkable* (New York, Horizon Press, 1962).
KENNAN, G. F. *Russia and the West Under Lenin and Stalin* (Boston, Atlantic-Little, Brown, 1961).
KISSINGER, H. A. *The Necessity of Choice* (New York, Harper, 1961).
MOSELY, P. E. *The Kremlin and World Politics* (New York, Vintage Books, 1960).
MYRDAL, G. *Beyond the Welfare State* (New Haven, Yale University Press, 1960).
NIEBUHR, R. *The Structure of Nations and Empires* (New York, Scribner's, 1959).
SCHUMAN, F. L. *The Cold War: Retrospect and Prospect* (Baton Rouge, Louisiana State University Press, 1962).
SLESSOR, SIR J. *What Price Coexistence?* (New York, Praeger, 1961).
WOLFERS, A. *Discord and Collaboration* (Baltimore, Johns Hopkins Press, 1962).

CHAPTER 5

ACHESON, D. G. *Power and Diplomacy* (Cambridge, Mass., Harvard University Press, 1958).
ALBRECHT-CARRIÉ, R. *A Diplomatic History of Europe Since the Congress of Vienna* (New York, Harper, 1958).
ALLEN, H. C. *Great Britain and the United States* (New York, St. Martin's Press, 1955).
BALDWIN, H. W. *The Great Arms Race: A Comparison of U.S. and Soviet Power Today* (New York, Praeger, 1958).
BERGER, M. *The Arab World Today* (New York, Doubleday, 1962).
BÖLLING, K. *The Republic in Suspense: West Germany Today* (New York, Praeger, 1964).
BOWLES, C. *The New Dimensions of Peace* (New York, Harper, 1955).

BUCHAN, A. *NATO in the 1960's: The Implications of Interdependence,* rev. ed. (New York, Praeger, 1962).

CAMPBELL, J. C. *Defense of the Middle East: Problems of American Policy* (New York, Harper, for Council on Foreign Relations, 1958).

CARR, E. H. *The Twenty Years' Crisis, 1919–1939,* 2nd ed. (New York, St. Martin's Press, 1946).

CARTER, G. M., HERZ, J. H., and RANNEY, J. C. *Major Foreign Powers: The Governments of Great Britain, France, Germany and the Soviet Union,* 3rd ed. (New York, Harcourt, Brace, 1958).

CORRY, J. A. *Soviet Russia and the Western Alliance* (Contemporary Affairs No. 27) (Toronto, Canadian Institute of International Affairs, 1958).

CREMEANS, C. D. *The Arabs and the World* (New York, Praeger, 1963).

DEUTSCH, K. W. *Political Community in the North Atlantic Area* (Princeton, N.J., Princeton University Press, 1957).

EARLE, E. M. (ed.) *Modern France* (Princeton, N.J., Princeton University Press, 1951).

FEIS, H. *Churchill–Roosevelt–Stalin: The War They Waged and the Peace They Sought* (Princeton, N.J., Princeton University Press, 1957).

Handbook of German Affairs. *German Federal Republic* (Washington, D.C., German Diplomatic Mission, 1954).

HERZ, J. H. *International Politics in the Atomic Age* (New York, Columbia University Press, 1959).

HITCH, C. J., and MCKEAN, R. N. *The Economics of Defense in the Nuclear Age* (Cambridge, Mass., Harvard University Press, 1960).

HOFFMANN, S. (ed.) *In Search of France* (Cambridge, Mass., Harvard University Press, 1962).

HOSKINS, H. L. *The Middle East: Problem Area in World Politics* (New York, Macmillan, 1954).

HUREWITZ, J. C. *Diplomacy in the Middle East: A Documentary Record,* vol. i, 1535–1914; vol. ii, 1914–1956. (Princeton, N.J., Van Nostrand, 1956).

—— *Middle East Dilemmas* (New York, Harper, for Council on Foreign Relations, 1953).

KENNAN, G. F. *Realities of American Foreign Policy* (Princeton, N.J., Princeton University Press, 1954).

—— *Russia, the Atom and the West* (New York, Harper, 1958).

KERTESZ, S. D.(ed.) *East Central Europe and the World: Developments in the Post-Stalin Era* (South Bend, Ind., University of Notre-Dame Press, 1962).

KISSINGER, H. A. *Nuclear Weapons and Foreign Policy* (New York, Harper, for Council on Foreign Relations, 1957).

LAQUEUR, W. Z. *Communism and Nationalism in the Middle East* (New York, Praeger, 1956).

—— (ed.) *The Middle East in Transition* (New York, Praeger, 1958).

LERNER, D. *The Passing of Traditional Society: Modernizing the Middle East* (Chicago, Free Press, 1958).

LEWIS, B. *The Emergence of Modern Turkey* (New York, Oxford University Press, 1961).

LISKA, G. *Nations in Alliance: The Limits of Interdependence* (Baltimore, Johns Hopkins Press, 1962).

LOWIE, R. H. *Toward Understanding Germany* (Chicago, University of Chicago Press, 1954).
MOORE, B. T. *NATO and the Future of Europe* (New York, Harper, for Council on Foreign Relations, 1958).
NOVE, A., and CONNELLY, D. *Trade With Communist Countries* (New York, Macmillan, 1961).
OSGOOD, R. E. *Limited War: The Challenge to American Strategy* (Chicago, University of Chicago Press, 1957).
—— *NATO: The Entangling Alliance* (Chicago, University of Chicago Press, 1962).
PERETZ, D. *Israel and the Palestine Arabs* (Washington, D.C., Middle East Institute, 1961).
PRYOR, F. L. *The Communist Foreign Trade System* (Cambridge, Mass., The M.I.T. Press, 1963).
ROBERTS, H. *Russia and America* (New York, Harper, 1956).
SMITH, J. E. *The Defense of Berlin* (Baltimore, Johns Hopkins Press, 1963).
STALEY, E. *The Future of the Underdeveloped Countries* (New York, Harper, for Council on Foreign Relations, 1954).
THAYER, P. W. (ed.) *Tensions in the Middle East* (Baltimore, Johns Hopkins Press, 1958).
WARD, B. *The Interplay of East and West: Points of Conflict and Cooperation* (New York, Norton, 1957).
WHEELER-BENNETT, J. W. *The Nemesis of Power*, 2nd ed. (London, Macmillan, 1964).
WILCOX, F. O., and HAVILAND, H. F. (eds.) *The Atlantic Community: Progress and Prospects* (New York, Praeger, 1963).

CHAPTER 6

BELOFF, M. *The United States and the Unity of Europe* (Washington, D.C., The Brookings Institute, 1963).
BENOIT, E. *Europe at Sixes and Sevens* (New York, Columbia University Press, 1961).
DIEBOLD, W. *The Schuman Plan: A Study in Economic Cooperation, 1950–1959* (New York, Praeger, for Council on Foreign Relations, 1959).
FRANK, J. *The European Common Market* (New York, Praeger, 1961).
HAAS, E. B. *The Uniting of Europe* (Stanford, Calif., Stanford University Press, 1958).
HALLSTEIN, W. *United Europe: Challenge and Opportunity* (Cambridge, Mass., Harvard University Press, 1963).
HERTES, C. A. *Toward an Atlantic Community* (New York, Harper & Row, 1963).
HUMPHREY, D. D. *The United States and the Common Market; A Background Study* (New York, Praeger, 1962).
KITZINGER, U. W. *The Challenge of the Common Market* (Oxford, Blackwell, 1964).
LIPPMANN, W. *Western Unity and the Common Market* (Boston, Atlantic-Little, Brown, 1962).

MARJOLIN, R. *Europe and the United States in the World Economy* (Durham, N.C., Duke University Press, 1953).
MAYNE, R. *The Community of Europe* (New York, Norton, 1963).
MEYER, F. V. *The European Free Trade Association* (New York, Praeger, 1960).
MIDDLETON, D. *The Supreme Choice: Britain and Europe* (New York, Knopf, 1963).
ROBERTSON, A. H. *European Institutions* (New York, Praeger, for the London Institute of World Affairs, 1959).
URI, P. *Partnership for Progress; A Program for Transatlantic Action* (New York, Harper & Row, 1963).
WEIL, G. *The European Convention on Human Rights* (Leiden, Sythoff, 1963).

CHAPTER 7

CARRINGTON, C. E. *The Liquidation of the British Empire* (London, Harrap, 1961).
COATMAN, J. *The British Commonwealth of Nations* (London, Harrap, 1950).
HANCOCK, W. K. *Argument of Empire*, new ed. (Harmondsworth, Penguin Special, 1943).
HARLOW, V. (ed.) *The Commonwealth of Nations, Origins and Purpose* (London, H.M.S.O., 1950).
JENNINGS, I. *The British Commonwealth of Nations* (London, Christophers, 1954).
MANSERGH, N. *The Multi-Racial Commonwealth* (London and New York, Royal Institute of International Affairs, 1955).
—— *et al. Commonwealth Perspectives* (Durham, N.C., Duke University Press, 1958).
MILLER, J. D. B. *The Commonwealth in the World* (Cambridge, Mass., Harvard University Press, 1958).
ROBERTSON, SIR D. H. *Britain in the World Economy* (London, Allen & Unwin, 1954).

CHAPTER 8

American Assembly (ed.) *The United States and the Far East*, 2nd ed. (Englewood Cliffs, N.J., Prentice-Hall, 1962).
BAINS, J. S. *India's International Disputes: A Legal Study* (Bombay, Asia Publications House, 1962).
BARNETT, A. D. *Communist China in Perspective* (New York, Praeger, 1962).
BOWLES, C. *Ambassador's Report* (New York, Harper, 1954).
BOYO, R. G. *Communist China's Foreign Policy* (New York, Praeger, 1962).
BUSS, C. A. *The People's Republic of China* (Princeton, N.J., Van Nostrand, 1962).
CARY, J. *Japan Today, Reluctant Ally* (New York, Praeger, 1962).
CLUBB, O. E., Jr. *The United States and the Sino-Soviet Bloc in Southeast Asia* (Washington, D.C., The Brookings Institute, 1962).

Documents on the Sino-Indian Boundary Question (Peking, Foreign Language Press, 1960).

EDWARDES, M. *Asia in the Balance* (Harmondsworth, Penguin Books, 1962).

EMERSON, R. *Representative Government in Southeast Asia* (Cambridge, Mass., Harvard University Press, 1955).

FIFIELD, R. H. *The Diplomacy of Southeast Asia, 1945–1958* (New York, Harper, 1958).

FURNIVALL, J. S. *Colonial Policy and Practice: A Comparative Study of Burma and Netherlands India* (Cambridge, Cambridge University Press, 1948).

GINSBURG, N. (ed.) *The Pattern of Asia* (Englewood Cliffs, N.J., Prentice-Hall, 1958).

HONEY, P. J. *North Vietnam Today* (New York, Praeger, 1962).

JORDAN, A. *Foreign Aid and the Defense of Asia* (New York, Praeger, 1962).

KING, J. K. *Southeast Asia in Perspective* (New York, Macmillan, 1956).

LATOURETTE, K. S. *Short History of the Far East* (New York, Macmillan, 1947).

LATTIMORE, O., and LATTIMORE, MRS. E. O. *The Making of Modern China, A Short History* (London, Allen & Unwin, 1945).

LUARD, E. *Britain and China* (Baltimore, Johns Hopkins Press, 1962).

MENDEL, D. H. *The Japanese People and Foreign Policy* (Berkeley, Calif., University of California Press, 1961).

MORAES, F. *Yonder One World: A Study of Asia and the West* (New York, Macmillan, 1958).

PALMER, L. H. *Indonesia and the Dutch* (New York, Oxford University Press, 1962).

PANNIKAR, K. M. *Asia and Western Dominance* (London, Allen & Unwin, 1953).

RAVENHOLT, A. *The Philippines* (Princeton, N.J., Van Nostrand, 1962).

ROSE, S. *Britain and Southeast Asia* (Baltimore, Johns Hopkins Press, 1962).

SANGHVI, R. *India's Northern Frontier and China* (Bombay, Contemporary Publishers, 1962).

SCALAPINO, R. (ed.) *North Korea Today* (New York, Praeger, 1963).

SHADI, Z. T. *Goa, A Case Study of the Formulation of Indian Foreign Policy* (Berkeley, Calif., University of California Press, 1962).

SNOW, E. *The Other Side of the River, Red China Today* (New York, Random House, 1962).

TALBOT, P., and POPLAI, S. L. *India and America: A Study of Their Relations* (New York, Harper, for Council on Foreign Relations, 1958).

TAYLOR, G. E. *The Philippines and the United States* (New York, Praeger, 1964).

THOMSON, I. *The Rise of Modern Asia* (New York, Pitman, 1958).

WARD, B. *India and the West* (New York, Norton, 1961).

WILLIAMS, L. F. R. *The State of Pakistan* (London, Faber & Faber, 1962).

WILSON, D. *Politics in Thailand* (Ithaca, N.Y., Cornell University Press, 1962).

WINT, G. *The British in Asia* (New York, Institute of Pacific Relations, 1954)

—— and PATTERSON, G. (eds.) *Asia: A Handbook* (New York, Praeger, 1964).

WOODMAN, D. *The Republic of Indonesia* (New York, Philosophical Library, 1955).

ZAGORIA, D. S. *The Sino-Soviet Conflict 1956–1961* (Princeton, N.J., Princeton University Press, 1962).

CHAPTER 9

BOUTRAS-GHALI, B. *The Addis Ababa Charter* (New York, International Conciliation No. 546, Jan. 1964).
CARTER, G. (ed.) *African One Party States* (Ithaca, N.Y., Cornell University Press, 1962).
—— *Five African States. Responses to Diversity* (Ithaca, N.Y., Cornell University Press, 1963).
COHEN, SIR A. *British Policy in Changing Africa* (Evanston, Ill., Northwestern University Press, 1959).
COLEMAN, J. S., and ROSBERG, C. G., Jr. (eds.) *Political Parties and National Integration in Tropical Africa* (Berkeley, Calif., University of California Press, 1964).
DIA, M. *The African Nations and World Solidarity* (New York, Praeger, 1961).
FRIEDLAND, W., and ROSBERG, C. *African Society* (Stanford, Calif., Stanford University Press, 1964).
GALLAGHER, C. F. *The United States and North Africa* (London, Oxford University Press, 1963).
GORDON, E. *North Africa's French Legacy* (Cambridge, Mass., Harvard University Press, 1963).
HAILEY, L. *An African Survey*, rev. ed. (Oxford, Oxford University Press, 1957).
HANCE, W. *The Geography of Modern Africa* (New York, Columbia University Press, 1964).
HERSKOVITS, M. J. *The Human Factor in Changing Africa* (New York, Knopf, 1962).
HUGHES, A. J. *East Africa: The Search for Unity* (Harmondsworth, Penguin African Library, 1964).
KEPPEL-JONES, A. *South Africa* (London, Hutchinson, 1953).
LEGUM, C. *Africa: A Handbook to the Continent* (New York, Praeger, 1962).
McKAY, V. *Africa in World Politics* (New York, Harper & Row, 1963).
OLIVER, R., and FAGE, J. S. *A Short History of Africa* (Harmondsworth, Penguin African Library, 1962).
PADMORE, G. *The Gold Coast Revolution* (London, Dobson, 1953).
PATON, A. *The Land and the People of South Africa* (Philadelphia, Lippincott, 1955).
RIVKIN, A. *Africa and the West* (New York, Praeger, 1962).
ROSBERG, C., and SEGAL, A. *An East African Federation* (New York, International Conciliation No. 543, May 1963).
SCHMITT, K., and BURKS, D. *Evolution or Chaos* (New York, Praeger, 1963).
THOMPSON, V. *French West Africa* (Stanford, Calif., Stanford University Press, 1958).
—— and ADLOFF, R. *The Emerging States of French Equatorial Africa* (Oxford, Oxford University Press, 1960).
WALLERSTEIN, I. *Africa: The Politics of Independence* (New York, Vintage Books, 1961).

CHAPTER 10

ADAMS, M. (ed.) *Latin America, Evolution or Explosion?* (New York, Dodd, Mead, 1963).

ADAMS, R. N., *et al. Social Change in Latin America Today* (New York, Harper, for Council on Foreign Relations, 1960).

BERLE, A. A. *Latin America: Diplomacy and Reality* (New York, Harper & Row, 1962).

DAVIS, H. (ed.) *Government and Politics in Latin America* (New York, Ronald Press, 1958).

DRAPER, T. *Castro's Revolution: Myths and Realities* (New York, Praeger, 1962).

HIRSCHMAN, A. *Journeys Toward Progress: Studies of Economic Policy-making in Latin America* (New York, Twentieth Century Fund, 1963).

LIEUWEN, E. *Arms and Politics in Latin America*, rev. ed. (New York, Praeger, 1961).

MARTZ, J. D. *Central America. The Crisis and the Challenge* (Chapel Hill, N.C., University of North Carolina Press, 1958).

MECHAM, J. L. *The United States and Inter-American Security, 1889–1960* (Austin, Tex., University of Texas Press, 1961).

PIERSON, W., and GIL, F. *Governments of Latin America* (New York, McGraw-Hill, 1957).

CHAPTER 11

California Institute of Technology. *Resources of the World: A Speculative Projection* (1956).

CARLSON, L. *Geography and World Politics* (Englewood Cliffs, N.J., Prentice-Hall, 1958).

HAUSER, P. M. (ed.) *Population and World Politics* (Glencoe, Ill., Free Press, 1958).

MOODIE, A. E. *Geography Behind Politics* (London, Hutchinson University Library, 1957).

P.E.P. *World Population and Resources* (London, 1955).

SCHECHTMAN, J. B. *Post-War Population Transfers in Europe* (Philadelphia, University of Pennsylvania Press, 1962).

SCHIMM, M. G. *Population Control* (New York, Oceana, 1961).

TAEUBER, I. B. *The Population of Japan* (Princeton, N.J., Princeton University Press, 1958).

THOMAS, B. (ed.) *Economics of International Migration* (London, Macmillan, 1958).

THOMPSON, W. S. *Population and Progress in the Far East* (Chicago, University of Chicago Press, 1959).

CHAPTER 12

ALMOND, G. A., and COLEMAN, J. S. (eds.) *The Politics of Developing Areas* (Princeton, N.J., Princeton University Press, 1960).

BERLINER, J. S. *Soviet Economic Aid* (New York, Praeger, 1958).

BLACK, E. R. *The Diplomacy of Economic Development* (Cambridge, Mass., Harvard University Press, 1960).

GALBRAITH, J. K. *Economic Development in Perspective* (Cambridge, Mass., Harvard University Press, 1962).

GERSCHENKRON, A. *Economic Backwardness in Historical Perspective* (Cambridge, Mass., Harvard University Press, 1963).

HEILBRONER, R. L. *The Great Ascent: The Struggle for Economic Development in Our Time* (New York, Harper & Row, 1963).

HIRSCHMAN, A. *The Strategy of Economic Development* (New Haven, Yale University Press, 1958).

MILLIKAN, M. F., and BLACKMER, D. L. M. (eds.) *The Emerging Nations* (Boston, Atlantic-Little, Brown, 1961).

MYRDAL, G. *An International Economy* (New York, Harper, 1956).

—— *Beyond the Welfare State* (New Haven, Yale University Press, 1960).

ROSTOW, W. W. *The Stages of Economic Growth* (Cambridge, Cambridge University Press, 1960).

STALEY, E. *The Future of Underdeveloped Countries, Political Implications of Economic Development*, rev. ed. (New York, Praeger, 1961).

INDEX

Bold type indicates a substantial treatment of the subject, as distinct from reference.